Made Up

Made Up

How the Beauty Industry Manipulates
Consumers, Preys on Women's Insecurities,
and Promotes Unattainable Beauty Standards

Martha Laham

ROWMAN & LITTLEFIELD
Lanham • Boulder • New York • London

Published by Rowman & Littlefield
An imprint of The Rowman & Littlefield Publishing Group, Inc.
4501 Forbes Boulevard, Suite 200, Lanham, Maryland 20706
www.rowman.com

6 Tinworth Street, London SE11 5AL, United Kingdom

British Library Cataloguing in Publication Information Available

Library of Congress Cataloging-in-Publication Data

Names: Laham, Martha, author.
Title: Made up : how the beauty industry manipulates consumers, preys on women's insecurities, and promotes unattainable beauty standards / Martha Laham.
Description: Lanham, Maryland : Rowman & Littlefield, 2020. | Includes bibliographical references and index.
Identifiers: LCCN 2020003493 (print) | LCCN 2020003494 (ebook) | ISBN 9781538138045 (cloth) | ISBN 9781538138052 (ebook)
Subjects: LCSH: Cosmetics industry—Social aspects. | Feminine beauty (Aesthetics)—Social aspects. | Beauty, Personal—Social aspects. | Beauty culture—Social aspects.
Classification: LCC HD9970.5.C672 .L34 2020 (print) | LCC HD9970.5.C672 (ebook) | DDC 338.4/766855—dc23
LC record available at https://lccn.loc.gov/2020003493
LC ebook record available at https://lccn.loc.gov/2020003494

To my family and friends

Contents

Foreword

Jerome R. Potozkin

I have had the privilege of working with Martha Laham for over two decades. She is a no-nonsense, bright, and insightful author and professor of advertising and marketing who has done extensive research on the beauty industry. *Made Up: How the Beauty Industry Manipulates Consumers, Preys on Women's Insecurities, and Promotes Unattainable Beauty Standards* represents the culmination of her research and is essential reading for anyone interested in this topic. The beauty industry generates billions of dollars annually, more than the gross domestic product of many nations. Professor Laham explores the origins of this industry and the factors leading to its continued growth. As a board-certified dermatologist specializing in cosmetic dermatology, I have seen firsthand what is described in the book, from the unrealistic pressures to look a certain way to how technology, with the growth of social media and the selfie, has led people to scrutinize their appearance as never before.

This book describes the history of the beauty industry dating back to ancient Egypt. It gives perspective to the power and impact of the industry's early pioneers, such as Josephine Esther Mentzer, born to Jewish immigrants and the founder of Estée Lauder. She was committed to her mission and recognized early on that "to sell a cream, you sold a dream." An enterprise that started in a kitchen ended up as a multibillion-dollar company. You will learn how the beauty industry is regulated and how cosmetics differ from pharmaceuticals in their regulation.

With her background and expertise in advertising and marketing, Professor Laham expertly dissects how the cosmetics industry targets people of all ages. Baby boomers are thought to be obsessed with youth and are targeted based on the "anti-aging" features of lotions and potions. On the other hand, the younger generations have been greatly affected by the selfie craze. The beauty industry has learned how to push the emotional buttons of each generation.

Have you ever wondered what defines beauty? You will learn how iconic figures such as Audrey Hepburn and Elizabeth Taylor helped define the feminine ideal. The book outlines "ideal" beauty trends over time and provides an insider's view of what cosmetic dermatologists and cosmetic surgeons have studied through the years. In addition to the ways that beauty is defined, Professor Laham provides great insight into how gender stereotypes are created and perpetuated in ads that use gender-stereotypic images. The reader is presented with multiple examples that illuminate the conditioning we are unwittingly exposed to. We also learn the impact of the feminist movement on advertisers, leading to regulatory action. Hand in hand with the beauty and cosmetics industry, advertisers have engaged in the objectification of women and have used sexually charged campaigns to promote beauty products. They have tapped into our obsession with celebrity to sell their products.

In my practice, I have noticed that most people are their own worst critics when it comes to their appearance. Professor Laham explores the concept of body image and the effect of advertising on our psyche. We learn how repeated exposure to idealized images lowers our self-perceptions of attractiveness. The deck is stacked against us, as many images are not "real." In the pre-digital era, images were idealized through airbrushing. Today's images can be easily altered with digital technology. The images that we are repeatedly exposed to affect us in a way that is far more than skin deep, and Professor Laham discusses the ill effects of trying to improve images of ourselves in the section "Photoshopping May Be Bad for Your Health," in chapter 8.

The final chapter delves into the growth of aesthetic medicine. Current trends have demonstrated the common acceptance of cosmetic surgery. The most dramatic growth that has trended nationwide, which I have seen in my practice over the past two decades, is in nonsurgical cosmetic procedures. Professor Laham accurately describes how increasing numbers of people, driven by unrealistic expectations, want to completely change their appearance or look like a celebrity as opposed to having a more realistic goal of looking like the best natural version of themselves. She details how the explosion of aesthetic medicine has also led to unskilled and unethical practitioners entering this arena.

Both entertaining and informative, *Made Up* is a must-read for anyone interested in the cosmetics, beauty, and advertising industry.

Jerome R. Potozkin, MD, is an award-winning board-certified dermatologist and the author of *Botox and Beyond: Your Guide to Safe, Nonsurgical, Cosmetic Procedures.*

Acknowledgments

I would like to express my genuine appreciation to several people without whose support and encouragement this book would not have been possible.

I owe a special debt of gratitude to my extraordinary copyeditor, Elissa Rabellino, for her incisive editorial skills and her invaluable assistance in preparing the manuscript. I am equally grateful to my attorney, Scott Dallas, for his helpful guidance on the legal and regulatory landscape of the cosmetics industry. I also wish to thank Lorna Garano and Peter Handel for their unfailing reassurance and their invaluable feedback on the book's concept.

I am much obliged to three generations of marketing and advertising students who joined me in spirited discussions and debates on gender representation in advertising. This book is in large part a response to their abiding interest in this topic.

I would also like to thank my colleagues in the Business Administration Department, the dean of the business division, the vice president of instruction, and the president of Diablo Valley College, for their validation of my research interests.

Thanks to everyone on the Rowman & Littlefield team who gave expert guidance, technical help, and editorial support. My special thanks go out to executive editor Suzanne Staszak-Silva and editorial assistant Charlotte Gosnell. I also wish to acknowledge Rowman & Littlefield's highly professional production staff, including senior production editor Alden Perkins, copyeditor Jocquan Mooney, designer Jen Huppert, typesetter Jason Rock, and proofreader Beth Easter.

And last but hardly least, I am most grateful to my family and friends for their unwavering love, optimism, and enthusiasm. Thank you for always believing in me and urging me to press on.

Introduction

When a woman stays young and beautiful forever, the world is hers.

—Queen Ravenna, *Snow White and the Huntsman* (2012)

Once upon a time over two hundred years ago, Jacob and Wilhelm Grimm, a pair of nineteenth-century university-trained philologists and librarians, published their compendium of European folktales called *Children's and Household Tales* (1812), more commonly known as *Grimm's Fairy Tales* in the English-speaking world. Over the next four decades, the German brothers went on to publish six more editions, tinkering with their tales from one edition to the next until the seventh and final edition in 1857, the one best known to us today.

Modern audiences are mostly familiar with "Disneyfied" versions of the Grimm brothers' timeless tales. These singsong, child-friendly confections with happily-ever-after endings sugarcoat the grittier narratives of the original stories. Initially intended for an adult audience, the first collection of folktales was hardly suitable for children's ears. Benign titles belied a tableau of perversion, torture, betrayal, jealousy, humiliation, and rejection set against fantastical milieus.

Feminine beauty is a common theme that runs throughout a number of Grimm stories, often conflated with spectacular wickedness or unflawed purity. More specifically, characters who are beautiful and virtuous are frequently targeted by characters who are beautiful and diabolical.

Consider the tale of "Little Snow White." In the modern retelling of this Grimm classic, Snow White's innate purity and beauty provokes her stepmother, the Evil Queen. Malignant and narcissistically invested in her physical appearance, the Evil Queen is obsessively preoccupied with nonpareil beauty. She seeks validation from her magic mirror by repeatedly asking it, "Mirror, mirror, on the wall, who

1

in this land is fairest of all?" The mirror always replies, "You, my queen, are the fairest of all."

Snow White's beauty blossoms with each passing day until one day the magic mirror breaks it to the Evil Queen that she's no longer the fairest in the land, declaring that little Snow White is fairer than she.

Consumed with envy, the Evil Queen flies into a murderous rage. She's determined to rid the land of Snow White and hatches a plan to snuff her out. The plan backfires and ultimately leads to the Evil Queen's undoing.

The unctuous male mirror in Snow White's story is an echo chamber. The reverberated message is a simple one: Women are judged and valued on their physical appearance and allure. In her book *The Annotated Brothers Grimm* (2004), Maria Tatar, John L. Loeb Research Professor of Germanic Languages and Literatures and of Folklore and Mythology at Harvard University, notes that the male mirror may be viewed as "a judgmental voice, representing the absent father or patriarchy in general, which places a premium on beauty." Tatar also suggests that the voice could be the inner monologue that induces habitual monitoring of physical appearance against cultural standards of beauty ("an echo of the queen's own self-assessment, one that is, to be sure, informed by cultural norms about physical appearances").

Whether in fairy tales or in real life, the importance of physical appearance and the fulfillment of expected gender roles are inculcated into women from an early age. This is especially true for my generation of women, who came of age during the 1960s. In those days, women were straitjacketed by socially endorsed views of gender and femininity that were promoted and reinforced by the mainstream media.

Take teen-zines, such as *Seventeen*, *Mademoiselle*, *Teen*, and *YM* (*Young Miss*). During the 1960s, these popular publications helped crystallize the identity formation of teenage girls. Editorial content chiefly focused on the trappings of traditional femininity, such as beauty, fashion, cooking, and decorating.

When I was a teenager, *Seventeen* was my favorite magazine. Each month, I'd make the pilgrimage to a grocery store to buy the latest edition. I grew up in an immigrant household that hadn't integrated fully into American society. My family clung to strict traditions and customs from the old country (such as an adherence to traditional gender roles of male dominance and female submissiveness), disapproved of permissive Western values, and derided American pop culture. They viewed teen magazines as a form of cultural propaganda. So I'd hide my copy of *Seventeen* in a yellow Pee-Chee folder and read it during alone time. *Seventeen* was a training manual that schooled me in becoming an American teenager.

I was in high school during the mid-1960s. The style icon of the moment was the British teen supermodel Twiggy. With her sideswept pixie cut and willowy figure, young girls everywhere tried to copy her mod look and achieve her reed-thin physique. Twiggy reportedly lived off water, lettuce, and a single daily portion of steak. To emulate Twiggy's gamine figure meant ditching junk food, controlling food cravings, and turning off the hunger switch.

The coltish thin ideal spilled over into the 1970s, when dieting was pursued with religious fervor. Many women sipped their way to skinniness by subsisting on diet drinks and sodas or tried one fad diet after the next. Others turned to quick-fix weight-loss drugs, such as amphetamine-laced "rainbow diet pills." These brightly colored pills were as effective as they were addictive and even deadly.

Prior to the 1970s, few people talked about eating disorders until the shocking death of 1970s singing sensation Karen Carpenter due to complications related to her years-long struggle with anorexia. Yet a heightened awareness of the dangers of eating disorders did little to change women's skinny obsession. What's more, women and girls were barraged with thin-ideal media images that portrayed thinness as a dominant view of beauty and equated slimness with success and happiness. There was no counternarrative then.

As an undergraduate student, I cultivated an interest in feminist literature. I was particularly moved by the works of trailblazing feminist authors and writers like Betty Friedan (*The Feminine Mystique*, 1963), Germaine Greer (*The Female Eunuch*, 1970), and Gloria Steinem (cofounder of *Ms.* magazine, 1972)—feminist voices that challenged scripted roles that women had inhabited largely because of prevailing cultural norms and female biology. These courageous feminists and others like them refused to cave in to age-old tactics of silencing women. They were loud, proud, and unbowed.

Some years later, I left the advertising and promotion industry to enter the education field. There, I became fascinated with—and dedicated to—exploring female role portrayals in advertising. This book is the culmination of a three-decades-long examination of gender representation in advertising.

Made Up: How the Beauty Industry Manipulates Consumers, Preys on Women's Insecurities, and Promotes Unattainable Beauty Standards takes a hard look at the multibillion-dollar beauty industry, which promotes unrealistic beauty standards, perpetuates gender stereotypes, and uses sexual objectification to sell products. The book is divided into four parts. Part I explores the global beauty industry, traces the cultural history of cosmetics, examines the regulatory climate of the cosmetics industry, and profiles the beauty consumer. Part II investigates the pervasiveness and persistence of the feminine beauty ideal, explores the globalization of Western standards of beauty, analyzes the myth-making power of beauty advertising, and decodes archetypal and stereotypical portrayals of women in beauty ads. Part III investigates the decorative and sexual depictions of women in beauty advertising and analyzes the power of celebrity beauty endorsements. Part IV looks at the interplay between images of physical perfection in advertising messages and the surge in body modification and enhancement.

In societies that worship youth and beauty, the appearance of aging is often met with escalating disdain. In her 2012 *New Yorker* article "Snow White: Beauty Is Power," which critiqued the film *Snow White and the Huntsman* (2012), Tatar wrote, "The queen's quest for lasting youth is part of the story's larger exploration (in the tradition of many great myths) of how humans relate to the natural world—whether we are of it or have mastered and moved beyond it. Efforts to remain forever young violate the natural order of generational succession and imperil life itself." The pathological pursuit of youth and beauty can swiftly spin out of control and lead us down a crooked path to self-destruction.

Martha Laham
Oakland, California
December 2019

I

THE BEAUTY INDUSTRY

1

The Beauty Industrial Complex

Never underestimate any woman's desire for beauty.

—Estée Lauder (1908–2004), cofounder, the Estée Lauder Companies Inc.

You may be familiar with the pioneers who shaped the modern beauty industry, such as Elizabeth Arden, Helena Rubinstein, Madam C. J. Walker, Max Factor, Charles Revson, Mary Kay Ash, and Estée Lauder. These grandes dames and grands seigneurs built billion-dollar empires on the sale of paints and potions primarily designed to satisfy aesthetic needs.

Consider Estée Lauder, cofounder of the Estée Lauder Companies Inc. Lauder was a natural-born entrepreneur and a visionary marketer. Her groundbreaking promotional tools, including innovative sampling programs and a high-touch approach to cultivating an emotional connection with beauty consumers, have become standard industry practices.

The cosmetics doyenne who changed the face of the beauty industry came from modest roots. Estée Lauder, née Josephine Esther Mentzer, was born and grew up in Queens, New York. She was the ninth child of Jewish immigrants; her mother was Hungarian, and her father was Czech.

Working in her father's hardware store gave Lauder her first exposure to retail merchandising at an early age. Her uncle, a chemist who created recipes for beauty creams, introduced her to the world of beauty. He took her under his wing and taught her how to combine ingredients to formulate skin creams straight out of the kitchen. During her teen years, she learned the significance of personal selling to create interest in a product and make a sale. Lauder sold her uncle's products to her high school classmates by giving them full makeovers.

While making continuous improvements to her uncle's formulas, Lauder created a market niche for the final product. Instinctively, she grasped the importance of focusing on the sensory attributes of cosmetic products. She often said, "To sell a cream, you sold a dream in the early days."[1]

Lauder was tireless in her pursuit of making a name for herself and her products, using direct sales to accomplish both. Employing an early form of one-to-one marketing, she gave free product demonstrations and makeovers at salons, in hotels, in the subway, on the street, and in private homes. Along the way, she cemented her reputation as a cosmetics purveyor and became a staple of New York's high society.

In 1946, Lauder and her husband, Joseph, launched the Estée Lauder brand with just four skin care products. The Lauders were determined to build a market for premium beauty products by targeting middle-class and wealthy women who had the means and motivation to purchase premium brands that were imbued with an aura of elegance and sophistication. To accomplish this business objective, Lauder made a crucial distribution decision. Instead of selling the company's products through mass-market retailers, such as drugstores, supermarkets, and variety stores, or making them available at company-owned salons, like Elizabeth Arden and Helena Rubinstein, Lauder set her sights on carriage-trade retailers.

Lauder approached many department store buyers to persuade them to carry Estée Lauder products. She finally landed her first department store account with Saks Fifth Avenue. The New York–based luxury department store placed an order for $800 worth of products, which sold out within two days. Lauder personally attended to every aspect of merchandising, from designing cosmetic display counters to supervising sales representatives and working behind the counter to interacting with customers. And it was around this time that Lauder launched a novel consumer promotion, a gift-with-purchase premium.

By the late 1950s, the Estée Lauder brand had become one of the most recognized beauty brands among department store shoppers. Other luxury department stores picked up the Estée Lauder collection, including Neiman Marcus, I. Magnin, and Marshall Field's. Then in 1953, Lauder launched her first fragrance, Youth Dew, which marked a turning point in the company's history. Youth Dew was a massive hit within a few years, accounting for 80 percent of company sales. The fledging startup took off and flourished into a multimillion-dollar juggernaut.[2]

During the 1960s and 1970s, the company prospered by adding new lines to its product portfolio, including its first prestige men's fragrance under the Aramis brand and the Clinique brand, the first-ever dermatologist-created prestige cosmetic brand. The company also experienced a period of rapid market expansion by entering into global markets, with Estée Lauder products sold in more than seventy countries.[3]

The 1980s and 1990s saw robust growth driven by new-product development, such as the introduction of Estée Lauder's Origins, the first prestige natural skin care brand, and through successful acquisitions, including MAC Cosmetics, La Mer, Aveda, and Bobbi Brown Cosmetics. By now the company employed approximately

10,000 employees and generated over $2 billion in sales, making it the third-largest cosmetics company in America.[4]

By 2019, Estée Lauder Companies Inc. ranked No. 591 on the *Forbes* Global 2000 rankings of the world's largest public companies, reached a market value of $61.5 billion, and managed a brand portfolio containing more than two dozen prestige brands.[5]

Lauder summed up her formula for success in a simple statement: "I was a woman with a mission and single-minded in the pursuit of my dream."[6] By every measure, Estée Lauder had accomplished her mission and made her dream a reality.

This chapter starts off with a brief history of cosmetics. Next, it dives into the makeup of the beauty industry. Finally, it looks at changes in the beauty industry landscape.

THE HISTORY OF COSMETICS: FROM THE STONE AGE TO THE INDUSTRIAL AGE

The Roman writer Titus Maccius Plautus (c. 205–184 BCE) satirized the importance of personal beauty in the following statement: "A woman without paint is like food without salt." Even before salt was produced, humans wore "body paint" 50,000 years ago. A 2010 *BBC News* article reported that scientists unearthed convincing evidence that Neanderthals used shells to mix and store pigments.[7] Prior to this finding, researchers had believed that only modern humans wore makeup for ritual and decorative purposes.

Cosmetics has been a cultural staple in most civilizations throughout the ages. Let's journey back in time and learn about cosmetics' colorful history, with the focus of our attention on the beautifying rituals of women in the West.

The Birthplace of Cosmetics

The ancient Egyptians were the first true makeup mixologists, dating as far back as 10,000 BCE. Using hundreds of organic substances, they created cosmetics for aesthetic and therapeutic purposes. Egyptian chemists blended many of the same ingredients that we find in all-natural makeup and skin care today, including rosemary, lavender, chamomile, lily, rose, henna, and olive oil.

Ancient Egyptian royals and the upper crust anointed themselves with scented oils and ointments; used cleansers, moisturizers, and deodorizers; dyed their hair and painted their nails; and applied makeup such as eye cosmetics. For example, you've probably seen pictures of ancient Egyptian men and women wearing an eye paint primarily made from green malachite and galena (a lead-based substance) called *kohl* (see figure 1.1).

In addition to their aesthetic value, cosmetics were believed to have mystical and medicinal powers. According to a 2010 article, scientists suggest that the eye makeup

Figure 1.1. Ancient Egyptian royals Cleopatra, Nefertiti, and Rameses II shown wearing an eye paint called *kohl*. © DigitalVision Vectors/ewg3D

commonly worn by ancient Egyptian royals also doubled as "an infection-fighter" to ward off or cure eye disease.[8] "Some Egyptians believed that this makeup also had a 'magical' role in which the ancient gods Horus and Ra would protect wearers against several illnesses," the article said.

The Beauty Secrets of the Orient

The ancient Chinese used nail color as a signifier of social class. The nail polish was created by combining beeswax, gelatin, egg whites, and gum arabic. During the Zhou dynasty (c. 1050–256 BCE), for example, royals wore gold or silver nail lacquer, while during the Ming dynasty (1368–1644 CE), they wore black or red nail color. Lower classes were forbidden from wearing bright nail colors.[9]

Women from the Tang dynasty (618–907 CE) followed a seven-step makeup routine, including applying powder, darkening eyebrows, painting dimples, coating cheeks with red rouge, and pasting the forehead with ornamental designs made from various materials like bird feathers, shell, fish bone, or gold leaf. Lip makeup was worn to please the gods, thus linking a woman's appearance to her spiritual worth.[10]

In ancient Japan, light skin was considered aesthetically pleasing. During the Nara period (710–794 CE), aristocratic women used rice powder to paint their faces and necks white. Removing natural eyebrows and painting smudgelike eyebrows on the forehead was popular in the Heian period (794–1185 CE), as well as painting the teeth gold or black.

Figure 1.2. The women of ancient Greece were renowned for their beauty rituals.
© DigitalVision Vectors/ZU_09

Ancient Beauty Rituals of the Greeks and Romans

In ancient times, the Mediterranean Sea was the central superhighway for commerce and trade, including the exportation of Egyptian cosmetic products to the emerging Greek and Roman civilizations spanning the third to the first millennia BC.

The origin of the word *cosmetic* comes from the Greek *kosmetike*, which means "the art of dress and ornament." The ancient Greeks were obsessed with cosmetics (see figure 1.2). Multiple ingredients went into the production of cosmetic products.

Skin moisturizers were made of honey; aromatic scents and emulsifiers contained olive oil; eye shadow was created by grinding charcoal to dust and mixing it with olive oil; and rouge was made from powdered iron oxide.

To lighten skin and deal with blemishes, both men and women used white lead face cream, which was highly toxic.[11] Ancient Greek women wore makeup sparingly and favored a natural look. In contrast, red lip paint, made of red dye and wine mixed with fetid substances like crocodile excrement, was largely worn by courtesans. Crimson lips served as a means of advertising (signaling) prostitution.

Ancient Romans initially used cosmetics for ritual purposes before they became part of Romans' everyday beautification rituals mainly among the rich and prostitutes. Milky-white skin was a stamp of Roman beauty and a sign of the leisure class. Prosperous women applied white lead to lighten their complexions and added a touch of red lead to achieve a rosy glow.[12]

Roman women followed certain skin care practices, such as using facial masks before bedtime. Recipes for these masks contained ingredients like sheep sweat (lanolin), excrement, honey, placenta, marrow, bile, animal urine, sulfur, and ground oyster shells. Women also bathed in donkey (ass) milk, which was believed to soften skin, preserve its whiteness, and erase wrinkles.

Killer Cosmetics of the Middle Ages

In medieval Europe, church leaders deemed the practice of wearing makeup to be sinful and immoral and imposed a ban on it, a prohibition that was ignored in brothels. For instance, in England, makeup use was considered "an incarnation of Satan."[13] Altering the face that God gave a woman was tantamount to challenging God and his craftsmanship. However, the clergy made an exception for women stricken with maladies that marred their appearance to such an extent that they were perceived as physically revolting to their husbands and onlookers.

In time, Italian theologian St. Thomas Aquinas reluctantly yielded and permitted the use of cosmetics, believing that a woman's physical attractiveness could discourage her husband from committing the sin of adultery. But he also cautioned that a woman who was too beautiful could attract other women's husbands.[14]

By the twelfth century, cosmetics came into regular use throughout Europe. Distribution was controlled by apothecaries and doctors, as the compounds were often toxic. Because of the frequency of smallpox outbreaks, which could leave permanent and disfiguring pockmarks, unblemished skin was coveted. A comely woman possessed pale skin, an even skin tone, and buttery blond hair. To achieve flawless skin, women were known to smear their faces with the blood of bull or hare. In Elizabethan England, society women achieved a pale skin tone by slathering egg whites all over their faces or by placing leeches behind the ears to drain blood from the region of the head, which resulted in a naturally pale look.

During the Renaissance, maintaining a pale complexion was compulsory among the upper echelons of European society. Skin whiteners were made from a deadly

Figure 1.3. Queen Elizabeth I was a royal user of Venetian Ceruse, also known as Spirits of Saturn. © PHOTOS.com/Getty Images Plus/Photos.com

combination of substances, such as lead oxide, white lead, hydroxide, carbonate, and mercury. These whiteners could cause facial muscle paralysis, scarring, or premature death. Ceruse, a foundation made of white lead and vinegar, was an extremely popular cosmetic. A royal user of the prestige product Venetian Ceruse, also called Spirits of Saturn, was Queen Elizabeth I (see figure 1.3).[15] The product produced a look known as "the Mask of Youth."[16]

The Age of Pallor

Paleness was still popular in Europe during the eighteenth century. The right shade of pallor was created by using white lead makeup and facial powder. Aristocratic women often wore face paint, a substance called *fucus*, as blush. Madder (an herb), cochineal (a dye made from insects), and ochre-based compounds were utilized to produce blush and lip color. Lips were commonly painted into a delicate rosebud shape to create a "bee-sting" effect.

During Queen Victoria's reign, heavy makeup fell out of fashion, and its use was discouraged. Queen Victoria herself proclaimed that makeup was improper, vulgar, and only appropriate for use by actors and prostitutes.[17]

By the mid-1800s, women took a subtler approach to wearing cosmetics. An ancestor of cold cream, Crème Céleste, which was made of a combination of white wax, spermaceti wax, sweet almond oil, and rosewater, was applied as a facial paste to moisturize the skin, hide blemishes, and create a light, silky complexion. To hide imperfections and create radiant skin, women dusted their faces with rice powder, zinc oxide, or pearl powder, a combination of bismuth chloride and talc (magnesium silicate). Clear lip balms often made of beeswax were applied to the lips to give them a shiny, moist appearance.

Some beauty rituals posed certain dangers. For example, both men and women took small quantities of arsenic by ingesting arsenical products, such as complexion wafers, liquids, and pills, to maintain a pale complexion, which could cause nervous system and kidney damage. Also, women were known to apply drops of belladonna to their eyes to dilate their pupils to create an alluring, wide-eyed look, which could lead to blindness.[18]

During the Edwardian era, pale skin remained in vogue, while fair hair became passé. The Edwardian beauty was a brunette with a milky complexion set off by rosy cheeks.[19] To attain an alabaster-white complexion, toxic substances like white lead makeup were still in use, as well as rice and pearl powders. To create a smoky eye, women used burnt matchsticks to darken eyelids, eyebrows, and eyelashes. Rouge, made from raw materials such as carmine (extracted from the cochineal insect), safflower, red sandalwood, and brazilwood mixed with talc, was applied to the cheeks to produce a rosy flush. Geranium and poppy petals were employed to lightly stain the lips and create a "bitten lip" effect.

The Mechanization of Makeup

The modern beauty industry arose in the second half of the nineteenth century, thanks in large part to rapid advances in mass-production methods and the development of mass marketing.[20] By then, cosmetics had gained wider acceptance and achieved broader use in most societies around the world, including America. Interestingly, the world of theater played a principal role in conventional makeup practices because actors were adept at applying theatrical makeup.

The mass availability of cosmetics gave rise to the field of cosmetology. Professional beauticians dispensed beauty advice to women on hair and makeup. Prominent makeup artists from stage and screen, such as Max Factor Sr., and early beauty innovators, like Elizabeth Arden, recognized the potential of a mass market for cosmetics and started to make and sell their own namesake products.

A whole new industry emerged to meet increased market demand for beauty products. The earliest skin care and cosmetics mass producers included Shiseido (Japan), Guerlain (France), L'Oréal (France), Maybelline (United States), Beiersdorf (Germany), Coty (France), Lancôme (France), and Garnier (France). As more department stores and chain stores carried cosmetics, a greater number of women had access to inexpensive cosmetic products. And the modern beauty industry was born.

THE MAKEUP OF THE BEAUTY INDUSTRY: RIPE FOR CONSOLIDATION

When you go up and down the health and beauty aids (HBA) aisle of a supermarket, you'll typically find a wide range of products, such as shampoos, cosmetics, moisturizing lotions, deodorants, nail polishes, and toothpastes. These products are made and marketed by firms within the *beauty and personal care* (BPC) *industry*, also referred to as the *personal care industry*, *cosmetics industry*, and *beauty industry*. Let's take a glance at the current state of the beauty industry.

The Beauty Industry Is Positively Glowing

Industry watchers often use phrases like "keenly competitive," "strong growth," "juicy returns," and "highly consolidated" to describe the beauty and personal care industry. Despite the competitive market pressures and challenges facing the retail industry ecosystem, the beauty and personal care industry has maintained robust growth in recent years. A 2014 *Forbes* article outlined the market attractiveness of the industry, including strong brand loyalty, high purchase frequency, nice profit margins, greater channel sales opportunities, and product development opportunities through acquisition or research and development (R&D) efforts.[21]

The beauty and personal care industry manufactures a broad spectrum of products, ranging from staples like toothpaste and shampoo to discretionary goods like eye makeup and fragrance. Products are of varying quality and, therefore, varying prices. For example, the industry produces prestige products commonly intended for department stores (e.g., Nordstrom and Macy's), as well as lower-priced "masstige" products ("premium but attainable"[22]) commonly sold through mass-market retailers, including big-box stores (e.g., Target) and drugstores (e.g., CVS). Given the diversity of these markets and products, overall industry revenue is somewhat shielded from dramatic changes in the economy. However, consumers tend to abandon pricier beauty products and substitute them with mid-tier or low-priced products during an economic downturn. After the economy rebounds, consumers generally go back to familiar products and brands.

The global beauty market is usually broken down into distinct product categories, including skin care, color cosmetics, hair care, fragrances, nail care, oral care, and personal care products. Many items in these categories have a complementary relationship, in which the items are used in conjunction with one another. For example, when you buy shampoo, you're probably going to buy hair conditioner. Therefore, the demand for one item influences the demand for another item.

Thanks to a rapidly aging global population, an increased adoption of digital technologies, and growth in emerging-market economies, the global beauty care products market was worth $532.43 billion in 2017, according to Orbis Research.[23] The industry is expected to climb to a market value of $805.61 billion by 2023 with a compound annual growth rate (CAGR) of 7.14 percent over a five-year period.[24]

Big Beauty Keeps Getting Bigger

Did you know that the most valuable cosmetics brand in the world is Johnson's (Johnson & Johnson)? This megabrand is valued at $14.1 billion, according to a report titled "Cosmetics 50 2019," prepared by Brand Finance. Chanel (Chanel S.A.), L'Oréal Paris (L'Oréal Group), Gillette (Procter & Gamble), Neutrogena (Johnson & Johnson), Nivea (Beiersdorf), Dior (LVMH Moët Hennessy Louis Vuitton), Clinique (Estée Lauder), Shiseido (Shiseido Group), and Guerlain (LVMH Moët Hennessy Louis Vuitton) rounded out the top ten global cosmetics brands.[25]

Despite the existence of hundreds of cosmetics companies, brands, and products, just a handful of billion-dollar conglomerates dominate the global beauty and personal care industry. In 2018, the world's largest beauty manufacturers included L'Oréal ($31.2 billion), Unilever ($24.8 billion), the Estée Lauder Cos. ($13.7 billion), Procter & Gamble Co. ($12.4 billion), Coty ($9.4 billion), Shiseido Co. ($8.9 billion), Beiersdorf ($6.9 billion), LVMH Moët Hennessy Louis Vuitton ($6.7 billion), Johnson & Johnson ($6.1 billion), Amorepacific Group ($5.6 billion), and Kao Corp. ($5.2 billion).[26]

A rapid succession of merger and acquisition (M&A) activity has resulted in a wave of consolidation within the industry, reaching a new high of 102 transactions in 2015. For instance, just in the first five months of 2015, Anglo-Dutch powerhouse Unilever snapped up a batch of premium skin care brands, including Murad, Dermalogica, Kate Somerville, and REN Skincare.[27] According to an article in the *Economist*, "Since this burst of transactions, six multinationals account for 80% of American makeup sales, while eight brands control 70% of the skin care market. With its Nivea brand, Beiersdorf is one of the few large independents left, desired by everyone from P&G and Unilever to L'Oréal."[28]

A 2017 Motley Fool article illustrated the stealth by which the largest beauty conglomerates have beefed up their brand portfolios. In 2016, Market Force polled about 8,000 beauty consumers to find out which beauty brands were their favorites and why. Both MAC Cosmetics and Clinique were voted as the most-loved beauty brands (both received 13 percent of the total vote), followed by bareMinerals by Bare Escentuals (10 percent), Urban Decay (7 percent), Lancôme (5 percent), and Estée Lauder (5 percent).[29] Of these popular brands, the Estée Lauder Companies Inc. owns MAC, Clinique, and Estée Lauder; L'Oréal owns Urban Decay and Lancôme; and Shiseido owns Bare Escentuals. With the exception of the Clinique and Estée Lauder brands, which were born from the Lauder group, the rest of the brands are acquisitions by these companies: the Estée Lauder Companies Inc. acquired MAC Cosmetics, L'Oréal bought Urban Decay and Lancôme, and Shiseido purchased Bare Escentuals.

THE ECONOMICS OF BEAUTY: "THE LIPSTICK EFFECT"

Do women spend more or less on beauty products during an economic recession? It turns out that women splurge on beauty products during economic downturns for almost entirely biological reasons. Dubbed "the lipstick effect" or the "leading lipstick indicator," when the misery index climbs, retail sales of beauty products post gains, making the beauty industry largely recession-proof, like the chocolate, beer, and video game industries (see figure 1.4).

Figure 1.4. During an economic downturn, consumers tend to spend money on small indulgences like expensive lipstick, a psychological phenomenon known as the "lipstick effect." © E+/sturti

A 2015 *Psychology Today* article presented findings from a series of psychology experiments that support the theory of the lipstick effect.[30] During a recession or economic downturn, women will refrain from making big-ticket luxury purchases, but they'll desire products that can enhance their attractiveness, like premium lipsticks. Because the lipstick effect generally operates below the level of conscious awareness, psychologists assert that precise experiments are necessary to pinpoint it. These experiments suggest that "this phenomenon is driven by women's desire to attract mates with resources," the article said.

The lipstick effect is "deeply rooted in women's mating psychology," according to a 2012 paper published in the *Journal of Personality and Social Psychology*.[31] The researchers found that when college-age women became aware of destabilization in the economy, they reported a heightened desire to purchase attractiveness-enhancing goods, along with a dampened desire to purchase goods that didn't enhance their physical appearance.[32]

This economic aberration seems to defy logic. In a 2011 *Time* article, Ken Goldstein, economist for the Conference Board, explained it in this way: "It's counterintuitive. In some cases, things are so bad and so tough that the consumer can't go on vacation. She can't buy a dress. . . . But at least she can buy some lipstick."[33] For proof of the lipstick effect, L'Oréal recorded sales growth of 5.3 percent during the first half of the Great Recession of 2008.[34]

Money Can Buy You Beauty

Economic factors such as income growth and income distribution can have a significant impact on the products that people are willing to spend on and how much they're willing to pay for those products. This is especially true for discretionary purchases like cosmetics. For example, state personal income, which includes earnings, property income, and government benefits, grew on average 3.1 percent in 2017, according to a Bureau of Economic Analysis (BEA) news release titled "State Personal Income Rises in 2017."[35] This means more pocket money to spend on those little indulgences like cosmetics and fragrances.

In the United States, the rich keep getting richer. Income inequality has been steadily rising since the 1970s. Who's the richest of them all? Baby boomers—the wealthiest generation in the United States for at least the next decade or so. "Their share of net household wealth will peak at 50.2 percent by 2020 and decline to 44.5 percent by 2030, quickly tapering off thereafter as mortality rates escalate," according to a November 2015 Deloitte University Press article, "The Future of Wealth in the United States."[36]

What does the wealth effect, the idea that people tend to spend more as the value of their assets rise,[37] have to do with the beauty industry? A great deal, it seems. According to a paper titled "Global Beauty Industry Trends in the 21st Century," published in "Active Citizenship by Knowledge Management & Innovation: Proceedings of the Management, Knowledge and Learning International Conference 2013," well-fixed baby boomers and a rising amount of discretionary income in the West are driving industry growth.[38] At the same time, growing middle classes in developing countries, such as China and Brazil, are becoming fertile markets.[39]

"POTS OF PROMISE": FINDING THE NEXT FOUNTAIN OF YOUTH

Speed to market of potentially game-changing new products can separate the winners from the losers in the cosmetics industry. Consider *nanotechnology*, an umbrella term that refers to the manipulation of tiny particles, commonly between 1 and 100 nanometers in size. Several cosmetics giants are racing to find cosmetic applications for nanotechnology. For example, shelling out about $600 million of its annual $17 billion in revenues to research, L'Oréal is the industry leader in nanotechnology patents, according to the *Bloomberg Businessweek* article "Nano, Nano on the Wall . . . ."[40] L'Oréal has already introduced its Revitalift anti-aging skin care brand that contains nanosomes of pro-retinol A, which are supposed to help reduce the appearance of fine lines and wrinkles. Nanosomes are tiny organic microspheres that act as carriers for the controlled release of active ingredients such as vitamins and nutrients. Other companies that produce nanocosmetics are Estée Lauder and Shiseido.

Let's take a critical look at key market opportunities that the beauty industry is chasing.

Anti-aging Skin Care Is the Beauty Industry's Shangri-La

If you've grown numb to skin care products that make anti-aging promises, such as turning back the clock and reversing the symptoms of premature aging, join the club. Most people over the age of forty aren't easily swayed by anti-aging claims used to sell many skin care products, but they buy the products anyway. After all, there very well could be "hope in a jar."

Thanks to baby boomers' desire to outwit the aging process, anti-aging has become an increasingly profitable segment of the skin care market. The global anti-aging market clocked in sales of $250 billion in 2016 and is expected to increase at a compound annual growth rate (CAGR) of 5.8 percent, climbing to $331.41 billion by 2021, according to a 2017 MarketersMedia press release.[41] The anti-aging market includes a whole slew of products, including anti-wrinkle products, retinol products, skin brighteners, anti-cellulite products, and hair color.

Some cosmetics companies claim that their anti-aging skin care products contain ingredients so powerful that they can perform wonders, like resetting the "skin's aging clock." The 2011 *Chicago Tribune* article "Do Anti-aging Skin Creams Work?" noted that anti-aging creams moisturize the skin, giving the appearance of healthier, suppler skin.[42] But inexpensive creams will do that too. Other product claims are harder to confirm because few studies have been produced and published in peer-reviewed medical journals to prove that these products fulfill their advertised promise. Simon Yoo, MD, is quoted as saying, "Efficacy is very vague in terms of over-the-counter products. Without any oversight, it is difficult to say whether these do anything."[43]

Cosmeceuticals: Real Science or Pseudoscience?

What qualifies a product to be called a *cosmeceutical*? Because the term refers to "a cosmetic product claimed to have medicinal or drug-like benefits,"[44] the FDA should be able to furnish us with an explanation. Not quite. The FDA doesn't recognize the term "cosmeceutical." Rather, cosmeceutical is a term of art used by the cosmetics industry to signify cosmetic products that are distinctive for their medicinal or drug-like benefits and can contain active ingredients, such as retinoids, peptides, depigmenting agents, alpha hydroxy acids, sunscreens, and others. Here's how the FDA explains it: "A product can be a drug, a cosmetic, or a combination of both, but the term 'cosmeceutical' has no meaning under the law."[45]

The global cosmeceuticals market is expected to reach $72.2 billion by 2022, according to a report titled "Global Cosmeceuticals Market Outlook 2022," published by ReportLinker. Consumers' desire to combat visible signs of aging has sparked market demand for cosmeceuticals.[46] Consumers are willing to pay a premium price for cosmeceuticals based on their perceived performance vis-à-vis other anti-aging skin care products. To justify higher prices, cosmeceutical companies typically use the term "cosmeceutical" in their sales messages. Consequently, consumers may mistakenly infer that a cosmeceutical is like a pharmaceutical-grade product and thus has met quality, safety, and effectiveness standards required for a drug, which it generally hasn't.

Some experts say that cosmeceuticals are nothing more than a subtype of pseudoscience. A 2014 WTOP article titled "The Truth about Anti-aging 'Cosmeceuticals'" cautioned consumers to be wary of product claims made about cosmeceuticals, which often appear in glossy magazine ads, on in-store print collateral at cosmetic counters, and through expert or celebrity testimonials.[47] Tina Alster, MD, explained that science has produced many excellent skin care products throughout the last decade, including some cosmeceuticals. "There are other ones that may claim they are doing something that don't, or may have ingredients that could be harmful to us in the long run," Alster said. She went on to say that some cosmeceuticals contain lesser-known ingredients that "haven't been around long enough to adequately judge their safety with extended use."[48]

As a footnote, with all the anti-aging breakthroughs in cosmetic science that promise to combat the effects of aging on skin, it's surprising that traditional beauty companies appear to be steering clear of entering the highly lucrative cosmetic procedures market. Rather, several cosmetics companies are positioning their products toward the competition (cosmetic plastic surgery)—in this case, anti-aging and cosmeceutical products suggesting that they're Botox alternatives, such as Dr. Brandt Skincare's Needles No More line.

Going Green Is Good for the Bottom Line

With growing awareness and rising concern over harmful chemicals in beauty and personal care products, many consumers are showing an interest in green beauty products, especially environmentally conscious millennials and health-conscious Gen Xers and baby boomers, as reported in the 2017 *Fast Company* article "What's Driving the Billion-Dollar Natural Beauty Movement?"[49]

A 2015 New Hope Network article titled "Natural Marketplace Sees Personal Care Industry Shift to Organic" reported that in 2014, the global natural and organic personal care market experienced a year-over-year increase of 9.3 percent, once more outstripping the traditional beauty category (see figure 1.5).[50] Beauty companies that have benefited from the demand for organic and natural beauty products include Bare Escentuals, The Body Shop, Burt's Bees, the Hain Celestial Group (with brands such as Zia Natural Skincare and Avalon Organics), Yves Rocher, Amway, Aveda, Kiehl's, and several small-batch beauty brands.

The Democratization of Beauty

Luxury beauty products are no longer reserved for affluent beauty consumers who can easily afford them. To address consumers' yen for luxury at affordable prices, many beauty companies have jumped on the premiumization bandwagon. *Premiumization*

Figure 1.5. Consumers' expanding interest in green beauty is driving growth in the global natural and organic personal care products market. © iStock/Getty Images Plus/ JulyProkopiv

is a branding term used to describe "the bridge between the desirability of the luxury world and the function and necessity of the mass market."[51]

Brands seek to premiumize their market offerings through differentiation (what makes a brand stand out) and relevance (how consumers see the brand fitting into their lives). A good example of a company that has successfully used a premiumization strategy is German color cosmetics brand BeYu, which is owned by the ART-DECO Cosmetic Group. As a masstige brand, BeYu has built a brand reputation for high-quality color cosmetics and eye-catching packaging, all at an affordable price.[52]

Move Over, Ladies

Once taboo, male primping has gone mainstream. Many millennial men have a positive attitude toward grooming, which is driving interest in "mampering," according to a 2014 CNBC article.[53] Matthew McCarthy, then senior marketing director of antiperspirants and deodorants at Unilever, is quoted as saying, "Younger guys are willing to try lots of stuff because they are growing up in a world where it's okay to care about your grooming."[54]

The global male grooming market is a major source of growth in the global beauty industry as well as one of its fastest-growing segments. In 2018, the size of the global male grooming products market was worth some $60 billion, and by 2024 it's expected to be valued at about $81 billion.[55]

Many cosmetics companies have heard the bugle call and are developing "just for men" lines. For example, department store brands, like Shiseido Men, Biotherm Homme, and Clinique for Men, and mass brands, like Dove Men+Care and L'Oréal Men Expert, are going after a slice of the male grooming market.

The Revenge of the Indie Brands

Indie beauty brands are steadily stealing market share from global beauty brands. The 2016 *Beauty Packaging* magazine article "Indie Brands Lead Beauty Industry Growth" noted new indie brands as highly differentiated, targeted, and directed at addressing a specific concern or offering a specific solution. "Packaging-wise, the new guard of niche brands is detail-oriented and simple, as classic silhouettes and monochromatic colors are favored, as are clean, technologically-driven formulas," the article said.[56]

This new generation of niche brands are nimble and can quickly respond to changes in the beauty marketplace. They are finding new—and often the shortest—marketing channels to get their products in the hands of beauty consumers. Their secret marketing weapon: digital marketing. In the 2016 *WWD* article "Social Media in the Beauty Landscape," Mary Beth Laughton, former executive vice president of omni retail at Sephora, is quoted as saying, "There is so much more content available to help clients over that decision-making threshold. The rise of visual social media has powered not only the ability for a client to explore more, but also make more informed decisions by seeing more images of product on faces and how to use products."[57]

Niche brands that primarily live in cyberspace include Sigma Beauty, Dose of Colors, and BH Cosmetics, which have built greater Instagram followership than established brands like CoverGirl and Revlon.[58] Some digital brands, such as Birchbox and Violet Grey, are using omni-channels, where they have set up brick-and-mortar stores in addition to their e-tailing activities, as reported in the 2015 CosmeticsDesign article "Retail Trend: Digital Beauty Brands Opening Storefront Shops."[59]

The New Beauty Battleground for Cosmetics Brands

The internet has revolutionized the way we shop for and buy cosmetics, with digital beauty sales going through the roof. The year-over-year growth in digital beauty sales rose to 14 percent in 2016, making the online beauty industry worth $1.2 billion, as cited in the 2017 TheStreet article "Who's Winning in Online Beauty Right Now."[60] Traditional beauty companies like Estée Lauder have taken the e-commerce plunge, while e-tailers like Amazon are swiftly making market-share gains in the beauty category. One in every five online beauty purchases was made through Amazon Marketplace in 2016, according to research by 1010data.[61] The findings also showed that MAC Cosmetics, an Estée Lauder brand, hit the jackpot to become the brand leader, with an overall 5.1 percent market share of the online cosmetics market. By category, MAC's lip products smeared the competition at 13 percent market share. In the number two spot is Estée Lauder's Clinique brand, which ranked number one for face makeup.

Market leaders in the beauty industry usually have a home court advantage at the store level, and some do in the social ecosystem as well. Engagement Labs produced data rankings of the top personal care and beauty brands in the United States based on social influence.[62] To perform the analysis, the company used its Engagement Labs TotalSocial® platform, which measures online social media listening and offline conversations. In the first half of 2018, the brands that received the highest TotalSocial® scores included Bath & Body Works, Ulta, Sephora, Dove, Colgate, Neutrogena, L'Oréal, Burt's Bees, Clinique, and Pantene, as compared with previous rankings from December 2017.[63]

In an Engagement Labs press release, Ed Keller, the company's CEO, commented on the results: "Our analysis really drives home the need for beauty brands to understand the importance of having a comprehensive view of social influence that embraces conversations as a powerful asset, regardless of where they take place."[64]

Prestige beauty brands aren't acclimating as quickly as other types of beauty products to the new digital terrain. One reason is that prestige brands must preserve an air and a promise of exclusivity and sophistication to appeal to their target markets. As more beauty consumers get their information about beauty brands and shop for beauty products online, prestige brands must weigh a desire to protect their upscale image against the business reality that they must be everywhere to compete with lesser-known beauty brands that have achieved digital dominance. The 2015 *Adweek* article "3 Ways Prestige Beauty Brands Can Preserve Their Allure in the Digital Age" described the dilemma faced by prestige beauty players: "The balance between connection and exclusion: Since the floodgates of access have opened beyond control, beauty brands need new ways of balancing belonging with longing."[65]

An Interbrand article titled "How Can Beauty Brands Adapt to the Digital World?" predicted that the digital marketing landscape would largely dictate the winners and the losers in the battle for market share.[66] To survive, mature brands must stretch across several marketing channels and reach multiple touchpoints to maintain their competitive footing. "In a crowded and highly competitive sector, standing out means expanding your brand's digital presence in order to get closer to the consumer, moving beyond that single point of in-person interaction to trace the journey the customer takes to get there. We are living in an environment where brands are omnipresent, and need to reach the customer at as many moments as possible," the article said.

In the next chapter, we'll learn some surprising facts about how beauty products are made and marketed.

2

The Beauty Industry Unmasked

Although men, women and children all use personal care products every day, the federal laws designed to ensure the safety of these products have remained largely unchanged since the late 1930s.

—From "Personal Care Products Safety Act Letter to Senate Leadership,"
August 30, 2016, from EWG.org

Have you ever noticed that fragrances don't generally contain a list of ingredients on their labels? The Food and Drug Administration (FDA) doesn't require fragrance manufacturers to list individual ingredients on the label, as those ingredients are most likely to be trade secrets.[1] FDA regulations may exempt a company from disclosing a certain ingredient that has been granted trade secret status under narrow circumstances and stringent FDA review. The legal argument is that a company that has spent heavily on research and development (R&D) to create a product with patented ingredients may legitimately protect this information.

What precisely is a trade secret? According to the Uniform Trade Secrets Act, which has been adopted by almost every state, a "trade secret" is defined as information that "derives independent economic value, actual or potential, from not being generally known to, and not being readily ascertainable by proper means by, other persons who can obtain economic value from its disclosure or use, and is the subject of efforts that are reasonable under the circumstances to maintain its secrecy."[2] For a cosmetic product, a clue that the FDA may have granted trade secret status to a certain ingredient is if you see the words "and other ingredients" at the end of the ingredients list.

Trade secret protection can provide a cosmetics company with an edge over its competitors. But is this protection being misused? A 2014 EcoWatch article suggested that nearly two dozen companies requested trade secret status to avoid letting the public know about toxic chemicals contained in about 1,500 cosmetic products listed in the California Safe Cosmetics Program Product Database.[3] The database is part of the California Safe Cosmetics Act of 2005, which requires cosmetics manufacturers to report the use of potentially hazardous ingredients to the state Department of Health Services (DHS), which in turn will warn consumers.[4] An analysis by Women's Voices for the Earth found that more than twenty companies may have tried to get around the intent of this legislation by evading public ingredient disclosure in the state's database.[5] Erin Switalski, executive director of Women's Voices for the Earth, is quoted as saying, "Trade secret status should never be allowed to conceal harmful chemicals such as carcinogens or reproductive toxins from consumers. . . . It's reasonable and prudent for consumers to want to avoid exposure to carcinogens, just as women of reproductive age may well want to avoid exposure to reproductive toxins."[6]

Let's unmask the truth about cosmetics regulation, manufacturing, testing, advertising, and other surprising facts.

COSMETICS AND THE LAW, PART 1: UNPACKING COSMETICS

To fully understand the complexities of cosmetic manufacturing and marketing, we must view it through the prism of the laws applicable to cosmetic products and the government agencies charged with their enforcement. The US Food and Drug Administration (FDA), a federal agency under the US Department of Health and Human Services, is responsible for safeguarding and advancing public health through the supervision and regulation of certain product classes, including cosmetics, the nation's food supply, human and veterinary drugs, medical devices, biological products, and products that release radiation. The FDA has some overlapping authority with its sister agencies: the Federal Trade Commission (FTC), the chief regulatory body responsible for protecting consumers and promoting competition by enforcing consumer protection and antitrust laws, as well as truth-in-advertising laws; the US Consumer Product Safety Commission (CPSC), an independent federal agency that promotes product safety by protecting the public from "unreasonable risks of injury or death" from consumer products under the agency's jurisdiction; and the US Environmental Protection Agency (EPA), a regulatory agency responsible for safeguarding public health and the environment and authorized by Congress to draft regulations to implement environmental laws.

Because cosmetics are applied to the largest organ in the body, the skin, you'd think that the FDA would approve cosmetic products and ingredients before they enter the market. Not so. Under the Federal Food, Drug, and Cosmetic Act (FD&C Act)—a set of laws that give the FDA the authority to oversee the safety of food, cosmetics, medical devices, and drugs—the agency doesn't require premarket approval for cosmetics, with the exception of color additives, as it generally does for drugs to prove

Figure 2.1. Major cosmetics companies produce millions of products every year. Cosmetic products and ingredients do not need to go through an FDA premarket approval process, except for color additives. © iStock/Getty Images Plus/brusinski

their safety and efficacy prior to marketing, although cosmetics are still subject to findings that products have been adulterated (either contain ingredients that are injurious to health or are missing a valuable constituent) under the Act (see figure 2.1).[7] However, the FDA can take enforcement actions against cosmetic products already on the market that don't comply with the law or against entities that disobey the law. For example, cosmetics companies can get themselves into hot water with the FDA when they make a drug claim about a cosmetic in their marketing, or if they market a drug as if it is a cosmetic, without following the legal requirements for drugs.

Some confusion lies in determining whether a product is a cosmetic or a drug under the law. According to the FDA: *Cosmetics* are "articles intended to be rubbed, poured, sprinkled, or sprayed on, introduced into, or otherwise applied to the human body . . . for cleansing, beautifying, promoting attractiveness, or altering the appearance," whereas *drugs* are "articles intended for use in the diagnosis, cure, mitigation, treatment, or prevention of disease" and "articles (other than food) intended to affect the structure or any function of the body of man or other animals."[8] Based on these definitions, a cosmetics company may run afoul of the law when it makes an implicit or explicit performance claim about a product that gives it the appearance of doing the same job as a drug.

But here's where it can get tricky: A product can be both a cosmetic and a drug. Take shampoo. Its intended use is to get your hair clean, making it a cosmetic. An anti-dandruff shampoo's intended use is to get rid of dry scalp flakes as it cleans your hair, making it both a cosmetic and a drug. Other examples include toothpastes containing fluoride, deodorants serving as antiperspirants, and moisturizers and foundations making sun-protection claims. These hybrid products must meet the guidelines for both a cosmetic and a drug under the law.[9] Moreover, over-the-counter hair growth products (e.g., Rogaine) meet the FDA definition of a drug, but few other cosmeceuticals for skin care and hair care do.

The FDA requires a product deemed both a drug and a cosmetic to provide scientific evidence supporting product safety, effectiveness, or therapeutic claims before that product can be marketed. A failure to do so carries serious regulatory ramifications, as the FDA could consider the cosmetic to be a misbranded drug.

"If You Can't Say It, Don't Wear It": Decoding Cosmetic Labels

Many ingredient labels on cosmetics and personal care products are difficult for consumers to decode. Unless you're a cosmetic chemist or a scientist, ingredients listed in technical language may look like a string of gibberish (see figure 2.2). In a *Herizons* magazine article titled "The Ugly Side of the Beauty Industry," Samuel Epstein, MD, coauthor of *The Safe Shopper's Bible* and former head of the Cancer Prevention Coalition, said that labeling is useless to anyone without a pharmacology degree: "I don't want to go shopping for my body products, my cosmetics, with a chemical dictionary telling me this one's okay, this one's not. I want to be able to walk in and buy it off the shelf with the understanding that it's safe."[10] Abby Lippman, a former professor in the department of Epidemiology, Biostatistics and Occupational Health at McGill University in Montreal, dispensed the following advice: "If you can't say it, don't wear it," adding that she didn't expect women to stop using cosmetics, nor did she wish to make women who wear cosmetics "sound like victims when they're making a conscious decision."[11]

Figure 2.2. Cosmetic product labels can be confusing to consumers buying a cosmetic product, because the ingredient list often includes unfamiliar chemical names. © E+/vgajic

So why don't cosmetics companies use plain English on cosmetic labels? Because the names of chemicals are the ingredients. Consider antiperspirants, which are considered both a cosmetic and a drug. On the product label, the first ingredient may be a drug ingredient. That ingredient may be marketed under a trade name, which doesn't tell us much about what the ingredient is and what it does. The terrain can get even murkier when products claim to contain "natural" ingredients. For instance, a body lotion may claim to contain vitamin E. If the label makes no mention of vitamin E and instead calls it something like "tocopherol," you may not know that tocopherol is a form of vitamin E.

As we've learned, the FDA doesn't regulate cosmetics in the same way as food or drugs or subject them to the same rigorous testing requirements to validate the safety of specific products or ingredients. However, it does have regulatory power over labeling under the authority of the Federal Food, Drug, and Cosmetic Act (FD&C Act) and the Fair Packaging and Labeling Act (FPLA). These laws are designed to protect consumers from health risks and deceptive marketing practices, as well as to aid consumers in making informed decisions about the cosmetics and personal care products that they buy. To hinder the distribution of false or misleading information, the FDA prohibits a manufacturer from making statements suggesting that the FDA has approved the product, whether in the labeling or advertising of that product.

What's cosmetics labeling? It refers to "all labels and other written, printed or graphic matter on or accompanying such article. This includes labels, inserts, risers,

display packs, leaflets, promotional literature or any other written or printed information distributed with a product,"[12] according to the FD&C Act. In addition, if
a cosmetic could be harmful to a consumer when used improperly, it must carry an
appropriate warning label as well as sufficient directions for safe use. Such statements
must be "prominent and conspicuous." For certain cosmetics, such as aerosol products, feminine deodorant sprays, and foaming detergent bath products (also known
as bubble bath products), specific language must be incorporated in their label warn-
ings and cautions. Know that the FDA regulates only the labeling that appears right
on the product but not false or misleading advertising about the product displayed
in different media, which is under the purview of the FTC.

COSMETICS AND THE LAW, PART 2:
TRUTH IN ADVERTISING

Assume that you have sensitive skin and want to find a facial cream that won't cause
an adverse skin reaction. You see an ad for a cream that claims to be hypoallergenic.
Like most consumers, you may believe that "hypoallergenic" means that the product is unlikely to cause an allergic reaction. Several cosmetics manufacturers make
the hypoallergenic claim for their products, including Neutrogena, Perricone MD,
Weleda, and Clinique. But before you purchase the hypoallergenic product that you
"reasonably" believe will not cause an unwanted skin irritation, know that the FDA
sets no federal standards, nor does it provide definitions, that rule on the use of the
term "hypoallergenic." Each manufacturer decides whatever it wants the term to
mean. In other words, a cosmetics manufacturer that labels its products hypoallergenic doesn't have to submit proof of its hypoallergenic claim to the FDA.[13]

For many years, the cosmetics industry has been under scrutiny by not only the
FDA but also the FTC, which has the power to investigate and prevent fraudulent
advertising and unethical or harmful marketing practices. Let's discuss the FTC's role
in monitoring, stopping, and combating false or misleading advertising for cosmetic
products in the media.

The FTC's Truth-in-Advertising Laws

In advertising, cosmetics companies frequently use sales messages designed to give
you practical reasons to purchase their products, which often involve making a *claim*,
a product-specific strategy based on a prediction or a promise of how the product
will perform. In most instances, a claim demands facts, proof, or explanations to
back it. For example, when an anti-wrinkle or anti-aging claim is made for a skin
care product, some sort of evidence is usually required to legitimize the claim. The
proof required to make a claim credible is called *support*, such as test results, research
findings, consumer surveys, expert validation, and other outside evidence.

The FTC's truth-in-advertising laws assert that any advertisement that appears in any medium (the internet, radio, television, print, and so on) must be truthful—that is, it must not mislead consumers—and, when appropriate, it must be supported by scientific evidence. The litmus test used by the FTC to determine whether an ad is deemed deceptive is the "reasonable person" standard; in other words, the ad is being seen from the point of view of the typical person. Prior to running an ad, "the advertiser must substantiate all claims—express *and* implied—that the ad conveys to reasonable consumers."[14]

The FTC's Enforcement Authority over Cosmetics Advertising

In 2014, the FTC accused L'Oréal USA of making "false and unsubstantiated claims" as to the specific benefits of its Génifique and Youth Code skin care products to target or boost the activity of users' genes and make their skin look younger, according to a 2014 *Fortune* article titled "L'Oréal USA Settles with FTC over Deceptive Skin Care Ads."[15] Jessica Rich, former director of the FTC's Bureau of Consumer Protection, is quoted as saying, "It would be nice if cosmetics could alter our genes and turn back time. But L'Oréal couldn't support these claims."[16] L'Oréal's ads claimed that Génifique products could bring about "visibly younger skin in just 7 days."[17] Likewise, ads for its Youth Code products claimed that they utilized "gene science" to "crack the code to younger acting skin."[18] Let's review enforcement strategies used by the FTC when it suspects an advertiser of publishing false or misleading advertising claims.

The agency has several enforcement tools at its disposal. According to *Major Principles of Media Law*, the simplest, most effective method to tamp down fraudulent advertising is to use publicity.[19] For example, in the L'Oréal case, several media outlets ran stories about the FTC's charges of deceptive advertising in addition to the company's settlement reached with the FTC.

The FTC also holds investigative and enforcement powers. For example, the FTC can pursue an advertiser when the agency has good reason to believe that the advertiser is making false and misleading claims about its products or services. As a first step, the FTC, often acting based on complaints from consumers, businesses, or other parties, will notify the advertiser that its ads are considered false or misleading and may also furnish a copy of a proposed *cease and desist order* with supporting documentation.[20] A cease and desist order would outline potential and/or actual violations and provide a warning that failure to remove or modify the misleading aspects of the ad could lead to fines, punishment, or other legal consequences.

To avoid a lengthy, costly legal proceeding over the challenged advertising, the advertiser may choose to sign a *consent agreement*, where the advertiser agrees to stop running the challenged advertising, with no admission of wrongdoing. The agreement is placed on the public record, usually for a 60-day comment period, after which the FTC may issue a *consent order* (a court order on which all parties involved have agreed), which carries the force of law with respect to future actions.[21] Rather than issuing an official consent order, the FTC may have the advertiser sign an affidavit called an *assurance of voluntary compliance* (AVC), a legal instrument entered into between the state attorney general and the advertiser that the attorney general believes has violated a consumer protection law (or may do so in the future). In either case, the agency ordinarily negotiates a settlement with the advertiser, as opposed to pursuing a formal legal proceeding. There are a couple of reasons to follow this legal strategy: it saves staff time; and the quicker the agency can get the advertiser to stop running the suspect advertising, the quicker the agency can protect the consumer from it.[22]

This is effectively what happened in the L'Oréal case. The FTC negotiated a settlement with L'Oréal over alleged false and unsubstantiated claims made about its Génifique and Youth Code products. Under the proposed consent order ("proposed order"), the cosmetics giant is prohibited from making certain product claims (such as the ability to target or boost the activity of genes to make skin appear or act younger) about any Lancôme brand or L'Oréal Paris brand facial skin care product unless the company can supply "competent and reliable scientific evidence substantiating such claims."[23] The proposed order was then placed on record for a public comment period—in L'Oréal's case, a 30-day period. According to an FTC press release, the FTC approved the final order following the public comment period, thus settling the charges against L'Oréal USA, Inc. for the deceptive advertisements.[24]

What happens if the advertiser refuses to sign a consent order? The FTC may start formal proceedings before an administrative law judge (ALJ). The ALJ will inquire fully into and consider all relevant facts, hear arguments from both the Commission and the advertiser, and issue an initial decision.[25] If the ALJ finds that the law has been violated, he or she may issue a formal cease and desist order, compelling the advertiser to stop the illegal practice. If either the advertiser or the Commission enforcement staff is not satisfied with the initial decision, it can appeal the Commission's decision to the federal courts.

Once a consent order or cease and desist order becomes final, the FTC staff monitors compliance. If the advertiser violates the terms of the order, it could face hefty civil penalties.[26]

Finally, the FTC has several other law enforcement tools in its arsenal. For instance, the agency can file a legal action against an advertiser in a federal district court, thus avoiding inordinate delays in the handling of cease and desist orders.[27]

Taking a Claim at Face Value

A 2012 *Los Angeles Times* article titled "Clamping Down on Beauty Product Claims" noted that many product claims made by beauty advertisers don't hold water.[28] The FDA has expressed a growing concern that product claims made by beauty manufacturers are insufficiently supported by scientific data. Then-FDA spokeswoman Tamara Ward was quoted in 2012 as saying, "Improper claims made in the labeling of cosmetics have escalated over the years. . . . FDA wants to ensure that labeling for cosmetic products is appropriate and that the products do not include claims that are not allowed."[29]

With respect to willingly accepting cosmetic claims, a *FindLaw* article titled "Cosmetics Labeling" recommended *caveat emptor* ("Let the buyer beware"), while also suggesting that advertising claims made for certain cosmetic ingredients may be "pure puffery."[30] John Bailey, a former director of the FDA's Office of Cosmetics and Colors, is quoted as saying, "Image is what the cosmetic industry sells through its products, and it's up to the consumer to believe it or not."[31] Moreover, an article in the *Economist* titled "The Beauty Business: Pots of Promise" issued a warning to the cosmetics industry: "Creams and cosmetics are making increasingly extravagant marketing claims. So far, women have been willing to buy into the illusion. Should that change (and there are signs it might), then manufacturers expose themselves to potentially ruinous litigation."[32]

The reality is that most consumers don't complain about specious claims because they assume that if the beauty industry makes a product claim, it must be true. This is largely because many consumers believe that cosmetics are tested and confirmed to work, which isn't always the case. Even in instances when a product is tested, the cited study used as proof in the cosmetic ads may not be rigorous enough to support the advertising claim. Rather than undertaking a rigorous clinical study in which it would perform skin biopsies to prove the formation of more skin collagen, the cosmetics company sponsoring the study may just ask women if they think their skin looks better, which is too subjective to produce statistically significant results. Even further, efficacy claims are often hazy if the cosmetics company relies on computer studies or animal studies to support these claims. In a 2011 *MarketWatch* article, Jessica Krant, MD, is quoted as saying, "What works in the lab doesn't always work in the real world."[33]

A 2015 *CBS News* article cited a study published in *Journal of Global Fashion Marketing: Bridging Fashion and Marketing* that analyzed the merits of product claims made about beauty products.[34] Using 289 makeup, hair care, fragrance, and skin care ads appearing in the April 2013 issues of seven women's fashion magazines, including *Vogue*, *Marie Claire*, and *Glamour*, the researchers found that fewer than one in five beauty claims was deemed to be truthful by a panel of readers. In addition, ads that contained scientific nomenclature to explain product benefits were "even less persuasive."[35]

The advertising claims were grouped according to the type of claims, such as scientific claims (e.g., "clinically proven") and endorsement claims (e.g., "dermatologists recommend"). A small panel of female judges, with differing degrees of knowledge about the beauty industry, were asked to sort the claims into four groupings: "outright lie," "omission," "vague," or "acceptable."

The results of the study were startling: A mere 18 percent of all claims fell into the "acceptable" category. A large majority (86 percent) of scientific claims were deemed "vague" or "false." Brag-and-boast claims, such as product superiority (e.g., "award-winning product"), and performance claims (e.g., "your skin feels softer") were considered "false." In contrast, most endorsement claims were considered "acceptable." Jie Fowler, one of the study's authors and an associate professor of marketing at Valdosta State University, is quoted as saying, "For the past 30 years a fundamental belief that advertisers hold is that women are more emotional, so whatever we write should be sensitive and emotional. But consumers today are more cynical so this type of plan may not work as well."[36]

FILLING IN THE REGULATORY GAPS: SELF-REGULATORY ORGANIZATIONS (SROS)

The FDA holds the cosmetics industry responsible for authenticating the safety of their products and the ingredients that go into those products prior to product launch. *Industry self-regulation* is "the process whereby members of an industry, trade, or sector of the economy monitor their own adherence to legal, ethical, or safety standards, rather than have an outside, independent agency such as a third-party entity or governmental regulator monitor and enforce those standards."[37] In the cosmetics industry, self-regulation takes several forms:

- *Voluntary Cosmetic Registration Program (VCRP)*: This post-market reporting system was established by the FDA and is used by cosmetics companies that sell their products to consumers in the United States. Information obtained through the VCRP can help the FDA pinpoint products that could be harmful and notify the manufacturers and distributors of those affected products.
- *Personal Care Products Council (PCPC)*: Formerly known as the Cosmetic, Toiletry, and Fragrance Association (CTFA), this Washington, DC–based national trade association has represented the global cosmetics and personal care products industry for over 120 years. The PCPC speaks on behalf of its more than 600 member companies that make and market a whole host of beauty and personal care products. In 2007, the PCPC developed the Consumer Commitment Code to exceed FDA requirements by taking a proactive approach toward product safety adopted by cosmetics companies.
- *Cosmetic Ingredient Review (CIR)*: With the support of the FDA and the Consumer Federation of America (CFA), this independent, nonprofit scientific body was formed and funded by the PCPC. The CIR program is responsible for scrupulously reviewing and assessing the safety of cosmetic product ingredients and publishing its findings in peer-reviewed scientific publications, such as the *International Journal of Toxicology*.
- *Advertising Self-Regulatory Council (ASRC)*: Established in 1971, the ASRC (formerly known as the National Advertising Review Council) sets the policies and procedures for advertising self-regulatory programs, including the National Advertising Division (NAD), Children's Advertising Review Unit (CARU),

National Advertising Review Board (NARB), Electronic Retailing Self-Regulation Program (ERSP), Direct Selling Self-Regulatory Council (DSSRC), and Digital Advertising Accountability Program ("Accountability Program"). In 2019, the ASRC merged into BBB National Programs, Inc., the national self-regulatory unit of the former Council of Better Business Bureaus (CBBB), and assumed all ASRC responsibilities. The NAD receives and reviews complaints concerning advertising claims filed by competitors, consumers, and local Better Business Bureaus, which are reviewed through the NAD's monitoring program.
- *Independent Third-Party Verification*: Independent verification and validation, such as testing services, claims substantiation, and cosmetics safety assessments, are provided by several organizations, including the NSF Cosmetics and Personal Care Program and Intertek. While cosmetics firms are under no legal obligation to get third-party verification, seeking it can serve as another line of defense if a product claim is disputed.

In addition to SROs, state legislatures and state attorneys general have stepped in to fill gaping holes in cosmetics regulation.

- *State Legislatures*: States have crafted and enforced cosmetic safety legislation. The state of Washington, for example, passed the Children's Safe Products Act (CSPA) in 2008. Under the Act, manufacturers that sell children's products, including personal care products, in the state are required to report the presence of "chemicals of high concern to children" in those products. Also, in 2013, Minnesota banned formaldehyde in children's personal care products, such as shampoos, lotions, and bubble baths.[38]
- *State Attorneys General*: Each state attorney general serves the public interest and has investigatory and enforcement powers. State attorneys general can bring legal action on behalf of the state against businesses and other organizations that violate laws intended to protect consumers.

Watchdog Organizations Keep the Cosmetics Industry on Its Toes

Nonprofit organizations are also watchdogging the cosmetics industry's business and marketing practices, such as Truth in Advertising, Inc. (TINA.org), and the Environmental Working Group (EWG). To disseminate product information about potentially hazardous cosmetics and personal care products, consumer and environmental organizations have harnessed the power of the internet. For example, EWG's Skin Deep® database makes it easy for consumers to find out if certain cosmetics and personal care products contain ingredients that are known or suspected to pose a health risk.

The American Cancer Society (ACS) is another organization that provides public information on the potential health and environmental risks of ingredients used to manufacture cosmetics. The ACS neither takes a stand on nor maintains ingredients lists on specific ingredients or cosmetics products. It does, however, supply consumers with neutral, third-party evidence to draw their own conclusions. The ACS position is that a direct association between cosmetics or their ingredients and short- or long-range health effects "is not entirely clear."[39] This is largely because cosmetic products are ordinarily only tested for short-term health effects, such as allergic or adverse reactions (for example, skin and eye irritation), and not longer-term health problems. According to the ACS,

> Because human studies of the long-term effects of most cosmetics (except, perhaps, hair dyes) don't exist, there is little evidence to suggest that using cosmetics, or being exposed to the ingredients in cosmetics during normal use of these products, increases cancer risk. Still, because there are no long-term studies, little is known about the health effects of long-term exposure to many ingredients in cosmetics. This means that we cannot claim that these products will not cause health problems in some people.[40]

Grassroots organizations are dedicated to studying and monitoring potentially harmful ingredients found in beauty products. For instance, the David Suzuki Foundation has developed a "dirty dozen" list of cosmetic ingredients.[41] The list includes BHA (butylated hydroxyanisole) and BHT (butylated hydroxytoluene), mainly used as preservatives in moisturizers, lipsticks, and other personal care products. These butylated compounds can cause skin reactions and pose health concerns, including endocrine disruption and organ-system toxicity.[42] As another example, San Francisco–based Campaign for Safe Cosmetics was started by a group of women who became curious about the safety of certain common cosmetics. They scoured neighborhood drugstores and spent hours reading labels on beauty products, only to find out that the ingredients were unrecognizable and unpronounceable. According to the 2013 *Mercury News* article, what started as a bootstrap effort evolved into a national movement that has changed the way consumers shop for personal care products, and has also driven the cosmetics industry to change the way it manufactures products.[43]

Finally, some nonprofits are committed to protecting public health and the environment. One such organization that you've probably heard of is Consumer Reports. This independent, nonprofit organization conducts unbiased product testing in addition to publishing product reviews and comparisons in its non-advertiser-sponsored magazine of the same name, which includes safety information and data on cosmetics.

Overhauling Cosmetics Laws in the US

Eighty-two years ago, the Federal Food, Drug, and Cosmetic Act (FD&C Act of 1938) was passed in response to the deaths of 107 people, including children, who were killed after ingesting a toxic elixir. Several amendments to the law have been instituted, but there's not been a major overhaul of the law. In 1954, Congress attempted to pass a bill to revise the law, but President Dwight D. Eisenhower vetoed it. Since then, however, no attempt has been made by Congress to strengthen the law—that is, until recently.

In 2015, senators Dianne Feinstein (D-CA) and Susan Collins (R-ME) introduced the Personal Care Products Safety Act, which amends the FD&C Act by ramping up federal oversight of cosmetics and personal care products. The proposed legislation addresses the agency's sluggishness in modernizing the current statute.[44] If the bill becomes law, cosmetics companies will be required to register their facilities and products with the FDA and to submit cosmetic ingredient statements, including the amounts of ingredients used in cosmetics. Each year, the FDA will review at least five ingredients to determine their safety and appropriate use. A domestic and foreign manufacturer, distributor, or packer whose name appears on a cosmetic label will be required to report harmful health events related to their cosmetics, as well as give the FDA authority to recall those products deemed dangerous, among other conditions.

Tougher Cosmetics Laws Outside the US

Both the European Union (EU) and Canada have far more stringent cosmetics regulations than the United States. For example, the EU has three sets of regulations—EU Cosmetics Directive (2003/2013 rev.); EU Cosmetic Products Regulation (2009); and Registration, Evaluation, Authorisation and Restriction of Chemicals (REACH) Regulation (2006)—that cosmetics manufacturers, importers, and exporters must meet if they wish to sell cosmetics products in the EU market. Under the current EU Cosmetics Directive, cosmetic ingredients are reviewed for safety by the EU Scientific Committee on Consumer Safety (SCCS). Currently, 1,328 chemicals have been banned from cosmetics because they are known to cause, or are suspected of causing, a variety of health problems, including cancer, organ dysfunction, genetic mutation, reproductive harm, or birth defects. In comparison, the FDA bans or restricts only about a dozen chemicals in cosmetics.

Another significant difference between the European Union and the United States is that the EU requires premarket safety assessments of the finished cosmetic product prior to placing it on the market, whereas the FDA does not. Also, EU regulation requires that all cosmetics containing nanomaterials identify them right on the ingredient label, plus these nanomaterials must be authorized by the European Commission prior to their use in cosmetic products, whereas the FDA regulation does not require either. Finally, EU laws prohibit animal testing for cosmetic purposes, whereas the FDA does not, although the agency supports the application and development of alternatives to animal testing.

Canada has two major pieces of cosmetics legislation, the Food and Drugs Act and the Cosmetic Regulations, both of which set forth safety requirements for all cosmetics sold in Canada. Health Canada, the federal department responsible for national public health, maintains a database called the Cosmetic Ingredient Hotlist, a data warehouse containing those ingredients prohibited for use in cosmetics for sale in Canada. More than 500 chemical ingredients are banned or restricted for use in cosmetics products by Health Canada.[45]

CHEMICAL EXPOSURE:
WHAT'S LURKING IN YOUR COSMETICS?

About how many personal care products do you think you use daily? If you're a woman and answered an average of twelve products, that's in line with the estimate given by the EWG. A dozen products doesn't sound like a lot. But the number of chemicals that you could be exposed to may shock you, according to the *ABC News* article "Women Put an Average of 168 Chemicals on Their Bodies Each Day, Consumer Group Says."[46] It's not just women who are at risk for exposure. Men are, too, but to a lesser extent because they use fewer products. Still, they're exposed to around eighty-five chemicals in the personal care products they typically use.

Studies show that teens, who use roughly seventeen personal care products daily, may be at greatest risk for exposure to chemicals.[47] Blood and urine tests conducted on twenty teens showed that chemicals from these products remained in the teens' bodies. Sixteen hormone-altering chemicals, many of which appear on the EWG's list of Dirty Dozen Endocrine Disruptors (e.g., phthalates), were identified in an EWG research report titled "Teen Girls' Body Burden of Hormone-Altering Cosmetics Chemicals: Adolescent Exposures to Cosmetic Chemicals of Concern."[48]

Women and girls are more vulnerable to exposure to cosmetic chemicals that could cause hormone imbalances. That's because many chemical toxins are fat-soluble and thus are more easily absorbed. Because women have more body fat than men, these fat-soluble chemicals can accumulate in women's bodies, especially in breast tissue, a fat depot where these chemicals can be stored.

The potential health risks posed by certain cosmetic chemicals can run deep. Let's look at two specific chemicals that have been under the microscope for a while: parabens and phthalates.

Parabens: Why They May Be Bad for You

According to the FDA, parabens are a group of chemicals that are commonly used as preservatives in cosmetics and personal care products, such as deodorants, makeup, moisturizers, hair care products, shaving products, and many others. Methylparaben, propylparaben, butylparaben, and ethylparaben are the most common parabens used in cosmetics to prevent the growth of harmful bacteria and mold. Parabens are so commonplace that product ingredient labels typically list more than one paraben in a product.[49]

The FDA hasn't established specific rules to cover preservatives in cosmetics. Rather, the law regards preservatives in cosmetics in the same manner as it does other cosmetic ingredients. At the same time, the FDA pledges to intervene if reliable scientific information demonstrates that a cosmetic is harmful to consumers when they use the product according to directions shown on the label or in a normal manner. With respect to health concerns swirling around parabens, such as breast cancer, the agency's position is as follows: "FDA scientists continue to review published studies on the safety of parabens. At this time, we do not have information showing that parabens as they are used in cosmetics have an effect on human health."[50]

So are parabens a problem? A 2004 *New Scientist* article reported that British scientists claimed to have found preservative chemicals in samples of breast tumor, which probably arose from use of underarm deodorants.[51] The chemical culprit: para-hydroxybenzoic acids, or parabens. The 2004 study showed high concentrations of parabens in eighteen out of twenty tumor samples. According to molecular biologist Philippa Darbre, a professor at the University of Reading's School of Biological Sciences who led the research team, "One would expect tumours to occur evenly, with 20 per cent arising in each of the five areas of the breast. . . . But these results help explain why up to 60 per cent of all breast tumours are found in just one-fifth of the breast—the upper-outer quadrant, nearest the underarm."[52] The findings appear in a 2004 paper titled "Concentrations of Parabens in Human Breast Tumours," published in the *Journal of Applied Toxicology*.

The authors assert that larger cell-based studies are needed to determine the presence and potency of parabens in breast tumors. In the *New Scientist* article, Philip Harvey, editor in chief of *Journal of Applied Toxicology*, said, "From this research it is not possible to say whether parabens actually caused these tumours, but they may certainly be associated with the overall rise in breast cancer cases."[53] Chris Flower, then–director general of the Cosmetic, Toiletry, and Perfumery Association (CTPA), disputed the study's conclusions. He is quoted in the *New Scientist* article as saying, "There are almost no deodorants and body sprays that contain parabens. . . . Although they are in most other creams and cosmetics, the safety margin is huge and they would not have any effect on enhancing growth of new tumours."

Phthalates: Why They're Named Chemical Enemy Number One

Environmental Health Perspectives published an article in 2005 titled "Chemical Exposures: The Ugly Side of Beauty Products" that explored the risks associated with low-level exposure to certain toxicants, especially phthalates, in cosmetics and personal care products. The article highlighted three reports produced by environmental groups: *Growing Up Toxic: Chemical Exposures and Increases in Developmental Diseases*; *Skin Deep: A Safety Assessment of Ingredients in Personal Care Products*; and *Shop Till You Drop? Survey of High Street Retailers on Risky Chemicals in Products 2003–2004*.[54] These reports indicated that several cosmetics and personal care products contain chemical ingredients for which safety data is lacking. They also mentioned that these ingredients have been linked in animal studies with "male genital birth defects, decreased sperm counts, and altered pregnancy outcomes."[55] One of the chemicals of concern was phthalates.

What's wrong with phthalates, and why should we care if they're in our cosmetic products? Phthalates are used to make plastics, thus earning the name of plasticizers. Phthalates are contained in hundreds of products, including vinyl flooring, detergents, lubricating oils, and personal care products such as soaps, shampoos, perfumes, lotions, hair sprays, and nail polishes.[56]

How do you know whether the personal care products you use contain phthalates? You may not know unless phthalates are listed on the cosmetic label. Some products include "phthalates" in an ingredient list, or they may be listed by different names, such as DEP, DBP, DEHP, and fragrance.[57]

The potential dangers of phthalates in cosmetics are well documented. An observational cohort study conducted from 2006 to 2008 found that women who had higher phthalate metabolite levels in their urine had a greater chance of delivering a baby before the full 37-week gestation period.[58] "As exposure to phthalates is widespread and because the prevalence of preterm birth among women in our study cohort was similar to that in the general population, our results are generalizable to women in the United States and elsewhere. . . . These data provide strong support for taking action in the prevention or reduction of phthalate exposure during pregnancy," according to the study's authors.[59]

Cosmetics Industry Response to Cosmetic Chemical Concerns

Some beauty and personal care products companies are voluntarily phasing out or eliminating the use of certain chemical ingredients that are suspected of being or known to be harmful. For example, the British cosmetics and skin care company The Body Shop has phased out phthalates in its products.

Other industry players are caving in to increased consumer pressure and are voluntarily removing potentially harmful chemical ingredients from their products. For instance, Johnson & Johnson pledged to eliminate harmful chemicals, notably formaldehyde and 1,4-dioxane (both chemicals have been linked to cancer), from its line of children's personal care products. The company also promised to discontinue the use of this unpopular chemical in its adult brands, such as Aveeno, Neutrogena, and Clean & Clear®, according to the 2012 *New York Times* article "Johnson & Johnson to Remove Formaldehyde from Products."[60] Two years later, the company made good on its promise to remove formaldehyde and 1,4-dioxane from its baby shampoo and 100 other baby products, as reported in the 2014 *New York Times* article "The 'No More Tears' Shampoo, Now with No Formaldehyde."[61]

Counterfeit Cosmetics: Peddling in Deadly Fakes

The 2019 MSN.com article "The World's Most Counterfeited Brands Revealed" cited that trade in fakes is worth an astronomical $462 billion a year, according to data from the Organization for Economic Co-operation and Development (OECD) and the European Union Intellectual Property Office (EUIPO). This figure could reportedly climb to a startling $2.3 trillion by 2022.[62] Popular brands of jewelry, watches, apparel, leather goods, sneakers, software, smartphones, entertainment material, toys, sunglasses, cigarettes, and pharmaceuticals are most vulnerable to counterfeiting, as well as name-branded cosmetics. In the makeup category, MAC Cosmetics is the world's most counterfeited makeup brand.[63]

There's no federal law that prohibits you from buying fake cosmetics for personal use. However, there are stiff penalties for peddling in fakes, including prison time and a hefty fine. For consumers, the real danger is that fake cosmetics could be harmful to your health because they could contain harmful substances, such as cyanide, lead, and mercury.

A 2013 CosmeticsDesign article titled "Reports of Counterfeit Estée Lauder Cosmetics Grow in the Bay Area" addressed the problem of contaminated counterfeit makeup, which has made its way onto the streets of San Francisco and over the internet.[64] The US Department of Homeland Security (DHS) has reported a spike in the number of counterfeit makeup manufacturing rings. These counterfeit rings are pushing fake cosmetics that often contain heavy metals, bacteria, and other potentially toxic substances, the article said.

Counterfeit cosmetics are mostly manufactured in the Far East, with China identified as one of the primary source countries, as reported in a 2015 *Guardian* article.[65] The potential harm that these copycats can cause is palpable. "Mercury, lead, arsenic, cyanide and even human urine and rat droppings are often found in counterfeit cosmetics made in China. The level of toxins in some of these products have led to severe allergic reactions including skin rashes and burns, disfigurement and long-term health problems such as high blood pressure and infertility," according to a 2015 *Mashable* article.[66]

SAVING CREATURES GREAT AND SMALL: COSMETICS ANIMAL TESTING

Layering mascara on rabbits? Adorning guinea pigs with lipstick? Putting volumizing mousse on mice? No, these aren't depictions of lovable cartoon characters. Rather, they're real creatures used for animal testing of cosmetics. Many Americans may not be aware that animal testing of cosmetic products and ingredients is still allowed in the United States. Even though US law doesn't require animal testing of cosmetics (see figure 2.3), it doesn't prohibit it either.

In the absence of federal legislation that halts this practice, many cosmetics laboratories across the nation are exposing thousands of animals, including mice, rabbits, rats, and guinea pigs, to substances that could cause the animals to suffer. Let's find out where other countries stand on cosmetics animal testing.

Figure 2.3. No laws or FDA regulations specifically require the use of animals in cosmetics testing for safety. © iStock/Getty Images Plus/Artfully79

Nations Banning Cosmetics Testing on Animals; the US May Finally Catch Up

More than thirty nations, including European Union member countries (such as Austria, Belgium, Greece, France, Germany, and Italy), India, Israel, Norway, and New Zealand, have passed legislation banning animal testing of cosmetics. The United Kingdom played a major role in getting the ball rolling. The 1970s and 1980s saw a groundswell of public discontent over animal testing of cosmetics in Britain, which led the British government to end cosmetics testing in 1998. During the 1990s, the whole of Europe followed Britain's lead, even in the face of industry resistance. By 2009, public and political support won the day, and Europe's laboratories suspended cosmetics animal testing ("the testing ban"). Four years later, all European countries banned the sale of cosmetics and ingredients tested on animals, regardless of whether alternative testing methods exist ("the marketing ban").[67]

Many countries that have banned cosmetics testing sell products in countries that still allow animal testing. For example, in 2014, China lifted its requirement of premarket animal testing of "ordinary" cosmetics, such as hair care and skin care products, on domestically produced and sold cosmetic products, although it still requires animal testing on cosmetics for "special use," such as hair color, sunscreen, and deodorants. However, the country requires post-market animal testing on foreign imported ordinary cosmetic products, among other test/no test requirements.[68] This means that if a cosmetic product made in Britain, which bans cosmetics testing on animals, is exported to China, which requires animal testing, the British product can no longer be considered cruelty-free.

In the United States, something is finally being done to institute cruelty-free cosmetics policies. In 2015, a bipartisan bill called the Humane Cosmetics Act to phase out animal testing of cosmetics and the sale of latterly animal-tested cosmetics was introduced in the US House of Representatives by Martha McSally (R-AZ), Don Beyer (D-VA), Joe Heck (R-NV), and Tony Cárdenas (D-CA). In a 2015 press release titled "Federal Bill to End Cosmetics Testing on Animals Introduced," issued by the Humane Society of the United States (HSUS), McSally said, "Subjecting animals to painful and inhumane testing is not who we are as a country. There's no reason to continue this cruel practice when we have cost-effective alternatives that can bring about safe products for consumers."[69]

Ending animal testing is widely supported by the American public. Most American adults (79 percent) favor a federal law to end animal testing of cosmetics, according to a SurveyUSA poll conducted in August 2019.[70] Wayne Pacelle, former president and CEO of HSUS, pointed out the senselessness of animal testing and the need to eliminate this practice in the following statement published in the HSUS press release: "Given the ready availability of alternatives, there is no compelling reason to continue using outdated animal testing methods that cause tremendous animal suffering. So many companies are already using non-animal tests for shampoos, makeups and other products sold around the world, and the United States can help accelerate that trend." Several celebrities, including Kesha, Ricky Gervais, and Jenna Dewan, have voiced support for the bill, in addition to more than 140 cosmetics companies, including Lush, Coty, The Body Shop, and Paul Mitchell.[71]

In the next chapter, we'll meet the beauty consumers and learn what makes them buy what they buy.

3

The Beauty Seekers

In the factory, we make cosmetics. In the store, we sell hope.

—Charles Haskell Revson (1906–1975),
cofounder, president, and chairman of Revlon, Inc.

Cosmetics magnate Charles Revson, who built an empire on the foundation of nail polish, captured the unvarnished truth about the beauty business in a single metaphor: hope in a jar. In the laboratory, cosmetic chemists create viscous lotions and miracle potions. In the marketplace, cosmetics companies create symbolic meanings, such as allure and desirability, and transfer those meanings into cosmetic products, like an $8 bottle of Revlon nail polish.

In 1931, Revson got his start in the cosmetics industry by selling nail polish for Elka Company, a small nail polish supplier to beauty salons. In the early days of nail polish, only dye-based polishes were available, either colorless or in a few shades of red. Elka had developed an opaque "cream enamel," which offered superior coverage and could be made in a wider range of colors.[1]

The market potential of this revolutionary product was not lost on Revson. He and his older brother, Joseph, distributed Elka nail polish as Revson Brothers. A year later, Revson parted company with Elka and went into partnership with Joseph and Charles R. Lachman, a chemist (who contributed the "l" in the Revlon company name), to market a new, creamy nail lacquer. In 1932, Revlon was born.[2]

A shrewd businessman with keen instincts, Revson could sniff out a trend and quickly respond to it. For example, he saw an opportunity for business growth by capitalizing on the permanent wave trend, which became all the rage in the 1930s.[3] The process of permanent-waving required the use of a contraption called a "permanent wave machine," which combined chemicals and long, electrically heated clamps that snaked out of an intimidating-looking machine and locked onto women's hair.

Observing that women were flocking to beauty salons to get perms and getting manicures during this daylong process, Revson swooped in and began distributing his nail polishes through salons, a calculated business risk that paid off with sales taking off.

Revson understood the importance of color variety and created a color wheel of shades, including seasonal shades. He believed that women should use polish to make a fashion statement, such as coordinating nail color with outfits, using shades as a reflection of their mood, and wearing the right nail color to mark a special occasion. Also, product naming was elevated to a fine art, often evoking a landscape of imagery, such as "Cherries in the Snow," "Fifth Avenue Red," "Fatal Apple," "Cinderella's Pumpkin," "Stormy Pink," and, the most popular of all, "Fire and Ice."

By 1939, Revson had extended the Revlon brand name by creating lipsticks to match nail color, a practice dating back to the 1920s and already used by Cutex, Revlon's biggest nail rival. Revson was no stranger to taking product ideas already tested by his competitors, improving upon them, and then using advertising and promotion to help create sales.[4]

He possessed keen marketing instincts and knew sales like the back of his well-groomed hand. For example, he created an innovative strategy in which he sold nail enamels in tandem with lipstick. He armed Revlon "salesgirls" with color charts to show customers how to match lip and nail color. To stimulate market demand, Revlon ran a print ad campaign that used rhyme in the ad copy: "matching lips and fingertips." By 1945, Revlon had become one of the top five beauty brands in the United States.[5]

In addition to valuing product innovation, Revson understood the relationship between pricing strategy and channel distribution. He recognized that price can signal prestige, and so he used image pricing to communicate something special about Revlon products. To attract both price sensitive and price insensitive consumers, Revlon products were sold in department stores, selected drugstores, and upscale beauty salons.[6] He avoided bargain and cut-rate stores, which could tarnish the Revlon brand image.

Revson was an audacious and tireless promoter. He recognized the power of print to establish cachet for the Revlon brand. The company frequently ran full-color photographic advertisements, often double-page spreads, to promote its products in fashion magazines like *Vogue* and *Harper's Bazaar*. Take, for example, the "Fire and Ice" launch in 1952. Revson instructed the company's then ad agency, Norman, Craig & Kummel, to work with Bea Castle, Revlon's in-house marketing executive, to create a glittering print ad featuring Dorian Leigh, one of the earliest modeling icons. Leigh wore a body-hugging sparkling silver dress with a brilliant red cape in the ad, which was shot by top fashion photographer Richard Avedon.

The "Fire and Ice" print ad was widely used in an umbrella campaign. *Vogue* made the shade the focal point of its November issue; other magazines carried the ad; and counter cards, window displays, and radio endorsements hyped up the ad.

The result: The "Fire and Ice" promotional effort was one of the most talked-about product launch campaigns in the beauty industry. The real success of the campaign, though, rested on its use of artful dramatization in telling an aspirational story to the American woman: that she could be a glamorous seductress. The ad copy read: "For you who love to flirt with fire . . . who dare to skate on thin ice . . . Revlon's 'Fire and Ice' for lips and matching fingertips. A lush-and-passionate scarlet . . . like flaming diamonds dancing on the moon!"[7]

Revson knew he was selling more than a shiny product wrapped in stylish packaging and promoted through glossy ads. He was selling the female consumer hopes, dreams, fantasies, status, and success in Technicolor. A 1975 *Time* magazine article described Revson's uncanny consumer insight as follows: "Charles Revson had an almost eerily unerring sense of what American women wanted—or could be persuaded to want."[8]

In this chapter, we'll look at what makes beauty consumers tick: who they are, what they buy, where they buy, and why. We'll also talk about advertising messages for beauty products. Finally, we'll discuss the ways that the beauty industry is changing the conversation with a new generation of beauty consumers.

BEAUTY BEFORE AGE: MEETING THE BEAUTY CONSUMER

How much do you think the average woman spends on beauty products? To put it in perspective, American consumers' yearly spending on beauty exceeds that spent on education.[9] A 2017 *Daily Mail* article cited a 2017 survey by beauty e-tailer SkinStore that found the average American woman will pony up around $300,000 on facial products alone in her lifetime.[10] Let's get to know the beauty consumer.

Who Is the Beauty Consumer?

Millennial women are the new marketing darlings of the beauty industry, yet Generation X and baby boomer women are just as important to market growth. Nielsen conducted an insight analysis on the consumption of beauty products among these generations and presented the findings in a 2015 article that revealed the spending power of these three groups, especially in combined households.[11]

Millennial-led households forked out $461 million on beauty products in the twelve-month period ending June 2014. The purchasing power of this cohort is even greater in combined households. "Millennial and Generation X families have the greatest potential for beauty sales: These multigenerational households spent $798 million in the same 12-month period. Meanwhile, millennial and baby boomer combined households spent an additional $699 million," according to Nielsen.[12] Together, these women make up the beauty industry's most valuable customers (see figure 3.1).

Figure 3.1. The one-size-fits-all approach to beauty no longer works. Today's beauty consumers expect diversity at the beauty counter. © E+/SDI Productions

"The Pig in the Python"

With staying and spending power, boomers remain a formidable consumer presence in the marketplace. According to Forrester Research, baby boomers are the "biggest spenders" because they have extra cash on hand from decades of saving and investing, as explained in the *Business Insider* article "Baby Boomers Are the Sexiest Consumers in Retail."[13]

Aging baby boomers are a growth driver in the beauty industry, especially for anti-aging products and services. "As technological advancements extend the average life expectancy in the United States, baby boomers will seek products to look as youthful as they feel. To this end, demand for cosmeceuticals, which are cosmetics with pharmaceutical capabilities, such as wrinkle-reducing moisturizers, will also rise over the next five years," as noted in a 2014 IBISWorld article."[14]

"The Middle Child"

Once called "the MTV generation," Generation X is sandwiched between two significantly larger generations. A 2014 Pew Research Center article described Gen Xers as "a low-slung, straight-line bridge between two noisy behemoths," the baby boomers that came before them and the millennials that came after them.[15]

Generation X women, with many pushing and passing fifty and hitting their peak earning years, are getting the beauty industry's attention. These women are redefining what middle-age looks like, with healthier lifestyles, greater life expectancies, and freer attitudes than their predecessor generation, according to a 2011 *Los Angeles Times* article.[16] As beauty consumers, the most important consumption-specific values of Gen X women are superior service and convenience. Moreover, affluent Gen X women are more willing to splurge on luxury products, such as prestige beauty brands. The article mentioned that a JWT study found that Gen Xers depend more on preventive anti-aging beauty routines than baby boomers do.[17]

"The Peter Pan Generation"

The millennial generation, also called Generation Y, has the unique distinction of being the most diverse adult population in the nation's history and possibly the greenest. Most millennial women in this sustainability-conscious generation are also beauty conscious. According to a 2015 Meredith Corporation press release, in 2014, a study found that a majority of female millennial consumers (73 percent) said that looking beautiful or sexy was important to them, as compared with slightly more than half (57 percent) of their baby boomer counterparts.[18]

Millennial women are fueling the natural beauty trend. A 2016 *Allure* article cited a 2016 and 2017 Kari Gran–sponsored study that found a majority of millennial women (73 percent) look for "cleaner, all-natural products."[19] Moreover, the younger generation is taking a preemptive strike at unwanted signs of aging skin by adopting a "beauty-from-the-inside-out approach," as noted in a 2016 *WWD* article.[20]

In addition to baby boomers, Generation X, and millennials, the Silent Generation and Generation Z shouldn't be forgotten, as they are viable markets, based on their unique beauty needs and wants. Let's get acquainted with them.

"The Lucky Few"

The Silent Generation, also known as Traditionalists, is caught between two more familiar generations: "the get-it-done G.I. and the self-absorbed Boom."[21] A 2013 Mintel article titled "The Mature Beauty Market—Time for Brands to Grow Up?" identified Mintel's Old Gold trend, explaining that manufacturers are presented with two conflicting developments. On the one hand, older consumers are living longer, working longer, and representing a greater proportion of the population in both developed and some developing countries, whereas the share of younger consumers is declining. On the other hand, beauty product usage drops after people reach their mid-fifties. Given these twin effects, manufacturers will need to figure out how to keep older consumers engaged and interested in beauty products. Mintel offers some advice on how beauty companies can do this: remain relevant. "Beauty companies must take the physiological and emotional needs of this demographic into account and formulate and market accordingly," the article pointed out.[22]

In 2016, *Marketing Week* said that beauty brands would miss the boat if they fixated on millennials and forsook older consumers. Marie Cesbron, L'Oréal's former director of customer insights and global innovation and now insight and strategy adviser at The Age of No Retirement, pointed out that the sacred cows of marketing were to chase the youth market. Cesbron said: "To be fair, targeting the young has worked in the past but age-agnostic marketing nowadays is crucial."[23]

"The Homeland Generation"

Generation Z (also known as post-millennials) is a rapidly rising group. The oldest Gen Zers only recently graduated from college, while the youngest are at an age when they're watching television shows on Disney Junior and Nickelodeon. An *ABC News* article noted that the tween makeup market rakes in sales north of $24 million annually (see figure 3.2).[24] Big-box retailer Walmart, for example, has introduced a line of cosmetics for young girls age twelve and under.[25]

Generation Z consumers are becoming fascinated with beauty products starting from an increasingly early age, thanks to social media and the selfie craze, as suggested in a 2016 *Beauty Packaging* article.[26] "The ability to share images on social media is a key part of this as communication is made through platforms such as Instagram, YouTube and Snapchat. Uploading a video, selfie or a product image is a way to start a conversation, show others a perfected look and gain peer social acceptance through likes and followers," the article said.

Figure 3.2 Young girls are being exposed to makeup routines earlier than ever. Many tween girls are experimenting with cosmetics and even wearing some form of makeup. © E+/PeopleImages

EMOTIONAL PERSUASION:
PUSHING THE RIGHT BUTTONS

In the 1950s, a black-and-white print ad showed a woman with a noose circling her neck, a gun to her temple, and a bottle of pills labeled "Poison" in one hand.[27] No, this wasn't a suicide-prevention ad. It was an ad for a lanolin-based hair care product called Charles Antell Formula 9. The ad copy read, "We overheard that plaint . . . 'If my hair looks such a mess *one more* night, I'll kill myself!'" Most beauty companies have ditched the use of this kind of outlandish shame-mongering to promote their products, although some aren't above tapping into consumers' fear of appearance-based rejection and playing on consumers' insecurities about their physical appearance.

To create deeper, more enduring, and stronger emotional brand attachments with consumers, beauty companies will often use *emotional branding*. From the 2014 *Adweek* article "Emotional Branding and the Emotionally Intelligent Consumer": "Emotional branding refers to the practice of building brands that appeal directly to a consumer's ego, emotional state, needs and aspirations. The purpose of emotional branding is to create a bond between the consumer and the product by provoking the consumer's emotion."[28] Let's look at a few ways that beauty companies build brand relationships.

Speaking to the Heart

You may have seen an ad or a product description for Ralph Lauren Tender Romance fragrance. In one ad, a young couple, sitting in a field of grass, is wrapped in a tender embrace.[29] A product description for the fragrance uses the following descriptive copy: "'Tender Romance evokes both the sweetness and innocence of falling in love for the first time.'—Ralph Lauren."[30] If this messaging resonates with you on a personal level, you may identify with the brand and wish to make it your signature fragrance.

Beauty companies often link their products to an *affective state*, such as happiness, love, fear, confidence, passion, disgust, and so on. A 2011 study found that consumers buy cosmetic products primarily for emotional reasons, which explains why emotional appeals used in cosmetics advertising tend to work.[31] Researchers asked women about their perceptions of the functional and emotional attributes of the cosmetic products they used, as well as the degree to which they were satisfied with these products. In a Psych Central article, the lead author of a report originally published in the *African Journal of Business Management*, Vanessa Apaolaza-Ibañez, is quoted as saying, "The study shows that both the emotional and utility aspect of cosmetic brands have a significant impact on consumer satisfaction, but that the emotional component has a greater effect." She added that the results demonstrated that "consumer satisfaction is greatest when the cosmetics brand helps to strengthen positive emotions through the perception of 'caring for oneself' and removing feelings of worry and guilt about not taking care of one's appearance."[32]

The irony is that for the brand to elicit a positive response from consumers, it must first provoke an unpleasant emotional state, such as dissatisfaction with or concern over their appearance. Beauty companies are quite clever in how they tap into consumers' anxiety about appearance. "One way of achieving this is by subtly telling them they are ugly—something that many cosmetics adverts achieve implicitly and very effectively by showing images of unusually beautiful women,"[33] the study explained.

The Power of Storytelling

Dermatologists say that beauty companies employ persuasion by convincing consumers that they should spend lavishly on expensive creams and lotions. These companies use persuasive strategies to speak to consumers at cognitive and psychological levels. In a 2011 *MarketWatch* article, Julie Moore, MD, pointed out that some of her patients buy expensive creams because they believe that those creams are better than drugstore brands and because the pricier brands are exclusively available at department stores.[34]

As a beauty consumer, you're probably familiar with some persuasive techniques employed in advertising messages for beauty products. For example, many beauty ads use evocative language to build a picture in your mind, utilize demonstration or dramatization to hold your attention, or create a visual narrative to get you engaged.

Consider the Clé de Peau Beauté brand. Calling itself "the premier luxury skincare and makeup brand from Shiseido Cosmetics—the ultimate expression of elegance and science,"[35] the brand often uses figurative language to promote its products. For example, a Clé de Peau Beauté eye shadow ad features this copy: "Dancing in the shadows, eyes shimmer in irresistible shades of radiance. Lustrously dewy, yet impossibly light. Even up close, the mystery remains."[36] Clé de Peau Beauté eye shadows can cost as much as $80, which is on the high side for eye shadow. This product would probably appeal to status-seeking beauty consumers with more discretionary income rather than value-conscious consumers with less discretionary income to spend on pricey beauty products.

Telling the Brand Story at a Glance: Names, Logos, and Slogans

Youth Code, Wrinkle Expert, Revitalift, Visible Lift, Excellence Age Perfect, and Root Rescue—these brand names belong to L'Oréal Paris products. Each brand name suggests something about the product's benefits. The same is true for these Estée Lauder brand names: Advanced Night Repair, Resilience Lift, Perfectionist, and Sumptuous, as well as the Re-Nutriv sub-brand, instantly let the consumer know what to expect from the brand.

Next, an attention-grabbing logo can quickly communicate a distinctive image that identifies the brand. In a 2015 *Entrepreneur* article, Alina Wheeler, a branding expert and author of *Designing Brand Identity* based in Philadelphia, pointed out the significance of a great logo design: "We have less time and less space to tell our stories in than ever before. To rise above the clutter, a symbol or a logo is the fastest communication known to man. It unlocks associations with your brand on sight, so it's important to get it right the first time around."[37] The logo for L'Oréal's Garnier brand is an example of a design that does double duty. The logo contains the name of the brand; it has an image of a green leaf that communicates the brand's green commitment; and it even combines a tagline in some communication messages, "Take care," which is personal and also fits the brand's promise to protect people and the planet.

Finally, a catchy and functional slogan can become the heart and soul of the brand. A slogan is a key element to a brand's identity and contributes to the brand's image and awareness. For example, you may recognize the following slogan for a hair-coloring product: "Does she . . . or doesn't she?" It belongs to Miss Clairol "hair color bath" and was used to successfully introduce the product in 1956. This slogan is as memorable now as it was then. In fact, it has been named one of the top ten slogans of the twentieth century by *Advertising Age*.[38] In another example, in 1997, CoverGirl launched an advertising campaign that debuted a catchy company slogan, "Easy, breezy, beautiful CoverGirl." In a few words, CoverGirl lets the consumer know that the brand will deliver a natural, fresh, clean look. And it worked: Sales increased during the campaign's run, and a new crop of teenage girls enthusiastically embraced the brand.

UP CLOSE AND PERSONAL: GETTING THE RIGHT MESSAGE TO THE RIGHT AUDIENCE

A 2015 Nielsen article titled "Age Before Beauty: Treating Generations with a Personal Touch in Beauty Advertising" noted that beauty ads can sometimes look alike across brands, thus falling short of telling a distinctive product story to connect with consumers. Therefore, beauty companies should tailor their advertising to address different target audiences.[39] The insights presented in the article were gained through Nielsen's TV Brand Effect and Online Brand Effect, which are tools for measuring ad resonance, over the twelve-month period ending in June 2014.

Beauty companies that got the message right used some form of market segmentation and targeting. To illustrate, women aged 18 to 39 and 40 to 54 had a mental picture of themselves as being young and doing what they could to stay young. Based on this self-portrait, ad copy that features youthful images and mentions "youth" would probably reel in these beauty consumers. In contrast, women older than fifty-five looked for skin care products that did battle with wrinkles, addressed skin dullness, and tackled the sagging skin that comes with age.[40] These beauty consumers would probably be swayed by ad copy that mentions "anti-aging," "reverse," "re-store," or "regenerate."

Microsegments emerged within each generation, in which beauty consumers responded to different elements of ads. Millennial women, for example, sought functionality and needed to see it to believe it. Also, millennials loved product dem-onstrations; however, this varied by the age of the millennial. Younger millennial women aged 18 to 25 were more attracted to product demonstration visuals than their older counterparts aged 26 to 34. These demonstrations were usually woven into the visual composition of the ad, with voiceovers stressing product benefits and efficacy. In addition to product demonstrations, younger millennial women appreci-ated a compelling story, with or without comic elements, taking place in a familiar setting, like a home. Older millennial women, on the other hand, were commonly drawn to ads that featured a mash-up of storylines or glamour shots, limited product information, and voiceovers that emphasized product benefits and how those ben-efits could result in a positive lifestyle change.[41]

Let's not forget men here. Men tended to be highly visual. They preferred visual content in ads for personal care products. As with women, age was a factor in how men responded to ads. For example, millennial men responded more favorably to flashy, animated ads for personal care products than did men in older generations. Story-based ads that stressed product benefits and ensured lifestyle changes appealed more to older millennial men aged 26 to 34 than to younger millennial men aged 18 to 25.[42]

Interestingly, older millennial men had more in common with baby boomer men than you'd expect, according to Nielsen. In terms of ad recall, older millennial males and baby boomer males both had stronger recall and enjoyed "a mix of the storyline commercials and the animation commercials." As the article reported, both older millennial males and baby boomer males "don't care for the female product com-mercials as much as younger millennial and Gen-X males."[43]

Finally, younger millennial men were partial to animations and active visuals, as compared with other male groups. In addition, younger millennial men reacted to "a single highlight within an ad, while Gen-X men respond to a story."[44]

From Hope in a Jar to Hope in a Better Tomorrow

Several beauty brands are creating female-empowering ads to reach young women who have grown weary or skeptical of glitzy beauty ads. Femvertising ad campaigns include Dove's #SpeakBeautiful, CoverGirl's #GirlsCan, and P&G's Always brand's #LikeAGirl.

How successful are female-empowering messages? Consider Estée Lauder's Cli-nique's #StartBetter. In 2014, Estée Lauder scrapped its time-honored sales message of "hope in a bottle" to communicate "the sort of hope embodied in a fresh start, be it a new job, new relationship or simply a new day," as noted in a 2014 *Advertising Age* article.[45] The centerpiece of the social-media-centric campaign is a video dubbed the "Clinique Start Better Manifesto," an inspirational message packaged as a dare to start something new.[46] The overall results of the campaign are nothing short of astonishing. Shortly after the campaign launched on YouTube, Facebook, Instagram, and Twitter, it raked up almost 10 million impressions, 284,000 total engagements, and more than 1.4 million total video views.[47]

A year later, Clinique followed up the #StartBetter campaign with another global digital campaign, #FaceForward. For the new digital campaign, Clinique swapped models for influencers and bloggers to deliver the brand message, according to a 2015 *Adweek* article.[48] This time, the motivating message was more of a question: "If you could give your future self any advice, what would it be?" The bloggers shared stories, imparted advice, stressed self-acceptance and confidence, and inspired others to participate. "In a general sense, the campaign follows on recent work supporting Always and Dove in offering audiences a more realistic portrait of the young, enterprising, thoroughly modern woman,"[49] the article said.

THE RISE OF THE DIGITAL BEAUTY CONSUMER

Think about the last time you went shopping for beauty products. Did you buy products online through an e-tailer, like Dermstore.com or SkinStore.com; a click-and-mortar, such as Sephora or Ulta Beauty; or a traditional retailer, like a drugstore or a department store? If you're like many beauty consumers, you're doing some, or all, of your shopping for beauty products through e-tailers. As a result, many retailers and brand owners are using multichannel marketing by making their products available at and promoting them through multiple touchpoints (see figure 3.3).

Let's find out how beauty brands are reaching consumers by tapping into their digital lives.

Beauty's Secret Weapon: Digital Marketing

Are you familiar with the term *digital competence*? It refers to "the confident, critical and creative use of information and communications technology (ICT) to achieve goals related to work, employability, learning, leisure, inclusion and/ or participation in society."[50] Like people, brands have digital competence, which involves quantifying a brand owner's investment in search, display, and e-mail marketing, among other things. For example, Gartner L2 Digital IQ index for beauty benchmarks the digital performance of beauty brands doing business in the United States. In 2018, out of 124 beauty brands, Tarte earned the highest digital IQ score, followed by Maybelline and NYX.[51]

Beauty companies are staring down the rabbit hole and coming to the realization that traditional media aren't enough to draw out millennials; they must add digital media to their advertising armory. Several beauty brands are already capitalizing on digital media, such as MAC Cosmetics, Bath & Body Works, and L'Oréal Paris. For

Figure 3.3.   Beauty consumers who want to save time and value convenience are shopping online for beauty products. © iStock/Getty Images Plus/Amax Photo

example, as of October 2019, Bath & Body Works topped the list of leading beauty brands with the most followers on Facebook (9.56 million followers), followed by Risqué (7.29 million followers), Mary Kay Brasil (6.31 million followers), Eudora (5.56 million followers), and Pantene Brasil (4.96 million followers).[52]

Increasingly, beauty companies are using social media marketing to widen and leverage their brands' media coverage and to influence consumers' buying decision process. A 2016 *WWD* article described social media's ability to drive consumer behavior.[53] A 2015 study by TABS Analytics found that 31 percent of millennials, the heaviest buyers of beauty products, said that Instagram was significant in how they made their buying choices for cosmetics, representing an 11 percent increase from 2014. Consider Kylie Jenner's Lip Kit. Priced at $29, the kit sold out in mere minutes when it was launched online. Then there's Becca's Champagne Pop highlighter, cocreated with YouTube personality Jaclyn Hill. The highlighter generated an estimated $20 million in sales during the second half of 2015, making it the biggest single-day seller in Sephora.com's history.[54]

The real star maker may be Instagram. From a Digiday article: "Image-oriented by their very nature, fashion and beauty companies are investing heavily in the platform as it gains in popularity: 98 percent of L2's top fashion brands are on Instagram as of this month (August 2015), and 95 percent of beauty brands are on the platform—up from 75 percent and 78 percent in October 2013."[55] Take Tarte Cosmetics, an indie brand offering a line of natural, cruelty-free cosmetics. To launch its 2016 spring collection, the company elected to use social media influencers to create buzz for its products before the scheduled launch, the *WWD* article said. This pre-launch strategy paid off. Prior to the collection's launch, Tarte netted 20 million Instagram impressions, saw a growth rate of 80 percent on Instagram, and experienced a 38 percent boost in engagement on the brand's Instagram account.[56]

Finally, with over three billion smartphone users worldwide,[57] many beauty companies are using mobile advertising to reach consumers on their mobile devices. For instance, using TV Guide's iPhone application, Unilever's Dove ran mobile ads as part of Dove's "Show Us Your Skin" campaign, which promoted healthy skin along with Dove products. The campaign encouraged "real women" to submit photos of themselves "looking their best with clean, healthy skin," according to a *Mobile Marketer* article.[58] Uploaded photos that met requirements appeared in campaign ads and on a Times Square billboard.

Beauty Ambassadors Take Over the Beauty Conversation

Brand ambassadors are the largest megaphones on social media. A 2015 *Entrepreneur* magazine article defined this social media maven as follows: "A brand ambassador, unlike a celebrity spokesperson, is someone who eats, lives and breathes your brand. This is someone your customers can connect and engage with, someone who has a solid, well-established online presence with a decent-size network."[59] Many beauty companies have enlisted these influencers to pitch their products. For example, several popular beauty bloggers have been recruited by beauty brands to generate buzz and sales. Consider fashion blogger Arielle Charnas of Something Navy. A 2016 *Los Angeles Times* article noted that Charnas posted about Peter Thomas Roth Rose Stem Cell Bio-Repair Gel Mask on her Snapchat story. Twenty-four hours after the story broke, the post led to the sale of 502 masks, the equivalent of $17,565 worth of product. "Do the math: that's equal to $123,000 in sales in a week, $527,000 in a month or almost $6.4 million in a year,"[60] the article said.

In a 2014 survey of women aged 18 to 64, Dove explored the question of what—and who—influences conceptions of beauty. "The results showed that women are more than twice as likely to say that their conception of beauty is shaped by 'women in the public domain' and social media (29 percent and 25 percent, respectively) than they were before they entered high school (11 percent and 10 percent, respectively)," as cited in a 2015 *Women in the World* article.[61] A more egalitarian view of beauty that came of widening and dismantling strict beauty standards was acknowledged by the survey participants. The authors of the Dove study said, "Whether women are rating beauty products, giving each other advice or sharing personal beauty/body image stories, or posting their own images or 'selfies,' beauty has become more personalized and more inclusive on the Internet."[62]

Generally, women tend to accept beauty influencers' endorsements because they're seen as trustworthy and genuine and not just out for endorsement dollars, although many beauty influencers are paid to develop content for beauty companies. Still, the most trusted source of beauty information is real people. A 2015 survey by SHE Media (formerly SheKnows Media) found that an overwhelming majority of women (86 percent) said that they largely trusted product and service recommendations from everyday people. With respect to social media platforms, over half (58 percent) of women looked to YouTube to learn about products from "everyday experts," followed by Facebook (52 percent), Pinterest (50 percent), and Instagram (46 percent), as cited in a 2015 *Fast Company* article.[63]

RECLAIMING BRAND LOVE:
A CRISIS OF BEAUTY BRAND LOYALTY

Historically, beauty consumers have exhibited high brand loyalty or at least brand preference for certain beauty brands and products. Over time, however, brand loyalty has declined, especially among millennials. A 2014 *Beauty Packaging* magazine article presented the results from a consumer insights study by TABS Group that found many beauty consumers aren't hard-core loyalists but instead price buyers or brand switchers.[64] According to Kurt Jetta, TABS founder and executive chairman, "The heaviest cosmetics shoppers demonstrate no brand loyalty, purchasing more than 8 brands, on average, and shopping at many more outlets than lighter buyers. . . . The bottom line is that more deals lead to more sales, particularly among the heaviest buyers who have no loyalty to specific brands."[65]

Baby boomers are also less brand loyal but not for the same reasons as millennials. Boomer women have outgrown brands that they used when they were younger because they have different skin care needs than they had ten or twenty years ago, as suggested in a 2012 MediaPost article.[66] Based on a survey by MediaPost, in 2012, boomer women said their top skin care concerns were "protecting skin from damage" (24 percent); "looking healthy" (20 percent); and "addressing specific skin conditions" (18 percent). Other findings suggest that boomer women make product purchases based on product performance and not self-image. Just 19 percent look for products that could make them look younger, and only 14 percent seek products that could make them look pretty.[67]

If beauty companies want to win back boomer women, a lucrative market segment, they must address boomer women's needs as those needs stand now and not as they stood twenty years ago, the MediaPost article concluded. From a communications standpoint, the beauty industry's emphasis on image, youth, and beauty in advertising may be less persuasive than advertising that stresses product benefits and performance.

In the next chapter, we'll examine the nature of beauty, discuss the feminine beauty ideal, and explore Western standards of feminine beauty.

II
THE BEAUTY IDEAL

4

The Perfect Woman

The beauty of a woman is not in the clothes she wears, the figure that she carries, or the way she combs her hair. The beauty of a woman is seen in her eyes, because that is the doorway to her heart, the place where love resides. True beauty in a woman is reflected in her soul. It's the caring that she lovingly gives, the passion that she shows and the beauty of a woman only grows with passing years.

—Audrey Hepburn (1929–1993), actor, fashion icon, and philanthropist

If you were asked to name some of history's most beautiful women, there's an odds-on chance that you'd mention Audrey Hepburn, who topped the list of all-time beauty icons in a 2016 survey commissioned by Superdrug, a British health and beauty retailer. The survey found that women tend to revert to the past to find beauty inspiration, with sex symbol Marilyn Monroe and steely beauty Grace Kelly rounding out the top three all-time beauties. In an article in the *Sun*, Sarah Gardner, the head of beauty at Superdrug, is quoted as saying, "The vintage style of Hepburn and Monroe now defines classic, and it is telling that the list is compiled mostly of beauties of yesteryear or more mature women."[1]

Belgian-born Audrey Hepburn, née Edda van Heemstra Hepburn-Ruston, spent part of her youth in England, where she attended boarding school. She studied ballet in the Netherlands during much of World War II.[2] There, she made her film debut in *Nederland in 7 Lessen* (*Dutch at the Double*) at the age of 19.[3]

After the war ended, Hepburn continued studying ballet in Amsterdam and later in London.[4] It was then that her life took a dramatic pivot when she was spotted by Colette, an acclaimed French author. Colette had written the popular novelette *Gigi* (1944), which was made into a French film and adapted into a play.[5] At Colette's urging, Hepburn went on to star in the Broadway production of *Gigi* (1951), which led to her first starring film role, in *Roman Holiday* (1953), for which she won an Academy Award for Best Actress. And a star was born.

Audrey Hepburn, with her doe-eyed gaze and famously lithe figure, redefined beauty standards at a time when voluptuous, toothsome actors of the 1950s and 1960s prevailed, like Marilyn Monroe, Brigitte Bardot, and Sophia Loren. David Wills, author of *Audrey: The 50s*, wrote the following passage in his article "The Importance of Being Audrey" for *Biography*: "In an era dominated by the atomic prurience of the bombshells and on the heels of the Forties glamazons, Audrey revolutionized movie glamour with an understated allure that had never been seen on-screen before. . . . Audrey's unique appearance—the short hair, the slender frame and petite bosom, the long neck, the prominent brow, the strong jawline, and the irregular smile—set her apart."[6]

Fan magazines took note of the rising star's cultural and cinematic significance. "*Silver Screen* proposed that Audrey was 'changing Hollywood's taste in girls,' while *Photoplay* described her as 'altogether un-Marilyn Monroe-ish. And yet . . . Audrey Hepburn is the most phenomenal thing that's happened to the film capital since Marilyn Monroe,'" Wills noted. The fashion world also jumped on the Hepburn bandwagon. In 1954, *Vogue* called Hepburn "today's wonder-girl. . . . She has so captured the public imagination and the mood of the time that she has established a new standard of beauty, and every other face now approximates the 'Hepburn look,'"[7] Wills said.

Never forgetting the aid that she had received from UNICEF as a young girl in post–World War II Holland, Hepburn became a goodwill ambassador for UNICEF, traveling the world to raise awareness of the plight of starving children. In recognition of her humanitarian work, she was posthumously given the Jean Hersholt Humanitarian Award at the 1993 Academy Awards. Since her death that year, Hepburn has continued to capture the public imagination and is proof that "what is beautiful is good."

Yet, how do we define beauty? What is the feminine beauty ideal? How have Western beauty ideals been exported to non-Western cultures? Let's explore.

THE MATHEMATICS OF BEAUTY: IS IT JUST 1:1.618?

The meaning and nature of beauty is one of the most litigated debates. People know it when they see it, even if they can't put their finger on exactly what makes a person beautiful. Psychologists and scientists have extensively studied—and cracked—the centuries-old mystery of beauty, and who has it.

Consider iconic actor Elizabeth Taylor. Taylor's mesmerizing violet eyes, milky white skin, and raven hair made her alluring. But her beauty was more than that—it was her "hyper-femininity" that made her beauty exceptional. Nancy Etcoff, a psychologist and faculty member of Harvard Medical School and Harvard University's Mind Brain Behavior Interfaculty Initiative, and author of *Survival of the Prettiest:*

The Science of Beauty, noted that it was the combination of these physical attributes that probably boosted her magnetism, according to the 2011 *ABC News* article "Science of Beauty: What Made Elizabeth Taylor So Attractive?" "A higher contrast tends to make the face look more feminine," Etcoff said.[8]

Taylor played up her best features with makeup, which amplified the effect. She favored a bold lip color to accentuate her rosebud lips and wore heavily lined eye makeup to accent her violet-hued eyes. "She also had a feature that most people wouldn't think of as contributing to attractiveness, but really does, which is a small, gracile jaw. Which means a jaw that is kind of small and very hyper-feminine," Etcoff explained.[9]

It's not enough that Taylor had a beautiful face. She also possessed an "exaggerated" hourglass figure, which is considered the perfect female body shape, according to science. Etcoff noted, "She combines that beautiful face with a very beautiful body, which is beautiful in a particular way. She's almost what we would call a super-normal stimulus, which means that her hourglass figure is exaggerated."[10]

Beauty Is in the Mind of the Beholder

You've probably heard various sayings on beauty, such as "Beauty is only skin deep," "Beauty is in the eye of the beholder," "Beauty is as beauty does," and "A thing of beauty is a joy forever." These maxims seize on whatever aspect of beauty is affecting to the observer, which makes beauty difficult to define with any precision.

Merriam-Webster's Collegiate Dictionary defines *beauty* as "the quality or aggregate of qualities in a person or thing that gives pleasure to the senses or pleasurably exalts the mind or spirit." The classical conception of beauty regards it as "an arrangement of integral parts into a coherent whole, according to proportion, harmony, symmetry, and similar notions." From Aristotle's *Metaphysics*: "The chief forms of beauty are order and symmetry and definiteness, which the mathematical sciences demonstrate in a special degree."[11]

In his book *Beauty: The Fortunes of an Ancient Greek Idea*, David Konstan introduces the reader to a classical Greek term that comes closest to the modern idea of beauty, *kállos*. Konstan wrote, "The primary meaning of *kállos* refers to physical beauty, above all the beauty associated with erotic attraction." He also stated that, as a Greek adjective, *kalós* ("beautiful") can mean different things depending on the specific context. It can describe tangible things, such as clothes; intangible qualities, such as laws, knowledge, and other abstract ideas; and moral concepts, such as "noble," "honorable," and "good."[12]

The beauty-is-good stereotype is originally derived from Greek lyric poetry. Sappho, an ancient Greek poet, was the first to observe and write, "What is beautiful is good, and who is good will soon be beautiful." This notion of beauty is captured in the Greek word *kalokagatia* ("beauty-good"). Generally, the Greeks were concerned with investigating the ethical and aesthetic proportions of beauty, and how it contributed to "the highest goodness."[13]

The Golden Ratio

Most of us associate the Italian Renaissance polymath Leonardo da Vinci with one of his most famous paintings, the *Mona Lisa*. This masterpiece was painted sometime between 1503 and 1519 and possibly created according to the *golden ratio*, also known as the *divine proportion*, *golden mean*, or *golden section* (see figure 4.1).[14] A special number approximately equal to 1:1.618, this mathematical pattern is the ideal proportion for the sides of a rectangle and is considered one of the most

Figure 4.1. Many experts claim that Leonardo da Vinci utilized the golden ratio to paint the *Mona Lisa*. The golden ratio is a mathematical formula presumed to define facial beauty. © DigitalVision Vectors/ilbusca

aesthetically pleasing of all geometric forms. You can find the divine proportion in art, architecture, and human anatomy.

If you've visited the Louvre and seen the *Mona Lisa*, you may have puzzled over her mysterious smile and noticed that she seems to have an uncanny ability to follow you with her eyes. With respect to the ideal female face, it turns out that the eyes—and the mouth—have it, as eye–mouth distances are believed to determine how attractive a woman's face is.

In a set of experiments, participants were given a paired comparison task, where they assessed the attractiveness between faces with the same features but different eye–mouth distances and different distances between the eyes. The researchers discovered two new "golden ratios" that closely correspond with the dimensions of the average face. While different feminine faces varied in attractiveness, those faces where the vertical distance between the eyes and mouth was roughly 36 percent of the face's length and the horizontal distance between the eyes was approximately 46 percent of the face's width were deemed more attractive.[15] The study's findings appear in a 2010 *Vision Research* article titled "New 'Golden' Ratios for Facial Beauty."[16]

Pamela Pallett, one of the study's authors, then a postdoctoral fellow in psychology at UC San Diego and an alumna of the department, is quoted as saying, "People have tried and failed to find these ratios since antiquity. . . . But there was never any proof that the golden ratio was special. As it turns out, it isn't. Instead of phi, we showed that average distances between the eyes, mouth and face contour form the true golden ratios."[17]

General conclusions about female facial attractiveness and facial averageness were drawn from the study. Kang Lee, one of the lead authors of the study and a distinguished professor at the University of Toronto's Dr. Eric Jackman Institute of Child Study, said, "Our study conclusively proves that the structure of faces—the relation between our face contour and the eyes, mouth and nose—also contributes to our perception of facial attractiveness. Our finding also explains why sometimes an attractive person looks unattractive or vice versa after a haircut, because hairdos change the ratios."[18]

The Attractiveness of Symmetry

Biologists suggest that symmetry between other physical features, even hands, is preferred. Furthermore, symmetry is believed to be a proxy for good health. "Symmetry suggests orderly development in the womb and during childhood, and thus, the theory has it, captures a range of desirable things from good genes to infection-resistance," as noted in a 2014 article in the *Economist*.[19] As this signals a favorable genetic endowment, then, we tend to prefer people with facial symmetry, or evenly balanced features, such as the symmetry found in famous faces like David Beckham, Brad Pitt, Natalie Portman, and Michelle Pfeiffer.

People give symmetrical faces significantly higher ratings on the dimension of attractiveness, as compared with faces perceived as less symmetrical. Interestingly, an attractive face may also be a rather average-looking face. "When presented with individual faces and a composite of those individual faces, participants will judge the composite as more attractive than the individual, more distinctive faces. And the more faces that contribute to the composite, the more attractive it becomes," according to a 2011 article titled "Beauty Is in the Mind of the Beholder," published in the Association for Psychological Science's *Observer* magazine. Prototypical faces, those faces that come closest to the average traits of the population, are viewed as the most attractive.[20]

We may wish to take such findings with a grain of salt because of the relatively small sample sizes in many of the earlier experiments, thus making it possible for fluke results to show up. Stefan Van Dongen at the University of Antwerp's Evolutionary Ecology Group (EVECO) discovered that the averageness effect vanishes when enough people are evaluated, and therefore, facial symmetry may say little about a person's health, as reported in a 2015 BBC article.[21] Furthermore, our notions of beauty may have something to do with the effect of conformity, or the bandwagon effect. "Study after study has found that if you hear or see that someone else is attracted to someone, you are more likely to fancy them yourself. In this way, tastes for certain types of people could spread throughout a population, shaping our norms for what we consider beautiful," the article said.

IS BEAUTY UNIVERSAL?

Did you know that babies as young as five hours old spend more time staring at pictures of faces that adults rate as attractive than at adult faces that are not so attractive?[22] The 1996 *Newsweek* article "The Biology of Beauty" cited a series of pioneering experiments carried out in the 1980s by Judith Langlois, now the Charles and Sarah Seay Regents' Professor Emerita at the University of Texas, Austin.[23] In the experiments, three- and six-month-old babies were placed in front of a screen and shown pairs of facial photo shots. Each pair included a photo that adult judges found to be attractive and one considered unattractive. The first study showed that the babies stared significantly longer at the faces of "attractive" white females than "unattractive" ones. Langlois repeated the experiment using white male faces, black female faces, and the faces of other babies. The same results were produced. Langlois is quoted as saying, "These kids don't read *Vogue* or watch TV. They haven't been touched by the media. Yet they make the same judgments as adults."[24]

From infancy into adulthood, we tend to prefer certain physical characteristics over others. Research has shown that these preferences are hardwired, and they tend to span borders, cross cultures, and pass down through generations. Additionally, these preferences aren't confined to Western cultures but are also observed in hunter-gatherer cultures with no exposure to mainstream media. For example, the Hadza people of Tanzania, a remote population of hunters and gatherers, displayed a greater preference for symmetry in the human form than people from Britain, as reported in a 2012 CNN article.[25] These findings and others like them suggest that there's a cross-cultural consensus on what constitutes attractiveness, and that what is perceived as physically attractive and unattractive is recognized across individuals and cultures.[26]

What physical features commonly communicate attractiveness? Research indicates that men tend to prefer women with large wide-set eyes, full lips, high cheekbones, a small nose, a narrow jaw, and full breasts; who are shorter than they are; and who have a low waist-to-hip ratio. Women tend to favor men with a heavy lower face; who are taller than they are; who display a high degree of facial symmetry and have masculine facial dimorphism (subtle or exaggerated sex-specific traits); and who have broad shoulders, a relatively narrow waist, and a V-shaped torso.[27] These preferences become cultural ideals of femininity and masculinity, which are reinforced by the media and other institutions.

The Globalization of the Western Ideal of Beauty

One of America's biggest exports is its pop culture. The US media and entertainment (M&E) industry is made up of all the businesses that produce and distribute movies, television programs, commercials, streaming content, music and audio recordings, radio shows, news, newspapers, magazines, books, and video games. These industries make, create, and distribute products and content unique to the American culture. Strikingly, as of 2019, the US M&E market was dominated by just four media conglomerates, which controlled roughly 90 percent of media: Comcast (via NBCUniversal), Disney, AT&T (via WarnerMedia), and ViacomCBS (controlled by National Amusements).[28] Given this corporate concentration, corporate media increasingly dominate the mass media, propagating "the image culture" and spreading Western ideals of beauty.

A classic example of the diffusion of Western ideals of beauty through the mass media is the NBC television series *Baywatch*. The series was canceled after only one season. It was then resuscitated when it switched over to first-run syndication and became an international hit. The 2013 *Huffington Post* article "How Baywatch Unknowingly Changed the World: The Untapped Power of TV Shows" noted the global reach and influence that the show had from its original release in 1989 leading up to its 2017 film adaptation. The show was translated into forty-four different languages; 1.1 billion people in 148 counties tuned in weekly to watch the heroics and interpersonal relationships of a team of Los Angeles, California–based lifeguards.[29] With its bikini-clad stunners, including Pamela Anderson, and handsome hunks, including David Hasselhoff, *Baywatch* introduced overseas audiences to the standards of physical attractiveness in the United States. "Within 24 months, *Baywatch* went from *that* show NBC canned to '[one of] the highest-rated of American imports.' From Belgium and Guatemala to Malaysia, Kenya, and the Philippines, the lionhearted Alpha Males and their beach-trophy pinups were awaited every night by all parts of the world—including the Middle East,"[30] the article said.

Figure 4.2. Glossy beauty and fashion magazines are the perfect medium for presenting and promoting Western beauty ideals. © E+/pixelfit

Print media is also a powerful agent of Western beauty ideals (see figure 4.2). Major American mass media companies, such as Hearst Communications Inc. (*Cosmopolitan, Seventeen, Marie Claire, Elle*, and *Harper's Bazaar*), Condé Nast (*Allure, Glamour*, and *Vogue*), and Time Inc. (*InStyle*), publish international editions of their women's fashion magazine brands. Consider *Cosmopolitan*, also called *Cosmo*. "A bible for fun, fearless females,"[31] the publication includes sixty-four international editions distributed in more than one hundred countries and in thirty-five languages.[32] *Cosmopolitan* has a wide reach, connecting with 81 million readers daily, according to *Cosmopolitan's* website. Based on these statistics, *Cosmo*, as a communication medium, has the capability to disseminate Western beauty ideals all around the world, as suggested in a 2012 *New York Times* article.[33]

THE PERFECT WOMAN: THE FEMININE BEAUTY IDEAL

Big is considered the epitome of beauty in some parts of western Africa. From an early age, girls are sent to feeding camps, where they're forced to consume 16,000 calories a day to reach a weight that will make them marriageable. In some parts of northern Thailand, Kayan women wear brass coils to give the appearance of an elongated neck, which is considered a sign of refinement and beauty (see figure 4.3). In China, the centuries-old practice of foot binding, which was first banned in 1911,

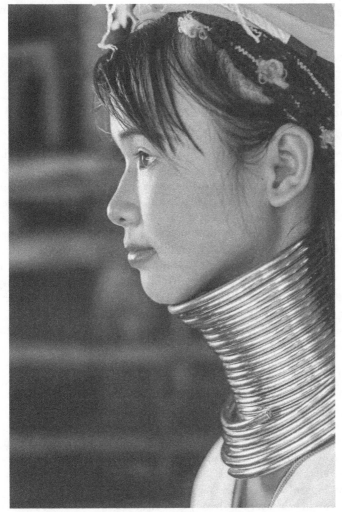

Figure 4.3. Kayan women in northern Thailand are famous for wearing brass coils around their necks. © E+/hadynyah

involved breaking the feet of young girls and bending them until they were permanently positioned under the sole of the foot. Foot binding was a display of status and beauty in the Chinese culture.[34] In the United States and other Western nations, many women are preoccupied with their weight and practically starve themselves to get thin, taking their cues from the beauty and fashion industry responsible for shaping and reinforcing "the cult-like worship of what physical attributes the public sees as beautiful," as noted in a 2011 CNN article.[35]

These stories illustrate the painful steps that many women go through to meet *the feminine beauty ideal*, "the socially constructed notion that physical attractiveness is one of women's most important assets, and something all women should strive to achieve and maintain."[36] Let's see how Western ideals of female beauty have evolved, against a backdrop of sociopolitical changes.

A Historical Look at Western Beauty Ideals

The *New York Times* published a review, titled "Curves In, Curves Out," of the book *American Beauty*, by Lois W. Banner, professor emerita of history at the University of Southern California's Dornsife College of Letters, Arts and Sciences.[37] In her book, Banner presented four prototypes of feminine beauty, all exemplars of the American white upper class. The first feminine prototype is the "steel-engraving lady" from the early nineteenth century. She is described as "frail, pale, willowy," bordering on anorexic. These upper-crust women restricted food intake to maintain their svelteness and consumed small quantities of arsenic to achieve pale skin.[38]

Around the mid-1850s until the 1890s, a new ideal of beauty came to the fore: the "Voluptuous Woman." Banner portrayed her as "buxom, hearty, and heavy." Lillian Russell, an American actor and singer, and Lydia Thompson, a burlesque dancer and actor on the London stage, typified this female. Thompson, with her popular troupe the "British Blondes," introduced American audiences to Victorian burlesque, and for the first time, blond hair became associated with feminine beauty, whether natural or bottled.[39]

Toward the end of the nineteenth century, the Voluptuous Woman was pushed aside to make room for the "Gibson Girl." Tall, fit, and aristocratic, she was leaner than her predecessor yet "large of bosom and hips." The focus on exaggerated female curves was exemplified in the "Grecian bend," so named after the graceful, slightly rounded shoulders found in ancient Greek art. For the modern interpretation of this stooping style, "the breasts and buttocks were so protruded by stays, corsets and high heels that women who affected the style 'could not sit upright in carriages, but rather had to lean forward and rest their hands on cushions on the floor.'"[40]

The fourth and final ideal of beauty arrived during the early twentieth century. The "small, boyish model" was epitomized by silent screen stars like Mary Pickford and Clara Bow. By 1921, Banner wrote, "the basic institutions of the American beauty culture had taken shape."[41]

Each era has defined the perfect woman. Let's meet them.

"The Voluptuous Woman" (1600s to 1800s)

Eurocentric beauty standards were widely adopted by American women during the seventeenth century. The public figure that had the most influence in establishing those standards was Peter Paul Rubens. This Flemish artist was famous for his depictions of fleshy, voluptuous, full-bodied women.[42] The term *Rubenesque* was

"THE FASHIONS" Expressly designed and prepared for the Englishwoman's Domestic Magazine.

The Skirts arranged upon THOMSON'S Crinolines.

AUGUST 1865

Figure 4.4. The Victorian hourglass emphasized an ample bust, small waist, and full hips. Women wore tightly laced corsets made of rigid materials, such as whalebone, ivory, steel, or wood, to create a V-shaped silhouette. © DigitalVision Vectors/duncan1890

coined to describe this vision of female beauty. She was a woman in the peak of good health and wealth.

During the Victorian era, the ideal woman was delicate, graceful, and helpless in nature. An hourglass figure was prized. To achieve this silhouette, women wore tightly laced corsets, ruffled blouses with billowy sleeves, and crinoline or hoop skirts (see figure 4.4).

"The Gibson Girl" (1890s to 1910s)

Starting in the 1890s, the progressive movement was a period marked by widespread social and political activism, with many American women taking up a moral-reform agenda. Meanwhile, many women began to chafe over a fundamental value system known as the "cult of domesticity," or what historians call the "cult of true womanhood," a concept of femininity firmly holding that the natural place for a woman was in the home.[43] Somewhere between these dual identities of womanhood—the activist and the conformist—emerged a portrait of a new American woman who grew out of the sketches of Charles Dana Gibson, an American graphic artist. Her name: the Gibson Girl.

The Gibson Girl was depicted as an effervescent, new feminine ideal who was the visual embodiment of the independently minded woman regarded as the "New Woman."[44] She increasingly sought and fought for her place in society. She was "honester, braver, stronger, more healthful and skillful and able and free, more human in all ways," as quoted in Martha H. Patterson's book *The American New Woman Revisited: A Reader, 1894–1930.*[45]

"The Flapper" (1920s)

If you've read F. Scott Fitzgerald's 1925 novel *The Great Gatsby* or seen film versions based on the novel, you probably remember literature's ultimate flapper: Daisy Fay Buchanan. In her 2013 *Daily Beast* piece titled "The Problem with The Great Gatsby's Daisy Buchanan," Katie Baker, managing editor of *The Daily Beast*, described Daisy to a T: "She's the most desirable debutante, the ever-evading maid. She's warm, feverish, thrilling, intoxicating—a siren, an enchantress, a blossoming flower."[46]

The flapper was the very opposite of her predecessor, the Gibson Girl. Curves were out, thin was in. A boyish frame thin enough to slip into a slim sheath was the signature look of the 1920s. Influenced by cubist artists such as Picasso, Braque, and Léger, who favored geometric shapes, the flapper look was basically a drop-waisted, rectangular-shaped, straight dress, like the ones worn by the female cast members of PBS's period drama *Downton Abbey.*[47] If a woman was naturally endowed, she'd wear certain types of undergarments, called "flatteners," to press the breasts tightly against the body to give her a flat-chested appearance.[48]

"The Soft Siren; the Star-Spangled Girl" (1930s and 1940s)

The *Time* magazine article "This Is What the Ideal Woman Looked Like in the 1930s" quoted the following passage from a 1938 *Life* magazine piece to describe the ideal female form in the 1930s: "The ideal figure must have a round, high bosom, a slim but not wasp-like waist, and gently rounded hips." Romance-inspired clothing placed the emphasis on the "soft feminine figure."[49]

By the early 1940s, an unprecedented number of women had joined the labor force, including the government munitions industry (see figure 4.5). And here's where we meet Rosie the Riveter, the poster girl for the government's recruitment efforts and the most iconic image of the working woman during wartime. According to a 2014 *Today* article, "Rosie the Riveter was a cultural icon during World War II. The bodacious Betty Grable pinup with the long legs was one ideal, but during the 1940s, a beautiful female body was curvaceous, although not exaggerated."[50]

"The Hourglass" (1950s)

America entered a postwar boom in the 1950s in more ways than one, from an economic boom to booming suburbs to the baby boom to blond bombshells.

Figure 4.5. The munitions industry recruited women workers during World War II. Rosie the Riveter was a pop-culture icon representing women defense workers. © Retrofile RF/George Marks

Hollywood produced a string of glamour girls with hourglass figures, such as Jayne Mansfield, Kim Novak, and Marilyn Monroe, who became icons of femininity. "The leggy, curvy blonde was the pinnacle of attractiveness during these years, and still remains one of the most beautiful women in American history," according to a 2015 *Medical Daily* article.[51]

But the 1950s were unkind to skinnier women. Ads depicted women who were thin as wanting and hopeless and in need of gaining weight to be popular or attractive. For example, a 1950s ad for Numal, an appetite stimulant and food supplement, shows a fetching woman cradled in the arms of a well-formed man, both dressed in bathing suits. The caption proclaims, "Skinny Girls Don't Have Oomph!" The ad copy reads, "If you're otherwise healthy but skinny, scrawny, rundown and lbs. underweight, try correcting this common mistake in eating."[52]

"The Twig" (1960s)

Iconic singer-songwriter Bob Dylan gave a lyrical account of the tectonic social, cultural, and political shifts rumbling through America during the 1960s in his song and album titled *The Times They Are A-Changin'* (1964). The 1960s was a decade of extremes: "flower children and assassins, idealism and alienation, rebellion and backlash."[53] Something else was changing too: a radical shift in the feminine beauty ideal.

In a complete about-face from the curvaceous figures of the 1950s, the new feminine ideal was willowy, almost to the point of emaciation, and androgynous, a throwback to the 1920s flapper look. The beauty icon of the moment was English model Twiggy, with her small bust, elfin crop, and boyish frame.

"The California Girl" (1970s)

Like a bad trip, the 1970s were a hallucinatory extension of the 1960s. "The sober, gloomy seventies seemed like little more than just a prolonged anticlimax to the manic excitements of the sixties," as cited in the book *The Seventies: The Great Shift in American Culture, Society, and Politics*, by Bruce Schulman.[54] Another carryover from the 1960s was the coltish thin ideal.

To achieve this body type, many women restricted their food intake, followed fad diets like the low-calorie craze, or took colorful diet pills such as amphetamine derivatives (commonly referred to as "speed"). A *Shape* magazine article "Dieting Through the Decades: What We've Learned from Fads" explained, "Tab cola and calorie counting books were all the rage during the disco era and according to every weight loss study ever published."[55] There was a potentially deadly side to the preoccupation with thinness. Eating disorders like anorexia nervosa were making the headlines, beginning with the death of 1970s singing sensation Karen Carpenter in 1983 due to complications related to her struggle with anorexia.

At the same time, a new beauty standard arrived on the sandy shores of SoCal: the classic California girl. She was bronzed, slender, and athletic, with flowing hair and a natural glow. Toothsome, tanned, and toned Farrah Fawcett, who holds the record for the best-selling pinup poster of all time, represented the prototypical healthy, athletic beauty.[56]

"The Supermodel" (1980s)

The *National Review* article "Decade of Greed?" captured the feeding frenzy of the 1980s in the following passage: "A *Time* magazine reporter declared, 'The past decade brought growth, avarice, and an anything-goes attitude,' and then glibly summarized the 1980s with five words: 'Get rich, borrow, spend, enjoy.'"[57] The "go-go years of big hair, big shoulders, and big curves" were exemplified by the female stars of ABC's prime-time television soap opera *Dynasty*, including Linda Evans and Joan Collins.[58]

The 1980s saw the emergence of "the supermodel phenomenon." Top models became household names, such as Linda Evangelista, Cindy Crawford, Iman, Paulina Porizkova, and Elle Macpherson.[59] Hitting the genetic lottery, supermodels, with

Figure 4.6.   The fitness and aerobic craze swept the country in the 1980s. Millions of women flocked to aerobics classes to tone up or slim down. © E+/RyanJLane

their uncommon proportions, represented the new normal, setting next to impossible beauty norms that young women felt pressured to emulate.

In the meantime, the fitness craze swept the country, which had a marked influence on beauty standards (see figure 4.6). Millions of women hit the gym and aerobicized their way to a better body, with many following the lead of Oscar-winning actor and fitness guru Jane Fonda, whose exercise studios, books, and videos were massively successful.[60]

"The Waif" (1990s)

From the 2015 *New York Times* article "The Best Decade Ever? The 1990s, Obviously": "Peace, prosperity, order—and the American culture was vibrant and healthy as well. There were both shockingly excellent versions of what had come before and distinctly new, original forms."[61] One of those new forms was the heroin chic waif.

A 2012 *Business Insider* article noted that "'heroin chic' is a fashion movement from the 1990s led by waif-like model Kate Moss."[62] It was marked by extreme thinness, pale skin, dark undereye circles, and a general state of untidiness, similar to a heroin-addict look. Members of the medical and therapeutic communities sounded the alarm over this potentially dangerous body type. From the 1993 *People* magazine article "How Thin Is Too Thin?": "Even without the deadly specter of anorexia, the skin-and-bones look, critics say, underlines the idea that thinness is a principal yardstick of a woman's worth."[63]

"Redefining Beauty; More Diverse, More Inclusive" (2000s and 2010s)

If you group together the opposing forces of the early twenty-first century, what emerges is a snapshot of the good, the bad, and the ugly, from the technological wonders of the digital age to the tragic events of September 11 to the global financial meltdown. So far, the 2000s have felt like an unprecedented series of highs and lows. According to the 2009 *ABC News* article "The 2000s: A Decade of Doom or Diversions?": "We gaped at reality TV, Paris Hilton, celebrity meltdowns, sex tapes and balloon boy—but also endured bursting economic bubbles at the start and end of the decade, and millions of Americans out of work."[64] A silver lining has been the body-positive movement, which has capsized rigid ideals of physical attractiveness for women.

According to a 2015 *Medical Daily* article, "The past several decades have largely revolved around an 'ideal' body image that involves skinny women (stick-thin actors; the heroin-chic waif; or tall, lean, and tanned Victoria's Secret models), but lately there's been pushback from women all over the world who are tired of glorifying impossible female figures."[65] That said, today's ideal body shape may be described as slender, fit, and healthy, like the figures of Jennifer Aniston and Jennifer Lawrence.

America has become a more multicultural, mixed nation. Narrow ideals of female beauty are peeling away. Increasingly, Americans are embracing beauty in diversity. To find out how the average American perceives beauty, *Allure* conducted a large beauty survey twenty years ago. At that time, people picked a blue-eyed blonde as their beauty ideal. *Allure* repeated the survey in 2010. Nearly two-thirds of the respondents (64 percent) believed that women of mixed race represented the height of beauty.[66]

In the next chapter, we'll describe prevailing gender stereotypes, scrutinize gender advertisements, and discuss governmental and industry efforts to shatter harmful stereotypes.

5

The Myth Makers

That's what she was, Joanna felt suddenly. That's what they all were, all the Stepford wives: actresses in commercials, pleased with detergents and floor wax, with cleansers, shampoos, and deodorants. Pretty actresses, big in the bosom but small in the talent, playing suburban housewives unconvincingly, too nicey-nice to be real.

—From the satirical thriller *The Stepford Wives* (1972)

If you've read Ira Levin's novel *The Stepford Wives*, or seen the 1975 film version based on the novel or its 2004 remake, then you've been introduced to the cozy community of Stepford, Connecticut. In this eerily antiseptic setting, the husbands, who belong to something of a fraternal order, rule the roost, while the wives, who are cheery homemakers, live to please their husbands. The wives appear strangely shapelier than the average woman and oddly obsessed with housecleaning.

Even a casual observer can see that something isn't quite right with the women of Stepford. They appear to be well-dressed, robotic mannequins. That's because they are. The men of Stepford have plotted to refashion their spouses, replacing them with more fetching, pliable, and sexually obedient facsimiles.[1]

The Stepford wife is a creepy throwback to the 1950s family sitcoms, like *Leave It to Beaver* and *The Adventures of Ozzie and Harriet*, featuring the all-purpose mom wearing a ruffled hostess apron, a perma-press smile, and a rope of pearls.

The timing of the release of the novel and the original film was around the second wave of feminism. During this phase, issues like gender equality in the workplace, women's reproductive rights, sexual objectification of women, and patriarchal oppression were tenaciously addressed. As Margaret Talbot wrote in her 2003 article for the *Atlantic* titled "A Stepford for Our Times": "In 1975, when the movie *The Stepford Wives* first came out, it was widely regarded as a chilling parable about men's fears of feminism, a tale of horror that also worked as a social satire on sexism."[2]

Today, the term "Stepford wife" has come to mean different things. For example, it is used to lampoon the antediluvian stereotype of the subservient wife. Also, it refers to an accomplished woman who gives up her life and/or career to support her husband's aims, while wholly being bound to him, no matter how badly he behaves publicly. Finally, America's preoccupation with physical perfection may have given rise to a "Stepford syndrome," according to a WebMD article.[3] Lawrence Reed, MD, suggests that if a Stepford syndrome does exist, it's media-driven: "The media is creating the impression that everyone has to be beautiful and have a perfect face. There is a perception generated today that if you are not perfect, you don't exist."[4]

In advertising, the dutiful wife is a stock character in ads used to hawk everything from soap to detergent to personal care products. For example, in a 1940s ad for Lysol disinfectant for feminine hygiene, an image of a 24-hour-clock pie chart traces the different roles that a wife dutifully and happily carries out throughout the day: "good mother," "good housekeeper," "good hostess," and "good cook." When the clock strikes six o'clock, she's reduced to tears of despair. The headline and caption of the ad carry a message of foreboding: "A perfect wife . . . until 6 P.M. But her marriage was marred by 'One Neglect' few husbands can forgive." If the headline wasn't enough to strike fear in the female reader, certainly the ad copy could: "Even the most loving husband may find it difficult to forget—or forgive—a wife's carelessness, or ignorance, about intimate personal cleanliness. That's why so many women use 'Lysol' regularly."[5]

In this chapter, we'll learn about gender stereotypes and female archetypes used in promoting beauty and personal care products. We'll also look at the role that feminism has played in combating sex-role stereotypes featured across the media. Finally, we'll find out what industries and institutions are doing to address potentially damaging gender stereotypes in advertising.

GENDER STEREOTYPES ARE MADE AND NOT BORN

The Donna Reed Show (1958–1966) was a popular American sitcom that portrayed the iconic image of the white, upper-middle-class, nuclear family living in the suburbs in the postwar era. Donna Stone is a gracious and wholesome housewife to her handsome husband, Alex, a pediatrician, and a loving mother to their teenage children, Mary and Jeff. These gender roles, a man as the breadwinner and a woman as a homemaker and caretaker, aren't merely reminiscent of a bygone era (see figure 5.1). Rather, they persist as recurring themes portrayed in the media and reinforced by advertising.

Studies have revealed that women are more likely to be portrayed as product users in ads than they are as authority figures, and they are three times more likely to be shown at home rather than at work, as reported in a 2014 *New Republic* article.[6] The author, Mya Frazier, wrote, "A 2010 study found that in the U.S., women were portrayed as professionals in only 5.4 percent of ads, while men were depicted in

Figure 5.1. Traditional gender portrayals, such as the happy homemaker, were a staple of mid-twentieth-century advertising and still persist today. © Retrofile RF/George Marks

professional settings nearly three times more often. When ads included images of housekeeping, men were virtually non-existent, showing up in only 1.4 percent of ads studied, while women were shown in housekeeping roles in 32.4 percent of the ads."[7]

Gender-stereotypic images pervade the media, which can amplify and strengthen fixed ideas of how women and men should behave. The rationale for using gender stereotypes in ads is that consumers commonly define themselves by gender, which can be "communicated at a glance."[8] This is especially useful when the brand story must be told in a matter of seconds.

Let's take a deeper look at gender representation in advertising.

The Shape-versus-Mirror Debate

A running debate about advertising's power to sway consumers raises the shape-versus-mirror question. For example, a common complaint is that advertisers portray women as sex objects. The question arises as to whether advertising is guilty of creating this stereotypical portrayal of women or is simply reinforcing an existing stereotype. The answer isn't straightforward. "Stereotyping women as sex objects is a practice that is deeply embedded in our culture. Using such strategies also makes advertising a participant in shaping and reinforcing that cultural value."[9]

A 2015 *Psychology Today* article cited a 2014 study that explored gender-role portrayals in advertising by poring over a month's worth of ads in Dutch and Italian newspapers.[10] Psychologists Stefano Tartaglia and Chiara Rollero chose Italy and the Netherlands as test cases because the two European countries exhibit very different gender-related values. Using Hofstede's cultural dimensions, a model of national culture, Italy is one of the countries that score highest on the masculinity dimension, whereas the Netherlands is considered a feminine society.

Earlier content analysis of newspaper ads found that men typically appeared in occupational roles, while women were mostly displayed in decorative roles. Therefore, the researchers fully expected to make the same discovery, which they did. "Italian men were more likely to be depicted in a working or professional role, and Italian women were more likely to be depicted in a non-functional, decorative role or a leisure activity like jogging,"[11] the article noted. With the Netherlands' commitment to gender equality, the research team fully expected the country to display gender-egalitarianism in the Dutch ads, which they didn't. "Surprisingly, the pattern in the Dutch ads was almost identical to the pattern in the Italian ads. More men than women were shown at work, while more women than men were shown at play or in a passive decorative role,"[12] the article said.

Hoping to contribute to the ongoing shaping-versus-mirroring debate on whether advertising reflects social and cultural values or creates them, the research team posed two hypothetical questions. The first was the mirroring hypothesis: Does advertising content reproduce and reflect cultural beliefs, norms, and values? According to the data, the answer was "yes" in Italy and "no" in the Netherlands. While the Dutch support gender equality, newspaper ads didn't emphasize it, as women were frequently depicted in decorative and sexualized roles.[13]

The second hypothetical question was the molding hypothesis: Does advertising content deliberately shape cultural beliefs, norms, and values? For Italy, the answer was possibly, as it was unclear whether Italian women chose to stay home because of the images they'd seen in newspaper ads or for other reasons. The results for the Netherlands disputed the viability of this hypothesis. "Dutch men and women work outside the home in nearly equal numbers, despite what is depicted in their newspaper ads,"[14] the article explained.

Through the Looking Glass

You're probably familiar with Lewis Carroll's classic 1871 novel *Through the Looking-Glass, and What Alice Found There*, the sequel to his extremely popular 1865 fantasy novel *Alice's Adventures in Wonderland*. In the later novel, the reader follows young Alice back into a whimsical world filled with a dizzying array of anthropomorphic creatures and characters. This time, however, instead of being transported into a fantasyland of the delightfully absurd by tumbling through a rabbit hole, Alice climbs through a mirror into an alternate reality. There, she must understand physical antipathies, or *opposites,* which at once amuse and confound.

As with Alice's altered perception of people and objects, when we peer into a mirror at ourselves, what bounces back at us may not be a reflection of our true selves but instead a version of ourselves based on how we imagine that we must appear to others; in effect, we take on the role of the other. In a phenomenon called the *looking-glass self,* we perceive and respond to what we feel or think others' judgments of our appearance are and then create our self on the basis of those judgments.[15] The significance of this concept isn't lost to marketers. They can use advertising as a powerful looking glass through which cultural narratives and images in the media are used to shape our view of the world—and ourselves.

The mass media functions as a looking glass to reflect and influence beliefs and attitudes about gender. Consider the depiction of females in advertising. Using women as cultural receptacles, some advertisers have been slow to abandon narrow and unrealistic portrayals of women, such as the happy homemaker, the sexpot, the sacrificial mother, the femme fatale, the girl next door, and others that pigeonhole women.

Take, for example, the advertising campaigns for Breck shampoo. Ads for the shampoo usually featured the iconic girl next door. In 1937, the first Breck Girl was a seventeen-year-old haloed golden girl. She appeared in Breck's first national advertising campaign in 1946.[16] Later ads featured models and actors as Breck Girls, such as Cheryl Tiegs, Cybill Shepherd, Kim Basinger, and Jaclyn Smith. The Breck Girl blossomed into a beauty icon in the 1940s and 1950s and remained relevant into the 1970s.

A 2000 *Smithsonian Magazine* article described the birth of the Breck Girls image: "The Breck Girls portraits were born during the Depression and came of age in the 1940s and '50s, times that shook cherished values, including long-held beliefs about the roles of men and women. Advertising executives responded by crafting and presenting idealized images of an American woman they thought everyone could love, a woman both desirable and chaste."[17]

When the feminist movement was in full swing in the 1970s, the company moved away from using younger models to stave off criticism claiming that the company was only using young women to sell hair products; however, the company did use a young, baby-faced Brooke Shields, holding a doll, in a 1974 ad.[18] Donna Alexander, the first African American Breck Girl—a Junior Miss Scholarship recipient and a college student of veterinary science—appeared in a 1975 ad.[19]

In 1978, the Breck Girl campaign was dropped to steer clear of feminist ire, only to be reprised with an updated name in 1987 "in response to hundreds of requests . . . and the public's desire for nostalgia," as quoted in a 1988 *Chicago Tribune* article.[20] Although the Breck Girl's narrative changed over the years, she still singularly projected an idealized and purified image of the American woman.

GENDER STEREOTYPES IN ADVERTISING: PERPETUATING THE MYTH OF NORMALITY

Actors Chris Evans and Evan Rachel Wood starred in a steamy ad campaign for Gucci Guilty fragrance for men in 2011. In one of the ads, Evans and Wood appear partially nude in the photograph and locked in an embrace. He is rising above her, his body pressed against her face and torso. Her face reaches for his, with her lips slightly parted.[21]

Using a well-choreographed stereotypical pose, this ad artfully presents an ideal portrayal of femininity and masculinity. Let's dive into a discussion of gender-role portrayals in advertising.

Gender Roles That People Play

You may remember a 2011 commercial titled "Even Angels Will Fall," for Axe/ Lynx Excite men's deodorant.[22] In the ad, set in a picturesque European village against a swelling orchestral backdrop, scantily clad, lithe female angels drop from the sky and land on the street. Awestruck villagers watch the possessed angels glide in a single direction. They arrive at their destination: a young guy standing next to a scooter. They fix their gaze upon the young guy and then defiantly peel off their haloes and smash them to the ground. The ad cuts to a bedroom scene of the young guy holding a can of Axe Excite and liberally spraying it over his chest. His eyes move up to an angel's feather falling from above. He glances down at the can. The voiceover: "New Axe Excite. Even angels will fall."[23]

This Axe ad is clearly aimed at a young male audience that probably won't find it to be offensive or sexist in terms of gender, although South Africa banned the commercial from the airwaves after a self-professed Christian complained.[24] Still, the ad, and generally all early Axe advertising campaigns, used portrayals of gender to get its message across.

People have historically defined themselves by their gender. *Gender role*, defined as "the pattern of behavior, personality traits, and attitudes defining masculinity or femininity in a certain culture,"[25] often determines how we behave, speak, or dress. These roles are picked up at an early age—in some cases, as early as age one. Personal and commercial sources of information provide instruction in gender socialization for both girls and boys. The most persuasive commercial source is advertising used to support cultural expectations concerning the proper way for girls and boys, women and men, to appear and act.

One article reported the findings of a 1996 study on gender-role stereotyping.[26] The experimental study involved two groups of high school students. One group viewed magazine ads with stereotypical images of women, while the other group viewed non-stereotyped images. Both groups were asked to respond to statements relating to a woman in a role-neutral photograph. Six out of the twelve questionnaire statements contained differences in gender-role expectations, although these differences weren't consistently associated with either experimental treatment or gender.

The results of the study provided further evidence that even transitory exposure to gender advertisements contributes to reinforcing gender roles. According to the study's authors, "The results of this study suggest that the process of learning about gender-appropriate behavior and observing the gendered nature of social life may lead to the development of gender-specific heuristics—or seeing the world through gendered lenses."[27] For example, both females and males who viewed the role-neutral image were more likely to state that the woman in the image did most of the household chores.

"Men Are from Mars, Women Are from Venus"

A 1955 ad for Max Factor's Color-Fast lipstick in "Crushed Rose" features an alluring photograph of an attractive woman and a handsome man. Her lips appear ready to greet his. The headline reads, "Nothing draws a man to a woman like Crushed Rose." The first line of ad copy makes this promise: "You smooth it on, and suddenly love is just a kiss away!"[28] This image depicts stereotypes of femininity and masculinity that fit or match a certain set of cultural expectations.

Advertising commonly displays gender roles and relationships through a variety of social cues. Some are subtle, while others are overt. But they nearly always leave a residual impact, especially when one is exposed repeatedly to the same advertising message. For example, men have been historically portrayed as powerful and dominant figures, while women have been depicted as fragile and vulnerable characters.

In his seminal work *Gender Advertisements*, first published in 1976, famed sociologist Erving Goffman framed the notion of gender display in this way: "If gender be defined as the culturally established correlates of sex (whether in consequence of biology or learning), then gender display refers to conventionalized portrayals of these correlates."[29] Using gender-coded language and portrayals, advertisers reinvent social reality and play it back to us as a believable approximation of reality. Goffman called this "commercial realism,"

the standard transformation employed in contemporary ads, in which the scene is conceivable in all detail as one that could in theory have occurred as pictured, providing us with a simulated slice of life; but although the advertiser does not seem intent on passing the picture off as a caught one, the understanding seems to be that we will not press him too far to account for just what sort of reality the scene has.[30]

WOMAN AND HER SYMBOLS: ARCHETYPES IN ADVERTISING

If you've studied psychology, you may remember the theories of personality proposed by noted psychologists like Sigmund Freud, Karen Horney, and Carl Jung. The last proposed the existence of *archetypes*, or "universally recognized ideas and behavior patterns."[31] Advertising heavily borrows from Jung's archetypes. For example, the "wise old woman" archetype often appears in advertising messages that feature professionals like doctors, lawyers, teachers, nurses, and caregivers, and, as the corresponding shadow or the dark side, witches.

In the context of advertising, an *archetype* is defined as "an artificial statistical construction in human form, an individual personification or representation drawn from research and observation of a group."[32] For example, when we divide a population according to demographic characteristics, such as age, education, gender, ethnicity, and so on, a snapshot of that segment of the population emerges, which can be viewed as an archetype.

An archetype shouldn't be confused with a *stereotype*, "a representation of a cultural group that emphasizes a trait or group of traits that may or may not communicate an accurate representation of the group."[33] A stereotype can carry a negative meaning when a group is inappropriately caricatured. For example, a common complaint is that women are too often depicted in ads as housewives, decorative or sex objects, submissive, incompetent, and incapable of making the big decisions.[34]

Jung's archetypes have inspired the creation of archetype models used by advertisers. For example, authors Margaret Mark and Carol S. Pearson propose a twelve-archetype model that aligns each archetype with a particular set of values, desires, characteristics, and motivational drivers.[35] These archetypes include categories such as "Hero," "Magician," "Jester," and "Lover."

Archetypes and stereotypes are helpful shorthand devices used by advertisers. In the case of stereotypes, advertisers must weigh the advertising efficiency of using them in advertising messages against the risks of offending the very audiences they're trying to reach. For example, the homemaker stereotype was a dominant portrayal of women through the 1930s. Early advertising messages relying on this stereotype often portrayed women as childlike, helpless, foolish, or deferential. For example, a 1939 print ad for Kellogg's Pep cereal uses an image of a husband and wife. The husband wears the conventional gray flannel suit, while the wife wears the "housewives' uniform" and holds a duster. His arm is wrapped around her waist. He gazes down at her approvingly. She girlishly smiles up at him. The text in the speech bubble reads: "So the harder a wife works, the cuter she looks!"[36]

Borrowing from Mark and Pearson's archetype model, let's look at a few examples of cosmetic and personal care brands and the archetypes that they embody.

- *"The Caregiver"*: Motivated by a desire to take care of and protect others, the Caregiver is inherently compassionate, nurturing, and selfless. Committed to the betterment of others, the Caregiver likes to help others for the sake of pure altruism.[37] An example of a Caregiver brand is Johnson & Johnson. For its baby products, the company makes a pledge "to create the gentlest baby products in the world."[38] Advertising messages typically capture touching moments between a mother and her baby, where the product is positioned as a helper.
- *"The Innocent"*: Guided by deeply held beliefs, the Innocent archetype may be described as an idealistic optimist who puts a positive spin on a difficult situation and encourages others to keep calm and carry on. The Innocent is eager to take up causes and opportunities where they can "put their personal values into action."[39] An example of an Innocent brand is Unilever's Dove. The brand exudes positivity, believing that "beauty should be for everyone." Dove products promise to help women reach their personal beauty potential. A good example of an advertising campaign that demonstrates Dove's firmly held values is its "Campaign for Real Beauty" (2004), which has been instrumental in changing the way that women are portrayed in beauty ads. The campaign was followed by the formation of the Dove Self-Esteem Project. The project's goal is to be "an agent of change to educate and inspire girls on a wider definition of beauty and to make them feel more confident about themselves."[40]
- *"The Lover"*: Building close relationships is the chief goal of the Lover. Passionate and romantic by nature, Lovers view themselves as being especially appreciative of others.[41] The Lover seeks opportunities to cultivate emotional connectedness and to become physically attractive in every way. Many cosmetic and fragrance brands fit the Lover archetype. Consider the Chanel brand and its Chanel N°5 fragrance, one of the world's most iconic perfumes. The fragrance embodies passion, intimacy, and sensual pleasure. Coco Chanel described the fragrance as "a woman's perfume, with the scent of a woman." A 2013 ad campaign for Chanel N°5 resurrects Marilyn Monroe to be reborn as the face of N°5. The print campaign uses a seductive black-and-white shot of Marilyn from 1955. She is coquettishly posing with a bottle of the perfume.[42]
- *The Magician"*: The primary desire of the Magician is to seek the fundamental laws of how things work and to apply these lessons to getting things accomplished. Charismatic, creative, and quixotic, the Magician strives to make dreams come true and urges others to believe that anything is possible.[43] An example of a Magician brand is Unilever's Axe/Lynx. For some time, the Axe brand was all about products that made guys "look, feel, and smell their most attractive." Employing "the Axe Effect," ads often showed a regular guy using the product and suddenly being transformed into a veritable babe magnet. Over the years, the brand has grown up and shed its one-dimensionality, acknowledging

that "the rules of attraction are changing and that it is about connection, not conquest." A 2016 ad campaign titled "Find Your Magic" recognizes that traditional masculinity is peeling away, and it's all about "embracing one's individual sense of how to be a man," according to the 2016 *Adweek* article.[44]

THE MYTH BUSTERS:
FROM FEMINISM TO FEMPOWERMENT

As the feminist movement of the 1960s and early 1970s shifted into high gear, the old advertising tricks of the trade employed by real-life Don Drapers of the *Mad Men* era weren't working as well. Many advertisers faced resistance from feminist groups, such as the National Organization for Women (NOW), which challenged sex-role stereotypes featured across the mass media. These groups argued that media portrayals of women operated "as a primary means for introducing and promoting female role stereotypes and sexism" and called for academic research endeavors to explore the problem. According to one piece, feminist theorists mainly studied and focused on the following images: "portrayals that were unrealistic and limited; pictures of women as sex objects, 'happy housewives' themes of females as incompetent, portrayals of women's dependency upon men; and underrepresentation of working women."[45]

Feminist Groups Take Resolute Action Against Sexism in Advertising

During the 1970s, feminist groups put their fighting words into action by holding advertisers to account. They held protests, boycotted products, filed lawsuits, and waged letter-writing campaigns.[46] Starting in 1970, NOW created the "Barefoot and Pregnant Award of the Week for Advertising Degrading to Women."[47] The certificate indicated the name of the offender, the ad, where the ad was seen or heard, and why the ad was deemed objectionable.

When the federal government failed to address sexism in the media, feminist groups sought the help of self-regulatory organizations, such as the National Advertising Review Board (NARB). In 1975, the NARB released a report titled "Advertising & Women" that confirmed what feminist groups were saying all along about the prevalence of sexism in advertising and the perpetuation of gender stereotypes. The NARB went one step further by providing advertisers with guidelines for updating their representations of women to reflect the new realities of a society that had apparently passed many advertisers by.[48]

By now, scores of academicians and scholars were conducting studies and publishing papers on gender depictions of women in the media, which put further pressure on advertisers to address potentially harmful gender stereotypes in ads. Feminist scholars and writers at the forefront of critiquing the role of women in society and the oppression of women that pervaded in the American mass media and culture included Betty Friedan (*The Feminine Mystique*, 1963), Gloria Steinem (cofounder of *Ms.* magazine), Germaine Greer (*The Female Eunuch*, 1970), Susan Brownmiller (*Against Our Will: Men, Women, and Rape*, 1975), and Kate Millett (*Sexual Politics*, 1970), to name a few.

In her seminal work *The Beauty Myth: How Images of Beauty Are Used Against Women*, first published in 1990, feminist writer Naomi Wolf argued that the persistence of unrealistic and unattainable standards of physical attractiveness, which were promoted through the commercial interests of the mass media, can trigger women to engage in unhealthy behaviors, such as disordered eating, and instigate an obsession with appearance. Wolf wrote, "A cultural fixation on female thinness is not an obsession about female beauty but an obsession about female obedience."[49]

The Rise of Fempowerment

By 2010, a new genre of advertising was emerging: "femvertising." More advertisers were challenging gender norms, empowering women and girls, and shattering stereotypes (see figure 5.2). From a 2016 *Adweek* article: "From Always' #LikeAGirl to Nike's #BetterForIt, women are being encouraged, celebrated, held up not for how they look but for what they can accomplish."[50]

Figure 5.2. Several beauty and personal care brands are communicating more positive and empowering messages to girls and shattering gender stereotypes. © E+/GlobalStock

In 2014, ad agency Leo Burnett created a groundbreaking digital and social media campaign for P&G's Always, titled "#LikeAGirl," which demonstrated the negative connotations of gendered language on young girls' self-esteem and confidence. In the video, young people are asked what it means to run, fight, and throw "like a girl." They respond by caricaturing what it means to perform these activities "like a girl." Then a series of young girls are asked the same set of questions. They respond by springing into action, with focus and determination. The others quickly recognize their blunder. The tagline reads, "Rewrite the Rules." The campaign resulted in "a social media movement that aims to redefine what it means to do something 'like a girl,'"[51] as reported in a 2014 *ABC News* article.

As refreshing as "fempowerment" advertising is, how do we know it works? Rely on research, which has found that fempowerment ads not only generate impressions but also leave impressions. According to the *Adweek* article, "Women ages 18 to 34 are twice as likely to think highly of a brand that made an empowering ad and nearly 80 percent more likely to like, share, comment and subscribe after watching one."[52]

Other beauty and personal care brands are using fempowerment ads to send a positive message to women and girls, as well as to depict them more accurately and realistically. One of the first campaigns to use this advertising approach was Dove's "Campaign for Real Beauty." Dove's real-beauty message has struck a chord across a broad swath of women across the globe. Examples of the campaign include a groundbreaking billboard ad in 2004 that featured women of all different shapes and sizes to promote Dove's firming collection ("New Dove Firming. As tested on real curves"); a striking time-lapse web video, titled "Evolution" (2006), showing a pretty, wholesome girl transformed into a billboard model through artificial means of makeup and digital manipulation ("No wonder our perception of beauty is distorted"); and Dove's "Real Beauty Sketches" viral ad in 2013, which used an FBI-trained forensic artist to demonstrate that women view themselves as far less attractive than strangers do ("You are more beautiful than you think").

All in all, progress has been made in addressing gender stereotypes in ads. The reality is, however, that stereotypes aren't easily extinguished. When faced with competing ideas or imagery, people are often slow to accept norms that may not conform to existing stereotypes about their social group. A 2016 *Daily Mail* article cited a study that found that gender stereotypes are as strong today as they were thirty years ago, and that "more people think men are more likely to avoid 'traditional' female roles such as taking care of children and looking after the house than they did in 1983."[53] The study concluded,

> Changes in the activities and representation of women and men in society have unquestionably occurred since the early 1980s. Nonetheless, those changes apparently have not been sufficient to alter strongly held and seemingly functional beliefs about the basic social category of gender, where a variety of psychological processes may be at work that lead to the continued maintenance of gender stereotypes. [54]

REGULATORS AND INDUSTRY PLAYERS LEAN ON ADVERTISERS TO DO THE RIGHT THING

The Advertising Standards Authority (ASA), Britain's advertising watchdog, has taken a tougher stance on ads that use potentially harmful and blatant gender stereotypes. The ASA has pledged to scrap ads that show women as solely responsible for cleaning up a family mess. A 2017 *Marketing Week* article noted that the ASA may yank ads suggesting that certain activities identified with girls are unsuitable for boys and vice versa.[55] Also, the ASA may get rid of ads that depict men as foolishly bungling simple parental duties or household chores. This initiative is outlined in a 2017 ASA report, titled "Depictions, Perceptions and Harm: A Report on Gender Stereotypes in Advertising," which found that gender stereotypes have the potential to "cause harm by inviting assumptions about adults and children that might negatively restrict how they see themselves and how others see them."[56]

By 2019, the ASA made good on its pledge and instituted a ban on ads in Britain that depict "'harmful gender stereotypes' or those which are likely to cause 'serious or widespread offence,'" as reported in a 2019 *BBC News* article.[57] ASA's chief executive, Guy Parker, is quoted as saying, "Our evidence shows how harmful gender stereotypes in ads can contribute to inequality in society, with costs for all of us. Put simply, we found that some portrayals in ads can, over time, play a part in limiting people's potential."[58]

The European Association of Communications Agencies (EACA), which represents more than 2,500 communications agencies and agency associations from thirty European countries and is a part of the European Advertising Standards Alliance (EASA), has pledged to redouble its commitment to deal with "irresponsible gender mainstreaming in media and advertising" across EU member states.[59] In a position statement, the EACA underscored its commitment to combating stereotypes and bringing about a balanced portrayal of women and men in ads.[60]

Where does the United States stand on ads that reinforce harmful gender stereotypes? The FTC's Division of Advertising Practices enforces federal laws pertaining to truth in advertising. The agency monitors the accuracy of claims for food, over-the-counter drugs, dietary supplements, alcohol, and tobacco; advertising to children; performance claims for high-tech products and conduct related to the internet; and other related matters. The FTC is *not* mandated to protect consumers against negative and potentially harmful gender stereotypes in advertising.

"You've Come a Long Way, Baby"—Maybe

In 1968, Philip Morris launched Virginia Slims, the first cigarette brand marketed specifically to women (and the last cigarette commercial to air on the national networks), with an ad campaign using the slogan "You've come a long way, baby." The question is, have we come far enough in vaporizing gender stereotyping in advertising?

Joint research done by the Geena Davis Institute on Gender in Media at Mount Saint Mary's University and J. Walter Thompson (JWT) New York, in collaboration with the University of Southern California's Viterbi School of Engineering, analyzed more than 2,000 films, in English only, from the Cannes Lions archive spanning a ten-year period. Among the reported findings, men received about four times as much screen time as women and spoke about seven times more often than women in advertising, as cited in a 2017 *Marketing Week* article.[61] "The research found there are twice as many male characters in ads as female characters and 25% of ads feature men only, in comparison to just 5% featuring women only. Similarly, 18% of ads feature male voices, while less than 3% of ads feature female voices only,"[62] the article said. The study, called "Unpacking Gender Bias in Advertising," was presented at the 2017 Cannes Lions International Festival of Creativity.[63]

Industry-wide efforts to do something about gender stereotyping in the media are finally getting somewhere. For example, the Unstereotype Alliance, spearheaded by Unilever in partnership with UN Women and other industry leaders and organizations, has pledged to eradicate stereotypical portrayals of gender in advertising and all brand content. Alliance members include Unilever, Procter & Gamble, Google, Microsoft, Mars, Johnson & Johnson, Twitter, Mattel, World Federation of Advertisers, and the Geena Davis Institute on Gender in Media.[64]

The initiative comes on the heels of Unilever's own global research revealing that sexist stereotypes exist in advertising. "Just 3% of ads featured women in a leadership or managerial role. And 40% of women did not identify with their portrayal in advertising spots," as cited in a 2017 *Fortune* article.[65] Unilever's research showed that gender stereotypes can be subtle yet pervasive across all types of ads, and the problem of stereotyping "is most acute in the portrayal of women," as reported in a 2016 article in the *Guardian*.[66] Keith Weed, former chief marketing and communications officer at Unilever, was quoted as saying, "The time is right for us as an industry to challenge and change how we portray gender in our advertising. Our industry spends billions of dollars annually shaping perceptions and we have a responsibility to use this power in a positive manner."[67]

A 2017 *Adweek* article pointed out that the American ad industry has wrestled with and debated the problem of gender stereotyping in advertising for some time.[68] Jess Greenwood, global chief marketing officer at New York–based ad agency R/GA, suggested that any meaningful regulation of sexist ads won't occur in the United States. She noted that advertisers on both sides of the pond are leaning toward "much more inclusive representations" driven by consumer demand. Gina Grillo, president and CEO of the nonprofit organization the Advertising Club of New York, echoed: "U.S. consumers vote [yea] or nay at the cash register. It's a new world, and companies that are delivering outdated stereotypes are no longer resonating."[69]

In the next chapter, we'll explore the decorative role of women in advertising. We'll also examine the objectification of women in advertising. Finally, we'll look at the use of sexual imagery in ads and put the theory that "sex sells" to the test.

III

THE MIRROR MAKERS

6

The Decorative Sex

The stereotype is the Eternal Feminine. She is the Sexual Object sought by all men, and by all women. She is of neither sex, for she has herself no sex at all. Her value is solely attested by the demand she excites in others. All she must contribute is her existence. She need achieve nothing, for she is the reward of achievement.

—From *The Female Eunuch,* by Germaine Greer (1970)

If you were asked to pick a single word to describe the Calvin Klein brand, you might choose *chic, minimalist, seductive, bold, sophisticated, supermodels,* or *androgynous.* You may also associate the brand with its provocative advertising campaigns, such as the 1980 eyebrow-raising campaign for Calvin Klein jeans featuring a then-15-year-old Brooke Shields cooing, "Do you know what comes between me and my Calvins? Nothing."[1] Calvin Klein has turned his name into a global brand powerhouse while repeatedly stress-testing the adage, "There's no such thing as bad publicity."

In 1985, Calvin Klein's Obsession fragrance sparked embers with its oriental spicy scent for women. The fragrance was launched using a sultry advertising campaign with the arousing tagline, "Between love and madness lies obsession." From a 2003 *AdAge* article: "The campaign shook up the world of scent advertising with shots of nude men and women. The shock effect worked for Calvin Klein: Obsession hit sales of $30 million in its first year."[2]

In 1988, polymath David Lynch, perhaps best known for the popular television crime drama *Twin Peaks,* was hired to direct a series of moody black-and-white TV spots for the fragrance.[3] In this campaign, Lynch cast two lead actors from *Twin Peaks* to appear in four vignette ads, which were inspired by the works of Gustave Flaubert's *Madame Bovary* (1856), D. H. Lawrence's *Women in Love* (1920), F. Scott Fitzgerald's *The Great Gatsby* (1925), and Ernest Hemingway's *The Sun Also Rises*

(1926). In each ad, a narrator delivered a passage about doomed love from the novel while the actors performed a dramatic reenactment.[4]

In just six years following its debut, Obsession generated more than $100 million in annual worldwide wholesale sales, making it one of the top-selling fragrances in the world.[5]

Calvin Klein's shock-and-awe approach to advertising continued to work for the brand, while also periodically igniting a firestorm of criticism. For example, in 1992, the designer's underwear ads featured a shirtless Mark Wahlberg cast with a topless Kate Moss. This time the controversy was over Moss's alarmingly thin frame. "She was too skinny, the arguments went, an unrealistic, unattainable role model for young women the commercials were targeting," as quoted in a 2015 *Vogue* article titled "Sex Sells: Calvin Klein's 1990s Ads Stirred Libidos and Controversies in Equal Measure."[6] The Moss campaign, juxtaposed with other campaigns from the early 1990s, stirred public sentiment. President Bill Clinton even personally weighed in on the ads. "The images were so shocking at the time for their depictions of waifish, adolescent beauty they were accused of promoting 'heroin chic' aesthetics and condemned by President Bill Clinton in 1995 and again in 1997," as noted in a 2017 *Vogue* article.[7] The brand didn't suffer a blowback from the controversy. The campaign struck gold, helping the company to gross $85 million within twelve months.[8]

Calvin Klein still courts controversy over its use of risqué ads. For example, in 2016, Calvin Klein's underwear campaign triggered a new round of debate. The 2016 *ABC News* article "Calvin Klein's New, Racy Ad Campaign Sparks Controversy" noted that social media ads asked users to complete this fill-in-the-blank sentence: "I _____ in my Calvins."[9] The campaign featured top models Abbey Lee Kershaw and Kendall Jenner and actor Klara Kristin. One of the photos that made headlines featured Kristin posing in a skirt above a camera. The caption read, "I flash in #mycalvins" together with #takeapeek. Once again, the fashion maestro of shockvertising managed not only to grab eyeballs but also to grab free headlines and sound bites.

In this chapter, we'll examine how women are portrayed in decorative roles in advertising, with a focus on cosmetics advertising. We'll also introduce the concepts of hypersexualization and objectification in preparation for our discussion of sexual objectification in advertising. Finally, we'll look at recent government and industry policies and measures that have been taken to combat female objectification in the media.

THE DECORATIVE ROLE: A CENTURY OF WOMEN IN COSMETICS ADVERTISING

For nearly 2,000 years, women all over the world have used some variation of cold cream to smooth skin and remove makeup. Cold creams are nothing more than water-in-oil emulsions, which are also used as the base for other cosmetic products, such as foundation cream, cleansing cream, vanishing cream, and moisturizing cream. Despite the sameness or near sameness of the products, early cosmetics advertising boasted their unique product benefits, with slogans emphasizing reliability ("Never hardens" and "The delicate fragrance lasts"), safety and health ("Never irritates" and "Good for your skin"), and youthfulness ("Keeps the schoolgirl complexion").[10]

Decades later, a substantial body of market research found that a consumer's response to cosmetics advertising was determined more by "the expectations and preferences of other women—what was called 'other-directed' pitches—than by her own 'inner-directed' goals such as age reduction or the promotion of health."[11] In 1967, a study analyzed ads from three American women's magazines between 1913 and 1964. Among the thirteen product categories surveyed, the study laid bare the fact that only cosmetics still stressed "an emotional, other-directed appeal," such as other-directed femininity in ads.[12]

Let's take a revealing look at the history of cosmetics advertising and its depiction of women.

It All Began with Powder

The first rough ads for cosmetics ran in European newspapers during the seventeenth and eighteenth centuries. Early ads were for lead-based powder used to whiten the skin and hair. Also, early American newspapers advertised products such as the beauty patch, which was used to hide facial blemishes and scars (such as smallpox scars), rouge, and lipstick.[13]

The first commercial American cosmetic products were Chesebrough's Vaseline Petroleum Jelly, created in 1859, and Pond's Cleansing Cream and Pond's Extract, first produced in 1846.[14] These products were promoted through testimonials, product brochures, and advertising trade cards (small brightly colored cards), which were distributed through apothecary shops. Pond's, for example, hired J. Walter Thompson Company, one of the earliest ad agencies in the United States, to develop its first national advertising campaign in 1886.[15] For Pond's, one of its first clients, the agency created the award-winning Pond's Girl ad campaign that carried the slogan "Avoid sunburn, freckles and chaps."[16]

The 1880s and 1890s ushered in advances in printing technology and an increased use of high-quality illustrations in print media, which contributed to the popularization of "pretty girl" pictures in advertising.[17] For example, in the 1880s, one of the earliest images of realistic ads featured the smiling "Sozodont Girl" for Sozodont toothpaste. The Sozodont Girl, an ultrafeminine image of ideal Victorian beauty, was first captured as a woodcut portrait and carried the headline "Pearls in the Mouth."[18] At the same time, advertising that emphasized public prudishness of the Victorian period was yielding to advertising that showed readers just a little skin. According to *Soap, Sex, and Cigarettes: A Cultural History of American Advertising*: "Advertisers then found that a peek at the forbidden could bring readers to a halt.

Since the Victorians covered their bodies from chin to toes, it took only a hemline lifted to the ankle to arrest the viewer."[19]

Advertising of cosmetic preparations was spotty during the 1800s, as the use of cosmetics was still frowned upon. "The discreet use of certain cosmetics—including hair tint, cheek rouge and body powder on the arms and neckline—to cover the signs of aging was permissible."[20]

The soap trade, which had grown into a budding industry, was one of the first to employ large-scale advertising. In the 1890s, N. K. Fairbank Co., a Chicago-based soap manufacturer, used the arts and crafts style in its ad for Fairy soap.[21] Around the same time, British-made Pears soap ran a string of full-page ads that used original paintings by well-known artists and illustrators and carried the tagline: "Good morning! Have you used Pears' soap?"[22] Also, Pears soap was one of the first commodities to use product endorsements, which featured stage celebrity Lillie Langtry and opera star Adelina Patti.[23]

The Soap Wars

The emergence of a modern consumer culture in the 1920s led to the development of urban retail forms, such as chain stores (Woolworth's) and department stores (Federated Department Stores), as well as the continued popularity of mail-order businesses, like Sears, Roebuck and Co., which published its first catalogue ("the Consumers' Bible") in 1888. With robust growth within the domestic market and the rise of mass markets, cosmetics use gained greater acceptance, which opened the door to a wave of cosmetics advertising. "With heightened national production capabilities and the development of a professional advertising industry, 20th-century producers were able to send positive messages about cosmetic consumption to a wide array of Americans," according to *The American Beauty Industry Encyclopedia*.[24] As a result, cosmetic ads flooded the pages of popular women's magazines, such as *Good Housekeeping, McCall's,* and *Ladies' Home Journal.*

As competition heated up, especially in the fiercely competitive beauty soap category, cosmetics manufacturers more aggressively promoted their products to stand out in a crowded marketplace. In advertising messages, emotional and psychological appeals, such as sex, status, esteem, well-being, pleasure, and so on, were employed to make products more aesthetically pleasing or interesting to consumers. For example, in 1911, J. Walter Thompson created a print ad for Woodbury's facial soap that used a painting of a good-looking couple in evening attire and had an enticing headline: "A skin you love to touch."[25] The ad broke new ground by using sex appeal to sell a product. Other soap makers tried to connect with consumers at an emotional level. Created by New York–based ad agency Benton and Bowles Inc. in 1928, a Palmolive soap ad features a picture of a young mother dotingly adjusting her young son's bow tie as he gazes at her adoringly. The caption reads, "His first love."[26]

The 1920s introduced an entirely new advertising medium: radio. At first, people weren't enthralled with the "talking box" and considered it to be in bad taste and intrusive. Still, the cosmetics industry embraced the new medium and spent heavily to promote their products by sponsoring radio programs and buying commercial spots. In 1931, Lady Esther became the first cosmetics firm to devote almost its entire advertising budget to radio.[27] The company sponsored national radio programs, such as *The Lady Esther Serenade*, featuring Wayne King and his orchestra, and *Lady Esther Presents Orson Welles*.

During the late 1920s and early 1930s, the Art Deco style, which used symmetrical, geometric, and streamlined images and forms, surfaced in cosmetics and toiletry ads. For example, Odorono, a toilet water (the equivalent of an antiperspirant) marketed to women, used colorful ads featuring "angular drawings of women with long necks and limbs that connote elegance."[28] In those days, most people didn't think they needed deodorant, especially men, who were expected to have a musky smell of body odor, or they believed that the product was harmful. Furthermore, it was taboo for women to broach such matters in public. Early ads created by J. Walter Thompson used a fear appeal, or "whisper copy," to convince women that "excessive perspiration" was an unseemly medical condition and that if they suffered from it, tongues would wag.[29]

Major cosmetics manufacturers thrived by producing and promoting new cosmetic products and makeup colors to meet consumer demand. For example, as many as 1,500 face creams greased up the marketplace. By the late 1920s, every woman purchased a pound of face powder annually.[30] Max Factor, famed makeup artist and founder of the cosmetics giant Max Factor & Company, pioneered the "color harmony" principles of makeup. In 1927, he introduced the Society Make-up line, the company's first cosmetic line to gain national distribution. For women who weren't accustomed to wearing makeup, the cosmetic line helped them choose makeup shades that "harmonized" with their complexion, hair, and eyes. Several ads for the collection featured glamorous actors of the day, such as Carole Lombard and Anita Page. In the ads, the stars tell women that they can look like a screen star if they use the makeup line ("Like the Screen Stars . . . Have Your Make-Up in Color Harmony").[31]

Connecting with the African American Consumer

During the late nineteenth and early twentieth centuries, cosmetics advertising attempted to reach African American consumers, which in turn helped to bolster support for African American newspapers and magazines. Products like commercial hair straighteners and skin-lightening preparations were frequently advertised in the press. For instance, banker and manufacturer Anthony Overton was the first African American to establish a multi-business industry. In 1898, he formed the Overton Hygienic Manufacturing Company.[32] Its nationally recognized High Brown Face Powder was "the first market success in the sale of cosmetics for Black women."[33] Overton promoted this powder and other toiletry products in Black newspapers.[34]

In 1905, Madam C. J. Walker, née Sarah Breedlove, made her fortune by creating and marketing a successful line of beauty and hair products for Black women through Madam C. J. Walker Manufacturing Company. Walker, who had picked up advertising techniques from her newspaperman husband, transformed the hair and beauty industry by inventing a treatment for hair loss, a common condition among Black and white women caused by an inadequate diet and harsh hair treatments. Like Overton's company, Walker's company became a leading advertiser in Black newspapers.[35]

In the Nude, in the Limelight

During the 1930s, cosmetics companies continued to use emotional and psychological appeals in their advertising, with an emphasis on beauty in a bar. For example, in 1930, ad agency Pedlar & Ryan created an ad for Procter & Gamble Co.'s Camay soap that issued this warning to women: "Someone's eyes are forever searching your face, comparing you with other women."[36] In another series of Camay ads, illustrations of beaming young women dressed in bridal gowns were featured alongside testimonials that spoke to Camay's ability to improve their skin complexion.[37]

In 1936, Woodbury facial soap was the first product to show a nude woman in its national advertising.[38] Its ad agency, J. Walter Thompson, hired renowned photographer Edward Steichen to create a nude series designed to give the product an artistic flair. The ad copy emphasized health and beauty, such as "Bathe all your skin for Beauty in the 'Filtered Sunshine' of Woodbury's Gentle Lather!"[39] Other cosmetics companies pushed the envelope of propriety. For example, a 1931 ad for Listerine deodorant displayed a photograph of a nude woman's back and the side of her breast.[40]

The arrival of color photographic film was a major turning point in the cosmetics industry, requiring manufacturers to create formulations that produced natural-looking skin tones.[41] In 1937, Max Factor, with his roots in the motion picture industry, quickly seized on this technological breakthrough by launching Max Factor's Pan-Cake Make-Up. Furnishing a matte finish and providing a natural complexion, the foundation was first used on actors' faces and then on consumers' faces when Factor introduced the product to general merchandisers in 1938. Factor recruited some of Hollywood's screen goddesses to appear in the print ads for the product, including Rosalind Russell, Loretta Young, Lana Turner, and Judy Garland. Each ad featured the celebrity and mentioned a current film in which she had a starring role. The ad copy made a direct link between the glamorous star and the product. In an ad featuring Judy Garland, the headline read: "A Glamorous NOW . . . a lovelier TOMORROW."[42]

By the 1940s, the cosmetics industry was booming. Market leaders like Max Factor, Maybelline, and Helena Rubinstein influenced the direction that the market took. Media use expanded to include television. Maybelline was the first cosmetic brand to use both radio and television. Maybelline also made extensive use of celebrity tie-ins and endorsements, including Hollywood film stars like Hedy Lamarr and Joan Crawford.[43]

Fire and Ice, Sugar and Spice

The cosmetics industry entered a golden age in the 1950s. Women were expected to take full advantage of beauty products, and many were afraid to leave home without wearing a full face of makeup (see figure 6.1). In 1952, Revlon developed one of the most talked-about beauty campaigns for the launch of its "Fire and Ice" lipstick and nail enamel. *Businessweek* called the campaign "the most effective ads

Figure 6.1. The 1950s makeup looks emphasized refinement, glamour, and sophistication. © Retrofile RF/George Marks

in cosmetics history," and *Advertising Age* named it the best ad of the year.[44] The magazine spreads featured raven-haired American model Dorian Leigh, who was one of the first Revlon Girls. Leigh was photographed wearing a sparkling silver gown framed by a billowy scarlet cape. Incidentally, the identical composition—same dress, same cape, same image—was used in a 2010 campaign featuring actor Jessica Biel to mark Revlon's rerelease of three "lip-and-tip" pairings in a "vintage inspired collection."[45]

Sexually suggestive ads, often disguised as visual metaphor, kept cropping up in cosmetics ads, even for deodorant. For example, in 1959, Bristol-Myers Squibb Co. hired ad agency Ogilvy, Benson & Mather to handle advertising for its Ban deodorant brand. At the time, broadcast networks didn't allow advertisers to show actual people putting on deodorant. So then, the decision was made to depict the human anatomy with a tableau of classical nude statues in the commercial and to use a British voiceover: "In the mature male and the mature female. . ."[46] Other advertisers turned up the heat. In the 1960s, Noxzema ran a commercial for its men's shaving cream that featured a man shaving to bump-and grind stripper music, with a sultry blonde, former Miss Sweden Gunilla Knutson, egging men on, "Take it off. Take it *all* off."[47]

The 1960s counterculture movement celebrated ideals of natural beauty, and the cosmetics industry responded in kind. Several brands stressed the ability to achieve a natural look. For instance, in 1961, New York ad agency Sullivan, Stauffer, Colwell & Bayles (SSC&B) created a print ad campaign for the launch of CoverGirl's cosmetics line. The ads used photographs of young, fresh-faced models appearing on fake covers of magazines such as *Woman's Day*, *Redbook*, *Vogue*, and *McCall's*.[48] The ads used this headline, "At last! A Cover Girl complexion . . . so natural you can't believe it's make-up!"[49]

Cosmetics companies also continued to capitalize on movie tie-ins and celebrity endorsements. For instance, in 1968, Yardley of London featured actor Olivia Hussey, who played Juliet in the 1968 film adaptation of *Romeo and Juliet*, in print ads for its Next to Nothing makeup line. The actor was photographed in a high-necked lacy top. The ad copy read: "Now You See It. Now You Don't."[50]

I Am Woman

By the 1970s, cosmetics companies provided a broader range of makeup looks geared toward the diverse needs of different women. Several major cosmetics companies started to tailor-make product lines geared toward people of color or acquired existing brands that had already built a reputation in this market segment. "Beginning in the 1970s, the major cosmetics marketers began adding product lines that catered to customers of color, buying African-American-owned competitors such as Johnson Products and Soft Sheen Products and using Black models in their advertising."[51]

Consider Somali-born model Iman, who, according to *Time* magazine, "challenged the notions of beauty in the pages of fashion magazines."[52] Iman became one of the first models of color to enter into an exclusive cosmetics contract with Revlon. In the 1980s, she appeared in an ad campaign that introduced the tagline, "The most unforgettable women in the world wear Revlon," which celebrated a broad spectrum of beauty.[53]

Several cosmetics brands conveyed the liberated woman in their advertising messages. For example, in 1973, Revlon Inc. released a new fragrance labeled Charlie. The company created an original advertising campaign for the launch, which revolutionized fragrance advertising. "The Charlie ad campaign shook up the fragrance market. Revlon's in-house Creative Workshop in 1973 created the best-known campaign, featuring model Shelley Hack as the 'Charlie girl,' an independent—perhaps even employed—female who selected her own scent."[54]

The Bold and the Beautiful

An October 1981 issue of *Life* magazine called Shelley Hack, Lauren Hutton, and Iman for Revlon; Margaux Hemingway for Fabergé; Karen Graham for Estée Lauder; Cristina Ferrare for Max Factor; and Cheryl Tiegs for CoverGirl the "million-dollar faces" of the beauty industry.[55] Consider Cheryl Tiegs, who was called "the all-time Cover Girl champ" in a 1992 *New York Times* article "All About/ Cover Girls; The Look That Sells Is Both Girl-Next-Door and Celebrity" for appearing in more than a dozen separate campaigns.[56] In the ad campaigns, Tiegs epitomized the very portrait of the shining all-American girl.

Many actors and models-turned-actors were used as spokespersons for cosmetics brands. Take raven-haired, blue-eyed actor Lynda Carter, best known as the first crime-fighting Wonder Woman. Carter became the face of Maybelline in 1980 and remained so until 1991. In 1980, Carter appeared in ads for Maybelline's Moisture Whip skin care and cosmetic line.[57] In another example, Sharon Stone appeared in a 1982 Finesse shampoo and conditioner commercial, where she played the woman about town. The ad used a jingle: "Sometimes you need a little Finesse—sometimes you need a lot."[58] Finally, in the early 1990s, naturally curly-haired, fresh-faced Rebecca Gayheart gained notice and recognition in a series of television and print ads for Noxzema. One slogan read: "For Healthy Looking Skin . . . Your Face Belongs to Noxzema."[59]

Sexual ads continued to dot the advertising landscape. In *Ogilvy on Advertising* (1985), advertising tycoon David Ogilvy addressed the use of sex in advertising.[60] He provided an example of the appropriate use of this type of message strategy in an Ogilvy & Mather commercial for Paco Rabanne men's cologne. The scene: A man, depicted as a bohemian artist occupying a loft, is shown lounging in bed in the morning and chatting on the phone with the woman with whom he just spent the night.[61] According to Ogilvy, "The most *risqué* copy I have seen was for Paco Rabanne men's cologne. Sales went up 25 percent, and the advertisement was voted the best to appear in magazines in 1981."[62] Ogilvy believed that the decision to use sex rested on "*relevance*."[63] He said, "To show bosoms in a detergent advertisement would not sell the detergent. Nor is there any excuse for the sexy girls you sometimes see draped across the hoods in automobile advertisements. On the other hand, there is a *functional* reason to show nudes in advertisements for beauty products."[64]

Blurred Gender Lines

As American society becomes more diverse, some cosmetics companies are using more inclusive messaging. For instance, a 2016 Brandchannel.com article high-lighted CoverGirl's borderless, genderless, and boundaryless advertising efforts.[65] In 2016, the company named James Charles, then a seventeen-year-old makeup artist and social media star, as its very first male spokesmodel. Also, the company chose makeup artist Nura Afia, a Muslim beauty vlogger, as a beauty brand ambassador.[66]

The nonbinary phenomenon has begun to grow exponentially. "According to a report by the Innovation Group at J. Walter Thompson, 56 percent of consumers aged 13 to 20 years say someone they know uses gender-neutral pronouns—'they,' 'them' or 'ze' versus 'he' or 'she'—significantly more than the 43 percent of millennials who do. Plus, more than one-third of Gen Z respondents in the study strongly agree that gender does not define a person as much as it used to,"[67] as cited in a 2016 *Adweek* article. In response, some cosmetics brands have come out with gender-creative products, like Giorgio Armani's gender-neutral lip balm called Him/Her Lipcare. MAC Cosmetics entered into a partnership with TV personality Caitlyn Jenner to create a limited-edition lipstick called "Finally Free."[68]

BODY PARTS: SEXUAL OBJECTIFICATION OF WOMEN IN ADVERTISING

In a 2011 photo spread for the French edition of *Vogue* magazine, *Vogue Paris*, sinewy models are stretched out on an assortment of exotic furs, their bodies coated in jewels and their faces tinted with rouge.[69] The models are staring alluringly into the camera. Not a terribly shocking scene if you're a reader of women's fashion magazines. In this instance, however, the models would be considered underage, some as young as ten.

This provocative spread drew fierce criticism from media observers and fashion bloggers, especially those in the United States, as reported in the 2013 *PBS News-Hour* article "Researchers Measure Increasing Sexualization of Images in Magazines."[70] In France, the *Vogue* controversy reached the French Senate, which opened an investigation to determine "whether there was a problem with hypersexualization affecting French children and if so what to do about it," the article said.

The American Psychological Association (APA) defines *hypersexualization* as "occurring when a person's value comes only from his or her sexual appeal or behavior to the exclusion of other characteristics."[71] Researchers have long examined the presence of hypersexualization of women in the media. For over twenty-five years,

Sarah Murnen, a social psychologist at Kenyon College, has explored the problem of hypersexualized images of females in the media. Over the past several years, Murnen and her colleagues found a dramatic increase in the volume of images in magazines that portrayed young women in "highly sexual ways."[72]

In an analysis of ads and articles appearing in *Seventeen* magazine, the research team discovered that "the average number of sexualizing characteristics almost tripled over three decades," with an increase in depictions of low-cut tops and tight-fitting clothing in particular. From the *PBS NewsHour* article, Murnen is quoted as saying, "We've seen three trends associated with these images. It's now common to see more parts of the body exposed. There is more emphasis on the size of women's breasts. And easy access to all these images has made it all more acceptable to us."[73]

Let's discuss the issue of objectification that continues to seep into advertising.

Objectification Theory

Objectification can be generally defined "as the seeing and/or treating a person, usually a woman, *as an object*."[74] Several feminist thinkers and scholars have studied and written about objectification. In a 1995 article titled "Objectification," in *Philosophy and Public Affairs*, Martha C. Nussbaum, the Ernst Freund Distinguished Service Professor of Law and Ethics at the University of Chicago, posited seven features indicative of treating a person as an object:

- *Instrumentality*: The person is treated as a tool for another's purposes.
- *Denial of autonomy*: The person is treated as lacking autonomy and self-determination.
- *Inertness*: The person is treated as lacking in agency (a person who's not allowed to act for herself) or the capacity to act.
- *Fungibility*: The person is treated as interchangeable with other objects.
- *Violability*: The person is treated as lacking in boundary-integrity, "as something that it is permissible to break up, smash, or break into."
- *Ownership*: The person is treated as something to be owned by another, can be bought or sold, and so on.
- *Denial of subjectivity*: The person is treated as if her experiences and feelings needn't be taken into account.[75]

Rae Langton, the Knightbridge Professor of Philosophy at the University of Cambridge, added to Nussbaum's list. Langton proposed the following three properties:

- *Reduction to body*: The person is treated as identified with their body or body parts.
- *Reduction to appearance*: The person is treated mainly in terms of how they look, or how they appear to the senses.
- *Silencing*: The person is treated as silent or incapable of speaking.[76]

Finally, proposed by Barbara L. Fredrickson, Kenan Distinguished Professor at the University of North Carolina at Chapel Hill, and Tomi-Ann Roberts, professor of psychology at Colorado College,[77] the objectification theory provides a framework for exploring the experiential ramifications "of being female in a culture that sexually objectifies the female body."[78] The theory asserts that "girls and women, more so than boys and men, are socialized to internalize an observer's perspective as their primary view of their physical selves."[79]

GENDER ADVERTISEMENTS: "SIZING UP THE SEXES"

One of the foremost researchers and authorities on the representation of women in advertising is speaker, author, and award-winning documentary filmmaker Jean Kilbourne. Her documentaries, including *Killing Us Softly: Advertising's Image of Women* (1979) and *Still Killing Us Softly: Advertising's Image of Women* (1987), are sobering commentaries on a systematic use of destructive gender stereotyping in advertising, the impact of advertising on women's self-image, and the sexual objectification of women in ads.

In *Killing Us Softly 4*, Kilbourne conducted a fresh examination of American advertising that promotes unrealistic and harmful ideals of femininity. Kilbourne anatomized more than 160 print and television ads and discovered that "the more things have changed, the more they've stayed the same."[80] The steady flow of sexist and misogynistic images and messages "lay bare a stunning pattern of damaging gender stereotypes—images and messages that too often reinforce unrealistic, and unhealthy, perceptions of beauty, perfection, and sexuality" (see figure 6.2).[81]

Let's explore representations of masculinity and femininity in advertising.

Goffman and Gender Displays

In chapter 5, we introduced Goffman's *Gender Advertisements*, which explored gender displays commonly used in advertising to reinforce gender-role stereotypes. Goffman asserted that these displays are essentially what advertising draws upon and are why ads seem familiar to us. He analyzed rituals of gender behavior appearing in a representational sample of print ads from selected magazines and newspapers. The pictures were sorted and grouped into common themes, or "genderisms."[82] Let's look at some of these themes.

- *Relative Size*: Men are frequently given greater social status (the position or rank of a person) than women by picturing men as taller than women. Goffman said that this tendency to show men with higher social status than women is, in part, explained by anatomical differences between the two sexes.[83]
- *The Feminine Touch*: Women are shown using their hands and fingers to showcase an object, such as tracing the outlines of it, fondling it, cradling its

Figure 6.2. A preponderance of idealized female images disseminated through advertising and various media often reinforce unrealistic expectations about beauty and body image. ©
E+/Juergen Sack

surface, or giving it a soft touch, whereas men are seen grasping or gripping objects.[84]

- *Function Ranking*: When performing a joint task, men typically play the executive role, specifically issuing instructions, within an occupational specialty. In contrast, women are usually seen acquiescing to the instructions and deferential to the instructors.[85]

- *The Ritualization of Subordination*: A quintessential stereotype is deference, in which women are positioned spatially on a lower plane than men, such as lying on beds and floors.[86]
- *Licensed Withdrawal*: Women, more often than men, are seen involved in activities that displace them psychologically from the given social situation, "leaving them unoriented in it and to it, and presumably, therefore, dependent on the protectiveness and goodwill of others who are (or might come to be) present."[87] Women are often pictured "mentally drifting" from the physical scene even while in close physical proximity with a male, and they appear lost and dreamy-eyed.[88]

Goffman contended that ritualized behaviors aren't machinations or inventions of advertisers but instead stylized portrayals of real life. He concluded,

> By and large, advertisers do not create the ritualized expressions they employ; they seem to draw upon the same corpus of displays, the same ritual idiom, that is the resource of all of us who participate in social situations, and to the same end: the rendering of glimpsed action readable. If anything, advertisers conventionalize our conventions, stylize what is already a stylization, make frivolous use of what is already something considerably cut off from contextual controls. Their hype is hyper-ritualization.[89]

Toxicity 101: Thingifying and Commodifying of Women in the Media

Women are often depicted as disconnected body parts in makeup ads and not as a whole being. Dana Heller, dean of the College of Arts and Sciences at Eastern Michigan University, described the nexus between commodity consumption and feminine appearance. She wrote, "Feminine identity or subjectivity can be likened to the commodity, not only in structural terms, but also in terms of appearance."[90] In cosmetics advertising, for example, the female body is often fragmented into divisible parts to make the sale and increase product consumption.

In her article "Beauty . . . and the Beast of Advertising," in the Winter 1990 *Media & Values*,[91] Jean Kilbourne observed the tyranny of advertising that promotes unattainable and idealized female images, as well as the threat of *self-objectification*, "when people view themselves as objects for use instead of as human beings."[92] Kilbourne said, "A woman is conditioned to view her face as a mask and her body as an object, as things separate from and more important than her real self, constantly in need of alteration, improvement, and disguise. . . . Objectified constantly by others, she learns to objectify herself."[93] Kilbourne explained that women are often sexualized and dismembered in ads; their bodies are disembodied parts requiring improvement or alteration. These images can directly or indirectly prompt women to see their bodies as separate parts and not as a whole person. Kilbourne said, "The mannequin has no depth, no totality; she is an aggregate of parts that have been made acceptable."[94]

SEX SELLS—OR DOES IT?

Sex in advertising is used to sell everything from burgers to perfume and beer to cars. Sexual imagery in advertising is designed to arouse the senses, shock the sensibilities, and create emotional overload. Factors driving an ever-rising proportion of "attractive flesh on display" include an increased acceptance of sexual messages in the mass media and a softening in media censorship of sexualized ads. Let's explore sex appeals in advertising.

Why Sex Sells

At no other time in our history have we been bombarded with so much advertising. The noisy profusion of messages has created *clutter*, "the multitude of messages all competing to get consumers' attention."[95] In a 2006 *CBS News* article, J. Walker Smith, former president of the market research firm Yankelovich and chief knowledge officer for brand and marketing at Kantar Consulting, emphasized the sheer volume of ads that people are exposed to daily: "Well, it's a nonstop blitz of advertising messages. . . . Everywhere we turn we're saturated with advertising messages trying to get our attention."[96] According to Smith, in the 1970s we were exposed to about five hundred ads a day. Today, that number has risen to as many as five thousand a day.[97] And here's where sex appeals in ads seem to work: They can break through clutter and grab eyeballs.

There's a whole body of academic research on the presence and prevalence of sexual content in advertising. For example, a study out of the University of Georgia looked at the use of visual sexual imagery in advertising for different product categories. Using six mainstream magazines, *Cosmopolitan, Redbook, Esquire, Playboy, Newsweek,* and *Time,* the researchers analyzed 3,232 full-page ads published in the years of 1983, 1993, and 2003, and found that sexual imagery was employed in 20 percent of the ads. The use of sexual themes to promote everything from alcohol to banking services climbed over the years. Only 15 percent of the ads sampled used sex as a selling point in 1983. That figure rose to 27 percent in 2003.[98] In a 2012 *Business News Daily* article, Tom Reichert, one of the study's authors and a former professor and head of the advertising and public relations department in the University of Georgia Grady College of Journalism and Mass Communication, is quoted as saying, "Our findings show that the increase in visual sexual imagery over the three decades of analysis is attributable to products already featuring sexual content in ads, not necessarily widespread adoption by other product categories. Specifically, alcohol, entertainment and beauty ads are responsible for much of the increase."[99]

Out of the 18 product categories used in the study, the ads containing the highest percentage of visual sexual imagery were health and hygiene products (38 percent), followed by beauty products (36 percent); drugs and medications (29 percent); apparel (27 percent); travel (23 percent); and entertainment (21 percent). Only two product categories did not use sex in their ads: charitable organizations and computer companies.[100]

Women were used to hawk products most often "when pitching sex." In the ads studied from 2003, an overwhelming majority (92 percent) of beauty ads displayed female models, while just under half of the ads did not include models.[101] In addition, females staggeringly populated the pages of sex-selling ads, with entertainment advertising being the exception. Of the 38 percent of provocative health and hygiene ads that contained models, nearly a third (31 percent) were females and a scant 7 percent were males.[102]

Reichert explained why we're witnessing an increase in sexual content in advertising. From the *Business News Daily* article, he is quoted as saying, "It takes more explicitness to grab our attention and arouse us than before. In the early 1900s, exposed arms and ankles of female models generated the same level of arousal as partially nude models do today. We can see during our lifetimes the changes in sexually explicit content on television, movies, books and other forms of media beyond just advertising."[103]

Sexy ads have stopping power, but their ability to produce sales lift can depend on the nature of the product. "Sexual appeals appear to be ineffective when marketers use them merely as a 'trick' to grab attention. They do, however, appear to work when the product is *itself* related to sex (e.g., lingerie or Viagra)."[104] For example, a 2013 Clorox Liquid-Plumr Urgent Clear commercial titled "Quickie," showing a woman grabbing a bottle of the drain cleaner from a store shelf and suddenly slipping into a fantasy of a brawny handyman showing up at her home, may get the viewer's attention but distract from the selling message.[105]

The Slippery Slope of Sexual Appeals

Whether we view sexual appeals in ads favorably or unfavorably can depend on our age. In general, younger audiences tend to be less affected by sexual content in ads, as compared with older audiences. Today's young generation of women appear to have a more tolerant attitude toward sexually themed ads. A 2008 *Journal of Advertising Research* article presented the results of a study that examined attitudes of college females toward sexual objectification in ads and whether those attitudes affected purchase intention.[106] The study concluded, "Young, educated women today appear far less offended by the portrayal of women as sex objects in advertisements than women in past generations, and it seems largely due to our culture."[107] Given that today's young college women are exposed to sexualized messages in ads at a much younger age than prior generations, the results of the study ring true.

Gender is also a determining factor. For example, research has shown that under controlled conditions women tend to exhibit more negative reactions toward the gratuitous use of sex in advertising, whereas men's reactions tend to be more positive.[108] There's a way that advertisers can use sex appeals in advertising without losing half of their audience. Portraying sex in a manner consistent with women's intrinsic values (for instance, associating sexual behavior with commitment and devotion) could improve women's attitudes toward sexual content in ads, according to a study in the *Journal of Consumer Research*.[109] The study's authors suggested that advertisers should "exercise caution" in using sex in advertising, especially if women are members of the target audience. The authors concluded, "The present experiments also revealed that the appropriate use of positioning and relationship context can improve women's attitudes toward the ad and brand."[110]

It's All in Your Head

Why sex sells is a question that has fascinated researchers for decades. Researchers at the University of California, Los Angeles (UCLA), and George Washington University discovered that two different types of ads create different levels of brain activity depending on whether they speak to the head ("logical persuasion," or LP, such as an ad that emphasizes a car's fuel efficiency) or to the heart ("nonrational influence," or NI, such as an ad that shows a pretty woman draped over the hood of a car).[111] The study findings were reported in the 2011 article "Regional Brain Activation with Advertising Images," published in the *Journal of Neuroscience, Psychology, and Economics (JNPE)*.[112]

The researchers found that viewing images of an attractive woman or man in an ad can stimulate regions of the brain that motivate impulse buying, thus bypassing the part of the brain responsible for rational thought, as reported in a 2011 *Daily Mail* article.[113] The reason is that NI images dodge the regions of the brain that process information logically and rationally.

Using experimental research involving electroencephalography (EEG), twenty-four healthy adults (eleven women and thirteen men) were monitored and their brain activity recorded as they viewed LP and NI ads. "The rate of activity in the emotional processing and decision-making parts of the brain was much lower during the NI than the LP adverts," the *Daily Mail* article said. Ian A. Cook, MD, is quoted as saying, "Watch your brain and watch your wallet. The lower levels of brain activity from ads employing NI images could lead to less behavioral inhibition, which could translate to less restraint when it comes to buying products depicted."[114] He added, "The finding reinforces the hypothesis that preferences for purchasing goods and services may be shaped by many factors, including advertisements presenting logical, persuasive information and those employing images or text that may modify behavior without requiring conscious recognition of a message."[115]

TAKING AIM AT SEXISM IN ADVERTISING: A GLOBAL PERSPECTIVE

In India, the government's Ministry of Information and Broadcasting issued a warning letter to television channels that instructed them not to run ads showing "voracious women and 'libidinous' men." Such images are increasingly appearing in deodorant ads targeted at young men, which flies in the face of India's ideals of chastity, as reported in a 2011 article in the *Telegraph*.[116]

Cultural differences can explain why advertising that sexually objectifies women is a red-line issue in some countries but not in others. Let's find out what some countries are doing to curb or stamp out sexism in advertising.

Regulatory Crackdown on Sexist Ads

Few countries have imposed an all-out ban on sexism in advertising. Rather, most countries regard it to be a bigger ethical issue. That said, some nations have addressed sexism in advertising as part of a more comprehensive set of laws governing the media's portrayals of race, gender, sexuality, and so on. For example, both Norway and Denmark have strict guidelines on the use of sexist images for commercial gain. In Norway, bans on sexist advertising went into effect back in 2003, according to a 2008 *BBC News* article.[117] The ban is part of a larger package of legislative guardrails on advertising, "protecting the depiction of religion, sexuality, race, and gender."[118]

In the United Kingdom, the advertising regulatory climate is harsher than in the United States. There, consumer protection laws are some of the toughest to be found.[119] The goal of Britain's Advertising Standards Authority (ASA) is "to make every UK ad a responsible ad."[120] Its sister organization, the Committee of Advertising Practice (CAP), is primarily responsible for revising, updating, monitoring, and enforcing the UK Code of Non-broadcast Advertising and Direct and Promotional Marketing (CAP Code). In response to public pressure, the ASA has recently pledged to toughen rules on ads that perpetuate sexist stereotypes, particularly those relating to objectification and body image, as reported in a 2017 *Guardian* article.[121]

Canada imposes comprehensive oversight on its advertising industry. At the national level, self-regulation is provided by Ad Standards (formerly Advertising Standards Canada), a nonprofit self-regulatory body committed to safeguarding the integrity and viability for advertising in Canada. Like the ASA, Ad Standards codified advertising standards under codes of conduct called the *Canadian Code of Advertising Standards* (*Code*). The *Code* provides guidelines for gender portrayals regarding the representation of women and men in ads.

The European Advertising Standards Alliance (EASA) is the organizing body for the advertising self-regulatory organizations across Europe. It strives to foster responsible advertising by providing guidance to its participating members on how best to implement advertising self-regulation to benefit consumers and businesses alike. This is done through advertising codes that follow a set of guidance principles to ensure that advertising is "legal, decent, honest and truthful,"[122] while taking into account cultural, business, legal, and economic contexts. Included in the guidance principles is a proviso regarding depictions of sex roles.

Some nations have instituted an all-out ban on nudity in advertising, as well as prohibited overt sexual references. For example, Israel bans billboard advertising that "depicts sexual humiliation or abasement, or presents a human being as an object available for sexual use," as stipulated by Israeli penal law governing obscene publication and display.[123]

The United States maintains a hands-off stance on sexism in advertising. Neither the FTC nor the FCC has established prohibitions against sexist ads.

THE HEAT IS ON: STAMPING OUT SEXUAL OBJECTIFICATION IN ADVERTISING

Sexualized ads may raise the temperature of regulators. Less overt forms of this type of advertising often slip under the radar—that is, unless complaints are lodged against the offending advertisement, and sometimes it only takes one. Take an ad for Rihanna's perfume Rogue. A 2014 *Guardian* article reported that a poster for Rihanna's perfume Rogue was given a placement restriction, with the goal of reducing the chances of children seeing it, because of the pop star's "sexually suggestive" image.[124]

"One person complained that the ad was offensive because it was overly sexual and demeaning to women and featured a 'sexualized and provocative' image which was inappropriate for children to see,"[125] the article said. The ASA looked into the complaint and didn't find the image to be "overtly sexual," but the regulator conceded that Rihanna's pose, with her legs thrust up in the air, was "provocative." As a result, the placement restriction wasn't lifted.

As public resistance grows against hypersexualized and objectified images of women to sell products, advertisers and their agencies will be forced to listen, respond, and change—and some are. Meet Madonna Badger, founder and chief creative officer of Badger & Winters, an ad agency that specializes in the creation of brand messages with a female perspective. Badger & Winters has pledged to never objectify women in their work. To raise awareness of the use of objectifying ads to sell everything from food to fashion to alcohol, in 2016, the agency made a two-minute video titled #WomenNotObjects.[126] The video affirms the agency's commitment to nonobjectifying creative work and urges other advertising agencies to do the same.

Badger asserts that the standard practice of "using 'shame and anxiety' to sell products is a 'dead paradigm.'"[127] In the 2016 *CNN* article "How to Create Ads That Don't Objectify Women," she is quoted as saying: "Agencies create advertising that promotes not only the product, but also the people who make it. Ads should never 'use people' or take advantage of women and men in any way, shape or form. It should never show people as objects that have NO power NO possibility and certainly are NOT equals."[128]

Spurred by efforts of the #WomenNotObjects initiative, the Cannes Lions International Festival of Creativity, the advertising and communication industry's equivalent of the Oscars, has taken a rare step by cautioning jurors not to recognize work that reflects gender bias and objectification, according to a 2017 *AdAge* article.[129] Philip Thomas, chairman of Cannes Lions and president of the marketing division at Ascential (which is the parent company of Cannes Lions Festival of Creativity), said that Badger worked with the organization to develop new judging criteria in jury briefings around gender bias and objectification, which would serve as more of a "guideline." Thomas noted that the move was part of an ongoing effort by Cannes Lions to address gender issues. He mentioned the addition of the Glass: The Lion for Change award, which acknowledges work that addresses gender inequality or prejudice, and See It Be It, a mentorship initiative for young women aimed at responding to the industry's gender imbalance problem.

In the next chapter, we'll find out why celebrity sells and discuss the use of celebrity endorsements to promote beauty products.

7

The Persuaders

Don't hate me because I'm beautiful.

—Advertising campaign and tagline for Pantene shampoo (1986)

Do you remember Kelly LeBrock and Iman in ads for Pantene shampoo from the 1980s? The fashion models attracted public notice as the first spokesmodels to deliver what has become one of the most famous and memorable taglines, "Don't hate me because I'm beautiful."

In 1985, Procter & Gamble (P&G) picked up the Pantene brand as part of the consumer-goods giant's acquisition of Richardson-Vicks, an over-the-counter drug company best known for its cold remedies. One year later, Pantene launched a campaign that would go down in advertising history as one of the most iconic campaigns of all time.

In the ads, the messaging emphasized the benefits of the product and its ability to transform the model's hair from limp and lifeless to healthy and shiny. In a 1986 TV spot, LeBrock tells a tale of troubled tresses until she discovers Pantene. She delivers the daring line "Don't hate me because I'm beautiful" at the start of the commercial and then backs into her hair-raising story. At the end of the commercial, she makes a promise: "No, it didn't happen overnight. But it did happen. You'll see." A male voice-over chimes in: "Pantene shampoos and conditioners. Serious care for beautiful hair." The same before-and-after approach was used in print ads featuring Iman and LeBrock.

Both LeBrock and Iman were recognizable faces at the time the ads broke. Le-Brock had had starring roles in *The Woman in Red* (1984) and *Weird Science* (1985), and Iman was a firmly established supermodel. As a result, they were believable and persuasive spokespersons to carry the aspirational message. Not everyone bought into it, however. Feminists criticized the message for its narcissistic undertones.

Pantene still uses diverse and recognizable spokesmodels in its ads. In 2016, Pantene launched a new campaign slogan, "Don't hate me because I'm strong," a play on the words used in the brand's 1980s campaign. Spokesmodels for the "Strong Is Beautiful" campaign included actor and women's bantamweight UFC champion Ronda Rousey and Indian actor and singer Priyanka Chopra.

The new campaign is part of a larger brand story for Pantene. In a 2016 *Los Angeles Times* article, Jodi Allen, former vice president and general manager for hair care for North America at Procter & Gamble, is quoted as saying, "'Strong Is Beautiful' is more than a campaign, it's the ethos and point of view of our brand, and all of our recent Ambassador choices are women who represent this idea."[1]

We begin the chapter by defining what *celebrity* is, and the reason why celebrity sells. Next, we'll describe how celebrities are used to promote products and influence consumer behavior, with special attention paid to celebrity beauty endorsements. Finally, we'll introduce the fresh faces of beauty endorsements.

WHAT IS CELEBRITY?

Scholars have variously defined celebrity as "a human pseudo-event, 'neither good nor bad, great nor pretty,' in lack of any human qualities"; "celetoid" to describe the fleeting and expendable nature of celebrity; and "status on speed."[2]

Because of the conceptual diversity of the term, a definitional consensus of celebrity is difficult to pin down. First, "celebrity" generally describes stars who are members of sports and show business (such as film stars and pop stars), or the wider cultural realm, where the person demonstrates a particular talent or attains something of note that attracts public attention, according to a 2013 article."[3]

Second, the late Daniel J. Boorstin, a prize-winning author and social historian, introduced one of the most widely cited definitions of celebrity in the following: "The celebrity is a person who is known for his well-knownness."[4] Therefore, celebrity can be ascribed through family ties, as with royals and blue bloods; gained through talent and achievements, as with actors, musicians, star athletes, or even notorious criminals; and primarily attributed by means of the media.[5]

Finally, in a contemporary context, a celebrity can be described as "a person who has a high public profile, usually promoted by appearances in the mass media and they are consequently readily recognized by others," according to *Celebrity Capital: Assessing the Value of Fame.*[6] Nowadays, a person can achieve celebrity by grabbing the media spotlight, regardless of whether she or he has cultivated a special skill or talent (see figure 7.1).[7]

Because of the proliferation of mass media and interactive media platforms, where an ordinary person can become famous by being seen on the right platform at the right time, celebrity may have lost some of its cachet, thus running the risk of being seen as a disposable commodity. In a 1995 *Psychology Today* article, Leo Braudy, university professor and the Leo S. Bing Chair in English and American Literature

Figure 7.1. The rise of celebrity culture has been fueled by the growth of new media, such as social media platforms, websites, blogs, live-streaming video, and online communities. © E+/StudioThreeDots

at the University of Southern California, is quoted as saying, "We're in the Kleenex phase of fame. We see so much of people, and in all branches of the media. We blow our nose on every new star that happens to come along and then dispose of them."[8]

Celebrity Power

If you see a makeup ad for Lancôme Paris featuring Spanish actor Penélope Cruz looking flawlessly beautiful, you may be persuaded by the message because of the believability of Cruz as the endorser. For a celebrity endorser to add value to a brand, he or she must be persuasive. An important aspect of persuasion is believability, which is attributed to the trustworthiness of the message sender or source.

Two important models of persuasion are *source credibility* and *source attractiveness*. A helpful explanation of these models is provided by anthropologist and author Grant McCracken.[9] First, under the source credibility model, message effectiveness depends on the communicator's "expertness" and "trustworthiness." Here, expertness is "the perceived *ability* of the source to make valid assertions," while trustworthiness is "the perceived *willingness* of the source to make valid assertions."[10] Consider Katy Perry and her collaboration with CoverGirl. In 2017, Perry announced her Katy Kat

Pearl Collection to her Twitter followers right before she walked the red carpet at the 2017 Grammy Awards.[11] Perry's fans and followers are most likely young females who will perceive Perry as a credible and trusted source. By extension, then, what she says about the CoverGirl brand, and more specifically the sub-brand inspired by her, will probably carry weight and be persuasive.

Second, under the source attractiveness model, message effectiveness principally hinges on the communicator's "familiarity," "likability," and/or "similarity."[12] According to McCracken, "Familiarity is defined as knowledge of the source through exposure, likability as affection for the source as a result of the source's physical appearance and behavior, and similarity as a supposed resemblance between the source and receiver of the message."[13] Katy Perry's breezy and frothy pop persona, superstar status, and physical attractiveness make her an effective endorser for CoverGirl, as the target audience will probably identify with her and view her as authentic.

Celebrity Influence

English actor Kate Winslet has been nominated for and won more prestigious awards than you can count on two hands, including six Academy Award nominations (with seven nominations in total) and an Oscar statuette in 2009 for Best Actress for *The Reader* (2008). One of the most lucrative roles that the actor has played is brand ambassador for Lancôme. Other global beauty brands have recruited Oscar nominees and winners to serve in the role of brand ambassador, such as Cate Blanchett for Giorgio Armani and Jennifer Lawrence for Dior.

Choosing the right celebrity to represent a corporate brand takes careful consideration. To take the guesswork out of determining a celebrity's effectiveness, advertisers usually rely on celebrity metrics, such as appeal, influence, familiarity, likability, and relevance. Like Nielsen's audience measurement system, celebrity indexes and scoring services furnish "a standard celebrity 'currency,'" according to *A Companion to Celebrity*.[14] These measurements help advertisers match the right celebrity to the right product. There are several ways to measure celebrity effectiveness. Here are the most common celebrity indexes.

- *Q Score*, or *Q-Rating*: A popular measurement that rates the familiarity and appeal of a celebrity, as well as a brand, a company, or an entertainment product, like a television show. Generally, the higher the Q-rating, the more likable the celebrity.
- *E-Score*: A consumer rating metric that assesses the appeal, equity, and endorsement potential of a celebrity, athlete, musician, brand, or television program, or even a character. E-Score publishes celebrity reports that aggregate data by categories or groupings, such as "celebrities with highest appeal by age group," "celebrities with biggest gains and declines in appeal," and "celebrity up & comers."
- *Davie-Brown Index* (*DBI*): This index quantifies the influence that a celebrity exerts on buying behavior. The DBI measures a celebrity's appeal, trust, awareness, and aspiration, as well as his or her relevance as a brand image.

Other measurements include *Variety* magazine's Vscore, a familiarity metric that tracks social listening, "the process of monitoring digital conversations to understand what customers are saying about a brand and industry online,"[15] and Nielsen's N-Score, a measure of the endorsement potential of actors, athletes, musicians, and well-known personalities.

Conventional celebrities aren't the only celebrity currency in town. Having achieved a sort of microcelebrity, several social media influencers (SMIs) have built up their following, gained visibility, and scored a certain level of influence and appeal, making them attractive endorsers. To measure an influencer's digital clout, social media analytics tools include Kred, PeerIndex, and Radian6.

CELEBRITY WORSHIP

We tend to like people who are like us, and in the case of celebrities, we tend to like those who personify characteristics that represent our ideal selves or self-concepts. If you see an ad featuring Brad Pitt for Chanel N°5, the first male ever to officially endorse the brand, you may be riveted by the ad because you like Pitt, and he may be someone you admire or who rocks your world. Whether it's Pitt for N°5, Kate Winslet for Lancôme, or Katy Perry for CoverGirl, one thing these celebrities all have in common is reference group appeal.

Let's learn about the marketing power of celebrities.

Celebrity Appeal

Do you belong to a group of people who have shared interests and aims, or just like to hang out together? If so, you belong to a *reference group*, "an actual or imaginary individual or group that significantly *influences* an individual's evaluations, aspirations, or behavior."[16] Reference groups appear in different forms. For our discussion on celebrity appeal, we're most interested in an *aspirational reference group*, people we don't know but admire and against whom we might compare ourselves.

Many people look up to celebrities and wish to emulate them. Celebrities exert this influence through their *referent power*, "the result of a person's perceived attractiveness, worthiness, and right to others' respect."[17] In effect, celebrities set the bar for those being influenced. So, if a person idolizes the qualities of a particular celebrity, he or she attempts to copy the celebrity's behavior to be more like, or appear like, him or her.

Marketers align a celebrity with their brand in such a way that the endorsed brand adopts an aspirational quality. Consider Burberry, an aspirational brand. You may have seen an ad for My Burberry Black fragrance featuring English actor Lily James of *Downton Abbey* fame. If you like James and relate to her, you may try the scent, like it, and buy it. The scent costs around $125. If the purchase isn't in this month's budget, it may be in next month's, which is an important characteristic of an aspirational brand.

Sprinkling Celebrity Stardust

Emma Watson for Lancôme. Jennifer Lopez for Gillette Venus razors. Natalie Portman for Miss Dior Chérie. Zoe Saldana for L'Oréal Paris. Clive Owen for Bulgari Man fragrance. These celebrity–product pairings work because of star power. Star power depends on the symbolic properties embodied in the celebrity and the transference of those properties to the brand, thus matching the celebrity image with the brand image.

Celebrities carry symbolic meaning based on identifiable traits, such as demographic and psychographic characteristics like age (offbeat millennial Jess in Fox's *New Girl*, played by Zooey Deschanel); gender (transgender hairstylist Sophia Burset in Netflix's *Orange Is the New Black*, played by Laverne Cox); social class, such as wealth (billionaire corporate raider Gordon Gekko of *Wall Street*, played by Michael Douglas); and personality types (the willing hero, such as secret agent 007 in the *James Bond* film franchise, played lately by Daniel Craig). Ideally, the marketer decides what meanings the product should convey (that is, how it should position the item in the marketplace) and then chooses a celebrity who embodies a similar meaning. Grant McCracken said, "Using a 'meaning transfer' perspective, these properties are shown to reside in the celebrity and to move from celebrity to consumer good and from good to consumer."[18]

Starstruck by Celebrity Endorsers

A 2014 *Daily Mail* article reported that women are more likely than men to be swayed by celebrity product endorsements, according to a 2014 British study.[19] Women were twice as likely to be starstruck than men. "Scientists discovered that women's brains respond differently to images of unknown people versus images of celebrities wearing the same pair of shoes. Females felt actual affection for the footwear when a celebrity was shown wearing it, report brain scanners, and create a memorable link which could more easily be recalled at a later date,"[20] the article said.

Using a sample of 854 Britons, researchers asked them if they ever purchased a product because it was endorsed by a celebrity. The data showed that more than twice as many women answered "yes" as men. In addition to gender, age was a factor in the results. Younger people were more likely to be wowed by celebrity association with a product or brand. "More than two fifths (41.2 per cent) of those who answered 'Yes' were in the youngest age bracket of 18–24."[21]

The study findings didn't come as a surprise to marketing experts such as Joanna Davies. She explained that women's celebrity fascination is an extension of the "Princess Phenomenon." Davies was quoted as saying, "Since Snow White with her porcelain complexion, itsy waist and perfectly pinned hair, women have been looking for guidance on how to look and chasing impossible perfection. Celebrity endorsement is just that Princess Phenomenon evolving."[22]

The popularity of celebrity endorsement is spreading across several global markets. A 2015 study found that consumers have an ardent desire to connect with celebrities and do this by buying personal care products endorsed by them, especially in Asian and Middle Eastern markets, as reported in a 2015 *Beauty Packaging* magazine article.[23] "According to a global survey conducted by Canadean, three out of 10 consumers in Asia-Pacific (27%) and the Middle East and Africa (30%) find it either important or very important that a personal care product is endorsed by a celebrity. This comes from a strong interest in celebrity culture and the latest fashions and styles in these two regions," the article cited. For example, Olay signed popular Indian actor Kajol to be its brand ambassador for its Olay Total Effects anti-aging skin care collection. Safwan Kotwal, an analyst at Canadean, is quoted as saying, "This was a shrewd move by Olay, choosing a household name to promote the product to middle-aged women. The slogan 'Join me in the battle against ageing' gives consumers the connection and makes Kajol someone they can relate to."[24]

"CELEBRITY SELLS"—MOSTLY

You may be familiar with Wedgwood luxury fine bone china. What you might not know is that eighteenth-century potter and entrepreneur Josiah Wedgwood, founder of the Wedgwood company and considered the "Father of English Potters," was responsible for one of the earliest uses of celebrity endorsements. In 1765, Wedgwood created a cream-colored tea set for Queen Charlotte, the wife of King George III. She permitted Wedgwood to fashion himself as "Potter to her Majesty" and to name the new set of vessels Queensware, "signaling its elegance and aspirational qualities."[25]

Celebrity endorsement has a long history in the United States. In the early 1900s, the cigarette industry recruited entertainment and sports personalities to become celebrity endorsers.[26] In 1905, Murad cigarettes used comedians Fatty Arbuckle and Harry Bulger in ads. From the 1930s on, many celebrities lined up to appear in cigarette ads, including Fred Astaire and Rita Hayworth (Chesterfield cigarettes), Henry Fonda (Camel cigarettes), Lucille Ball and Desi Arnaz (Philip Morris cigarettes), and John Wayne (Camel cigarettes).

In 1934, New York Yankees first baseman Lou Gehrig was the first athlete to appear on a box of Wheaties.[27] Over the years, scores of other star athletes have lent their images to "The Breakfast of Champions," including Babe Ruth, Michael Jordan, Lindsey Vonn, and Stephen Curry.

Today, celebrities pitch products for everything from bottled water (Jennifer Aniston for Smartwater) to cars (Matthew McConaughey for Lincoln Motors) and cosmetics (Taylor Swift for CoverGirl). In 2004, celebrities appeared in about 20 percent of all American ads, although that figure is believed to have dropped to 9 percent by 2012, according to a 2016 *Adweek* article.[28]

Let's find out how much celebrity endorsements are worth to companies and their brands.

Monetizing Celebrity

In *Celebrity Sells*, Hamish Pringle described celebrity as "anyone who is familiar enough to the people a brand wishes to communicate with to add values to that communication by association with their image and reputation."[29] As a powerful form of advertising, celebrity endorsement can enhance message recall; build believability; create brand liking and trust; increase name awareness and recognition; influence consumers' attitude toward the brand; and create a distinct personality for the endorsed brand. Celebrity endorsement can also intensify conviction for the brand and give the consumer a compelling reason to believe a product claim or selling premise.

The halo effect of celebrity endorsement can rub off on the company and its brand before the ink is even dry on an endorsement deal. From a 2016 *Forbes* article titled "How Brands Should Use Celebrities for Endorsements": "The brand value added by celebrities is immediate and palpable. When a celebrity signs an endorsement deal with a product, an element of legitimacy is suddenly present in the company, simply because of the power of the name backing it up."[30]

The million-dollar question is, do celebrity endorsements work? Yes, according to a 2012 article titled "The Economic Value of Celebrity Endorsements" in *Journal of Advertising Research*.[31] The study examined the impact of celebrity endorsements on sales and stock returns, with a focus on athlete endorsements. The findings proved that celebrity endorsements can have a positive impact on brand-level sales and the firm's stock returns. "Signing the kinds of endorsers that featured in this study on average generates a 4% increase in sales—which corresponds with around $10 million in additional sales annually—and nearly a 0.25% increase in stock returns."[32] Moreover, if the athlete enjoys a winning streak or earns a prestigious award, like an Olympic Gold medal, sales can edge up further.

Using celebrity endorsements can also affect how much firms can charge for their products, as well as consumers' purchase intention and brand consideration. A 2009 Knowledge@Wharton article cited the findings from a study showing that consumers were willing to pay up to 20 percent more for the same product, depending on who was representing it.[33] In addition, ads using celebrity endorsers can lead to greater purchase intent and brand evaluation, as compared with ads that don't have them, according to a 2013 article titled "The Role of Culture in Creative Execution in Celebrity Endorsement: The Cross-Cultural Study" in the *Journal of Global Marketing*.[34]

But not everyone is starry-eyed over celebrity endorsement, because the strategy doesn't always produce the results that marketers hoped for, according to a University of Colorado Boulder study cited in a 2014 *Forbes* article.[35] Research leader Margaret C. Campbell, provost professor of marketing at the University of Colorado Boulder's Leeds School of Business, is quoted as saying, "The overall message to marketers is be careful, because all of us, celebrities or not, have positives and negatives to our personalities, and those negatives can easily transfer to a brand."[36] Additionally, the tactic may be no more effective than noncelebrity ads, according to a 2011 *AdAge* article.[37] The article cited an *AdAge* study, titled "2010 Celebrity Advertisements:

Exposing a Myth of Advertising Effectiveness, 2010," that found "fewer than 12% of ads using celebrities exceeded a 10% lift, and one-fifth of celebrity ads had a negative impact on advertising effectiveness."[38]

THE TROUBLE WITH CELEBRITY ENDORSEMENTS

Using a high-flying celebrity spokesperson can be either a bang or a bust, according to the 2013 *Fast Company* article "Is Celebrity Branding Worth the Price Tag?"[39] For instance, celebrities have been known to go off the rails, such as golf great Tiger Woods (infidelity scandal), legendary Tour de France cyclist Lance Armstrong (doping allegations), and tennis megastar Maria Sharapova (testing positive for a banned performance-enhancing drug). "Celebrities can go terribly off script and take the brand with them. Plus there are other potential downsides, such as the additional cost of hiring a celebrity, which will impact your budget. And when watching ads, consumers may focus more on the celebrity and less on your brand,"[40] the article said.

Let's consider the potential pitfalls of celebrity endorsements.

Risky Business of Celebrity Endorsement

Celebrity endorsement is a powerful testimonial technique, but it can be risky. When not wearing their stage persona, celebrities are ordinary people, and people make mistakes. Advertisers may be able to control the message, but they can't always control the messenger. A damaging crisis in a celebrity's personal life can collide with his or her stage or public persona and deal a death blow to an endorsement.

There are potential drawbacks to celebrity endorsement. First, the "vampire effect," also known as the "overshadowing effect" in marketing circles, can suck the life out of a celebrity endorsement. From a 2015 *Psychology Today* article: "Rather than helping to sell the brand and enhancing its stature, the celebrity's presence reduces the ad's effectiveness and hurts the brand."[41] Second, celebrity fatigue can be a problem. When celebrities appear in too many brand endorsements, they can lose credibility. Third, overexposure can occur. When a celebrity takes on too many brand endorsements at any one time, the brand-boosting power of any one endorsement can be reduced.

Corporate brands aren't the only parties shouldering the risks. Issues like image control and power are concerning to many stars. Collaborations and co-branded celebrity products, a strategic alliance between the star and the brand, are ways for stars to protect their image and retain power. These arrangements are common in licensed fragrances. For example, in 2002, Jennifer Lopez first entered into a partnership with Coty Inc. to launch her debut fragrance, Glow by JLo. With one of the most successful fragrance launches in history, the brand alliance was beneficial to both parties. Glow brings in more than $100 million a year for Coty. Although details of Lopez's license agreement aren't publicly available, on average, most celebrities get between 5 percent and 10 percent of sales for lending their name to perfume marketers, as noted in a 2005 *Fortune* article.[42]

CELEBRITY BEAUTY ENDORSEMENTS: "MAGICAL CONTAGION"

The beauty industry has a long and storied history of using celebrities and star models as product endorsers in beauty ads, such as Max Factor's early use of top actors like Rosalind Russell, Lana Turner, and Judy Garland. As cultural symbols of beauty and glamour, Hollywood celebrities have stayed at the top of the endorsement heap, although a blip occurred during the late 1980s and 1990s, when advertisers traded in superstars for supermodels. Celebrities in beauty endorsements didn't entirely disappear; they sped off to foreign markets to chase handsome endorsement deals under the radar.[43] By 2006, celebrity endorsement made a comeback, and there was "no more shame in the celebrity-endorsement game,"[44] according to a 2006 *Time* article.

Let's delve further into celebrity endorsement used to promote beauty brands.

The Evolving World of Celebrity Endorsement in Beauty

Global market research firm Mintel charted the well-traveled road that celebrity endorsement has taken from traditional advertising to digital advertising in a 2017 article titled "The Evolution of Celebrity Endorsement in Beauty."[45] By the 1980s, as celebrity power rose, companies recognized the potential of riding the coattails of celebrity influence and creating brand/celebrity partnerships to not only build brand equity but also forge a believable link between the brand and the celebrity.

Following the Great Recession of 2008–2009, many consumers found themselves in a financial straitjacket and began to look for cheaper substitutes for their favorite brands. At the same time, social media and other digital media changed the way that people interfaced with celebrities, which increased organic brand engagement with celebrities the likes of which we've never seen before.

In 2016, the proportion of people who said that they were influenced by celebrity beauty endorsements slipped, even for celebrity-branded fragrances, which had ordinarily posted robust sales prior to hitting this dry spell. According to Mintel data, "Only 6% of fragrance buyers were influenced by celebrity endorsements in the 12 months to June 2016, with British men in particular less influenced by celebrity endorsements in the BPC [beauty and personal care] sector."[46]

Tepid news for celebrity beauty endorsements but not the nail in the coffin, by any means. In recent years, many celebrities have gone from merely being the face of or name on the brand to having a hand in designing new products through cocreation arrangements. For example, in 2011, actor Salma Hayek entered into a

Figure 7.2. Many beauty brands are teaming up with beauty bloggers and vloggers to boost their sales and increase brand exposure. © iStock/Getty Images Plus/Weedezign

partnership with CVS Pharmacy to launch its beauty brand Nuance Salma Hayek, which is exclusively sold at CVS stores and on the company's website.

Beauty endorsements aren't the sole dominion of mainstream celebrities. Popular influencers, such as beauty bloggers, are snatching up beauty endorsement deals (see figure 7.2). This trend is fueled by more women wanting to see recognizable role models as beauty brand endorsers. "Only 7% of women are interested in seeing a celebrity as a make-up brand ambassador, with 28% wanting to see someone who is known for being a strong female role model and 19% wanting to see someone who is popular/relevant in today's culture," according to Mintel's "Face Colour Cosmetics—UK—2015" report.[47]

The New Faces of Celebrity Beauty Endorsements

Thumb through any glossy magazine and you'll see beauty in all its diversity: Halle Berry for Revlon; Penélope Cruz and Lupita Nyong'o for Lancôme; Kerry Washington for L'Oréal Paris; Queen Latifah for CoverGirl; Ellen DeGeneres for CoverGirl and Olay; Eva Longoria for L'Oréal Paris; and Sui He for Shiseido.

Many beauty brands recognize that different celebrities appeal to different consumer segments. Consider the mature market. According to a 2015 *Telegraph* article, some beauty brands are tapping an older generation of ambassadors to appeal to this market, such as Charlotte Rampling for NARS, Helen Mirren for L'Oréal, and Jessica Lange for Marc Jacobs, all of whom are pleasantly over 50.[48]

Several beauty brands are using endorsers who are more closely associated with professional sports. For example, in 2015, Bobbi Brown Cosmetics partnered with GoPro-sponsored athletes as brand ambassadors—American World Cup alpine ski racer and Olympic Gold Medalist Julia Mancuso, X Games Medalist and Olympian snowboarder Hannah Teter, professional surfer Kelia Moniz, and world record base jumper Roberta Mancino—to launch its Long-Wear Life-Proof campaign.[49]

Popular male celebrities are also picking up beauty endorsement deals. Consider British actor Clive Owen. Lancôme selected Owen to be the brand's male spokesperson for Lancôme's men's skin care range and its fragrance Hypnôse Homme. Because men in the 35-plus age group are taking better care of their skin and waging their own battle against aging, the men's grooming market is rapidly picking up steam. As a result, global beauty brands have enlisted some of Hollywood's most popular leading men as endorsers, especially those with global appeal.[50]

In the next chapter, we'll examine the connection between body image and thin-ideal media images. We'll also consider the controversial use of digital photo manipulation in beauty and fashion advertising.

IV

THE CHANGELINGS

8

The Shapeshifters

Andy Sachs: So none of the girls here eat anything?
Nigel: Not since two became the new four and zero became the new two.
Andy Sachs: Well, I'm a six . . .
Nigel: Which is the new fourteen.

—From *The Devil Wears Prada* (2006)

Have you seen the film *The Devil Wears Prada*, or read the 2003 novel by Lauren Weisberger that the film is based on? If so, you probably remember that the story is about Andrea "Andy" Sachs (played by Anne Hathaway), a freshly minted college graduate and an aspiring journalist who lands a dream job as a junior personal assistant to the imperious editor in chief, Miranda Priestly (Meryl Streep), of the prestigious *Runway* magazine. Between Andy's toxic boss and her backstabbing coworkers, she struggles to find her sea legs. Her underdeveloped sense of style and lack of interest in and knowledge of the fashion industry make her feel like a fish out of water.

Andy is told that "a million girls would kill for" her job, and that if she survives a year in her current position, she can get a job at any magazine that she wants. Andy decides to soldier on.

The magazine's art director, Nigel (Stanley Tucci), takes Andy under his wing and gives her a head-to-toe makeover. She starts to dress more fashionably and perform her job more capably.

After a series of fast-moving events, the final straw comes when Miranda throws Nigel under the bus by tossing him out on his couture to save her own skin.

Miranda tells Andy that if she wants to get anywhere in her career, she must be willing to make the hard choices. Andy is repelled. She realizes that she has lost what really matters to her: her sense of self.

Andy liberates herself from *Runway* and the world of fashion, where a woman's worth is measured by her dress size and how many pairs of Jimmy Choo shoes she has in her closet.

Restored to her former self with a dash more style, Andy lands on her feet. She gets offered a job as a newspaper reporter, largely helped by a glowing recommendation from Miranda to Andy's prospective employer.

The *New York Times*' review of the movie describes how it illustrated the concept of conspicuous consumption—where consumers are driven by the urge to buy gratuitously expensive items to display their wealth and social status.

> In this version the vicarious thrill is not payback but rather conspicuous consumption: all those lovingly photographed outfits and accessories, those warehouses' worth of Chanel and Jimmy Choo, those skinny women decked out (by the tirelessly inventive Patricia Field) in expensive finery. "The Devil Wears Prada" does exactly what the real-life counterparts of Runway magazine do every month, which is to deliver the most sumptuous goods imaginable—or fantasy images of them, in any case—to the eager eyes of the masses.[1]

In this chapter, we'll define what body image is. Next, we'll explore the thin ideal and the impact of exposure to thin-ideal media images on women and girls. We'll also consider how the use of digital image manipulation in fashion magazines has bent our perception of beauty. Finally, we'll look at the relatively new trend of presenting more realistic body images in beauty and fashion advertising.

WHAT IS BODY IMAGE?

Do you ever have a negative or punishing thought about your body? If so, you're not alone. A 2011 survey by *Glamour* asked more than 300 women of all shapes to count the number of negative thoughts that they had about their bodies in a typical day. The results were startling: On average, women have thirteen negative thoughts about their bodies each day, as cited in the 2011 *Glamour* article about the survey, "Shocking Body-Image News: 97% of Women Will Be Cruel to Their Bodies Today."[2] This figure is even higher for many women who admit to having as many as thirty-five, fifty, or even one hundred punishing thoughts daily. Some women say that this inner speech is fleeting, while others say it's more like a running conversation (see figure 8.1).

Let's describe what body image is and how it affects our lives.

Our Bodies, Our Selves

How we think about, evaluate, and perceive ourselves is an important part of our overall self-concept. The internal representation of our outer appearance, which reflects physical and perceptual dimensions, is known as *body image*.[3] Body image influences not only how we feel about ourselves but also what we do with our lives, whom we meet and marry, and what purchases we make.

Figure 8.1. **Most women harbor negative feelings and thoughts about their bodies.** ©
iStock/Getty Images Plus/KatarzynaBialasiewicz

Body image is closely tied to self-esteem. Marketers use marketing communications, especially advertising, to impact our self-esteem. For example, beauty ads that
use thin-ideal media images serve as a constant reminder that beauty equates to thinness. These images can activate a process of advertising-induced social comparison
in which viewers are driven to evaluate themselves in comparison with the people
depicted in the images, which could have a negative effect on self-esteem.[4]

Finally, body image can fluctuate widely and be subject to perceptual distortions.
For example, a study found that brief exposures to thin-ideal images and programming led young females to overstate their body size after watching just thirty min-
utes' worth of television.[5] From a 1992 article titled "The Elastic Body Image: The
Effect of Television Advertising and Programming on Body Image Distortions in
Young Women," published in *Journal of Communication*: "This suggests that television messages that are fixated on the representation of the ideal female body imme-
diately led female subjects to thoughts about their own bodies. This in turn led to
the measurable fluctuations and disturbances in their body image. In their mind's
eye, their body shape had changed."[6]

Measuring Up: Social Comparison Theory

The drive to assess and compare our opinions and abilities with those of others,
particularly if we don't have objective criteria to go by, is a natural human tendency,
according to social psychologist Leon Festinger in his 1954 paper "A Theory of

Social Comparison Processes" in the journal *Human Relations*.[7] This theory can be applied to physical attractiveness, whereby we may appraise our own appearance in relation to someone else's and then draw a comparison. Two comparison outcomes can occur in this situation: We can find the other person not up to par (downward comparison), or we can come up short (upward comparison).[8] If the comparison is being made against someone whom we perceive to be quite different from ourselves, like an ultrathin fashion model in a magazine ad, we may experience body dissatisfaction and do something about it, such as get on a weight-loss program or seek cosmetic surgery, to measure up to the standard.

Studies have explored the effect of exposure to idealized images in advertising with respect to comparison standards and/or lowering self-perceptions of attractiveness. One study found that exposure to idealized images in advertising can reduce body satisfaction among young female adults.[9] Another study revealed that exposure to images of good-looking people raised standards of comparison among preadolescent and adolescent females; however, these images didn't lower their self-perception of physical attractiveness.[10] "These two studies, taken together, suggest that perhaps the negative impact of advertising (in terms of lowering body-image satisfaction) occurs in later teen years and early adulthood,"[11] the article said.

Finally, a 2006 article suggested that viewing advertisements containing thin female models can make young women feel poorly about themselves, particularly if they have body-image concerns.[12] Generally, women almost automatically evaluate themselves in part by contrasting their physical attractiveness to idealized images in fashion ads.

MIRROR, MIRROR: THE THIN IDEAL

One of the most widely cited country-specific studies on the relationship between media and body image involved Fiji, an island nation that has traditionally held a full-figured beauty ideal for women. Since the arrival of television in 1995, Harvard researchers said, an increase in eating disorders followed Fijians' exposure to Western-based values and media images communicated via the medium.[13]

At the time when the study began, Fiji had just one television station that aired television series from the United Kingdom, the United States, and New Zealand, such as *Melrose Place* and *Xena: Warrior Princess*. A survey of teenage girls was conducted in 1998, thirty-eight months after the television station went live. The results were astonishing: 74 percent of the teen girls felt that they were "too big or fat."[14]

For a Pacific island that didn't even have electricity until 1985, the impact of television was profound, as adolescent girls became more aware of Western standards of beauty, according to anthropologist and psychiatrist, and the Maude and Lillian Presley Professor of Global Health and Social Medicine at Harvard Medical School, Anne Becker, MD, who carried out the survey. Becker is quoted as saying, "Nobody was dieting in Fiji 10 years ago. . . . An alarmingly high percentage of adolescents are dieting now." She added, "The teenagers see TV as a model for how one gets by in the modern world. They believe the shows depict reality."[15]

Let's first define the thin ideal, and then examine the impact of thin-ideal media images on women's health and well-being.

What Is the Thin Ideal?

Ana Carolina Reston was a fashion model from Brazil. At the time of her death at age twenty-one from complications resulting from anorexia, she weighed just 40 kilograms, or 88 pounds, as reported in the *New York Times*."[16]

Official studies that irrefutably prove the link between the fashion industry and eating disorders aren't available, although many experts assert that the two are connected. In a letter to the British Fashion Council from forty doctors and health professionals at the Eating Disorders Service and Research Unit at King's College London, Professor Janet Treasure wrote, "There is no doubt there is cause and effect here. The fashion industry showcases models with extreme body shapes, and this is undoubtedly one of the factors leading to young girls developing disorders," as reported in the *Guardian*."[17]

Generally, *the thin ideal*, the ultraslender ideal-body image, refers to a feminine physique with a small waist and low body fat.[18] In its extreme form, the thin ideal is believed to be an unhealthy aspiration. For example, a *Daily Mail* investigative report ran a probe into fashion models used by eleven British High Street fashion chains. The 2015 *Daily Mail* article said, "At least six High Street models have a body mass index (BMI, worked out by dividing a person's weight by their height squared) of between 16 and 18.4—indicating malnutrition. A healthy BMI lies between 18.5 and 24.9."[19]

For most adult women, the thin ideal is an impossible ideal. Most fashion models are leaner than 98 percent of American women (see figure 8.2).[20] The average American woman is 5-foot-4 and weighs 140 pounds, as compared with the average American model, standing at 5-foot-11 and tipping the scales at just 117 pounds. These feather-weighted models meet the body mass index for anorexia, as noted in the 2012 *ABC News* article "Most Models Meet Criteria for Anorexia, Size 6 Is Plus Size: Magazine."[21]

The Thin-Ideal Media

On the face of it, the impact of exposure to thin-ideal media images may seem relatively benign. They are, after all, nothing more than pictures, which we may barely glance at as we're thumbing through magazine pages or scrolling through web pages. The harm may be inflicted when women and girls start to assiduously compare their actual appearance against an unrealistic or manipulated ideal, and the gap

Figure 8.2. Most runway models are significantly thinner than the average woman. ©
iStock/Getty Images Plus/1001nights

between the real and ideal becomes large enough to cause body-image disturbance or an increased risk of eating pathology. According to Michael R. Solomon, professor of marketing in the Haub School of Business at Saint Joseph's University, "Some marketers exploit consumers' tendencies to distort their body images when they prey on our insecurities about appearance. They try to create a gap between the real and the ideal physical selves and consequently motivate a person to purchase products and services he or she thinks will narrow that gap."[22]

Thin-ideal media, media that incorporate extremely thin female images or characters in their messaging or programming, promote the notion that thinness is an advantageous physical trait and equate that trait to the most "beautiful, desirable, successful protagonists,'" as cited in a 2012 article.[23] Researchers found that women who are heavy viewers of thin-ideal media tend to accept thinness as a norm. One researcher explained that dissatisfaction occurs when these heavy viewers start to view "this thin-ideal not only as realistic, but also physically attainable." Therefore, if a woman acknowledges these ideal body shapes as the norm and evaluates herself against them, body dissatisfaction can occur.[24]

The negative impact of thin-ideal media images on women can vary according to levels of internalization. One study showed that high internalizers who viewed thin female models in ads reported greater body-focused anxiety than when they saw ads featuring average-size models or ads without models.[25] Therefore, exposure to thin-ideal media may activate a salient gap between a woman's actual and ideal body, which can lead to increased body-focused anxiety.

From the Inside Out

Internal influences, such as a person's baseline self-esteem, combined with external influences, such as social influences (like peers and parents), can determine whether thin-ideal media images may magnify body dissatisfaction. For example, one study involving predominately white female college students explored the effect of exposure to ads of ultrathin models and body satisfaction. Using ads from *Glamour* and *Vogue*, half of the students viewed apparel ads showing thin female models, while the rest of them saw ads for products without apparel and without models. After viewing the ads, the students completed a set of surveys to rate items like depression, self-esteem, and urge to lose weight. According to the 2006 *CBS News* article "Thin Ads + Low Body Image = Stress," the students who viewed the ads with ultrathin female models rated worse on all the surveys, especially if they had preexisting body image concerns.[26] Researcher Gayle Bessenoff, an associate professor of psychology at Southern Connecticut State University, is quoted as saying, "Women who already have low opinions of their physical appearance are at an even greater risk for negative effects from media images."[27] The findings appear in a 2006 paper titled "Can the Media Affect Us? Social Comparison, Self-Discrepancy, and the Thin Ideal," published in *Psychology of Women Quarterly*.[28]

Figure 8.3.   Research shows that spending a lot of time on social media can exacerbate body-image concerns. © iStock /KatarzynaBialasiewicz

Social media has increasingly added to the problem of cultural expectations of thinness as an unnatural extreme. The 2016 *Time* article "How Social Media Is a Toxic Mirror" noted that social media platforms, such as Facebook, Instagram, and Snapchat, provide users with online photo editors and enhancement tools that can be used to doctor their own photos to elicit positive reactions on their appearance.[29] Studies have shown that the users who are most susceptible to this kind of behavior are those who spend an inordinate amount of time posting, commenting on, and comparing themselves with photos (see figure 8.3). One study revealed that female college students who engaged in this kind of online behavior on Facebook were more apt to associate their self-worth with their looks. Although girls have reported more body dissatisfaction and eating disturbances than boys, studies have shown that both could be similarly harmed by social media.

Finally, studies have shown that young women whose peers view thinness as an important physical trait are inclined to also value thinness while also experiencing negative body image. For example, a study done by Texas A&M University showed that peer competition, rather than social media habits or television viewing preferences, was associated with poor body image and eating disorders, as reported in a 2013 *Huffington Post* article.[30] The study's authors asserted, "Our results suggest that only peer competition, not television or social media use, predicts negative outcomes for body image. This suggests that peer competition is more salient to body and eating issues in teenage girls."[31]

What You View Can Hurt You

If the beauty and fashion industry were to make a concerted—and sustained—effort to show more images of models with more meat on their bones, do you think people would be less concerned with being thin? Probably. A study conducted by a team of psychologists from Durham University in the United Kingdom discovered that the size of models shown in images exerts a profound influence on body image attitudes, as reported in the 2012 *BBC News* article "Thinness in Media Feeds Body Size Obsession, Researchers Say."[32] A preference for thinness diminished significantly after the female participants in the study were shown pictures of larger models, whereas the opposite occurred after viewing similar pictures containing slender models. Lynda Boothroyd, a professor of psychology at Durham University, explained, "Although we don't yet know whether brief exposure to pictures of larger women will change women's attitudes in the long term, our findings certainly indicate that showing more 'normal' models could potentially reduce women's obsession for thinness."[33]

The decision to use fuller-figured models hasn't been an unequivocal success for brands. One study found that featuring plus-size models in ads and catalogs may fall flat on the intended customers, according to a 2010 *ASU Now* article titled "Study: Ads with Plus-Size Models Unlikely to Work."[34] Naomi Mandel, marketing professor in the W. P. Carey School of Business at Arizona State University, who conducted the study with colleagues at the University of Cologne in Germany and Erasmus University in the Netherlands, noted, "We found that overweight consumers demonstrated lower self-esteem—and therefore probably less enthusiasm about buying products—after exposure to any size models in ads (versus ads with no models). Also, normal-weight consumers experienced lower self-esteem after exposure to moderately heavy models . . . than after exposure to moderately thin models."[35]

THE TOXIC MIRROR:
TECHNOLOGIES OF ENHANCEMENT

Gawker's Jezebel, a popular blog that outs digitally doctored photos of the faces and bodies of celebrities and models, runs a column called "Photoshop of Horrors." In one example, country-western sensation Faith Hill appeared on a 2007 cover of *Redbook*. According to Jezebel, not only did Hill's photo undergo "the *standard* amount of digital altering that goes into a cover," but it involved "11 different kinds of alterations" before it made the cover of the magazine.[36]

Let's examine how digital technologies have altered our perceptions of beauty.

Photoshopping May Be Bad for Your Health

The relentless pressure to measure up to beauty standards has never been worse, often driving people to spend thousands of dollars for temporary or permanent solutions to their body concerns. But the easiest—and cheapest—procedure of them all is right at their fingertips: photo editing apps. In a matter of clicks, people can erase years off their age and achieve the body they have always dreamed of. It's a seemingly harmless practice on the surface, but possibly damaging to a person's health, says the American Medical Association (AMA).

The AMA has come out against photo retouching of images, claiming that such alterations can fuel unrealistic expectations of people's body images and beauty aspirations, especially among children and young adolescents, as noted in a 2011 *New York Daily News* article.[37] The AMA's policy goal is to discourage the manipulation of photographs to "promote impossible-to-achieve expectations of body image and proportions."[38] Barbara McAneny, MD, is quoted as saying, "We must stop exposing impressionable children and teenagers to advertisements portraying models with body types only attainable with the help of photo editing software."[39]

Heavy-handed uses of photo manipulation have occurred in fashion ads. Consider Ralph Lauren's poster ad for its Blue Label jeans. In 2009, Ralph Lauren was pilloried for radically distorting the image of an otherwise healthy model, as reported in the 2009 *Daily Mail* article "Ralph Lauren Apologizes for Digitally Retouching Slender Model to Make Her Head Look Bigger Than Her Waist."[40] Filippa Hamilton, the model used in the ad, was chiseled to such a degree that her head appears wider than her waist. "Size zero models have been accused of contributing to the development of eating disorders. Magazines have also been condemned for doctoring cover photos of celebrities to make them look skinnier,"[41] the article noted. Ralph Lauren swiftly issued an apology for the strangely doctored image. Yet critics seized the moment to raise the alarm over the dangerous impact that such images can have on young girls.

Hany Farid, a professor at the University of California, Berkeley, with a joint appointment in electrical engineering and computer sciences and the School of Information, warned that photo editing has taken idealized images to a whole new level. In a 2008 *ABC News* article titled "Real? Or Photoshopped? 'Airbrushing' Run Amok," he is quoted as saying, "The more and more we use this editing, the higher and higher the bar goes. They're creating things that are physically impossible. We're seeing really radical digital plastic surgery. It's moving towards the Barbie doll model of what a woman should look like—big breasts, tiny waist, ridiculously long legs, elongated neck."[42]

Marketers should probably rethink the use of doctored images in their brand advertising. The Advertising Association and its research unit Credos, a United Kingdom–based advertising think tank, said that a majority of women (76 percent) preferred more natural images in ads, while 84 percent objected to altering the way women appear in advertising images, as cited in a 2011 *Marketing Week* article.[43] Their findings are published in a report titled "Pretty as a Picture." Nearly half (48 percent) of the young women were "less trusting of brands that use airbrushing to change the way women look in ads,"[44] the article mentioned.

"DEADLY PERSUASIONS": REGULATORS FORCE
THE BEAUTY AND FASHION INDUSTRY'S HAND

Model Kate Moss famously said, "Nothing tastes as good as skinny feels."[45] In many instances, skinny has left a bad taste in the mouths of consumers and regulators. The 2016 *New York Times* article reported that the ASA, Britain's advertising watchdog, barred the Italian fashion brand Gucci from using the image of a young, rail-thin model in a geometric print dress that hung off her frail body in ads in Britain.[46] "The ruling comes amid a longstanding debate on both sides of the Atlantic about the perils of overly thin models projecting an unhealthy body image for women," the article said. In a similar move, in 2015, the ASA ruled against an Yves Saint Laurent ad featuring a model with a visible ribcage and reed-thin legs as she lay on the floor, because the authority said the model looked "unhealthily underweight."[47]

A 2016 survey of 3,000 models working at every major modeling agency in the world found that 94 percent of them "are woefully underweight," as cited in a 2016 *New York Post* article.[48] The ever-shrinking model is a social phenomenon that had been observed and documented nearly two decades ago. The 2000 *Guardian* article mentioned a report by the British Medical Association that found the media continue to use rail-thin female models, which can contribute to distorted body image among young women and trigger or perpetuate eating disorders.[49] According to the report, "Female models are becoming thinner at a time when women are becoming heavier, and the gap between the ideal body shape and reality is wider than ever. . . . There is a need for a more realistic body shape to be shown on television and in fashion magazines."[50]

As public outrage grows over the use of abnormally thin models, the fashion industry has found itself occasionally backed into a corner. For example, after getting blasted on social media for using an underweight model in a 2015 issue, via the hashtag "#covergate" (which ignited the Reddit thread titled "Corpse or model?"), the publisher of Danish fashion magazine *Cover* was compelled to make a public apology after using the severely thin model, as reported in a 2015 *New York Post* article.[51] Then–minister for taxation in Denmark, Benny Engelbrecht, added to the din of disapproval by taking to Twitter: "I seriously thought that the fashion industry had understood that anorexia is a problem that should be taken seriously."[52]

Let's see what governments and regulators are doing to restrict the increasing glamorization of thinness.

Governments Unleashing an Anorexia Crackdown

In 2006, Spain instituted the world's first ban preventing excessively thin models from strutting Madrid's fashion week catwalks, to the chagrin of modeling agencies and to the applause of eating-disorder activists. The fashion week ban followed a rash of complaints that young women and girls were trying to emulate skinny looks and, in turn, developing eating disorders. "Organizers say they want to project an image of beauty and health, rather than a waif-like, or heroin chic look," according to a 2006 CNN article titled "Skinny Models Banned From Catwalk."[53]

As the sponsor of the show and the institution responsible for the banning order, Madrid's regional government said that it wasn't laying the blame on designers and models for anorexia. Rather, the government felt that the fashion industry bore a responsibility to show healthy body images. Concha Guerra, a regional official, is quoted as saying, "Fashion is a mirror, and many teenagers imitate what they see on the catwalk."[54]

Italy's government and fashion industry officials combined forces to crusade against the use of anorexic models, as reported by the Associated Press in a 2006 article on *CBS News*, "Italy Bans 'Too-Thin' Models."[55] At the same time, the officials drew attention to full-figured Mediterranean women and made a pledge to include larger sizes in designer collections to show young women that "bigger can also be beautiful."[56] The death of a twenty-one-year-old Brazilian model from anorexia helped serve as an impetus for "the campaign against unhealthily rail-thin models on fashion show runways,"[57] the article said.

In 2015, France passed a law that banned dangerously thin models from sashaying down Paris catwalks. According to a 2017 *CBS News* article, the BBC reported that models in France are required to produce a doctor's note saying that "they're in good physical health," while their BMI must fall within the normal range.[58] If models fall outside this range and get compensated for their work, their employers may face fines up to $82,000 (75,000 euros) and up to six months in jail. Also, the new law requires digitally retouched photos to carry the label "photographie retouchée" ("retouched photograph"). In a statement to French media, Marisol Touraine, France's former minister of social affairs, health, and women's rights, is reported as saying, "Exposing young people to normative and unrealistic images of bodies leads to a sense of self-depreciation and poor self-esteem that can impact health-related behavior."[59]

Dueling Factions: Beauty Industry versus the Regulators

In 2012, senior marketing executives from some of the world's biggest beauty brands appeared before the All-Party Parliamentary Group (APPG) on Body Image in Westminster, England, and refuted claims that, as advertisers, they perpetuate low self-esteem by contriving an unachievable image of women in the media, according to a 2012 *Marketing Week* article.[60]

On behalf of L'Oréal, Louise Terry, then–group director of communications for the company, justified the firm's advertising practices as "aspirational" and "sincere."[61] Elizabeth Fagan, nonexecutive chair and former marketing director of Boots, a UK-based pharmacy-led health and beauty chain, also rejected the claim made during the inquiry: "We want all our brand communications to be engaging, inspirational and make people feel good. We don't want it to be unattainable but want women to think 'on a good day I could look like that.'"[62]

The all-party group had some sobering words for the marketers with respect to the promotion of body-perfect ideals in advertising. According to Rosi Prescott, former CEO of Central YMCA, which was acting as secretariat of the inquiry, "All sectors need to take action to tackle the growing anxiety young people have with their body image. Advertisers stand accused of body bigotry in the images they use, and from our research we know the public feel that they are still too reliant on using ultra-thin or highly muscular body types in advertising and marketing."[63]

BODY DIVERSITY DOES A BODY GOOD: ARE WE TURNING THE PAGE ON BODY IMAGE?

In 2012, Dove won top honors for its self-esteem ad campaign titled "Growing Up," at the inaugural Body Confidence Awards, hosted by the All-Party Parliamentary Group (APPG) on Body Image.[64] The Campaign for Body Confidence was co-founded by Jo Swinson, MP, and Lynne Featherstone, MP, following the immense response to their Real Women campaign, which calls for a ban on the use of air-brushing in advertising. With some of its winnings, Dove has pledged to invest in self-esteem education for young girls in the United Kingdom.[65]

Let's see what beauty and fashion brands are doing to promote a more positive body image in their advertising and marketing.

"Authenticity" Is the Watchword for Beauty and Fashion

Today's watchword for beauty and fashion brands is *authenticity*, beauty in sub-stance and not just in form. Betabrand, a San Francisco–based online clothing label that makes men's and women's fashions using community input, brought in women who hold doctorates and doctoral candidates to model one of their collections, ac-cording to a 2014 *New Yorker* article.[66]

Betabrand may be an isolated test case. Most marketers aren't inclined to bow to pressure from consumer and advocacy groups that advocate for a more realistic pre-sentation of the female form. "Any revolution in the depiction of women's bodies is not going to come from marketers, whose job it is to construct a narrative in which a person is incomplete until a product is purchased—and so must create feelings of unworthiness and desire, as well as an impulse to change,"[67] the article said.

Many advertisers that target their ads to a female audience, especially to millennial women, haven't shifted gears but rather added a new gear: "aspirational authenticity." The 2016 *Ad Age* article noted that these advertisers are instructing their ad agencies to make advertising more "'relatable' by mirroring the consumer's everyday reality."[68] According to the article, "Authentic brands are those that best tap into the emotional truths of their consumers. This is often a harder task than simply depicting 'relatable' scenarios and lifestyles, but when done insightfully, it can create truly breakthrough work that still connects deeply with an audience."[69]

Embracing Body Diversity Can Pay Off

There's unmistakable evidence that the beauty and fashion industries may be seeing the regulatory handwriting on the wall, or they may be listening to consumers who are clamoring for more realistic and relatable models in their advertising (see figure 8.4). Consider curvy models like Ashley Graham in ads for fashion labels Marina Rinaldi and Lane Bryant; Robyn Lawley in campaigns for brands like Barneys and Ralph Lauren; and Tess Holliday, who starred in an H&M sustainable fashion campaign and landed on the cover of *People* magazine's 2015 body issue as "The World's First Size 22 Supermodel!"[70]

The 2016 *Adweek* article "Why More Brands Are Embracing Plus-Size Models" observed that brands are finally getting the body diversity message, partly because of the global proliferation and power of social media.[71] Social media has given women, who have felt left out of the mainstream fashion industry, a platform to post body-positive selfies, create body-confidence hashtags, and run plus-size fashion blogs. Beauty and fashion brands have observed this pattern and gained insight into what these women want.

Celebrating body diversity and inclusiveness makes good business sense. For example, clothier Lane Bryant's #ImNoAngel and #PlusIsEqual campaigns contributed to same-store sales increases of 6 percent, while retailer Aerie's body-positive campaign #AerieREAL lifted parent company American Eagle Outfitters' growth by 4 percent in 2015, the *Adweek* article cited.[72]

Figure 8.4. Diversity and inclusivity are the watchwords for the fashion and beauty industries. © E+/Delmaine Donson

The mainstream fashion media are increasingly recognizing that at least half of their readership are average American women who are a size 16, not a size 0—and are doing something about it. For example, trendy fashion and lifestyle magazines like *Glamour* and *Cosmopolitan* are generating buzz for featuring plus-size women on covers as well as in editorial shoots. Also, *Redbook* includes full-figured models and regular women throughout the magazine.

There are other signs that the mainstream fashion media are moving the needle on the portrayal of beauty and body image. For example, according to the 2012 *Adweek* article, thanks to the courage of a fourteen-year-old girl who organized a successful petition campaign asking *Seventeen* magazine to publish one unretouched photo spread each month, the teen magazine addressed the girl's and her supporters concerns and launched the Body Peace Treaty, an extension of its continuing Body Peace Project, which pledges to "never change girls' body or face shapes . . . always feature real girls and models who are healthy," and "be totally up-front about what goes into our photo shoots."[73]

In the next chapter, we'll explore the "looks industry" and the use of cosmetic surgery and procedures to meet beauty standards promoted through the media.

9

The Skin Trade

Now there're questions that come to mind. Where is this place, and when is it? What kind of world where ugliness is the norm and beauty the deviation from that norm? You want an answer? The answer is, it doesn't make any difference. Because the old saying happens to be true. Beauty is in the eye of the beholder, in this year or a hundred years hence. On this planet or wherever there is human life, perhaps out amongst the stars. Beauty is in the eye of the beholder. Lesson to be learned—in the Twilight Zone.

—Rod Serling's epilogue in the "Eye of the Beholder" episode of *The Twilight Zone* (1960)

Imagine a world where beauty standards are institutionalized and under government control, where people who are unable to meet those standards are labeled as social pariahs and shipped off to a colony for the grotesquely deformed.

Meet Miss Janet Tyler, hospital patient 307, labeled as misshapen and physically defective by "the State." She lies in a hospital bed. Her face is entirely wrapped in bandages following her eleventh and final state-allowed procedure to make her appear like "normal-looking" people.

The medical staff, whose faces are obscured by shadows, describe Tyler as a "pitiful twisted lump of flesh." They tell her that if this final procedure isn't successful in making her look like everyone else, she'll be exiled to a segregated community for people with her affliction to live out their days.

Tyler can't bear the thought of being labeled as an outcast. She wants to be a productive, accepted member of society. She'll do anything to belong, even wear a mask to hide her hideous appearance.

On tenterhooks, Tyler begs and finally persuades her doctor, who feels compassion for her, to remove the bandages early. Sensing the doctor's empathy for Tyler, a nurse voices her concern to the doctor. Struck by the nurse's comments, the doctor questions why anyone in society should be evaluated on their physical beauty. The nurse reminds the doctor that to speak in such terms is a treasonous act.

The doctor unravels Tyler's bandages. The procedure has failed. We now see Tyler's face. She is a stunning beauty by contemporary standards. Her appearance is in sharp contrast to everyone else's in the hospital. In this world, facial attractiveness is indicated by very thick brows, hollowed eyes, swollen and contorted lips, and creased noses shaped like a pig's snout.

In a hysterical state, Tyler races through the hospital, dodging twisted faces at every turn. Projected on flat-screen televisions hung throughout the hospital is the snarling face of the State's leader. The leader speechifies on the necessity of upholding a single norm and achieving greater conformity, going so far as to call for the removal of "the ugly" from society.

A man arrives to retrieve a weary, despondent Tyler. Like Tyler, he'd be considered very good-looking by contemporary standards, and like hers, his appearance doesn't conform to established norms. He tells her that he's taking her to a settlement with others of her "own kind"—a safe place where her "ugliness" won't cause disruption to the State. He explains that she will find love, belonging, and acceptance in the restricted area—and that "beauty is in the eye of the beholder."

The takeaway from this episode is that there's no authoritative perspective on personal beauty and ugliness. Every perspective is authoritative in its own right.

Rod Serling, the creator, host, narrator, and head writer of *The Twilight Zone*, explored the homogenized representation of beauty in another episode, titled "Number 12 Looks Just Like You" (1964). This time, Serling transports us to a dystopian society where its citizens, once they enter adulthood, must undergo a procedure, called "The Transformation," to look like one of a set number of physically attractive models ("patterns"). From Serling's opening narration:

> Given the chance, what young girl wouldn't happily exchange a plain face for a lovely one? What girl could refuse the opportunity to be beautiful? For want of a better estimate, let's call it the year 2000. At any rate, imagine a time in the future where science has developed a means of giving everyone the face and body he dreams of. It may not happen tomorrow, but it happens now . . . in the Twilight Zone.[1]

The plastic surgery industry was in its nascent stage when *The Twilight Zone* first aired in 1959. Today, cosmetic surgery is commonplace. Ever the prophetic storyteller, Serling foresaw a real world where cosmetic surgery would become normalized.

In this chapter, we'll look at the evolution of the "looks industry." We'll also explore demographic and sociocultural trends that are driving demand for cosmetic procedures. Finally, we'll discuss the connection between media-portrayed idealized images and the surge in cosmetic surgery and procedures.

Know that the terms *cosmetic surgery* and *plastic surgery* aren't the same. Cosmetic surgery is the "surgery of appearance," while "plastic surgery" is focused on repairing or reconstructing facial and body defects. Some sources conflate these terms. Therefore, the two terms may be used interchangeably.

PLASTIC SURGERY THEN AND NOW: A BRIEF HISTORY

In his 1887 autobiography, British naturalist Charles Darwin observed a "universal passion for adornment," often involving "wonderfully great" suffering.[2] This passion has taken rather unnatural twists and contortions over the centuries.

Around the early 1900s, early beauty culturists created physical contouring, often involving straps, tapes, or bandages, to combat the effects of gravity on human skin. Consider chin straps, sometimes called "tie-ups," which were used to lift sagging neck muscles and reduce double chins.[3] Ads for chin straps were run by salons that used them for facial treatments, as well as merchandisers like Sears, Roebuck and Co. that sold them directly to consumers. A 1937 direct mail ad for the Contuce Chinstrap shows an illustration of an attractive woman wearing the manufacturer's chin strap with the accompanying ad copy: "Take that disfiguring double chin into your own hands! Decide that while you rest or sleep a 'Contuce' Chinstrap shall restore to you the shapely facial contours of youth."[4]

Let's take a brief look at the evolution of plastic surgery.

It Began Long, Long Ago in the Land of Mystery

The first recorded history of people receiving medical treatment for facial injuries dates as far back as 4,000 years ago. In ancient India, physicians used skin grafts for facial reconstruction as early as 800 BCE.[5]

By 1000 CE, rhinoplasty, often referred to as a "nose job" or "nose reshaping," had become a common procedure to reconstruct soldiers' noses and upper lips that had been lopped off in battle. A sixteenth-century Italian surgeon, Gaspare Tagliacozzi, called the "the father of plastic surgery," re-created noses slit off in sword duels by using a flap of skin from the upper arm to restore the nose, a procedure also used to correct saddle nose deformities caused by syphilis.[6]

The word *plastic surgery* comes from the Greek word *plastikos* ("capable of being shaped or molded"). In the late eighteenth century, French anatomist and surgeon Pierre-Joseph Desault coined the term *plastic surgery* as a classification of surgical procedures to repair deformities of the face.[7]

During the nineteenth and early twentieth centuries, plastic surgery was made safer, thanks to developments in anesthesia and antiseptics to prevent surgical-site infections. At the same time, plastic surgery evolved and advanced scientifically in Europe and the United States. Bodily injuries sustained by soldiers during World War I were believed to have elevated the plastic surgery profession to a new height.[8]

Cosmetic surgery grew out of the American eugenics movement aimed at improving the human race through selective breeding. According to a 2006 *Medscape* article, "The American eugenics movement, with its 'Better Baby Contests,' post–World War II prosperity, and the advent of motion pictures and television all helped to usher in the modern era of cosmetic surgery. The first modern cosmetic rhinoplasty was performed in 1923, followed by the first public face lift in 1931."[9]

Today, the cosmetic surgery industry is booming in large part due to more advanced and less invasive technologies and a greater emphasis on professionalization. Also driving demand is an ever-expanding menu of cosmetic procedures and services to improve and enhance one's appearance and combat the "tyranny" of middle age.

Facing the Facts

Plastic surgery is no longer just for the rich and famous. Americans are spending more on cosmetic plastic surgery than ever before. In 2018, they forked out $16.5 billion on cosmetic procedures.[10] According to the American Society of Plastic Surgeons (ASPS), 17.7 million surgical and minimally invasive cosmetic procedures were performed in the United States in 2018.[11] In rank order of appearance, the top five cosmetic surgical procedures were breast augmentation, liposuction, nose reshaping, eyelid surgery, and tummy tuck. Botulinum toxin type A (Botox is a common brand name), soft tissue fillers, chemical peel, laser hair removal, and microdermabrasion were the top cosmetic minimally invasive procedures.[12]

The United States isn't the only country with a hunger for cosmetic surgery. On a global scale, the demand for cosmetic surgery procedures has swelled. The International Society of Aesthetic Plastic Surgery (ISAPS) reported an overall increase of 5.4 percent in surgical and nonsurgical cosmetic procedures in 2018. The United States and Brazil accounted for 28.4 percent of the world's cosmetic procedures alone, followed by Mexico, Germany, India, Italy, Argentina, Colombia, Australia, and Thailand to round out the top ten country rankings for total procedures.[13]

GILD THE LILY: OUR CULTURAL OBSESSION WITH APPEARANCE

For women who wish to enhance their décolletage without downtime or invasive surgery, now they can accomplish this in a half-hour or less. Called "Insta Breast," the procedure calls for injecting saline solution into one's breasts, giving the patient instant breast enlargements, according to a 2014 *ABC News* article.[14] The effect isn't long lasting, deflating within about 24 hours.

Instant glamour is only an appointment away. Laser treatments, Botox injections, wrinkle fillers, and many other cosmetic procedures can be done during a lunch hour. Norman Rowe, MD, is quoted as saying, "The saline gets absorbed by the body. . . . It's for the women who don't have time for implants."[15] But the procedure doesn't come cheap. Each procedure could run between $2,500 and $3,500, Rowe said. If the cost doesn't give one pause, the potential for side effects just may. Jennifer Ashton, MD, warned that any break in the skin could run risks for infection, hematoma, or nerve damage, "whether it's with a needle or a scalpel."[16]

Let's examine the factors that are driving the increase in popularity of cosmetic surgery and procedures.

The Surge in Cosmetic Surgery:
From Fighting Father Time to Getting Selfie-Ready

Many physicians from various medical specialties are taking the cosmetic plunge. A 2009 CNN article noted the growing number of physicians who are adding aesthetic services to their practices.[17] "If your doctor hasn't gone cosmetic yet, it may just be a matter of time. As the cosmetic business booms (noninvasive procedures—including microdermabrasion, lasering, injectables, and chemical peels—are up 747 percent since 1997), more and more OB-GYNs and general practitioners (GPs) are branching out into aesthetic procedures,"[18] the article said.

Physicians' timing couldn't be better. Data show that the trend toward seeking cosmetic treatments has climbed by more than 200 percent, as cited in a 2015 *New York Daily News* article.[19] Several factors are driving this trend. Here are some.

- *Aging America*: Americans are living longer, with the average life expectancy historically higher today than ever before. According to the US Census Bureau, "Because of increases in life expectancy at older ages, people 90 and older now comprise 4.7 percent of the older population (age 65 and older), as compared with only 2.8 percent in 1980. By 2050, this share is likely to reach 10 percent."[20] Given this demographic trend, many people want to slow—and even reverse—the "aging clock." They want to look good at any age, but the challenge is looking good at older ages. Healthy eating and exercise won't fight gravity, but cosmetic procedures can.
- *Profit Motive*: Money is a motivator for both manufacturers and practitioners. Take injectables like Botox. Sales for the "miracle poison" reached $3.6 billion in 2018, with $1.55 billion derived from cosmetic uses.[21] Botox treatments range from $300 to $1,200 depending on the amount the individual wants and the medical practitioner who administers it,[22] and they aren't covered by insurance for cosmetic reasons.
- *Media's Obsession with Appearance*: There's no denying that popular culture and the mass media have contributed to the increasing popularity of cosmetic surgery procedures. Reality television shows that are centered on plastic surgery, such as *I Want a Famous Face, Extreme Makeover,* and *The Swan,* can stimulate viewers' interest in cosmetic procedures, according to a study published in *Plastic and Reconstructive Surgery*.[23] John A. Persing, MD, is quoted as saying, "The more they watched the shows, the more interested" they became in plastic surgery.[24]
- *Selfie Craze*: The selfie trend is stoking demand for facial plastic surgery. A study conducted by the American Academy of Facial Plastic and Reconstructive Surgery (AAFPRS) found that the surge in selfies has increased demand for cosmetic procedures, especially among the under-thirty crowd (see figure 9.1). One in three facial plastic surgeons reported an increase in the number of requests for procedures resulting from patients' self-awareness of how they look on social media. In a 2014 AAFPRS press release, Edward Farrior, MD,

Figure 9.1. The selfie craze is driving demand for cosmetic surgery, especially among millennials. © iStock/Getty Images Plus/Alessandro Biascioli

is quoted as saying, "Social platforms like Instagram, Snapchat and the iPhone app Selfie.im, which are solely image based, force patients to hold a microscope up to their own image and often look at it with a more self-critical eye than ever before. These images are often the first impressions young people put out there to prospective friends, romantic interests and employers and our patients want to put their best face forward."[25]

- *Celebrity Influence*: Plastic surgery is all over the media these days. Some celebrities have admitted to or been outed for getting cosmetic work done, making cosmetic procedures more acceptable and commonplace. Celebrity influence is a major factor in consumers' decisions to pursue cosmetic surgery. According to a 2016 AAFPRS annual survey, nearly all AAFPRS members (99 percent) gave a nod to celebrity influence as a factor. "Consumers are constantly bombarded with images of ageless stars, and want access to that fountain of youth."[26]

- *Cultural Acceptance of Cosmetic Surgery*: The increased acceptance of cosmetic surgery has begun to lift the stigma once attached to it. The normalization of cosmetic procedures has led to greater public acceptance.[27] A 2011 survey by American Society for Aesthetic Plastic Surgery (ASAPS) showed that over half (53 percent) of women and nearly half of men (49 percent) said that "they approve of cosmetic surgery." The same poll revealed that more than two-thirds (67 percent) of Americans said that "they would not be embarrassed if their friends or family knew they had cosmetic surgery."[28]

FOREVER YOUNG: THE CHANGING FACE
OF THE COSMETIC SURGERY MARKET

Exposing adolescent girls as young as eight years old to cosmetic surgery procedures may seem inconceivable, but that's exactly what's occurring through cosmetic surgery apps, according to a 2017 article in the *Telegraph*, "Girls as Young as Eight Being Groomed by Cosmetic Surgery Games."[29] Some experts warn that grooming youngsters for cosmetic procedures is a "revolting" marketing tactic.

A report produced by the Nuffield Council on Bioethics, a United Kingdom–based independent body that examines ethical issues raised by biological and medical research, asserted that children under the age of eighteen should be barred from cosmetic procedures, such as fillers, Botox, or plastic surgery, unless they're for medical reasons, the *Telegraph* article noted.[30] The organization also recommended "sweeping restrictions on online games which promote such ideals." An inquiry conducted by the Council found that online games, including plastic surgery simulators like "Plastic Surgery & Plastic Doctor & Plastic Hospital Office for Barbie," are encouraging children and teens to experiment with plastic surgery virtually.

Jeanette Edwards, who chaired the Council's inquiry and is a professor of social anthropology at the University of Manchester, is quoted as saying, "There is a daily bombardment from advertising and through social media channels like Facebook, Instagram and Snapchat that relentlessly promote unrealistic and often discriminatory messages on how people, especially girls and women, 'should look.'" Edwards added, "Under 18s should not be able to just walk in off the street, and have a cosmetic procedure. It's unethical. There are legal age limits for having tattoos or using sunbeds. Invasive cosmetic procedures should be regulated in the same way."[31]

The 2015 *New York Post* article noted that the celebrity drive to seek perfection is "trickling down to the masses, and even teenagers are getting plastic surgery in record numbers."[32] According to the American Society of Plastic Surgeons (ASPS), in 2018 nearly 227,000 cosmetic procedures were performed on patients ages nineteen and younger.[33]

Let's find out who's getting cosmetic surgery and why.

"Cosmetic Surgery Is the New Makeup"

Several demographic and psychographic characteristics affect the market size and growth of the cosmetic surgery market. Here are some.

- *It's Not Just a Woman Thing.* No longer are cosmetic procedures exclusively obtained by women. The number of men getting cosmetic procedures is on the rise (see figure 9.2). In comparison, women continue to dominate the cosmetic surgery market, making up 92 percent, or 14.7 million, of total cosmetic procedures in 2018. For the same period, men received 8 percent, or 1.3 million, of total procedures.[34] The most popular nonsurgical cosmetic treatment among

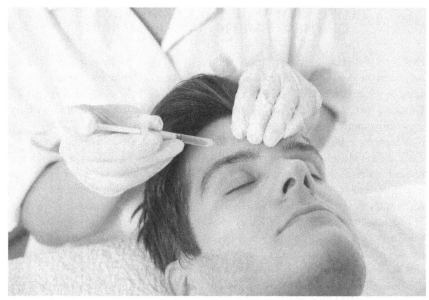

Figure 9.2.   A growing number of men are getting cosmetic procedures, such as Botox injections. © iStock/Getty Images Plus/AndreyPopov

men is Botox procedures. In 2018, more than 450,000 men received "Brotox" (aka Botox for men), a sharp increase of 381 percent since 2000.[35]

Several reasons have been given for men's interest in seeking noninvasive procedures, such as the lifting of societal stigmatization of getting cosmetics enhancement; the airing of reality television programs showing male cast members getting procedures; and the emergence of the American metrosexual, who's preoccupied with self-image and lifestyle.

- *Gen Xers Top Baby Boomers in Cosmetic Work*: In the United States, Generation X has outstripped the number of baby boomers getting cosmetic work, including surgical and minimally invasive procedures.[36] Nearly half (49 percent) of all cosmetic procedures were received by people aged 40 to 54 (7.8 million), while about a quarter (24 percent) of these procedures were received by people aged 55 and over (4.2 million total procedures).[37]

A 2011 *Los Angeles Times* article noted that Gen Xers are exhibiting a desire to keep aging at arm's length and are willing to spend more money on preventive anti-aging beauty regimens than their baby boomer counterparts, according to a study by ad agency J. Walter Thompson.[38] This generation is feeling a greater pressure to look younger for their age than prior generations, according to an *Allure* survey cited in the article. Part of the pressure could be coming from the media, especially glossy magazines like *InStyle*, *Glamour*, and *Allure*, which frequently feature youthful-looking celebrities and beauty icons of this generation, including Jennifer Lopez, Catherine Zeta-Jones, Jennifer Aniston,

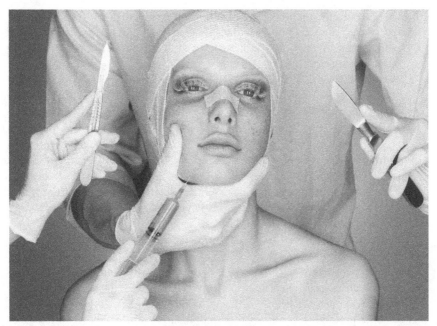

Figure 9.3. The face of cosmetic surgery keeps getting younger, with a sharp uptick in the under-thirty crowd getting nips and tucks. © iStock/Getty Images Plus/Romariolen

and Eva Mendes. These celebrities set the beauty bar, and many Gen X women aspire to emulate them.

- *Millennials Are Getting "Prejuvenation"*: The face of cosmetic surgery is getting younger (see figure 9.3). Many millennials under thirty are attempting to preserve their youth even before they get their first wrinkle. According to the 2017 *Los Angeles Times* article "Are the Kardashians, Millennials Seeking to Look Young Causing Cosmetic Procedures Boom?": "The past two to three years have seen an explosion in the popularity of noninvasive cosmetic procedures—with the Millennial and Baby Boomer generations now flocking to clinics in almost equal measure."[39]

  Both millennial men and women are getting work done, as reported in a 2014 press release from the American Academy of Facial Plastic and Reconstructive Surgery.[40] "Thirty-four percent of facial surgeons surveyed stated that women under 35 are looking after their skin to prevent visible signs of aging for longer, while 23 percent of facial surgeons surveyed stated that men under 35 are seeking rhinoplasty, neck liposuction, chin implants, and acne scar reduction procedures,"[41] the press release said.

- *Mommy Makeovers*: Who is the typical cosmetic surgery patient? A clue: It's not the popular cliché of an older woman paired with a younger man or a younger woman paired with an older man, according to a 2009 study.[42] The study looked at the demographic characteristics and motivations of cosmetic surgery patients, as well as their ages in relation to their partners. Data showed that the average cosmetic surgery patient is a married, college-educated, employed mother.[43] Interestingly, in the fillers category, half (50 percent) of women were older than their partner.[44]

- *Body Dissatisfaction Is the Best Predictor of Cosmetic Surgery*: If you're dissatisfied with some aspect of your appearance, you're hardly alone. The 2015 *New York Daily News* article "One in 5 American Women Actively Considering Plastic Surgery: Study" reported that a 2015 survey of 5,053 American women found that an overwhelming majority (85 percent) of women aged 55 to 64 were unhappy with "at least one" body part, as compared with more than 90 percent of women in the 18–24 age group, according to a study commissioned by RealSelf.com.[45] The study showed that young adult women, especially those between the ages of 25 and 34, were most likely to seek help to alter a body part (86 percent), while 40 percent said they were most likely to seek surgery. "The trend to seek help from a cosmetic doctor is on the rise by more than 200 percent,"[46] the article said.

The main takeaway is that the typical cosmetic patient is no longer the typical cosmetic patient: an older female who's trying to turn back the clock. In the *New York Daily News* article, RealSelf CEO and founder Tom Seery is quoted as saying, "As cosmetic procedures continue to become mainstream, millions of women are overcoming social stigma to pursue cosmetic changes they have been researching, often for years."[47]

THE REPLICANTS: THE DOPPELGÄNGER EFFECT OF COSMETIC SURGERY

For over half a century, young girls' first exposure to the feminine beauty ideal often began with acquiring their first Barbie doll. Stepping off toy maker Mattel's assembly line in 1959, Barbie quickly became a cultural phenomenon and the best-selling fashion doll in America. The symbol of the all-American girl made her European debut in 1961. Today, Barbie is sold in 150 countries,[48] with three Barbie dolls sold every second.[49]

The traditional Barbie doll was endowed with improbable body proportions—if she were a real woman, her body measurements would be 32-16-29.[50] A 2016 BBC article explained Barbie's manufactured appeal: "Boasting a physique based on the dream (read: unrealistic) vital statistics of Hollywood stars like Liz Taylor and Marilyn Monroe, Barbie's first outfit, a zebra-striped bustier swimsuit, was designed to be telegenic for the brand's black-and-white TV commercials."[51]

But it's not all been playtime for Barbie. She faced mounting criticism from feminists and other observers over her unrealistic body shape. The concern: Girls may attempt to emulate Barbie's molded proportions. In fact, some women have done just that by transmogrifying into Barbie look-alikes, as featured in the 2015 *Cosmopolitan* article "16 Insane Photos of Women Living as Human Dolls."[52]

Let's investigate the media-driven makeover culture.

Celebrity Copycat Surgery on the Rise

Many people take their makeover cues from famous faces that they see in the media. Cosmetic surgery patients routinely come to consultations armed with clippings of celebrity faces, or parts of faces, to instruct their doctors on what changes they'd like to make to their appearance. Whose famous facial feature is the most coveted of them all? It belongs to Kate Middleton, the Duchess of Cambridge, based on requests from women who are about to pursue cosmetic surgery.

Julian De Silva, MD, has maintained a running log of the most popular famous facial features that women request prior to undergoing cosmetic surgery, according to a 2016 *New York Post* article.[53] Kate Middleton's "mathematically perfect" nose was the most popular facial feature that women wanted, while Keira Knightley's eyelids came in second. Jennifer Lopez for eyebrows, Penélope Cruz for lips, Angelina Jolie for cheeks, Reese Witherspoon for skin, Miley Cyrus for forehead, Selena Gomez for chin, and Cher for jawline rounded out the top nine most-wanted facial features belonging to celebrities. De Silva said that patients frequently wish to "copy" the appearance of their favorite celebrity: "You will often have a consultation with a patient who will present you with a picture of a well-known person and will say: 'I want to look like that.'"[54]

Plastic surgeons say that anyone who thinks that he or she can be cloned into someone or something else through plastic surgery should think again. In a 2014 *New York Times* article, Steven Teitelbaum, MD, explained, "We really cannot make someone 'pass' for someone else. At most, we can try to mimic a feature, such as a nice nose, or even to put in a grossly disproportionate chin implant to mimic the nearly cartoonish visage of Jay Leno."[55]

Medical and ethical concerns arise when patients insist on getting surgery to look like a famous face. Part of a doctor's job is determining which patients' requests are medical or aesthetic in nature and which ones may be triggered by *body dysmorphic disorder* (BDD). Amy Wechsler, MD, shared a story of a patient who tried to find a doctor to get surgery to look like Brad Pitt. "There was this sense of, 'My life will be so much better if I had this person's X, Y or Z.' It can become an obsession," as quoted in the *New York Times* article.

Preoccupation with Perfection: Cosmetic Surgery and Body Dysmorphic Disorder

BDD is often shrugged off "as a 'first world' problem and a 'bad case of vanity' caused by today's obsession with appearance and celebrity," said the 2015 *BBC News* article "The 'Ugly Truth' About Body Dysmorphic Disorder."[56] Yet this serious condition afflicts up to one in fifty people, many of whom "'self-medicate' by undergoing frequent and repeated plastic surgery procedures,"[57] the article said.

The *Diagnostic and Statistical Manual of Mental Disorders, Fourth Edition* (*DSM-IV*) defines BDD as a "disorder that is characterized by a distressing or impairing preoccupation with slight or imagined defect(s) in one's physical appearance."[58] According to a 2013 article, "Body dysmorphic disorder affects about 1% to 2% of the general population but has been found to be up to 15 times more prevalent in patients seeking plastic surgery."[59] Although the onset of BDD usually occurs during adolescence (at an average age of sixteen), patients generally obtain their surgical consultation for the first time in their thirties. A symptom of BDD is intense body image dissatisfaction. People with BDD may also engage in compulsive behaviors, including "mirror gazing, comparing personal features, excessive camouflaging, skin picking, reassurance seeking, and even 'self-surgery' practices,"[60] the article said.

THE GLOBALIZATION OF BEAUTY: COSMETIC SURGERY AND THE WESTERN LOOK

If you were asked which country is the vainest of them all, the country with the most cosmetic procedures performed, which country would you name? If you said the United States, you hit the nail on the head. According to the International Society of Aesthetic Plastic Surgery (ISAPS), the United States topped the list of countries whose citizens got the most cosmetic tweaks in 2018, accounting for 18.7 percent of the world's procedures, followed by Brazil (9.7 percent), Mexico (4.5 percent), and Germany (4 percent).[61]

The story that the numbers don't tell us is how cosmetic surgery has become a cultural prerogative or a rite of passage in some countries. Nor do the figures explain how the desire to appear "westernized" has created a globalized beauty standard. Let's look at three examples from different regions of the world to tell this story.

Seoul, South Korea: The Plastic Surgery Capital of the World

Much has been reported on America's increasing obsession with beauty and the surge in plastic surgery to achieve it based on beauty ideals disseminated through the media and advertising. Statistically, though, it's not Americans who are getting the most cosmetic work done—it's South Korean women. According to data produced by the ISAPS, one in five South Korean women has gone under the knife, as compared with roughly one in twenty American women, as cited in a 2014 *ABC News* article.[62]

Many young South Korean women are getting Gangnam-style plastic surgery, a fusion of Western beauty ideals and the doll-like features of K-pop girls. From a 2013 article in the *Atlantic*: "K-pop has created a completely new beauty aesthetic that nods to Caucasian features but doesn't replicate them."[63]

The importance of physical appearance is deeply embedded in South Korean culture, where it's believed to improve one's employability and marriageability. "Children are considered an embodiment and reflection of their parents' status, and to this end they are shaped and molded—through intense schooling, but also through surgery to be the best they can be. Notions of beauty and productivity are married together,"[64] the article said.

A 2013 *Daily Mail* article noted that the popularity of plastic surgery, especially among the young, has been ascribed by some to "a desire to look more 'western' fueled by an obsession with celebrity culture."[65] This type of surgery is called the "Korean plastic face look" because so many women getting the facial surgery look as if they've come from the same gene pool. "Without the plastic surgery, Korean women are very diverse looking and easily can be told apart,"[66] the article said.

Iran: Beneath the Hijab

A 2013 *Daily Mail* article reported on Iran's rapacious appetite for cosmetic surgery.[67] Girls as young as fourteen are getting cosmetic work done to achieve "the Hollywood 'doll face'" seen on television programs and films exported from Western nations.

In Iran, many women alter their noses through plastic surgery to "reflect an 'Anglo American' aesthetic" as an almost silent protest against the country's rigid observance of Islamic dress, as suggested in the 2017 *Los Angeles Times* article.[68] Other reasons to do the surgery include boosting self-esteem, increasing marriageability, addressing medical issues, and reacting to the Muslim veiling tradition that some women find limiting when it comes to beauty. These add up to making Iran the world's leader in rhinoplasty surgeries.[69]

Brazil: Silver Medalist in the Olympics of Plastic Surgery

Called "the philosopher of plastic surgery" and "the maestro" by Brazilians, the late Ivo Pitanguy, MD, Brazil's pioneer of plastic surgery, is famous for saying, "The poor have a right to be beautiful too."[70] Pitanguy's tireless mission to extend this body-and-soul philosophy of plastic surgery made Brazil a world leader in plastic surgery, according to the 2016 *Forbes* article "In Plastic Surgery, Brazil Gets the Silver Medal."[71]

Brazil's preoccupation with plastic surgery has led to a shortage of doctors to deliver general medical care. The country brings in thousands of doctors from Cuba to deliver care to the poor and people living in remote communities, according to a 2014 *Guardian* article.[72] Since plastic surgery has practically become a cultural pastime, few Brazilians are complaining. In fact, plastic surgery is a source of national pride, with kiosks selling magazines such as *Plástica e Beleza* ("Plastic and Beauty"), displaying the newest cosmetic procedures and revealing who's getting cosmetic work done.

SELLING COSMETIC SURGERY:
ETHICS AND COSMETIC SURGERY ADVERTISING

The British Association of Aesthetic Plastic Surgeons (BAAPS) called for a ban on ads for cosmetic surgery procedures like breast enlargement and tummy tucks, warning that the industry is "an under-regulated 'wild west,'" as reported in a 2012 *Guardian* article.[73] Of chief concern is the broad use of cosmetic surgery advertising by private cosmetics chains in tabloids and women's magazines. Fazel Fatah, a past president of BAAPS, is quoted as saying, "We [BAAPS] have warned against the unrealistic expectations set by reality 'makeover' shows and against crass competition prizes promising 'mummy makeovers' and body overhauls. In no other area of surgery would one encounter Christmas vouchers and 2-for-1 offers—the pendulum has swung too far, and it is time for change."[74]

Let's consider the ethics of cosmetic surgery advertising.

Is Advertising Cosmetic Surgery Ethical?

In *De Curtorum Chirurgia per Insitionem* ("On the surgical restoration of defects by grafting"), first published in 1597, Gaspare Tagliacozzi, the pioneer of plastic and reconstructive surgery, described the role of the plastic surgeon:

> We bring back, refashion, and restore to wholeness the features which nature gave but chance destroyed, not that they may charm the eye but that they may be an advantage to the living soul. . . . For although the original beauty of the face is indeed restored, yet this is only accidental, and the end for which the physician is working is that the features should fulfill their offices according to nature's decree.[75]

In these words, Tagliacozzi foresaw a possible ethical dilemma when the physician offered aesthetic interventions.

As we've discussed, a cultural obsession with image and appearance has increased consumer interest in aesthetic enhancements. Given the competitive and profitable nature of the industry, marketing tactics are employed to stimulate demand for elective procedures, which can pose ethical concerns, according to a 2010 article.[76] First, physicians may advance their own "product/service interests" over those of their patients, who may feel subtle yet undue pressure when they're being marketed to by the physician. Exerting such influence can result in multiple elective procedures being done on otherwise healthy patients, which could put them at physical risk.[77]

Second, the medical community has voiced concern over the use of traditional marketing to promote cosmetic surgery procedures and services, including print, billboard, and television ads as well as sales promotion tools, which may negatively impact the standing of the medical profession.[78] For example, the 2008 *New York Times* article reported that some physicians use sales inducements, like twofers, discounts, rebates, and treatment packages, to bring prospective cosmetic surgery patients through the door.[79] "But such price-cutting blurs the line between the tactics of commerce and the practice of medicine, in which physicians have traditionally encouraged treatments based on a patient's condition or concerns, not on the doctor's bottom line,"[80] the article said.

Finally, selling cosmetic surgery by using sexual appeals or sexual content in advertising has added fuel to the controversy swirling around cosmetic surgery marketing, which could also be damaging to the reputation of the medical profession.[81] For example, the Advertising Standards Authority (ASA), Britain's advertising watchdog, received multiple complaints about an ad for breast enlargement surgery because the ad exploited young women's insecurities about their bodies by suggesting that women could only be happy with their bodies if they had undergone that surgical procedure.[82] The ad showed young women, dressed in largely revealing outfits, posing and cavorting around a swimming pool, on the beach, and on a yacht.[83]

Controversies and Conversations:
Social Media Driving People to Plastic Surgery

Social media has become a primary source for communicating the miracles—and the disasters—of cosmetic procedures. A 2016 article pointed out that cosmetic patients use social media to find surgeons and share stories about procedures and results, including whether the procedures were worth the expenditure.[84] In addition, social media allows current and potential plastic surgery patients to interact with plastic surgeons. Furthermore, some plastic surgeons use social media as a patient-engagement platform, which is a cost-effective way to promote their practice and elevate the perception of the surgeon as an expert.

A 2017 *MarketWatch* article noted that Americans look to celebrities and celebrity plastic surgeons online not only to learn about procedures but also to view them.[85] For instance, Michael Salzhauer (aka Dr. Miami) has attracted more than 500,000 followers by sharing details of his surgeries on Instagram, as well as live-streaming them in real-time Snapchats.[86]

Consumers should exhibit caution in taking ads for plastic surgery services on Instagram at face value, according to a study cited in a 2017 *Chicago Tribune* article.[87] The survey pored over approximately 1.8 million posts with twenty-one plastic surgery–associated hashtags on Instagram. Only 17.8 percent of the top posts had been published by board-certified plastic surgeons. The rest of the postings were by foreign surgeons, other physicians who weren't board certified, dentists, spas with no physician affiliation, and even a hair salon, the study noted. Clark Schierle, MD, senior author of the study, is quoted as saying, "I see examples of patients who've been botched by providers who were inadequately credentialed, and patients who were misled by false advertising or social media. Sometimes, if things seem too good to be true, they just might be."[88]

Still, some experts claim that consumers shouldn't be too concerned about getting procedures done by doctors who aren't board-certified plastic surgeons. Physicians who aren't plastic surgeons can receive additional training to certify them to perform cosmetic surgery from organizations like the American Board of Cosmetic Surgery. Joe Niamtu, MD, is quoted as saying, "There are a lot of great surgeons in the world, and they're not all plastic surgeons. . . . It boils down to your training, your experience and your outcomes."[89]

BOTCHED: THE DEADLY DANGERS
OF COSMETIC PROCEDURES

Almost any product can be illegally knocked off and sold as the authentic product, from luxury goods to software to prescription drugs like Botox Cosmetic. In 2004, the Office of Criminal Investigations (OCI) of the FDA was brought in to investigate a case involving four people who had suffered paralysis after allegedly getting Botox Cosmetic injections at a Florida medical clinic.[90] The paralysis of the four patients, who had been hospitalized with acute botulism poisoning caused by being injected with "potent, unapproved botulinum toxin," was temporary. The doctor who had administered the injections of the powerful neurotoxin had misrepresented it as the FDA-approved version of the drug used to reduce the cosmetic appearance of wrinkles.

The scope of the OCI investigation subsequently widened to include 210 investigations of health care professionals throughout the United States, leading to arrests and convictions of those individuals who intentionally injected the unapproved, cheaper substitute of the neurotoxin into almost one thousand unwitting patients.

Let's examine the underbelly of the cosmetic surgery industry.

The Dark Side of Cosmetic Enhancement

Many people have resorted to black-market cosmetic options, primarily due to the costliness of cosmetic procedures. The problem with this alternative to medical-grade skin care and aesthetic treatments is twofold. One, consumers aren't getting authentic products but instead knockoffs or defective products. Two, procedures are typically being administered by unqualified individuals rather than board-certified plastic surgeons or other qualified specialists. These procedures are almost always illegal, and the outcomes can be deadly.

Women across the United States are putting their lives at risk to get bigger, rounder derrieres in instances where they have been shot up with building materials, such as industrial-grade silicone, by people with no medical training, as reported in a 2013 *Fox News* article.[91] The article pointed out that deaths from black-market buttocks injections have been reported in several states, including Alabama, Florida, Pennsylvania, Nevada, and New York.

Doctors have observed a rise in the number of people getting illegal injections. Illicit cosmetic procedures are becoming commonplace, frequently occurring at "pumping parties" where multiple people queue up for injections in hotel rooms.

Illicit silicone isn't being used only to increase butt size. Some people are having it injected into their faces, which can cause bulging and solid nodules.[92]

Removing enormous quantities of silicone from the buttocks is so knotty that many doctors won't even attempt it. In the *Fox News* article, John Martin, MD, is quoted as saying, "When you put in a large amount of silicone, it can drift. If I fill your butt with this huge amount of silicone, it can run down your leg and you have to get your leg amputated."[93]

Driving the big-booty trend among women of all races and ethnicities are celebrities like Jennifer Lopez, Nicki Minaj, and Kim Kardashian. The 2014 *New York Post* article "Big Butts Are Becoming a Booming Business" noted that more women are trying to emulate the curvaceous figures of their favorite stars with fuller backsides.[94]

Silicone isn't the only foreign substance being injected into women to enhance their buttocks. A 2015 *Live Science* article indicated that reports have surfaced of women being injected with tire sealant, mineral oil, baby oil, and even cement, according to Tansar Mir, MD.[95]

THE SYNTHETICS: THE NORMALIZATION OF COSMETIC ENHANCEMENT

The sci-fi film *Ghost in the Shell* (2017), starring Scarlett Johansson, is set in a not-too-distant future where most people routinely get cybernetic enhancements. Today many people are getting enhanced or altered, although not with cybernetic parts—at least not yet. Are we witnessing a normalization of cosmetic enhancement?

A 2015 *Time* article provided clear evidence of Americans' increased acceptance of the notion of cosmetic enhancement.[96] A 2014 survey by MSN found that 62 percent of people would respond approvingly if they found out that a friend had work done. According to a survey conducted by the American Society for Dermatologic Surgery (ASDS), nearly half (52 percent) of people were considering aesthetic treatments in 2014, an increase of 30 percent from two years earlier.[97] "Cosmetic surgery has become the new makeup,"[98] the article said.

Not Everyone Is Buying In to Cosmetic Enhancement

Although cosmetic surgery has become more socially acceptable, most Americans are still shying away from it, according to a 2016 Pew Research Center article.[99] Just 4 percent of Americans said they'd had elective cosmetic surgery, and only 2 percent of them said they'd had noninvasive procedures like injectables, according to a 2016 Pew research survey. Women were about three times as likely as men to say they underwent cosmetic surgery; this gender gap was witnessed across age groups. Finally, six in ten Americans said that people are "too quick to undergo cosmetic procedures," while fewer than a third said that cosmetic surgery "almost always" boosts people's confidence and makes them feel better about themselves.[100]

Despite the mixed opinions on the appropriateness of cosmetic surgery, most people would probably approve of aesthetic results that fall within a range of beauty norms. In the *Time* article, Victoria Pitts-Taylor, professor of feminist, gender, and sexuality studies at Wesleyan University and author of *Surgery Junkies: Wellness and Pathology in Cosmetic Culture*, is quoted as saying, "Our unease with the technological modification of the body hasn't gone away. We've merely refined our judgment about it. We have this increasing tolerance for the anatomically improbable for women. A 36D breast size doesn't look nonhuman to us even if the waist is 21 inches. Anything more than that in either direction makes us increasingly uncomfortable."[101]

Eventually, we must ask ourselves: Is plastic surgery creating a class distinction, with cosmetic surgery haves and have-nots? "There's a plastic-surgery look that doesn't compete with the natural look and indicates class privilege to the time and money it takes to maintain such a face. My concern is the same way bad teeth are a risk in the business world, soon having certain natural facial features as far as aging might be a class signifier," said Kjerstin Gruys, an assistant professor of sociology at the University of Nevada, Reno, according to the *Time* article.[102]

In cultures that worship youth and beauty, where aging is seen almost as a disease, cosmetic surgery can stave off the aging process as well as combat negative age stereotypes related to declines in physical fitness and appearance. A 2010 article titled "The Ethics of Aesthetic Surgery," in the *Journal of Cutaneous and Aesthetic Surgery* (*JCAS*), cautioned:

> Aesthetic surgery makes profit from the ideology of a society that serves only vanity, youthfulness and personal success, and one which is losing sight of the real values. The real value of a person cannot be reduced to his or her appearance, and medicine as an art, should feel the obligation to resist these modern ideologies and should attempt to help people get a more authentic attitude about themselves.[103]

True self-worth should not be measured by how closely we can approximate the ideal of human perfection. Rather, it should be determined by our character and integrity.

Conclusion

Advertisers in general bear a large part of the responsibility for the deep feelings of inadequacy that drive women to psychiatrists, pills, or the bottle. You keep telling us over and over that if we could use that or have this or look like that, we would be forever desirable, forever happy. So we spend our time worrying over the grey streak or the extra pound or the dry skin instead of our minds, our hearts, and our fellow men.

—From *But Will It Sell?* by Marya Mannes (1964)

Yardley. Does this cosmetic brand ring a bell? The 250-year-old quintessentially British perfume and cosmetics house is known for its iconic flower-based scents, not least its 147-year-old signature scent, English Lavender.

The history of the House of Yardley, one of the oldest brands in the beauty market, is as alluring as the violet blue fields of English lavender that helped build Yardley's international reputation. Since 1921, the brand has held six Royal Warrants, which are granted by either the queen, the Duke of Edinburgh, or the Prince of Wales to people and companies doing business with the royal household for at least five years.[1]

Fast-forward to swinging London in the 1960s: the world capital of cool, Mary Quant miniskirts, John Lennon glasses, psychedelics, the Rolling Stones, and Soho's Carnaby Street. At the center of it all was Yardley. English models Jean Shrimpton, declared "the symbol of Swinging London," and Twiggy, named "the face of 1966," fronted Yardley's ad campaigns during an "era of high times, bold style, and wild possibilities."[2]

As the decade-long high of the 1960s wore off, Yardley began to lose its cool. As its customer base grew older, it slipped back into a staid image.

Starting in the late 1960s, Yardley's fate was determined by a succession of corporate parents. In 1967, Yardley was acquired by British American Tobacco (BAT). In addition to Yardley, the British-based tobacco company had acquired other cosmetics and fragrance firms. In 1970, BAT combined these acquisitions to create a wholly owned subsidiary, British American Cosmetics (BAC).[3]

In 1985, BAT sold Yardley to the British pharmaceutical company Beecham Group, which later merged with the Philadelphia-based pharmaceutical and health care–products company SmithKline Beckman Corp. Then in 1990, SmithKline Beecham sold off Yardley to Old Bond Street Corporation of the United States.[4]

In the ensuing years, Yardley tried to slough off its "granny image" by reinventing itself. Between 1993 and 1996, English actor Helena Bonham Carter became the face of Yardley until the brand broke from the actor for supermodel Linda Evangelista.[5]

By 1998, Yardley was struggling to keep its head above water amid mounting losses and debts. As a last-gasp effort to hunt for a new owner and avoid going bust, Yardley was placed in receivership to be run by accounting giant KPMG.[6]

In the following decade, Yardley had a string of corporate parents. In 2001, it was sold to the German hair care firm Wella,[7] which was bought by Procter & Gamble (P&G) in 2003.[8] Two years later, P&G off-loaded Yardley to Lornamead Group, a marketer of personal care brands. In 2009, Lornamead sold off some pieces of Yardley to Wipro Ltd., a large India-based software services exporter.[9]

In 2012, Wipro Consumer Care & Lighting, Wipro's fast-moving consumer goods (FMCG) arm, purchased Yardley's business in the United Kingdom and several other European countries. In the same year, Yardley London ran its first ad campaign in sixteen years to promote the launch of a new range of bath and body care products.[10] In 2018, Yardley made a move to enliven the brand by releasing a new fragrance line, called the Collection, intended for older millennials.[11]

From surviving the Great Fire of London in 1666 to changing hands several times over five decades, Yardley London has proven its resilience—and its long and winding history continues to be written.

There's a lesson to be learned from Yardley's story: Even the mightiest of beauty brands can stumble, lose its relevance, or fall behind the times. As it happens, some established beauty houses are struggling to maintain their foothold or staging comebacks in the marketplace.[12]

Whether it was complacency that took the wind out of their sails or digital disruption that caught them off guard, the biggest beauty brands have been forced to rewrite their marketing playbook as they fend off market-moving cosmetics brands that use guerrilla digital marketing tactics to grab market share. Proving that small really is beautiful, these nimble upstarts are integrating social media into the brand experience and, in turn, winning customer loyalty one post, one tweet, one video, and one app at a time.

If you can't beat them, buy them. Several large cosmetics companies have acquired small cosmetics brands and added them to their brand portfolio. In 2016, the beauty and personal care industry gobbled up fifty-two acquisitions, representing the biggest buying spree in a decade.[13]

The body-positive movement has steadily gathered momentum. Many women are breaking free from strict beauty norms and making fashion and beauty trends work for them by infusing their own personal sense of style. Several fashion and beauty companies have picked up on—and responded to—consumers' desire to see a more diverse range of models featured in ad pages and glossy spreads.

However, the vicious cycle of negative body image among women and girls persists and, with it, the specter of eating disorders as well as body dysmorphic disorder. Experts warn that social media and the pressure to look good are stoking mental health problems. Making matters worse, body shaming looms in every corner of the internet, and no one is immune to it.

The normalization of cosmetic enhancement has erased much of the stigma attached to plastic surgery. Some people have spent their entire life savings on cosmetic procedures to look like their favorite celebrities, models, animals, aliens, fashion dolls, pets, anime idols, and cartoon characters. Reality television series that center on cosmetic surgery reveal the extreme lengths to which people have gone to achieve physical perfection, leaving some marred or worse.

Ad regulators in such countries as Great Britain and Canada are instituting measures to eradicate sexism and sexist stereotypes in advertising. At the government level, the United States has made no such attempt to address potentially damaging and outdated gender stereotypes or outrageous and unrestrained sexism in advertising. To their credit, some advertisers and ad agencies are calling for eliminating gender stereotypes in ads and pledging not to create objectifying ads that use women as decorative props.

The beauty industry is long overdue for a makeover as it applies to strengthening cosmetic product regulations and upholding truth-in-advertising standards for beauty products. For real change to occur and real measures to be taken, it is up to each one of us to reject those beauty brands that use advertising that devalues who we are, as we are, to sell us useless or potentially harmful products while at the same time promoting homogenized, contrived, or unhealthy beauty standards. Beauty brands should celebrate our individuality, embrace the beauty in diversity, and speak to us honestly and authentically. Because we *are* worth it.

Notes

CHAPTER 1

1. "Estee Lauder: The Sweet Smell of Success," *Entrepreneur*, October 10, 2008, accessed July 21, 2017, https://www.entrepreneur.com/article/197658.

2. "Estee Lauder: The Sweet Smell of Success," *Entrepreneur*.

3. "Estee Lauder: The Sweet Smell of Success," *Entrepreneur*.

4. "Estee Lauder: The Sweet Smell of Success," *Entrepreneur*.

5. Andrea Murphy et al., "Global 2000: The World's Largest Public Companies," *Forbes*, May 15, 2019, accessed August 19, 2019, https://www.forbes.com/companies/estee-lauder/?list=global2000#2bf4a1e95b58.

6. "Estee Lauder: The Sweet Smell of Success," *Entrepreneur*.

7. "Neanderthal 'Make-up' Containers Discovered," *BBC News*, January 9, 2010, accessed July 21, 2017, http://news.bbc.co.uk/2/hi/sci/tech/8448660.stm.

8. American Chemical Society, "Ancient Egyptian Cosmetics: 'Magical' Makeup May Have Been Medicine for Eye Disease," American Chemical Society press release, January 11, 2010, accessed July 21, 2017, https://www.acs.org/content/acs/en/pressroom/newsreleases/2010/january/ancient-egyptian-cosmetics.html.

9. "Ancient Chinese Make Up," Ancient China Facts, accessed July 17, 2018, http://www.ancientchinalife.com/ancient-chinese-make-up.html.

10. "Ancient Chinese Make Up," Ancient China Facts.

11. Diane Mapes, "Suffering for Beauty Has Ancient Roots," *NBC News*, January 11, 2008, accessed July 21, 2017, http://www.nbcnews.com/id/22546056/ns/health/t/suffering-beauty-has-ancient-roots/.

12. Mapes, "Suffering for Beauty Has Ancient Roots."

13. Sally Feldman, "The Enduring Appeal of Makeup," *New Humanist*, January 25, 2016, accessed July 21, 2017, https://newhumanist.org.uk/articles/4990/the-enduring-appeal-of-makeup.

165

14. "A Brief History of Cosmetics 2: Dark Ages to Mid-20th Century," BareFacedTruth. com, January 25, 2012, accessed July 21, 2017, http://barefacedtruth.com/2012/01/25/cosmetics-through-history-part-2-dark-ages-to-mid-20th-century/.

15. "Venetian Ceruse," in *Wikipedia*, last modified May 22, 2019, accessed August 8, 2019, https://en.wikipedia.org/wiki/Venetian_ceruse.

16. Amy Oliver, "Vanity Mirror Used by Tragic 18th Century Society Beauty, 27, Who Died of Make-up Poisoning Sells for £300,000," *Daily Mail*, May 29, 2012, accessed September 21, 2019, https://www.dailymail.co.uk/news/article-2151541/Vanity-mirror-used -tragic-18th-century-society-beauty-27-died-make-poisoning-sells-300-000.html.

17. Molly Edmonds, "How Makeup Works: History of Makeup," HowStuffWorks, accessed August 21, 2019, https://people.howstuffworks.com/about-makeup1.htm.

18. Therese Oneill, "6 Terrifying Beauty Practices from History," *Mental Floss*, February 2, 2018, accessed October 19, 2019, https://mentalfloss.com/article/69360/7-terrifying-beaut y-practices-history.

19. "Beauty History: Cosmetics in the Edwardian Era," Beautiful with Brains, accessed August 8, 2019, https://www.beautifulwithbrains.com/beauty-history-cosmetics-in-the -edwardian-era/.

20. Geoffrey Jones, "Globalizing the Beauty Business before 1980," Harvard Business School, July 11, 2006, accessed March 15, 2020, https://hbswk.hbs.edu/item/globalizing-the -beauty-business-before-1980.

21. Ryan Caldbeck, "Why You Should Think about Investing in Beauty Instead of Bitcoin," *Forbes*, February 6, 2014, accessed July 22, 2017, https://www.forbes.com/ sites/ryancaldbeck/2014/02/06/why-you-should-think-about-investing-in-beauty-instead-of -bitcoin/#a125ea16f841.

22. "Masstige," in *Wikipedia*, last modified June 6, 2019, accessed August 8, 2019, https:// en.wikipedia.org/wiki/Masstige.

23. "Global Cosmetics Products Market Expected to Reach USD 805.61 Billion by 2023—Industry Size & Share Analysis," Reuters, March 13, 2018, accessed July 17, 2018, https://www.reuters.com/brandfeatures/venture-capital/article?id=30351.

24. "Global Cosmetics Products Market Expected to Reach USD 805.61 Billion by 2023—Industry Size & Share Analysis."

25. Brand Finance, "Cosmetics 50 2019: The Annual Report on the Most Valuable and Strongest Cosmetics Brands," May 2019, accessed October 23, 2019, https://brandfinance .com/knowledge-centre/reports/brand-finance-cosmetics-50-2019/.

26. M. Shahbandeh, "Revenue of the Leading 20 Beauty Manufacturers Worldwide in 2018 (in Billion U.S. Dollars)," Statista, last modified March 11, 2019, accessed August 29, 2019, https://www.statista.com/statistics/243871/revenue-of-the-leading-10-beauty -manufacturers-worldwide/.

27. Olivia Pearce, "Unilever to Acquire Murad Skincare; Follows Acquisitions of Dermalogica, Kate Somerville & REN," World Branding Forum, July 6, 2015, accessed July 13, 2017, https://brandingforum.org/news/unilever-to-acquire-murad-skincare-follows -acquisitions-of-dermalogica-kate-somerville-ren/.

28. "The Beauty Business: Pots of Promise," *Economist*, May 22, 2003, accessed July 13, 2017, https://www.economist.com/special-report/2003/05/22/pots-of-promise.

29. Bradley Seth McNew, "This Cosmetics Giant Owns Most of America's Favorite Brands," Motley Fool, February 10, 2017, accessed July 13, 2017, https://www.fool.com/ investing/2017/02/10/this-cosmetics-giant-owns-most-of-americas-favorit.aspx.

30. Raj Persaud and Peter Bruggen, "The Lipstick Effect: How Boom or Bust Effects Beauty," *Psychology Today*, October 10, 2015, accessed August 21, 2017, https://www.psychologytoday.com/us/blog/slightly-blighty/201510/the-lipstick-effect-how-boom-or-bust-effects-beauty.

31. Sarah E. Hill et al., "Boosting Beauty in an Economic Decline: Mating, Spending, and the Lipstick Effect," *Journal of Personality and Social Psychology* 103, no. 2 (2012): 287, accessed July 17, 2017, doi: 10.1037/a0028657.

32. Hill et al., "Boosting Beauty in an Economic Decline," 282.

33. Brad Tuttle, "Consumer Phrase of the Day: 'Lipstick Effect,'" *Time*, April 19, 2011, accessed July 10, 2017, http://business.time.com/2011/04/19/consumer-phrase-of-the-day-lipstick-effect/.

34. Larry Elliott, "Into the Red: 'Lipstick Effect' Reveals the True Face of the Recession," *Guardian*, December 21, 2008, accessed August 21, 2019, https://www.theguardian.com/business/2008/dec/22/recession-cosmetics-lipstick.

35. US Bureau of Economic Analysis, "State Personal Income Rises in 2017," BEA press release, March 22, 2018, accessed July 10, 2018, https://www.bea.gov/news/blog/2018-03-22/state-personal-income-rises-2017.

36. Val Srinivas and Urval Goradia, "The Future of Wealth in the United States: Mapping Trends in Generational Wealth," Deloitte Insights, November 9, 2015, accessed July 17, 2017, https://www2.deloitte.com/insights/us/en/industry/investment-management/us-generational-wealth-trends.html.

37. Daniel Liberto, "The Wealth Effect," Investopedia, June 26, 2019, accessed October 19, 2019, https://www.investopedia.com/terms/w/wealtheffect.asp.

38. Aleksandra Lopaciuk and Miroslaw Loboba, "Global Beauty Industry Trends in the 21st Century," paper presented at the Management, Knowledge and Learning International Conference, Zadar, Croatia, June 19–21, 2013, 1079, accessed July 17, 2017, https://pdfs.semanticscholar.org/c7bc/0b3d86f7245829db20b64f0531c942f12c6c.pdf.

39. Lopaciuk and Loboba, "Global Beauty Industry Trends in the 21st Century," 1084.

40. "Nano, Nano on the Wall . . . ," *Bloomberg Businessweek*, December 11, 2005, accessed July 17, 2017, https://www.bloomberg.com/news/articles/2005-12-11/nano-nano-on-the-wall-dot-dot-dot.

41. "Global Anti-aging Market 2017 Is Growing Rapidly and Expected to Reach $331.41 Billion by 2021—Orbis Research," MarketersMedia press release, June 19, 2017, accessed July 17, 2018, https://marketersmedia.com/global-anti-aging-market-2017-is-growing-rapidly-and-expected-to-reach-331-41-billion-by-2021-orbis-research/209086.

42. Trine Tsouderos, "Do Anti-aging Skin Creams Work?," *Chicago Tribune*, January 31, 2011, accessed July 31, 2017, http://www.chicagotribune.com/lifestyles/health/ct-met-skin-creams-20110131-story.html.

43. Tsouderos, "Do Anti-aging Skin Creams Work?"

44. William C. Shiel Jr., "Medical Definition of Cosmeceutical," MedicineNet, last modified December 21, 2018, accessed August 25, 2019, https://www.medicinenet.com/script/main/art.asp?articlekey=25353.

45. US Food and Drug Administration, "Is It a Cosmetic, a Drug, or Both? (Or Is It Soap?)," last modified March 6, 2018, accessed August 2, 2018, https://www.fda.gov/Cosmetics/GuidanceRegulation/LawsRegulations/ucm074201.htm.

46. ReportLinker, "Global Cosmeceuticals Market Outlook 2022," RNCOS, May 2019, https://www.reportlinker.com/p01103487/Global-Cosmeceuticals-Market-Outlook.html.

47. Paula Wolfson, "The Truth about Anti-aging 'Cosmeceuticals,'" *WTOP News*, July 31, 2014, accessed July 18, 2017, https://wtop.com/news/2014/07/the-truth-about-anti-aging-cosmeceuticals/.

48. Wolfson, "The Truth about Anti-aging 'Cosmeceuticals.'"

49. Rina Raphael, "What's Driving the Billion-Dollar Natural Beauty Movement?," *Fast Company*, May 26, 2017, accessed July 31, 2017, https://www.fastcompany.com/3068710/whats-driving-the-billion-dollar-natural-beauty-movement.

50. Jessica Rubino, "Natural Marketplace Sees Personal Care Industry Shift to Organic," New Hope Network, May 11, 2015, accessed July 18, 2017, https://www.newhope.com/nfm-market-overview/natural-marketplace-sees-personal-care-industry-shift-organic.

51. Sophie Maxwell, "What Is Premiumization?," *Brandingmag*, April 9, 2014, accessed August 24, 2019, https://www.brandingmag.com/2014/04/09/what-is-premiumization/.

52. Simon Pitman, "German Color Cosmetics Brand BeYu Targets US Masstige Market," CosmeticsDesign.com-USA, February 16, 2016, accessed July 18, 2017, https://www.cosmeticsdesign.com/Article/2016/02/16/German-color-cosmetics-brand-BeYu-targets-US-masstige-market.

53. Barbara Booth, "Real Men Don't Cry—but They Are Exfoliating. Say Hello to 'Mampering,'" CNBC, September 16, 2015, accessed July 18, 2017, https://www.cnbc.com/2014/12/05/real-men-dont-cry-but-they-are-exfoliating.html.

54. "Real Men Don't Cry—but They Are Exfoliating. Say Hello to 'Mampering.'"

55. M. Shahbandeh, "Size of the Global Men's Grooming Products Market from 2018 to 2024 (in Billion U.S. Dollars), Statista, October 29, 2019, accessed November 10, 2019, https://www.statista.com/statistics/287643/global-male-grooming-market-size/.

56. Belisa Silva, "Indie Brands Lead Beauty Industry Growth," *Beauty Packaging*, November 2, 2016, accessed July 12, 2017, http://www.beautypackaging.com/issues/2016-10-01/view_features/indie-brands-lead-beauty-industry-growth.

57. Rachel Brown, "Social Media in the Beauty Landscape," *Women's Wear Daily*, February 16, 2016, accessed July 12, 2017, https://wwd.com/beauty-industry-news/beauty-features/beauty-industry-social-media-10347599/.

58. Brown, "Social Media in the Beauty Landscape."

59. Deanna Utroske, "Retail Trend: Digital Beauty Brands Opening Storefront Shops," CosmeticsDesign.com-USA, last modified July 30, 2015, accessed July 12, 2017, https://www.cosmeticsdesign.com/Article/2015/07/30/Retail-Trend-Digital-beauty-brands-opening-storefront-shops.

60. Kaya Yurieff, "Who's Winning in Online Beauty Right Now," TheStreet.com, February 17, 2017, accessed July 12, 2017, https://www.thestreet.com/story/14003281/1/who-s-winning-in-online-beauty-right-now.html.

61. Yurieff, "Who's Winning in Online Beauty Right Now."

62. Engagement Labs, "Engagement Labs Releases TotalSocial® Ranking of Top Personal Care and Beauty Brands," Engagement Labs press release, June 14, 2018, accessed August 25, 2019, https://www.engagementlabs.com/press/engagement-labs-releases-totalsocial-ranking-top-personal-care-beauty-brands/.

63. Engagement Labs, "Engagement Labs Releases TotalSocial® Ranking of Top Personal Care and Beauty Brands."

64. Engagement Labs, "Engagement Labs Releases TotalSocial® Ranking of Top Personal Care and Beauty Brands."

65. Wolfgang Schaefer, "3 Ways Prestige Beauty Brands Can Preserve Their Allure in the Digital Age," *Adweek*, May 3, 2015, accessed July 7, 2017, https://www.adweek.com/brand -marketing/3-ways-prestige-beauty-brands-can-preserve-their-allure-digital-age-164458/.

66. Brittany Waterson, "How Can Beauty Brands Adapt to the Digital World?," Interbrand, accessed July 7, 2017, https://www.interbrand.com/views/how-can-beauty-brands -adapt-to-the-digital-world/.

CHAPTER 2

1. US Food and Drug Administration, "'Trade Secret' Ingredients," last modified November 4, 2017, accessed July 16, 2018, https://www.fda.gov/cosmetics/cosmetics-labeling/ trade-secret-ingredients.

2. Uniform Trade Secrets Act, drafted by the National Conference of Commissioners on Uniform State Laws, as amended 1985, Section 1(4)(i) and (ii), accessed September 26, 2019, https://www.wipo.int/edocs/lexdocs/laws/en/us/us034en.pdf.

3. Laura Beans, "22 Cosmetics Companies File for 'Trade Secret' Status to Skirt Toxins Law," EcoWatch, January 30, 2014, accessed July 8, 2017, https://www.ecowatch.com/22 -cosmetics-companies-file-for-trade-secret-status-to-skirt-toxins-la-1881858579.html.

4. Cynthia Washam, "Legislation: California Enacts Safe Cosmetics Act," *Environmental Health Perspectives* 114, no. 7 (2006): A402, accessed March 15, 2020, https://doi.org/ 10.1289/ehp.114-a402.

5. Women's Voices for the Earth (WVE), "Cosmetics Companies File for 'Trade Secret' Status," Women's Voices for the Earth press release, January 28, 2014, accessed July 8, 2017, https://www.womensvoices.org/2014/01/28/cosmetics-companies-file-for-trade-secret -status/.

6. Women's Voices for the Earth, "Cosmetics Companies File for 'Trade Secret' Status."

7. Scott R. Dallas Esq., e-mail message to author, April 12, 2018.

8. US Food and Drug Administration, "Is It a Cosmetic, a Drug, or Both? (Or Is It Soap?)," last modified March 6, 2018, accessed August 2, 2018, https://www.fda.gov/ Cosmetics/GuidanceRegulation/LawsRegulations/ucm074201.htm.

9. US Food and Drug Administration, "Is It a Cosmetic, a Drug, or Both? (Or Is It Soap?)."

10. Misha Warbanski, "The Ugly Side of the Beauty Industry," *Herizons* 21, no.1 (2007): 24, accessed July 7, 2017, http://www.herizons.ca/node/227.

11. Warbanski, "The Ugly Side of the Beauty Industry," 24.

12. US Food and Drug Administration, "Cosmetics Labeling Guide," accessed August 21, 2019, https://www.fda.gov/cosmetics/cosmetics-labeling-regulations/cosmetics-labeling -guide.

13. US Food and Drug Administration, "'Hypoallergenic' Cosmetics," last modified November 3, 2017, accessed January 13, 2018, https://www.fda.gov/Cosmetics/Labeling/ Claims/ucm2005203.htm.

14. Federal Trade Commission, "Advertising Substantiation Principles," accessed July 17, 2017, https://www.ftc.gov/sites/default/files/attachments/training-materials/substantiation .pdf.

15. Tom Huddleston Jr., "L'Oréal USA Settles with FTC over Deceptive Skin Care Ads," *Fortune*, June 30, 2014, accessed August 1, 2017, http://fortune.com/2014/06/30/loreal-usa -ftc/.

16. Huddleston Jr., "L'Oréal USA Settles with FTC over Deceptive Skin Care Ads."

17. Huddleston Jr., "L'Oréal USA Settles with FTC over Deceptive Skin Care Ads."

18. Huddleston Jr., "L'Oréal USA Settles with FTC over Deceptive Skin Care Ads."

19. Genelle Belmas, Jason M. Shepard, and Wayne E. Overbeck, *Major Principles of Media Law: 2017 Edition* (Boston, MA: Cengage Learning, 2017), 604–5.

20. Belmas, Shepard, and Overbeck, *Major Principles of Media Law,* 604.

21. Belmas, Shepard, and Overbeck, *Major Principles of Media Law,* 604.

22. Belmas, Shepard, and Overbeck, *Major Principles of Media Law,* 604.

23. Federal Trade Commission, "FTC Approves Final Order Settling Charges That L'Oréal USA, Inc. Made Deceptive Advertising Claims for Its Anti-aging Cosmetics," FTC press release, September 26, 2014, accessed July 17, 2017, https://www.ftc.gov/news-events/press -releases/2014/09/ftc-approves-final-order-settling-charges-loreal-usa-inc-made.

24. Federal Trade Commission, "FTC Approves Final Order Settling Charges That L'Oréal USA, Inc. Made Deceptive Advertising Claims for Its Anti-Aging Cosmetics."

25. Belmas, Shepard, and Overbeck, *Major Principles of Media Law: 2017 Edition,* 604.

26. Belmas, Shepard, and Overbeck, *Major Principles of Media Law: 2017 Edition,* 605.

27. Belmas, Shepard, and Overbeck, *Major Principles of Media Law: 2017 Edition,* 605.

28. Alene Dawson, "Clamping Down on Beauty Products Claims," *Los Angeles Times*, October 28, 2012, accessed July 10, 2017, http://www.latimes.com/fashion/alltherage/la-ig -beauty-crackdown-20121028-story.html#axzz2lTrOmZ00.

29. Dawson, "Clamping Down on Beauty Products Claims."

30. Judith E. Faulke, "Cosmetic Labeling," *FindLaw*, September 24, 1996, accessed July 16, 2017, https://corporate.findlaw.com/law-library/cosmetic-labeling.html.

31. Faulke, "Cosmetic Labeling."

32. "The Beauty Business: Pots of Promise," *Economist*, May 22, 2003, accessed July 13, 2017, https://www.economist.com/special-report/2003/05/22/pots-of-promise.

33. AnnaMaria Andriotis, "10 Things the Beauty Industry Won't Tell You," *MarketWatch*, April 20, 2011, accessed July 10, 2017, https://www.marketwatch.com/story/10-things-the -beauty-industry-wont-tell-you-1303249279432.

34. Amy Kraft, "Most 'Scientific' Beauty Product Claims Are Bogus, Study Finds," *CBS News*, July 28, 2015, accessed July 16, 2017, https://www.cbsnews.com/news/most-beauty -product-claims-are-bogus/.

35. Kraft, "Most 'Scientific' Beauty Product Claims Are Bogus, Study Finds."

36. Kraft, "Most 'Scientific' Beauty Product Claims Are Bogus, Study Finds."

37. "Industry Self-Regulation," in *Wikipedia*, last modified July 21, 2019, accessed August 24, 2019, https://wiki2.org/en/Industry_self-regulation.

38. "State Laws," Campaign for Safe Cosmetics, accessed August 22, 2019, http://www .safecosmetics.org/get-the-facts/regulations/state-laws/.

39. American Cancer Society, "Cosmetics," May 28, 2014, accessed July 17, 2017, https:// www.cancer.org/cancer/cancer-causes/cosmetics.html.

40. American Cancer Society, "Cosmetics."

41. David Suzuki Foundation, "'The Dirty Dozen' Cosmetic Chemicals to Avoid," May 4, 2010, accessed July 17, 2017, https://davidsuzuki.org/queen-of-green/dirty-dozen-cosmetic -chemicals-avoid/.

42. "Butylated Compounds," Campaign for Safe Cosmetics, accessed August 22, 2019, http://www.safecosmetics.org/get-the-facts/chemicals-of-concern/butylated-compounds/.

43. Heather Somerville, "Women's Consumer Advocates Take on Cosmetics Industry," *Mercury News*, August 12, 2016, accessed July 15, 2017, https://www.mercurynews.com/2013/10/08/womens-consumer-advocates-take-on-cosmetics-industry/.

44. Senator Dianne Feinstein, "Senators Introduce Bill to Strengthen Personal Care Product Oversight," US Senator for California Dianne Feinstein press release, April 20, 2015, accessed July 17, 2017, https://www.feinstein.senate.gov/public/index.cfm/2015/4/feinstein-collins-introduce-bill-to-strengthen-oversight-of-personal-care-products.

45. Government of Canada, "Cosmetic Ingredient Hotlist: Prohibited and Restricted Ingredients," November 11, 2011, accessed July 28, 2018, https://www.canada.ca/en/health-canada/services/consumer-product-safety/cosmetics/cosmetic-ingredient-hotlist-prohibited-restricted-ingredients.html.

46. Sydney Lupkin, "Women Put an Average of 168 Chemicals on Their Bodies Each Day, Consumer Group Says," *ABC News*, April 27, 2015, accessed July 14, 2017, https://abcnews.go.com/Health/women-put-average-168-chemicals-bodies-day-consumer/story?id=30615324.

47. Lupkin, "Women Put an Average of 168 Chemicals on Their Bodies Each Day, Consumer Group Says."

48. Environmental Working Group, "Teen Girls' Body Burden of Hormone-Altering Cosmetics Chemicals: Cosmetics Chemicals of Concern," September 24, 2008, accessed July 14, 2017, https://www.ewg.org/research/teen-girls-body-burden-hormone-altering-cosmetics-chemicals/cosmetics-chemicals-concern#.W32ez_ZFxPY.

49. US Food and Drug Administration, "Parabens in Cosmetics," last modified February 22, 2018, accessed August 24, 2019, https://www.fda.gov/cosmetics/cosmetic-ingredients/parabens-cosmetics.

50. US Food and Drug Administration, "Parabens in Cosmetics."

51. Gaia Vince, "Cosmetic Chemicals Found in Breast Tumours," *New Scientist*, January 12, 2004, accessed July 15, 2017, https://www.newscientist.com/article/dn4555-cosmetic-chemicals-found-in-breast-tumours/.

52. Vince, "Cosmetic Chemicals Found in Breast Tumours."

53. Vince, "Cosmetic Chemicals Found in Breast Tumours."

54. Julia R. Barrett, "Chemical Exposures: The Ugly Side of Beauty Products," *Environmental Health Perspectives* 113, no. 1 (2005): A24, accessed July 15, 2017, doi: 10.1289/ehp.113-a24.

55. Barrett, "Chemical Exposures: The Ugly Side of Beauty Products."

56. Centers for Disease Control and Prevention, "Phthalates Factsheet," National Biomonitoring Program, last modified April 7, 2017, accessed August 24, 2019, https://www.cdc.gov/biomonitoring/Phthalates_FactSheet.html.

57. Campaign for Safe Cosmetics, "Phthalates," accessed March 16, 2020, http://www.safecosmetics.org/get-the-facts/chemicals-of-concern/phthalates/.

58. Kelly K. Ferguson, Thomas F. McElrath, and John D. Meeker. "Environmental Phthalate Exposure and Preterm Birth," *JAMA Pediatrics* 168, no. 1 (2014): 61–67, accessed July 14, 2017. doi:10.1001/jamapediatrics.2013.3699.

59. Michelle Castillo, "Phthalate Exposure in Pregnancy May Increase Preterm Birth Risk," *CBS News*, November 19, 2013, accessed July 14, 2017, https://www.cbsnews.com/news/phthalate-exposure-in-pregnancy-may-increase-preterm-birth-risk/.

60. Katie Thomas, "Johnson & Johnson to Remove Formaldehyde from Products," *New York Times*, August 15, 2012, accessed July 14, 2017, https://www.nytimes.com/2012/08/16/business/johnson-johnson-to-remove-formaldehyde-from-products.html.

61. Katie Thomas, "The 'No More Tears' Shampoo, Now with No Formaldehyde," *New York Times*, January 18, 2014, accessed July 7, 2017, https://www.nytimes.com/2014/01/18/business/johnson-johnson-takes-first-step-in-removal-of-questionable-chemicals-from-products.html?_r=0.

62. "The World's Most Counterfeited Brands Revealed," MSN.com, May 12, 2019, accessed August 8, 2019, https://www.msn.com/en-ph/money/personalfinance/the-worlds-most-counterfeited-brands-revealed/ss-AABhajU.

63. "The World's Most Counterfeited Brands Revealed."

64. Chris Barker, "Reports of Counterfeit Estee Lauder Cosmetics Grow in the Bay Area," Cosmetics Design.com-USA, last modified December 12, 2013, accessed July 14, 2017, https://www.cosmeticsdesign.com/Article/2013/11/27/Reports-of-counterfeit-Estee-Lauder-cosmetics-grow-in-the-Bay-area.

65. Rachel Williams, "Deadly Beauty: The Fake Makeup That May Contain Cyanide or Arsenic," *Guardian*, May 18, 2015, accessed July 14, 2017, https://www.theguardian.com/uk-news/shortcuts/2015/may/18/deadly-beauty-fake-makeup-contain-cyanide-arsenic-counterfeiters.

66. Joanna Chiu, "The Very Real Danger of Fake Cosmetics from China," *Mashable* (blog), November 10, 2015, accessed July 14, 2017, https://mashable.com/2015/11/10/fake-makeup-china/#UabKuFALxPqj.

67. "Prohibitions on Cosmetics Testing in the EU and Elsewhere," Cruelty Free International, accessed August 24, 2019, https://www.crueltyfreeinternational.org/what-we-do/corporate-partnerships/eu-ban-cosmetics-testing.

68. Humane Society International, "China Implements Rule Change in First Step Towards Ending Animal Testing of Cosmetics," HSI press release, June 30, 2014, accessed July 15, 2017, http://www.hsi.org/news/press_releases/2014/06/china-implements-rule-change-063014.html.

69. Humane Society of the United States, "Federal Bill to End Cosmetics Testing on Animals Introduced," Humane Society of the United States press release, June 23, 2015, accessed July 8, 2017, https://www.humanesociety.org/news/federal-bill-end-cosmetics-testing-animals-introduced.

70. "New Poll Reveals US United against Cosmetics Animal Tests," Cruelty Free International, September 12, 2019, accessed October 19, 2019, https://www.crueltyfreeinternational.org/what-we-do/latest-news-and-updates/new-poll-reveals-us-united-against-cosmetics-animal-tests.

71. Humane Society of the United States, "Federal Bill to End Cosmetics Testing on Animals Introduced."

CHAPTER 3

1. James Bennett, "Revlon," Cosmetics and Skin, last modified March 2, 2018, April 4, 2018, http://cosmeticsandskin.com/companies/revlon.php.

2. "Revlon Inc.—Company Profile, Information, Business Description, History, Background Information on Revlon Inc.," in *Reference for Business*, accessed July 11, 2017, http://www.referenceforbusiness.com/history2/10/Revlon-Inc.html.

3. Bennett, "Revlon."

4. Bennett, "Revlon."

5. "Our Company—Our Founders," Revlon, Inc., accessed August 8, 2019, https://www.revloninc.com/our-company/our-founders.

6. Bennett, "Revlon."

7. Marlen Komar, "Revlon's Fire & Ice Campaign in 1952 Was the First Ad to Acknowledge Women Wear Makeup for Themselves," *Bustle*, October 9, 2018, accessed November 10, 2019, https://www.bustle.com/p/revlons-fire-ice-campaign-in-1952-was-the-first-ad-to-acknowledge-women-wear-makeup-for-themselves-12159808.

8. "Entrepreneurs: Merchant of Glamour," *Time*, September 8, 1975, accessed July 11, 2017, http://content.time.com/time/magazine/article/0,9171,917802,00.html.

9. "The Beauty Business: Pots of Promise," *Economist*, May 22, 2003, accessed July 13, 2017, https://www.economist.com/special-report/2003/05/22/pots-of-promise.

10. Sarah Ferguson, "How Much Does Your Face Cost? A New Survey Finds That the Average Woman in the U.S. Will Spend Up to $300,000 on Beauty Products in Her Lifetime," *Daily Mail*, April 6, 2017, accessed July 31, 2017, http://www.dailymail.co.uk/femail/article-4383930/How-Women-U-S-Spend-Beauty-Products.html#ixzz4wGrd8onn.

11. Nielsen, "Age Before Beauty: Treating Generations with a Personal Touch in Beauty Advertising," February 5, 2015, accessed July 12, 2017, http://www.nielsen.com/us/en/insights/news/2015/age-before-beauty-treating-generations-with-a-personal-touch-in-beauty-advertising.html.

12. Nielsen, "Age Before Beauty: Treating Generations with a Personal Touch in Beauty Advertising."

13. Ashley Lutz, "Baby Boomers Are the Sexiest Consumers in Retail," *Business Insider*, June 2, 2015, accessed July 17, 2017, https://www.businessinsider.com/baby-boomers-spend-the-most-money-2015-6.

14. "Booming: Industries Benefiting from the Aging Population," IBISWorld, November 17, 2014, accessed July 31, 2017, https://www.ibisworld.com/media/2014/11/17/booming-industries-benefiting-aging-population/.

15. Paul Taylor and George Gao, "Generation X: America's Neglected 'Middle Child,'" Pew Research Center, June 5, 2014, accessed July 18, 2017, http://www.pewresearch.org/fact-tank/2014/06/05/generation-x-americas-neglected-middle-child/.

16. Alene Dawson, "Gen X Women, Young for Their Age," *Los Angeles Times*, September 25, 2011, accessed July 11, 2017, http://articles.latimes.com/2011/sep/25/image/la-ig-beauty-genx-20110925.

17. Dawson, "Gen X Women, Young for Their Age."

18. Meredith Corporation, "Women 2020: Meredith's Exclusive Research Study Reveals Weight Acceptance and Wage Equality Top Issues Facing Millennial Women Today," Meredith Corporation press release, August 6, 2015, accessed July 18, 2017, http://meredith.mediaroom.com/2015-08-06-Women-2020-Merediths-Exclusive-Research-Study-Reveals-Weight-Acceptance-And-Wage-Equality-Top-Issues-Facing-Millennial-Women-Today.

19. Sarah Kinonen, "Millennial Women Want More Green Beauty Products," *Allure*, November 24, 2016, accessed July 28, 2019, https://www.allure.com/story/millennial-women -green-beauty.

20. Allison Collins, "Millennials Disrupt Beauty Industry's Antiwrinkle Agenda," *Women's Wear Daily*, April 27, 2016, accessed July 7, 2017, https://wwd.com/beauty-industry-news/ skin-care/millennial-beauty-antiwrinkle-baby-boomer-10419202/.

21. William Strauss and Neil Howe, *Generations: The History of America's Future, 1584 to 2069* (New York: William Morrow, 1991), 281.

22. Vivienne Rudd, "The Mature Beauty Market—Time for Brands to Grow Up?," Mintel (blog), September 24, 2013, accessed July 7, 2017, http://www.mintel.com/blog/beauty -market-news/mature-beauty-market.

23. Steve Hemsley, "Brands Need to Ensure Their Designs Are Age-Agnostic," *Marketing Week*, March 24, 2016, accessed July 18, 2017, https://www.marketingweek.com/ 2016/03/24/appeal-to-consumers-across-generations-by-adopting-an-age-agnostic-approach -to-design/.

24. Amanda Vanallen, Vanessa Weber, and Sarah Kunin, "Are Tweens Too Young for Makeup?," *ABC News*, January 27, 2011, accessed July 18, 2017, https://abcnews.go.com/US/ tweens-young-makeup/story?id=12777008.

25. "Now Walmart Targets EIGHT-year-olds with a New Range of 'Anti-aging' Make-Up," *Daily Mail*, January 26, 2011, accessed July 15, 2017, https://www.dailymail.co.uk/news/ article-1350857/Walmart-Geo-Girl-anti-aging-make-targets-EIGHT-year-olds.html.

26. Karla Rendle, "Millennial and Gen-Z Beauty Consumers," *Beauty Packaging*, March 6, 2016, accessed July 7, 2017, http://www.beautypackaging.com/issues/2016-03-01/view_ columns/millennial-and-gen-z-beauty-consumers.

27. Emily Chan, "'Successful Marriages Start in the Kitchen!' Outrageous Retro Advertising Slogans Reveal the Sexist Marketing Ploys Once Used to Sell Everything from Lingerie to Washing Machines," *Daily Mail*, January 9, 2018, accessed July 10, 2018, http://www .dailymail.co.uk/femail/article-5249797/Adverts-1940s-50s-60s-world-changed.html.

28. Christie Barakat, "Emotional Branding and the Emotionally Intelligent Consumer," *Adweek*, January 12, 2014, accessed July 30, 2017, https://www.adweek.com/digital/ emotional-branding-emotionally-intelligent-consumer/.

29. "Ralph Lauren Tender Romance Fragrance 2016," Models.com, accessed September 19, 2019, https://models.com/work/ralph-lauren-tender-romance-fragrance-2016/505964.

30. "Ralph Lauren Tender Romance," Sephora.com, accessed September 19, 2019, https:// www.sephora.com/product/tender-romance-P405915.

31. Vanessa Apaolaza-Ibañez et al., "Women Satisfaction with Cosmetic Brands: The Role of Dissatisfaction and Hedonic Brand Benefits," *African Journal of Business Management* 5, no. 3 (2011): 792–802, accessed July 7, 2017, doi: 10.5897/AJBM10.305.

32. Rick Nauert, "Cosmetics Industry Driven by Emotions," Psych Central, July 25, 2011, accessed July 7, 2017, https://psychcentral.com/news/2011/07/25/cosmetics-industry-driven -by-emotions.

33. Nauert, "Cosmetics Industry Driven by Emotions."

34. AnnaMaria Andriotis, "10 Things the Beauty Industry Won't Tell You," *MarketWatch*, April 20, 2011, accessed July 10, 2017, https://www.marketwatch.com/story/10-things-th e-beauty-industry-wont-tell-you-1303249279432.

35. Clé de Peau Beauté, "Company Information," accessed August 16, 2019, https://www .cledepeaubeaute.com/company-info.html.

36. Clé de Peau Beauté, eye shadow ad featuring Amanda Seyfried, Code MM, accessed August 16, 2019, http://www.code-mm.com/work/creative-direction/cle-de-peau-beaute -2012-aw-david-sims.

37. Kim Lachance Shandrow, "10 Questions to Ask When Designing Your Company's Logo," *Entrepreneur*, February 25, 2015, accessed August 1, 2017, https://www.entrepreneur .com/article/243181.

38. "Ad Age Advertising Century: Top 10 Slogans," *Advertising Age*, March 29, 1999, accessed July 15, 2017, http://adage.com/article/special-report-the-advertising-century/ad-age -advertising-century-top-10-slogans/140156/.

39. Nielsen, "Age Before Beauty: Treating Generations with a Personal Touch in Beauty Advertising."

40. Nielsen, "Age Before Beauty: Treating Generations with a Personal Touch in Beauty Advertising."

41. Nielsen, "Age Before Beauty: Treating Generations with a Personal Touch in Beauty Advertising."

42. Nielsen, "Age Before Beauty: Treating Generations with a Personal Touch in Beauty Advertising."

43. Nielsen, "Age Before Beauty: Treating Generations with a Personal Touch in Beauty Advertising."

44. Nielsen, "Age Before Beauty: Treating Generations with a Personal Touch in Beauty Advertising."

45. Jack Neff, "Clinique Sees Hope in a Fresh Start," *Advertising Age*, July 28, 2014, accessed July 15, 2017, http://adage.com/article/cmo-strategy/clinique-sees-hope-a-fresh -start/294329/.

46. Clinique, "Clinique Start Better Manifesto," YouTube, published May 20, 2014, accessed August 27, 2019, https://www.youtube.com/watch?v=19_JUAw_Zeg.

47. Shorty Awards, from the 7th Annual Shorty Awards, "Clinique #StartBetter, Entered in Fashion, Beauty and Luxury," accessed July 15, 2017, https://shortyawards.com/7th/ clinique-startbetter.

48. Patrick Coffee, "Clinique Drops Models for Influencers in New Campaign," *Adweek*, July 14, 2015, accessed July 15, 2017, https://www.adweek.com/digital/clinique-drops -models-for-influencers-in-new-campaign/.

49. Coffee, "Clinique Drops Models for Influencers in New Campaign."

50. Information Resources Management Association, ed., *Digital Multimedia: Concepts, Methodologies, Tools, and Applications* (Hershey, PA: IGI Global, 2018), 51.

51. Gartner, "Gartner L2 Digital IQ Index: Beauty U.S. 2018," March 9, 2018, accessed August 27, 2019, https://www.gartner.com/en/marketing/research/beauty-us-2018.

52. J. Clement, "Leading Beauty Brands with the Most Followers on Facebook as of October 2019 (in Millions)," Statista, October 16, 2019, accessed October 23, 2019, https://www .statista.com/statistics/300050/beauty-brands-follower-facebook/.

53. Rachel Brown, "Social Media in the Beauty Landscape," *Women's Wear Daily*, February 16, 2016, accessed July 12, 2017, https://wwd.com/beauty-industry-news/beauty-features/ beauty-industry-social-media-10347599/.

54. Brown, "Social Media in the Beauty Landscape."

55. Shareen Pathak, "Why Fashion and Beauty Brands Love Instagram," *Digiday*, August 11, 2015, accessed July 17, 2017, https://digiday.com/marketing/fashion-beauty-brands -instagram/.

56. Brown, "Social Media in the Beauty Landscape."

57. Arne Holst, "Number of Smartphone Users Worldwide from 2016 to 2021 (in Billions)," Statista, last modified July 26, 2019, accessed August 29, 2019, https://www.statista.com/statistics/330695/number-of-smartphone-users-worldwide/.

58. Lauren Johnson, "Unilever's Dove Promotes Beauty Products through Multichannel Digital Effort," *Mobile Marketer*, accessed July 17, 2017, https://www.mobilemarketer.com/ex/mobilemarketer/cms/news/advertising/12710.html.

59. Jeffrey Hayzlett, "What Does It Mean to Be a Good Brand Ambassador?," *Entrepreneur*, June 25, 2015, accessed July 16, 2017, https://www.entrepreneur.com/article/246773.

60. Rachel Strugatz, "Bloggers and Digital Influencers Are Reshaping the Fashion and Beauty Landscape," *Los Angeles Times*, April 10, 2016, accessed July 16, 2017, http://www.latimes.com/fashion/la-ig-bloggers-20160809-snap-story.html.

61. Brigit Katz, "New Study Shows Impact of Social Media on Beauty Standards," *Women in the World*, April 3, 2015, accessed July 12, 2017, https://womenintheworld.com/2015/04/03/new-study-shows-impact-of-social-media-on-beauty-standards/.

62. Katz, "New Study Shows Impact of Social Media on Beauty Standards."

63. Elizabeth Segran, "Female Shoppers No Longer Trust Ads or Celebrity Endorsements," *Fast Company*, September 28, 2015, accessed July 28, 2019, https://www.fastcompany.com/3051491/female-shoppers-no-longer-trust-ads-or-celebrity-endorsements.

64. "No Brand Loyalty among Millennials, Cosmetics Consumer Study Says," *Beauty Packaging*, December 24, 2014, accessed July 30, 2017, http://www.beautypackaging.com/contents/view_breaking-news/2014-12-24/no-brand-loyalty-among-millennials-cosmetics-consumer-study-says.

65. "No Brand Loyalty among Millennials, Cosmetics Consumer Study Says," *Beauty Packaging*.

66. Stephen Reily, "What Do Boomer Women Want from Cosmetic Companies? Not What They're Selling," Mediapost.com, March 12, 2012, accessed July 11, 2017, https://www.mediapost.com/publications/article/169776/what-do-boomer-women-want-from-cosmetic-companies.html.

67. Reily, "What Do Boomer Women Want from Cosmetic Companies? Not What They're Selling."

CHAPTER 4

1. Sara Kamouni, "Beauty Icons: How Audrey Hepburn Is the Ultimate Beauty Icon, According to New Survey," *Sun*, December 21, 2016, accessed July 7, 2017, https://www.thesun.co.uk/news/2449770/how-audrey-hepburn-is-the-ultimate-beauty-icon-according-to-new-survey/.

2. "Audrey Hepburn," Biography.com, last modified June 18, 2019, accessed August 29, 2019, https://www.biography.com/actor/audrey-hepburn.

3. "Audrey Hepburn: Style Icon," *BBC News*, last modified May 4, 2004, accessed July 7, 2017, http://news.bbc.co.uk/2/hi/entertainment/3667517.stm.

4. "Audrey Hepburn," Biography.com.

5. Pete Croatto, "History Lesson! Learn How Colette, Audrey Hepburn, Leslie Caron & Vanessa Hudgens Transformed *Gigi*," Broadway.com, April 6, 2015, accessed July 10, 2018,

https://www.broadway.com/buzz/180286/history-lesson-learn-how-colette-audrey-hepburn
-leslie-caron-vanessa-hudgens-transformed-gigi/.

6. David Wills, "The Importance of Being Audrey," Biography.com, January 19, 2017, accessed July 7, 2017, https://www.biography.com/news/audrey-hepburn-style-david-wills.

7. Wills, "The Importance of Being Audrey."

8. Ki Mae Heussner, "Science of Beauty: What Made Elizabeth Taylor So Attractive?," *ABC News*, March 23, 2011, accessed July 6, 2017, https://abcnews.go.com/Technology/elizabeth-taylor-science-great-beauty/story?id=13203775.

9. Heussner, "Science of Beauty: What Made Elizabeth Taylor So Attractive?"

10. Heussner, "Science of Beauty: What Made Elizabeth Taylor So Attractive?"

11. Crispin Sartwell, edited by Edward N. Zalta, "Beauty," in *Stanford Encyclopedia of Philosophy*, last modified October 5, 2016, accessed July 6, 2017, https://plato.stanford.edu/archives/win2017/entries/beauty/.

12. David Konstan, *Beauty: The Fortunes of an Ancient Greek Idea* (Oxford: Oxford University Press, 2015), 31–35.

13. "Beauty," in *New World Encyclopedia*, accessed July 6, 2017, http://www.newworldencyclopedia.org/entry/Beauty.

14. Marcus Chown, "The Golden Rule," *Guardian*, January 15, 2003, accessed October 10, 2019, https://www.theguardian.com/science/2003/jan/16/science.research1.

15. "Researchers Discover New 'Golden Ratios' for Female Facial Beauty," *(e) Science News*, December 16, 2009, accessed July 31, 2019, http://esciencenews.com/articles/2009/12/16/researchers.discover.new.golden.ratios.female.facial.beauty.

16. Pamela M. Pallett, Stephen Link, and Kang Lee, "New 'Golden' Ratios for Facial Beauty," *Vision Research* 50, no. 2 (2010): 149–54, accessed July 4, 2017, doi: 10.1016/j.visres.2009.11.003.

17. "Researchers Discover New 'Golden Ratios' for Female Facial Beauty," *(e) Science News*.

18. "Researchers Discover New 'Golden Ratios' for Female Facial Beauty," *(e) Science News*.

19. "Facing the Facts," *Economist*, August 13, 2014, accessed July 6, 2017, https://www.economist.com/science-and-technology/2014/08/13/facing-the-facts.

20. Eric Wargo, "Beauty Is in the Mind of the Beholder," *Observer*, April 2011, accessed July 4, 2017, https://www.psychologicalscience.org/observer/beauty-is-in-the-mind-of-the-beholder#.WWdhrIjytPY.

21. David Robson, "The Myth of Universal Beauty," BBC, June 23, 2015, accessed July 4, 2017, http://www.bbc.com/future/story/20150622-the-myth-of-universal-beauty.

22. Michael R. Solomon, *Consumer Behavior: Buying, Having, and Being*, 8th ed. (Hoboken, NJ: Pearson, 2009), 197.

23. "The Biology of Beauty," *Newsweek*, June 2, 1996, accessed July 23, 2017, https://www.newsweek.com/biology-beauty-178836.

24. "The Biology of Beauty," *Newsweek*.

25. Elizabeth Landau, "Beholding Beauty: How It's Been Studied," CNN, March 3, 2012, accessed July 4, 2017, https://www.cnn.com/2012/03/02/health/mental-health/beauty-brain-research/index.html.

26. Anthony C. Little, Benedict C. Jones, and Lisa M. DeBruine, "Facial Attractiveness: Evolutionary Based Research," *Philosophical Transactions of the Royal Society B: Biological Sciences* 366 (2011): 1638–59, doi:10.1098/rstb.2010.0404.

27. "Physical Attractiveness," in *Wikipedia*, last modified August 29, 2019, accessed August 29, 2019, https://en.wikipedia.org/wiki/Physical_attractiveness.

28. "Media Conglomerate," in *Wikipedia*, last modified August 29, 2019, accessed August 29, 2019, https://en.wikipedia.org/wiki/Media_conglomerate.

29. Abhishek Seth, "How Baywatch Unknowingly Changed the World: The Untapped Power of TV Shows," *Huffington Post*, November 25, 2013, accessed July 6, 2017, https://www.huffingtonpost.com/abhishek-seth/how-baywatch-unknowingly-changed-the-world_b_3891368.html.

30. Seth, "How Baywatch Unknowingly Changed the World: The Untapped Power of TV Shows."

31. *Cosmopolitan*, Hearst Corporation, 2019, accessed July 6, 2017, https://www.hearst.com/magazines/cosmopolitan.

32. Edith Zimmerman, "99 Ways to Be Naughty in Kazakhstan," *New York Times*, August 3, 2012, accessed July 30, 2017, https://www.nytimes.com/2012/08/05/magazine/how-cosmo-conquered-the-world.html.

33. Zimmerman, "99 Ways to Be Naughty in Kazakhstan."

34. Sadie Whitelocks, "Being Force Fed 16,000 Calories and Wearing a Lip Plate: The Most Bizarre Beauty Trends around the World Revealed," *Daily Mail*, September 23, 2016, accessed July 6, 2017, http://www.dailymail.co.uk/travel/travel_news/article-3803885/Being-force-fed-16-000-calories-wearing-lip-plate-bizarre-beauty-trends-world-revealed.html.

35. Alene Dawson, "What Is Beauty and Who Has It?," CNN, June 29, 2011, accessed July 4, 2017, http://www.cnn.com/2011/LIVING/06/29/global.beauty.culture/index.html.

36. Joan Z. Spade and Catherine G. Valentine, eds., *The Kaleidoscope of Gender: Prisms, Patterns, and Possibilities*, 3rd ed. (Thousand Oaks, CA: Sage, 2010), 185.

37. Carl N. Degler, "Curves In, Curves Out," review of *American Beauty*, by Lois W. Banner, *New York Times*, April 7, 1983, accessed July 6, 2017, https://www.nytimes.com/1983/04/17/books/curves-in-curves-out.html.

38. Degler, "Curves In, Curves Out."

39. Degler, "Curves In, Curves Out."

40. Degler, "Curves In, Curves Out."

41. Degler, "Curves In, Curves Out."

42. Jacqueline Howard and Anna Ginsburg, "The History of the 'Ideal' Woman and Where That Has Left Us," CNN, March 9, 2018, accessed August 30, 2019, https://www.cnn.com/2018/03/07/health/body-image-history-of-beauty-explainer-intl/index.html.

43. "Cult of Domesticity," in *Wikipedia*, last modified August 7, 2019, accessed August 30, 2019, https://en.wikipedia.org/wiki/Cult_of_Domesticity.

44. "The Gibson Girl's America: Drawings by Charles Dana Gibson," Library of Congress, accessed August 30, 2019, https://www.loc.gov/exhibits/gibson-girls-america/the-gibson-girl-as-the-new-woman.html.

45. Martha H. Patterson, ed., *The American New Woman Revisited: A Reader, 1894–1930* (New Brunswick, NJ: Rutgers University Press, 2008), 4.

46. Katie Baker, "The Problem with *The Great Gatsby*'s Daisy Buchanan," *Daily Beast*, May 10, 2013, accessed July 21, 2018, https://www.thedailybeast.com/the-problem-with-the-great-gatsbys-daisy-buchanan.

47. Emily Spivack, "The History of the Flapper, Part 3: The Rectangular Silhouette," *Smithsonian Magazine*, February 19, 2003, accessed July 6, 2017, https://www.smithsonianmag.com/arts-culture/the-history-of-the-flapper-part-3-the-rectangular-silhouette-20328818/.

48. "Flatteners," in *Encyclopedia of Fashion*, accessed July 6, 2017, http://www.fashionencyclopedia.com/fashion_costume_culture/Modern-World-1919-1929/Flatteners.html.

49. Eliza Berman, "This Is What the Ideal Woman Looked Like in the 1930s," *Time*, July 2, 2015, accessed July 5, 2017, http://time.com/3860561/ideal-woman-1930s/.

50. "The 'Perfect' Body: 100 Years of Our Changing Shape," *Today*, last modified February 24, 2014, accessed November 25, 2017, https://www.today.com/slideshow/perfect-body -100-years-our-changing-shape-54454777.

51. Lecia Bushak, "History of Body Image in America: How the 'Ideal' Female and Male Body Has Changed over Time," *Medical Daily*, November 6, 2015, accessed July 4, 2017, https://www.medicaldaily.com/history-body-image-america-how-ideal-female-and-male -body-has-changed-over-360492.

52. Amy Graff, "'Don't Let Them Call You Skinny': Vintage Ads Push Women to Gain Weight," *SFGate*, July 16, 2012, accessed September 25, 2019, https://blog.sfgate .com/sfmoms/2012/07/16/dont-let-them-call-you-skinny-vintage-ads-push-women-to-gain -weight/#photo-129217.

53. Kenneth T. Walsh, "The 1960s: A Decade of Promise and Heartbreak," *US News & World Report*, March 9, 2010, accessed November 10, 2019, https://www.usnews.com/news/ articles/2010/03/09/the-1960s-a-decade-of-promise-and-heartbreak.

54. Bruce J. Schulman, *The Seventies: The Great Shift in American Culture, Society, and Politics* (New York: Free Press, 2001), 1.

55. "Dieting through the Decades: What We've Learned from Fads," *Shape*, accessed July 5, 2017, https://www.shape.com/blogs/weight-loss-coach/dieting-through-decades-what -weve-learned-fads.

56. Elise Taylor, "Farrah Fawcett Almost Didn't Get to Wear Her Iconic Red Swim-suit," *Vanity Fair*, August 27, 2015, accessed August 30, 2019, https://www.vanityfair.com/ style/2015/08/farrah-fawcett-red-swimsuit-bruce-mcbroom-history-of-fashion.

57. Richard McKenzie, "Decade of Greed?," *National Review*, June 10, 2004, accessed July 5, 2017, https://www.nationalreview.com/2004/06/decade-greed-richard-mckenzie/.

58. "The 'Perfect' Body: 100 Years of Our Changing Shape," *Today*.

59. Lauren Valenti, "The Supermodels of the 1980s," *Marie Claire*, April 7, 2014, accessed March 15, 2020, https://www.marieclaire.com/fashion/g2168/supermodels-of-the-80s/.

60. "Jane Fonda's First Workout Video Released," History.com, April 24, 1982, last modi-fied July 27, 2019, https://www.history.com/this-day-in-history/jane-fondas-first-workout -video-released.

61. Kurt Andersen, "The Best Decade Ever? The 1990s, Obviously," *New York Times*, February 6, 2015, accessed August 30, 2019, https://www.nytimes.com/2015/02/08/opinion/ sunday/the-best-decade-ever-the-1990s-obviously.html.

62. Ashley Lutz, "The Fashion World Is Embracing 'Heroin Chic' Again," *Business Insider*, September 6, 2012, accessed September 19, 2019, https://www.businessinsider.com/heroin -chic-looks-at-new-york-fashion-week-2012-9.

63. Louise Lague, "How Thin Is Too Thin?," *People*, September 20, 1993, accessed August 2, 2017, https://people.com/archive/cover-story-how-thin-is-too-thin-vol-40-no-12/.

64. Michael S. James, "The 2000s: A Decade of Doom or Diversions?," *ABC News*, November 25, 2009, accessed November 25, 2017, https://abcnews.go.com/Technology/ Decade/defining-2000s-decade-doom-digital-divas/story?id=9174978.

65. Bushak, "History of Body Image in America: How the 'Ideal' Female and Male Body Has Changed over Time."

66. Elizabeth Angell, "What's Beautiful Now?," *Allure*, March 29, 2011, accessed August 1, 2017, https://www.allure.com/story/whats-beautiful-now.

CHAPTER 5

1. Nathaniel Rich, "American Dreams: 'The Stepford Wives' by Ira Levin," *Daily Beast*, August 24, 2012, accessed August 1, 2017, https://www.thedailybeast.com/american-dreams -the-stepford-wives-by-ira-levin.

2. Margaret Talbot, "A Stepford for Our Times," *Atlantic*, December 2003, accessed July 4, 2017, https://www.theatlantic.com/magazine/archive/2003/12/a-stepford-for-our -times/302852/.

3. "The Stepford Syndrome," WebMD, accessed July 3, 2017, https://www.webmd.com/ beauty/features/stepford-syndrome#1.

4. "The Stepford Syndrome," WebMD.

5. "A Perfect Wife . . . until 6 p.m.," Lysol Disinfectant for Feminine Hygiene, https:// i.pinimg.com/736x/6f/36/43/6f3643072eeaa8e9a7dd31b9653d5bb5.jpg.

6. Mya Frazier, "Honor Your Mother: Don't Watch That Patronizing Viral Ad," *New Republic*, May 8, 2014, accessed July 3, 2017, https://newrepublic.com/article/117693/mothers -advertising-regressive-stereotypes-dominate-pg-and-others.

7. Frazier, "Honor Your Mother: Don't Watch That Patronizing Viral Ad."

8. "Gender Advertisement," in *Wikipedia*, last modified June 3, 2019, accessed August 31, 2019, https://en.wikipedia.org/wiki/Gender_advertisement.

9. Sandra Moriarty et al., *Advertising & IMC: Principles and Practice*, 11th ed. (Hoboken, NJ: Pearson, 2019), 545.

10. Lawrence T. White, "Does Advertising Content Reflect or Shape Societal Values?," *Psychology Today*, December 26, 2015, accessed July 3, 2017, https://www.psychologytoday.com/ us/blog/culture-conscious/201512/does-advertising-content-reflect-or-shape-societal-values.

11. White, "Does Advertising Content Reflect or Shape Societal Values?"

12. White, "Does Advertising Content Reflect or Shape Societal Values?"

13. White, "Does Advertising Content Reflect or Shape Societal Values?"

14. White, "Does Advertising Content Reflect or Shape Societal Values?"

15. Michael R. Solomon, *Consumer Behavior: Buying, Having, and Being*, 12th ed. (Hoboken, NJ: Pearson, 2016), 182.

16. Mimi Minnick, "Breck Girls," *Smithsonian Magazine*, January 1, 2000, accessed July 4, 2017, https://www.smithsonianmag.com/arts-culture/breck-girls-60936753/#1Q7YV mcd8Tk4iUbi.99.

17. Minnick, "Breck Girls."

18. Victoria L. Sherrow, *For Appearance Sake: The Historical Encyclopedia of Good Looks, Beauty, and Grooming* (Westport, CT: Greenwood, 2001), 66–68.

19. Jesa Marie Calaor, "Beauty by Numbers: 12 Fun Facts Shampoo and Its History," *Allure*, February 16, 2018, accessed November 15, 2019, https://www.allure.com/story/ shampoo-facts-history.

20. Darlene Gavron, "Portrait of the Times Is Winner," *Chicago Tribune*, July 17, 1988, accessed August 8, 2019, https://www.chicagotribune.com/news/ct-xpm-1988-07-17 -8801160123-story.html.

21. "Chris Evans for Gucci Guilty Pour Homme Fragrance," Design Scene, accessed August 31, 2019, https://www.designscene.net/2010/12/chris-evans-gucci-guilty-pour-homme -fragrance.html.

22. "Axe Excite: Angels," *Advertising Age*, January 30, 2011, accessed September 20, 2019, https://adage.com/creativity/work/angels/22274.

23. "Axe/Lynx Excite Variant—Even Angels Will Fall Making-of," Ad Forum, BBH London, United Kingdom, accessed August 16, 2019, https://www.adforum.com/creative-work/ad/player/34462167/even-angels-will-fall-making-of/axelynx-excite-variant.

24. Lindsay Goldwert, "Axe 'Angels' Deodorant Ad Yanked for Offending Christians," *New York Daily News*, October 29, 2011, accessed July 4, 2017, http://www.nydailynews.com/life-style/fashion/axe-angels-deodorant-ad-yanked-offending-christians-article-1.968858.

25. N., Pam M.S., "Gender Role," in *PsychologyDictionary.org*, May 11, 2013, accessed August 31, 2019, https://psychologydictionary.org/gender-role/.

26. Sue Lafky, Margaret Duffy, Mary Steinmaus, and Dan Berkowitz, "Looking through Gendered Lenses: Female Stereotyping in Advertisements and Gender Role Expectations," *Journalism and Mass Communication Quarterly* 73, no. 2 (1996): 379–88, accessed July 8, 2017. doi: 10.1177/107769909607300209.

27. Lafky et al., "Looking through Gendered Lenses: Female Stereotyping in Advertisements and Gender Role Expectations," 386.

28. Dodai Stewart, "Max Factor: The Man Behind the Makeup," *Jezebel*, August 25, 2008, accessed August 16, 2019, https://jezebel.com/max-factor-the-man-behind-the-makeup-5041399.

29. Erving Goffman, *Gender Advertisements* (New York: Harper & Row, 1979), 1.

30. Goffman, *Gender Advertisements*, 15.

31. Solomon, *Consumer Behavior: Buying, Having, and Being*, 12th ed., 224.

32. "Archetype/Stereotype," *Advertising Age*, September 15, 2003, accessed July 3, 2017, http://adage.com/article/adage-encyclopedia/archetype-stereotype/98323/.

33. Sandra Moriarty et al., *Advertising: Principles and Practice*, 11th ed., 545.

34. Mary Lou Roberts and Perri B. Koggan, "How Should Women Be Portrayed in Advertisements?—A Call for Research," *NA—Advances in Consumer Research* 06 (1979): 66–72, http://acrwebsite.org/volumes/9532/volumes/v06/NA-06.

35. Young Entrepreneur Council, "Is Your Brand a Rebel, Lover or Hero?," *Inc.*, April 24, 2015, accessed July 3, 2017, https://www.inc.com/young-entrepreneur-council/is-your-brand-a-rebel-lover-or-hero.html; Solomon, *Consumer Behavior: Buying, Having, and Being*, 12th ed., 224–26; 255; Margaret Mark and Carol S. Pearson, *The Hero and the Outlaw: Building Extraordinary Brands Through the Power of Archetypes* (New York: McGraw-Hill, 2001); Carol S. Pearson, "Branding," Archetypal Narrative Intelligence, accessed July 3, 2017, http://www.carolspearson.com/archetypal-branding/archetypes/organizational-branding/.

36. "50+ Sexist Vintage Ads So Bad, You Almost Won't Believe They Were Real," Click Americana, accessed August 16, 2019, https://clickamericana.com/topics/culture-and-lifestyle/50-sexist-vintage-ads-so-bad-you-almost-wont-believe-they-were-real.

37. Carol S. Pearson, "Caregiver," Archetypal Narrative Intelligence, http://www.carolspearson.com/archetypes/caregiver/.

38. Johnson & Johnson Consumer Inc., "Our Mission," last modified July 9, 2018, accessed August 16, 2019, https://www.johnsonsbaby.com/our-mission.

39. Carol S. Pearson, "Innocent," Archetypal Narrative Intelligence, http://www.carolspearson.com/archetypes/innocent/.

40. Unilever USA, "Personal Care—Dove," accessed August 16, 2019, https://www.unileverusa.com/brands/personal-care/dove.html.

41. Carol S. Pearson, "Lover," Archetypal Narrative Intelligence, http://www.carolspearson.com/archetypes/lover/.

42. Michael Ochs Archives, "Marilyn Monroe with Chanel No. 5," Photos.com by Getty Images, accessed August 16, 2019, https://photos.com/featured/marilyn-monroe-with-chanel -no-5-michael-ochs-archives.html.

43. Carol S. Pearson, "Magician," Archetypal Narrative Intelligence, http://www.carol spearson.com/archetypes/magician/.

44. Tim Nudd, "Ad of the Day: Axe Gets Inclusive in a Remarkable Ad That's Really Pretty Magical," *Adweek*, January 14, 2016, accessed November 23, 2017, https://www .adweek.com/brand-marketing/ad-day-axe-gets-inclusive-remarkable-ad-thats-really-pretty -magical-168996/.

45. Yorgos C. Zotos and Eirini Tsichla, "Female Stereotypes in Print Advertising: A Retro- spective Analysis," *Procedia—Social and Behavioral Sciences* 148 (2014): 446, accessed July 3, 2017, doi: 10.1016/j.sbspro.2014.07.064.

46. "Feminism, Impact of," *Advertising Age*, September 15, 2003, accessed July 2, 2017, http://adage.com/article/adage-encyclopedia/feminism-impact/98471/.

47. "Women: Representations in Advertising." *Advertising Age*, September 15, 2003, ac- cessed July 3, 2017, http://adage.com/article/adage-encyclopedia/women-representations -advertising/98938/.

48. "Feminism, Impact of," *Advertising Age*.

49. Naomi Wolf, *The Beauty Myth: How Images of Beauty Are Used Against Women* (New York: Harper Perennial, 2002), 187.

50. Susan Wojcicki, "Ads That Empower Women Don't Just Break Stereotypes—They're Also Effective," *Adweek*, April 24, 2016, accessed July 3, 2017, https://www.adweek .com/brand-marketing/ads-empower-women-don-t-just-break-stereotypes-they-re-also -effective-170953/.

51. Mattie Kahn, "Always Redefines What It Means to 'Run Like a Girl,'" *ABC News*, July 1, 2014, accessed August 12, 2019, https://abcnews.go.com/Lifestyle/redefines-means-run -girl/story?id=24377039.

52. Wojcicki, "Ads That Empower Women Don't Just Break Stereotypes—They're Also Effective."

53. Abigail Beall, "Gender Stereotypes Are Holding Strong: Beliefs about the Roles of Men and Women Are 'as Firmly Held Now as They Were in 1980,'" *Daily Mail*, last modified March 9, 2016, accessed August 31, 2019, https://www.dailymail.co.uk/sciencetech/article-3482589/ Gender-stereotypes-holding-strong-Beliefs-roles-men-women-firmly-held-1980.html.

54. Elizabeth L. Haines, Kay Deaux, and Nicole Lofaro, "The Times They Are A- Changing . . . or Are They Not? A Comparison of Gender Stereotypes, 1983–2014," *Psy- chology of Women Quarterly* 40, no. 3 (2016): 353–63, accessed July 2, 2017, doi: 10.1177/ 0361684316634081.

55. Leonie Roderick, "Brands Face Crackdown on Gender Stereotypes in Advertis- ing," *Marketing Week*, July 18, 2017, accessed July 30, 2017, https://www.marketingweek .com/2017/07/18/brands-stricter-rules-gender-stereotypes/.

56. Advertising Standards Authority, "Depictions, Perceptions and Harm: A Report on Gender Stereotypes in Advertising," last modified October 9, 2017, accessed November 1, 2017, https://www.asa.org.uk/genderresearch.html.

57. "'Harmful' Gender Stereotypes in Adverts Banned," *BBC News*, June 14, 2019, ac- cessed September 1, 2019, https://www.bbc.com/news/business-48628678.

58. "'Harmful' Gender Stereotypes in Adverts Banned," *BBC News*.

59. European Association of Communications Agencies, "Gender Portrayal and Stereotyping," accessed July 2, 2017, http://eaca.eu/wp-content/uploads/2018/03/Position-paper-gender-2018.pdf.

60. European Association of Communications Agencies, "Statement of Gender Portrayal," accessed July 29, 2019, https://eaca.eu/wp-content/uploads/2018/03/EACA-position-statement-2018.pdf.

61. Rachel Gee, "The Representation of Women in Advertising Hasn't Improved in a Decade," *Marketing Week*, June 21, 2017, accessed July 2, 2017, https://www.marketingweek.com/2017/06/21/representation-women-ads/.

62. Gee, "The Representation of Women in Advertising Hasn't Improved in a Decade."

63. J. Walter Thompson Worldwide, "Unpacking Gender Bias in Advertising," June 21, 2017, accessed July 31, 2017, https://www.jwt.com/en/news/unpacking-gender-bias-in-advertising.

64. Unilever, "Launch of Unstereotype Alliance Set to Eradicate Outdated Stereotypes in Advertising," Unilever press release, June 20, 2017, accessed September 1, 2019, https://www.unilever.com/news/Press-releases/2017/launch-of-unstereotype-alliance-set-to-eradicate-outdated-stereotypes-in-advertising.html.

65. Claire Zillman, "How Some of the World's Biggest Brands Are Fighting Sexism in Advertising," *Fortune*, June 20, 2017, accessed July 4, 2017, http://fortune.com/2017/06/20/advertising-gender-stereotypes/.

66. Mark Sweney, "Unilever Vows to Drop Sexist Stereotypes from Its Ads," *Guardian*, June 22, 2016, accessed July 2, 2017, https://www.theguardian.com/media/2016/jun/22/unilever-sexist-stereotypes-ads-sunsilk-dove-lynx.

67. Sweney, "Unilever Vows to Drop Sexist Stereotypes from Its Ads."

68. Kristina Monllos and Patrick Coffee, "Why the U.S. Ad Industry Will Never Regulate Gender Stereotypes," *Adweek*, July 20, 2017, accessed July 20, 2017, https://www.adweek.com/brand-marketing/why-the-u-s-ad-industry-will-never-regulate-gender-stereotypes/.

69. Monllos and Coffee, "Why the U.S. Ad Industry Will Never Regulate Gender Stereotypes."

CHAPTER 6

1. "1980: Brooke Shields Sparks Controversy in Calvin Klein Jeans," 4A's, accessed September 1, 2019, https://www.aaaa.org/timeline-event/brooke-shields-sparks-controversy-calvin-klein-jeans/.

2. "Perfume," *Advertising Age*, September 15, 2003, accessed July 2, 2017, http://adage.com/article/adage-encyclopedia/perfume/98816/.

3. "David Lynch: Commercials, Ads and Promos," LynchNet: The David Lynch Resource, accessed August 5, 2018, http://www.lynchnet.com/ads/.

4. Paul Farhi, "Obsession for 'Twin Peaks,'" *Washington Post*, August 16, 1990, accessed July 19, 2018, https://www.washingtonpost.com/archive/lifestyle/1990/08/16/obsession-for-twin-peaks/8c83b84a-2d10-4c58-aacf-7987c1c9e28e/.

5. Kim Foltz, "The Media Business: Advertising; A New Twist for Klein's Obsession," *New York Times*, August 15, 1990, accessed July 19, 2018, https://www.nytimes.com/1990/08/15/business/the-media-business-advertising-a-new-twist-for-klein-s-obsession.html.

6. Nicole Phelps, "Sex Sells: Calvin Klein's 1990s Ads Stirred Libidos and Controversies in Equal Measure," *Vogue*, September 1, 2015, accessed July 2, 2017, https://www.vogue.com/article/calvin-klein-jeans-90s-ads-kate-moss-mark-wahlberg-controversy.

7. Steff Yotka, "Calvin Klein's New Campaign Proves There's No Age Limit to Being an Underwear Model," *Vogue*, April 18, 2017, accessed July 2, 2017, https://www.vogue.com/article/calvin-klein-lauren-hutton-underwear-ads.

8. "Calvin Klein, Inc.—Company Profile, Information, Business Description, History, Background Information on Calvin Klein Inc.," in *Reference for Business*, accessed August 15, 2019, https://www.referenceforbusiness.com/history2/92/Calvin-Klein-Inc.html.

9. Kelly McCarthy, "Calvin Klein's New, Racy Ad Campaign Sparks Controversy," *ABC News*, May 12, 2016, accessed July 2, 2017, https://abcnews.go.com/Lifestyle/calvin-kleins-racy-ad-campaign-sparks-controversy/story?id=39057405.

10. John McDonough and Karen Egolf, *The Advertising Age Encyclopedia of Advertising*, 1st ed. (New York: Routledge, 2002), 410.

11. "Cosmetics," *Advertising Age*, September 15, 2003, accessed July 5, 2017, https://adage.com/article/adage-encyclopedia/cosmetics/98419.

12. McDonough and Egolf, *The Advertising Age Encyclopedia of Advertising*, 410.

13. McDonough and Egolf, *The Advertising Age Encyclopedia of Advertising*, 407.

14. "Cosmetics," *Advertising Age*.

15. Ellen Gartrell, "Emergence of Advertising in America: 1850–1920, Pond's Advertisements," John W. Hartman Center for Sales, Advertising & Marketing History, Duke University Rare Book, Manuscript, and Special Collections Library, accessed August 9, 2019, https://library.duke.edu/rubenstein/scriptorium/eaa/ponds.html.

16. "Cosmetics," *Advertising Age*.

17. Juliann Sivulka, *Soap, Sex, and Cigarettes: A Cultural History of American Advertising*, 2nd ed. (Boston: Wadsworth, 2012), 56.

18. Sivulka, *Soap, Sex, and Cigarettes*, 57–58.

19. Sivulka, *Soap, Sex, and Cigarettes*, 56.

20. "Cosmetics," *Advertising Age*.

21. Sivulka, *Soap, Sex, and Cigarettes*, 60–61.

22. Sivulka, *Soap, Sex, and Cigarettes*, 64–65.

23. "Cosmetics," *Advertising Age*.

24. Julie Willett, ed., *The American Beauty Industry Encyclopedia* (Westport, CT: Greenwood, 2010), 71.

25. Sivulka, *Soap, Sex, and Cigarettes*, 104–5.

26. McDonough and Egolf, *The Advertising Age Encyclopedia of Advertising*, 409.

27. Kathy Peiss, *Hope in a Jar: The Making of America's Beauty Culture* (Philadelphia: University of Pennsylvania Press, 2011), 105.

28. Alys Eve Weinbaum et al., eds., *The Modern Girl Around the World: Consumption, Modernity, and Globalization* (Durham, NC: Duke University Press, 2008), 32.

29. Jeff Suess, "Our History: Odorono Ads Made Us Realize We Needed Deodorant," *USA Today*, last modified February 14, 2017, accessed July 6, 2017, https://www.usatoday.com/story/news/2017/02/14/odorono-ads-made-us-realize-we-needed-deodorant/97922010/.

30. "Cosmetics," *Advertising Age*.

31. James Bennett, "Max Factor," Cosmetics and Skin, last modified March 30, 2018, accessed July 27, 2018, http://www.cosmeticsandskin.com/companies/max-factor.php.

32. "Cosmetics," *Advertising Age*.

33. "Anthony Overton," in *Wikipedia*, modified August 8, 2018, accessed July 27, 2017, https://en.wikipedia.org/wiki/Anthony_Overton.

34. "Cosmetics," *Advertising Age*.

35. "Cosmetics," *Advertising Age*.

36. "Cosmetics," *Advertising Age*.

37. "1930s USA Camay Magazine Advert," Advertising Archives, accessed August 16, 2019, http://www.advertisingarchives.co.uk/index.php?service=search&action=do_quick_search&language=en&q=camay.

38. "Cosmetics," *Advertising Age*.

39. Sivulka, *Soap, Sex, and Cigarettes*, 180–81.

40. "Women: Representations in Advertising," *Advertising Age*, September 15, 2003, accessed July 3, 2017, http://adage.com/article/adage-encyclopedia/women-representations-advertising/98938/.

41. "Cosmetics," *Advertising Age*.

42. Max Factor, "A Glamorous NOW . . . a lovelier TOMORROW" (1947), Duke University Libraries Digital Repository, John W. Hartman Center for Sales, Advertising & Marketing History, accessed August 17, 2019, https://idn.duke.edu/ark:/87924/r4wd3qn8g.

43. "Cosmetics," *Advertising Age*.

44. "Cosmetics," *Advertising Age*.

45. Lesley Goldberg, "Jessica Biel Goes Glam for Revlon," *Hollywood Reporter*, November 13, 2010, accessed September 1, 2019, https://www.hollywoodreporter.com/news/jessica-biel-glam-revlon-44803.

46. "Bristol-Myers Squibb Co.," *Advertising Age*, September 15, 2003, accessed August 21, 2018, https://adage.com/article/adage-encyclopedia/bristol-myers-squibb/98360.

47. "Sex in Advertising," *Advertising Age*, September 15, 2003, accessed July 2, 2017, http://adage.com/article/adage-encyclopedia/sex-advertising/98878/adage.com/article/adage-encyclopedia/sex-advertising/98878/.

48. "Cosmetics," *Advertising Age*.

49. James Bennett, "Cover Girl," Cosmetics and Skin, last modified February 28, 2018, accessed August 17, 2019, http://www.cosmeticsandskin.com/companies/cover-girl.php.

50. James Bennett, "Yardley (post-1945)," Cosmetics and Skin, last modified January 22, 2018, accessed August 17, 2019, http://cosmeticsandskin.com/companies/yardley-1945.php.

51. "Cosmetics," *Advertising Age*.

52. Nadia Mustafa, "Iman," *Time*, February 9, 2004, accessed July 5, 2017, http://content.time.com/time/specials/packages/article/0,28804,2015519_2015510_2015477,00.html.

53. "Behind the Color, Legacy," Revlon, accessed August 17, 2019, http://en.revlon.com.hk/behind-the-color/legacy.

54. "Perfume," *Advertising Age*.

55. "Supermodel," in *Wikipedia*, last modified September 6, 2018, accessed July 19, 2018, https://en.wikipedia.org/wiki/Supermodel.

56. Kim Foltz, "All About/Cover Girls; The Look That Sells Is Both Girl-Next-Door and Celebrity," *New York Times*, May 24, 1992, accessed July 19, 2018, https://www.nytimes.com/1992/05/24/business/all-about-cover-girls-the-look-that-sells-is-both-girl-next-door-and-celebrity.html.

57. "Cosmetics," *Advertising Age.*

58. Caitlin Heikkila, "21 Beauty Products That Every '80s Kid Remembers," *Allure*, August 18, 2015, accessed August 9, 2019, https://www.allure.com/gallery/80s-beauty-products.

59. Brian Galindo, "'Noxzema Girl' Was Rebecca Gayheart's Biggest Contribution to the '90s," *BuzzFeed*, March 25, 2013, accessed August 17, 2019, https://www.buzzfeed.com/briangalindo/noxzema-girl-was-rebecca-gayhearts-biggest-contribution-to-t.

60. David Ogilvy, *Ogilvy on Advertising* (New York: Vintage Books, 1985), 25–30.

61. McDonough and Egolf, *The Advertising Age Encyclopedia of Advertising*, 1432.

62. Ogilvy, *Ogilvy on Advertising*, 28.

63. Ogilvy, *Ogilvy on Advertising*, 25.

64. Ogilvy, *Ogilvy on Advertising*, 25–26.

65. Sheila Shayon, "CoverGirl Redefines Role Models with Diversity, Inclusivity," Brandchannel, November 3, 2016, accessed July 4, 2017, https://www.brandchannel.com/2016/11/03/covergirl-diversity-inclusivity-110316/.

66. Deanna Pai, "CoverGirl's New Brand Ambassador Is Muslim Beauty Blogger Nura Afia," *Glamour*, November 2, 2016, accessed September 2, 2019, https://www.glamour.com/story/covergirl-nura-afia-muslim-beauty-blogger.

67. Kristina Monllos, "Brands Are Throwing Out Gender Norms to Reflect a More Fluid World," *Adweek*, October 17, 2016, accessed July 4, 2017, https://www.adweek.com/brand-marketing/brands-are-throwing-out-gender-norms-reflect-more-fluid-world-174070/.

68. Imogen Matthews, "Genderless Beauty Creates New Opportunities for Brands," Cosmetics Business, April 18, 2017, accessed July 31, 2017, https://www.cosmeticsbusiness.com/news/article_page/Genderless_beauty_creates_new_opportunities_for_brands/128205.

69. Saskia De Melker, "Researchers Measure Increasing Sexualization of Images in Magazines," PBS, December 28, 2013, accessed July 1, 2017, https://www.pbs.org/newshour/nation/social_issues-july-dec13-sexualization_12-21.

70. De Melker, "Researchers Measure Increasing Sexualization of Images in Magazines."

71. De Melker, "Researchers Measure Increasing Sexualization of Images in Magazines."

72. De Melker, "Researchers Measure Increasing Sexualization of Images in Magazines."

73. De Melker, "Researchers Measure Increasing Sexualization of Images in Magazines."

74. Evangelia Papadaki, edited by Edward N. Zalta, "Feminist Perspectives on Objectification," in *Stanford Encyclopedia of Philosophy*, last modified December 1, 2015, accessed July 18, 2018, https://plato.stanford.edu/archives/sum2018/entries/feminism-objectification/.

75. Martha C. Nussbaum, "Objectification," *Philosophy and Public Affairs* 24, no. 4 (1995): 257, accessed July 2, 2017, doi: 10.1111/j.1088-4963.1995.tb00032.x.

76. Papadaki and Zalta, "Feminist Perspectives on Objectification."

77. Barbara L. Fredrickson and Tomi-Ann Roberts, "Objectification Theory: Toward Understanding Women's Lived Experiences and Mental Health Risks," *Psychology of Women Quarterly* 21, no. 2 (1997): 173–206, accessed July 2, 2017, doi: 10.1111/j.1471-6402.1997.tb00108.x.

78. Roy F. Baumeister and Kathleen D. Vohs, eds., "Objectification Theory," in *Encyclopedia of Social Psychology*, 631, http://dx.doi.org/10.4135/9781412956253.n377.

79. Baumeister and Vohs, eds., "Objectification Theory," 631.

80. Jean Kilbourne, *Killing Us Softly 4: Advertising's Image of Women*, Media Education Foundation, accessed August 21, 2018, https://shop.mediaed.org/killing-us-softly-4-p47.aspx.

81. Kendra Hodgson, Jeremy Earp, and Jason Young, eds., *Media Education Foundation Study Guide: Killing Us Softly 4: Advertising's Image of Women* (Media Education Foundation), 3.

82. Erving Goffman, *Gender Advertisements* (New York: Harper & Row, 1979), 24.

83. Goffman, *Gender Advertisements*, 28–29.

84. Goffman, *Gender Advertisements*, 29–31.

85. Goffman, *Gender Advertisements*, 32–37.

86. Goffman, *Gender Advertisements*, 40–56.

87. Goffman, *Gender Advertisements*, 57–83.

88. Goffman, *Gender Advertisements*, 65.

89. Goffman. *Gender Advertisements*, 84.

90. Dana Heller, ed., *Makeover Television: Realities Remodelled* (London: I. B. Tauris, 2007), 183.

91. Jean Kilbourne, "Beauty . . . and the Beast of Advertising," *Media & Values: Redesigning Women* 49 (Winter 1990), accessed July 1, 2017, https://www.medialit.org/media-values.

92. "Self-objectification," in *Wikipedia*, last modified March 29, 2018, accessed June 15, 2018, https://en.wikipedia.org/wiki/Self-objectification.

93. Kilbourne, "Beauty . . . and the Beast of Advertising."

94. Kilbourne, "Beauty . . . and the Beast of Advertising."

95. Sandra Moriarty et al., *Advertising & IMC: Principles and Practice*, 11th ed. (Hoboken, NJ: Pearson, 2019), 126.

96. Caitlin Johnson, "Cutting through Advertising Clutter," *CBS News*, September 17, 2006, accessed July 1, 2017, https://www.cbsnews.com/news/cutting-through-advertising-clutter/.

97. Johnson, "Cutting through Advertising Clutter."

98. Jeanette Mulvey, "Why Sex Sells . . . More Than Ever," *Business News Daily*, June 7, 2012, accessed July 1, 2017, https://www.businessnewsdaily.com/2649-sex-sells-more.html.

99. Mulvey, "Why Sex Sells . . . More Than Ever."

100. Mulvey, "Why Sex Sells . . . More Than Ever."

101. Mulvey, "Why Sex Sells . . . More Than Ever."

102. Mulvey, "Why Sex Sells . . . More Than Ever."

103. Mulvey, "Why Sex Sells . . . More Than Ever."

104. Michael R. Solomon, *Consumer Behavior: Buying, Having, and Being*, 12th ed., (Hoboken, NJ: Pearson, 2016), 298.

105. Emma Bazilian, "Ad of the Day: Liquid-Plumr Gives Housewives More Erotic Cleaning Fantasies," *Adweek*, July 25, 2013, accessed August 17, 2019, https://www.adweek.com/brand-marketing/ad-day-liquid-plumr-gives-housewives-more-erotic-cleaning-fantasies-151441/.

106. Amanda Zimmerman and John Dahlberg, "The Sexual Objectification of Women in Advertising: A Contemporary Cultural Perspective," *Journal of Advertising Research* 48, no. 1 (2008), accessed July 2, 2017, doi: 10.2501/S0021849908080094.

107. Zimmerman and Dahlberg, "The Sexual Objectification of Women in Advertising: A Contemporary Cultural Perspective," 77.

108. Darren W. Dahl, Jaideep Sengupta, and Kathleen D. Vohs, "Sex in Advertising: Gender Differences and the Role of Relationship Commitment," *Journal of Consumer Research* 36, no. 2 (2009): 216, accessed July 1, 2017, doi: 10.1086/597158.

109. Dahl, Sengupta, and Vohs, "Sex in Advertising," 215–31.

110. Dahl, Sengupta, and Vohs, "Sex in Advertising," 228.

111. Remy Melina, "How Advertisements Seduce Your Brain," *Live Science*, September 11, 2011, accessed September 2, 2019, https://www.livescience.com/16169-advertisements-seduce-brain.html.

112. Ian A. Cook et al., "Regional Brain Activation with Advertising Images," *Journal of Neuroscience, Psychology, and Economics* 4, no. 3 (2011), 147–60, accessed July 28, 2019, doi: 10.1037/a0024809.

113. "Sex DOES Sell . . . and Here's Why: Attractive Men and Women in Adverts Affect Our Capacity for Rational Thought," *Daily Mail*, September 22, 2011, accessed July 1, 2017, http://www.dailymail.co.uk/sciencetech/article-2040218/Sex-DOES-sell-Attractive-men-women-ads-affect-capacity-rational-thought.html.

114. "Sex DOES Sell . . . and Here's Why," *Daily Mail*.

115. "Sex DOES Sell . . . and Here's Why," *Daily Mail*.

116. Dean Nelson, "India Bans 'Overtly Sexual' Deodorant Ads," *Telegraph*, May 27, 2011, accessed July 2, 2017, https://www.telegraph.co.uk/news/worldnews/asia/india/8541292/India-bans-overtly-sexual-deodorant-ads.html.

117. Stephanie Holmes, "Scandinavian Split on Sexist Ads," *BBC News*, April 25, 2008, accessed July 2, 2017, http://news.bbc.co.uk/2/hi/europe/7365722.stm.

118. Holmes, "Scandinavian Split on Sexist Ads."

119. Barbara Mueller, *Dynamics of International Advertising: Theoretical and Practical Perspectives*, 2nd ed. (New York: Peter Lang, 2011), 312.

120. "Our Purpose and Strategy," Advertising Standards Authority, accessed August 11, 2019, https://www.asa.org.uk/about-asa-and-cap/about-regulation/our-purpose-and-strategy.html.

121. Mark Sweney, "Standards Body Unveils Plan to Crack Down on Sexist Advertisements," *Guardian*, July 17, 2017, accessed July 30, 2017, https://www.theguardian.com/media/2017/jul/18/new-measures-announced-to-crack-down-on-sexist-adverts.

122. European Advertising Standards Alliance, "Welcome to EASA," accessed October 12, 2019, https://www.easa-alliance.org/.

123. "Sexism," in *Wikipedia*, last modified July 12, 2019, accessed August 9, 2019, https://en.wikipedia.org/wiki/Sexism.

124. "Rihanna Rogue Perfume Ad Restricted Due to 'Sexually Suggestive' Image," *Guardian*, June 4, 2014, accessed July 1, 2017, https://www.theguardian.com/media/2014/jun/04/rihanna-rogue-perfume-ad-restricted-sexually-suggestive.

125. "Rihanna Rogue Perfume Ad Restricted Due to 'Sexually Suggestive' Image," *Guardian*.

126. "#WomenNotObjects," by Badger & Winters, posted on YouTube on January 11, 2016, accessed October 12, 2019, https://www.youtube.com/watch?v=5J31AT7viqo.

127. Emanuella Grinberg, "How to Create Ads That Don't Objectify Women," CNN, last modified February 18, 2016, accessed July 4, 2017, https://www.cnn.com/style/article/women-not-objects-madonna-badger-feat/index.html.

128. Grinberg, "How to Create Ads That Don't Objectify Women."

129. Lindsay Stein, "Cannes Bans Gender Bias with Help from #WomenNotObjects," *Ad Age*, February 6, 2017, accessed July 1, 2017, http://adage.com/article/agency-news/cannes-bannes-gender-bias-womennotobjects/307847/.

CHAPTER 7

1. Ellen Thomas, "Pantene Signs Priyanka Chopra for 'Strong Is Beautiful' Campaign," *Los Angeles Times*, December 22, 2016, accessed July 24, 2017, http://www.latimes.com/fashion/la-ig-wwd-pantene-priyanka-chopra-20161220-story.html.

2. Olivier Driessens, "Celebrity Capital: Redefining Celebrity Using Field Theory," *Theory and Society* 42, no. 5 (2013): 545, accessed July 24, 2017, doi: 10.1007/s11186-013-9202.

3. Driessens, "Celebrity Capital," 544.

4. Neal Gabler, "The Brief Half-Life of Celebrity," *New York Times*, October 16, 1994, accessed September 27, 2019, https://www.nytimes.com/1994/10/16/arts/the-brief-half-life-of-celebrity.html.

5. Driessens, "Celebrity Capital," 544.

6. Barrie Gunter, *Celebrity Capital: Assessing the Value of Fame* (London: Bloomsbury, 2014), 2.

7. Gunter, *Celebrity Capital*, 35.

8. Jill Neimark, "The Culture of Celebrity," *Psychology Today*, May 1, 1995, accessed July 24, 2017, https://www.psychologytoday.com/us/articles/199505/the-culture-celebrity.

9. Grant McCracken, "Who Is the Celebrity Endorser? Cultural Foundations of the Endorsement Process," *Journal of Consumer Research* 16, no. 3 (1989): 310–21, accessed July 24, 2017, doi: 10.1086/209217.

10. McCracken, "Who Is the Celebrity Endorser? Cultural Foundations of the Endorsement Process," 310–11.

11. Marissa G. Muller, "Katy Perry Wore Brand New CoverGirl Makeup to the 2017 Grammy Awards," *Self*, February 12, 2017, accessed July 26, 2017, https://www.self.com/story/katy-perry-covergirl-makeup-2017-grammy-awards.

12. McCracken, "Who Is the Celebrity Endorser? Cultural Foundations of the Endorsement Process," 311.

13. McCracken, "Who Is the Celebrity Endorser? Cultural Foundations of the Endorsement Process," 311.

14. P. David Marshall and Sean Redmond, eds., *A Companion to Celebrity* (Hoboken, NJ: Wiley-Blackwell, 2015), 200.

15. "Social Listening," TrackMaven, accessed August 10, 2019, https://trackmaven.com/marketing-dictionary/social-listening/.

16. Michael R. Solomon, *Consumer Behavior: Buying, Having, and Being*, 12th ed. (Hoboken, NJ: Pearson, 2016), 394.

17. "French and Raven's Five Forms of Power," MindTools, accessed August 10, 2019, https://www.mindtools.com/pages/article/newLDR_56.htm.

18. McCracken, "Who Is the Celebrity Endorser? Cultural Foundations of the Endorsement Process," 310.

19. Deni Kirkova, "Are YOU Swayed by a Famous Face? Women Buy Twice as Many Celebrity-Endorsed Products as Men," *Daily Mail*, May 30, 2014, accessed July 27, 2017, http://www.dailymail.co.uk/femail/article-2641476/Susceptible-women-buy-twice-celebrity-endorsed-products-men.html#ixzz4rjgoLh7j.

20. Kirkova, "Are YOU Swayed by a Famous Face? Women Buy Twice as Many Celebrity-Endorsed Products as Men."

21. Kirkova, "Are YOU Swayed by a Famous Face? Women Buy Twice as Many Celebrity-Endorsed Products as Men."

22. Kirkova, "Are YOU Swayed by a Famous Face? Women Buy Twice as Many Celebrity-Endorsed Products as Men."

23. "How Important Are Celebrity Endorsements in Personal Care Purchases?," *Beauty Packaging*, August 12, 2015, accessed July 27, 2017, http://www.beautypackaging.com/contents/view_breaking-news/2015-08-12/how-important-are-celebrity-endorsements-in-personal-care-purchases.

24. "How Important Are Celebrity Endorsements in Personal Care Purchases?," *Beauty Packaging*.

25. "How to Get a Celebrity Endorsement from the Queen of England," with Harvard retail historian, Nancy Koehn, National Public Radio, May 21, 2012, accessed September 3, 2019, https://www.npr.org/sections/money/2012/05/21/153199679/how-to-get-a-celebrity-endorsement-from-the-queen-of-england.

26. C. Robert Clark and Ignatius J. Horstmann, "A Model of Advertising Format Competition: On the Use of Celebrities in Ads," *Canadian Journal of Economics/Revue Canadienne D'Economique* 46, no. 4 (2013): 1606–7, accessed July 24, 2017, doi: 10.1111/caje.12056.

27. Clark and Horstmann, "A Model of Advertising Format Competition," 1607.

28. "Why Peer-to-Peer Marketing Does More Than Celebrity Endorsements," *Adweek*, August 12, 2016, accessed July 11, 2017, https://www.adweek.com/digital/why-peer-to-peer-marketing-does-more-than-celebrity-endorsements/.

29. Hamish Pringle, *Celebrity Sells* (Hoboken, NJ: Wiley, 2004), xxiv.

30. Steve Olenski, "How Brands Should Use Celebrities for Endorsements," *Forbes*, July 20, 2016, accessed July 26, 2017, https://www.forbes.com/sites/steveolenski/2016/07/20/how-brands-should-use-celebrities-for-endorsements/#3e3c4b755593.

31. Anita Elberse and Jeroen Verleun, "The Economic Value of Celebrity Endorsements," *Journal of Advertising Research* 52, no. 2 (2012): 149–65, accessed July 24, 2017, doi: 10.2501/JAR-52-2-149-165.

32. Elberse and Verleun, "The Economic Value of Celebrity Endorsements," 163.

33. Wharton School of the University of Pennsylvania, "Celebrity Advertising: What Is the ROI?," Knowledge@Wharton, November 4, 2009, accessed July 24, 2017, http://knowledge.wharton.upenn.edu/article/celebrity-advertising-what-is-the-roi/.

34. Nam-Hyun Um, "The Role of Culture in Creative Execution in Celebrity Endorsement: The Cross-Cultural Study," *Journal of Global Marketing* 26, no. 3 (2013): 157, accessed July 24, 2017, doi: 10.1080/08911762.2013.804613.

35. Kevin Harrington, "Save Your Money: Celebrity Endorsements Not Worth the Cost," *Forbes*, January 31, 2014, accessed August 1, 2017, https://www.forbes.com/sites/kevinharrington/2014/01/31/save-your-money-celebrity-endorsements-not-worth-the-cost/#1120578c24f3.

36. Harrington, "Save Your Money."

37. Peter Daboll, "Celebrities in Advertising Are Almost Always a Big Waste of Money," *Advertising Age*, January 12, 2011, accessed August 1, 2017, http://adage.com/article/cmo-strategy/celebrities-ads-lead-greater-sales/148174/.

38. Daboll, "Celebrities in Advertising Are Almost Always a Big Waste of Money."

39. Mark McNeilly, "Is Celebrity Branding Worth the Price Tag?," *Fast Company*, January 22, 2013, accessed July 25, 2017, https://www.fastcompany.com/3004910/celebrity-branding-worth-price-tag.

40. McNeilly, "Is Celebrity Branding Worth the Price Tag?"

41. Utpal Dholakia, "Can a Celebrity Endorsement Hurt the Brand?," *Psychology Today*, November 3, 2015, accessed July 26, 2017, https://www.psychologytoday.com/us/blog/the -science-behind-behavior/201511/can-celebrity-endorsement-hurt-the-brand.

42. Julia Boorstin, "The Scent of Celebrity," *Fortune*, November 14, 2005, accessed July 27, 2017, http://archive.fortune.com/magazines/fortune/fortune_archive/2005/11/14/8360679/ index.htm.

43. Christine Lennon, "Beauty: Smiling for Dollars," *Time*, September 11, 2006, accessed July 26, 2017, http://content.time.com/time/magazine/article/0,9171,1533550,00.html.

44. Lennon, "Beauty: Smiling for Dollars."

45. Roshida Khanom, "The Evolution of Celebrity Endorsement in Beauty," Mintel (blog), April 12, 2017, accessed July 27, 2017, http://www.mintel.com/blog/beauty-market -news/the-evolution-of-celebrity-endorsement-in-beauty.

46. Khanom, "The Evolution of Celebrity Endorsement in Beauty."

47. Khanom, "The Evolution of Celebrity Endorsement in Beauty."

48. Katy Young, "All Hail the Pro-ageing Revolutionaries: The Celebrities Challenging Anti-ageing," *Telegraph*, April 15, 2015, accessed July 5, 2017, http://fashion.telegraph.co.uk/ beauty/news-features/TMG11537319/All-hail-the-pro-ageing-revolutionaries-the-celebrities -challenging-anti-ageing.html.

49. Ann-Christine Diaz, "Extreme Sports Athletes Put Bobbi Brown's Makeup to the Test," *Advertising Age*, April 21, 2015, accessed September 4, 2019, https://adage.com/article/ behind-the-work/extreme-sports-athletes-put-bobbi-brown-s-makeup-test/298138.

50. Simon Pitman, "Rise of Male Star Endorsed Cosmetics," Cosmetics Design.com-USA, last modified July 19, 2008, accessed July 27, 2017, https://www.cosmeticsdesign.com/ Article/2007/01/11/Rise-of-male-star-endorsed-cosmetics.

CHAPTER 8

1. A. O. Scott, "In 'The Devil Wears Prada,' Meryl Streep Plays the Terror of the Fashion World," review of *The Devil Wears Prada*, directed by David Frankel, *New York Times*, June 30, 2006, accessed July 27, 2017, https://www.nytimes.com/2006/06/30/movies/30devi .html?mcubz=1.

2. Shaun Dreisbach, "Shocking Body-Image News: 97% of Women Will Be Cruel to Their Bodies Today," *Glamour*, February 3, 2011, accessed July 9, 2017, https://www.glamour .com/story/shocking-body-image-news-97-percent-of-women-will-be-cruel-to-their-bodies -today.

3. J. Fan, "Perception of Body Appearance and Its Relation to Clothing," in *Clothing Appearance and Fit* (2004), Internal Representation, *ScienceDirect*, accessed September 4, 2019, https://www.sciencedirect.com/topics/engineering/internal-representation.

4. Ramesh Venkat and Harold Ogden, "Advertising-Induced Social Comparison and Body-Image Satisfaction: The Moderating Role of Gender, Self-Esteem and Locus of Control," *Journal of Consumer Satisfaction, Dissatisfaction and Complaining Behavior* 15 (2002): 53, accessed July 27, 2017.

5. Philip N. Myers Jr. and Frank A. Biocca, "The Elastic Body Image: The Effect of Television Advertising and Programming on Body Image Distortions in Young Women," *Journal*

of Communication 42, no. 3 (1992): 125–26, accessed July 29, 2017, doi: 10.1111/j.1460-2466.1992.tb00802.x.

6. Myers Jr. and Biocca, "The Elastic Body Image," 126.

7. Leon Festinger, "A Theory of Social Comparison Processes," *Human Relations* 7, no. 2 (1954): 117–40, accessed July 29, 2017, doi: 10.1177/001872675400700202.

8. Venkat and Ogden, "Advertising-Induced Social Comparison and Body-Image Satisfaction," 52.

9. Venkat and Ogden, "Advertising-Induced Social Comparison and Body-Image Satisfaction," 51.

10. Venkat and Ogden, "Advertising-Induced Social Comparison and Body-Image Satisfaction," 51.

11. Venkat and Ogden, "Advertising-Induced Social Comparison and Body-Image Satisfaction," 51.

12. Gayle R. Bessenoff, "Can the Media Affect Us? Social Comparison, Self-Discrepancy, and the Thin Ideal," *Psychology of Women Quarterly* 30, no. 3 (2006): 247, accessed July 29, 2017, doi:10.1111/j.1471-6402.2006.00292.x.

13. "'TV Brings Eating Disorders to Fiji,'" *BBC News*, May 20, 1999, accessed July 26, 2017, http://news.bbc.co.uk/2/hi/health/347637.stm.

14. "'TV Brings Eating Disorders to Fiji,'" *BBC News*.

15. "'TV Brings Eating Disorders to Fiji,'" *BBC News*.

16. Kimberly Conniff Taber, "With Model's Death, Eating Disorders Are Again in Spotlight—Americas—International Herald Tribune," *New York Times*, November 20, 2006, accessed July 29, 2019, https://www.nytimes.com/2006/11/20/world/americas/20iht-models.3604439.html.

17. Tom Phillips, "'Everyone Knew She Was Ill. The Other Girls, the Model Agencies . . . Don't Believe It When They Say They Didn't,'" *Guardian*, January 13, 2007, accessed July 27, 2017, https://www.theguardian.com/lifeandstyle/2007/jan/14/fashion.features4.

18. "The Thin Ideal," in *Wikipedia*, last modified June 22, 2019, accessed September 5, 2019, https://en.wikipedia.org/wiki/The_Thin_Ideal.

19. Sarah Rainey, "High Street Skeletons: We All Know about Painfully Thin Catwalk Stars. Here We Reveal the Deeply Worrying Vital Statistics of Models for High Street Chains," *Daily Mail*, October 28, 2015, accessed July 27, 2017, http://www.dailymail.co.uk/femail/article-3294113/High-street-skeletons-know-painfully-catwalk-stars-reveal-deeply-worrying-vital-statistics-models-high-street-chains.html#ixzz4sJ7nYQIq.

20. "Perfect Illusions: "Eating Disorders and the Family," PBS.org, accessed July 27, 2017, http://www.pbs.org/perfectillusions/eatingdisorders/preventing_facts.html.

21. Edward Lovett, "Most Models Meet Criteria for Anorexia, Size 6 Is Plus Size: Magazine," *ABC News*, January 12, 2012, accessed July 9, 2017, https://abcnews.go.com/News/most-models-meet-criteria-for-anorexia-size-6-is-plus-size-magazine/blogEntry?id=15350058.

22. Michael R. Solomon, *Consumer Behavior: Buying, Having, and Being*, 12th ed. (Hoboken, NJ: Pearson, 2016), 200.

23. Kristen E. Van Vonderen and William Kinnally, "Media Effects on Body Image: Examining Media Exposure in the Broader Context of Internal and Other Social Factors," *American Communication Journal* 14, no. 2 (2012): 43, accessed July 27, 2017, https://ac-journal.org/journal/pubs/2012/SPRING%202012/McKinnally3.pdf.

24. Van Vonderen and Kinnally, "Media Effects on Body Image: Examining Media Exposure in the Broader Context of Internal and Other Social Factors," 43.

25. Emma Haliwell and Helga Dittmar, "Does Size Matter? The Impact of Model's Body Size on Women's Body-Focused Anxiety and Advertising Effectiveness," *Journal of Social and Clinical Psychology* 23, no. 1 (2004): 119, accessed July 30, 2017, doi: 10.1521/jscp.23.1.104.26989.

26. Miranda Hitti, "Thin Ads + Low Body Image = Stress," *CBS News*, October 27, 2006, accessed July 9, 2017, www.cbsnews.com/2100-500368_162-2134194.html.

27. Hitti, "Thin Ads + Low Body Image = Stress."

28. Bessenoff, "Can the Media Affect Us? Social Comparison, Self-Discrepancy, and the Thin Ideal," 239–51.

29. Rachel Simmons, "How Social Media Is a Toxic Mirror," *Time*, August 19, 2016, accessed July 27, 2017, http://time.com/4459153/social-media-body-image/.

30. Carolyn Gregoire, "Body Image Issues among Young Women More Influenced by Peers Than TV, Study Finds," *Huffington Post*, January 31, 2013, accessed July 9, 2017, https://www.huffingtonpost.com/2013/01/31/body-image-issues-for-you_n_2590719.html.

31. Gregoire, "Body Image Issues among Young Women More Influenced by Peers Than TV, Study Finds."

32. "Thinness in Media Feeds Body Size Obsession, Researchers Say," *BBC News*, November 8, 2012, accessed July 27, 2017, https://www.bbc.com/news/uk-england-tyne-20251825.

33. "Thinness in Media Feeds Body Size Obsession, Researchers Say," *BBC News*.

34. Arizona State University, "Study: Ads with Plus-Size Models Unlikely to Work," *ASU Now*, March 22, 2010, accessed July 28, 2017, https://asunow.asu.edu/content/study-ads-plus-size-models-unlikely-work.

35. Arizona State University, "Study: Ads with Plus-Size Models Unlikely to Work."

36. Dodai Stewart, "Photoshop of Horrors Hall of Shame, 2000–2009," *Jezebel*, December 16, 2009, accessed July 17, 2017, https://jezebel.com/5426296/photoshop-of-horrors-hall-of-shame-2000-2009/.

37. Lindsay Goldwert, "AMA Takes Stand on Photoshop; Medical Association: Altering Contributes to Unrealistic Expectations," *New York Daily News*, June 24, 2011, accessed July 27, 2017, http://www.nydailynews.com/life-style/fashion/ama-takes-stand-photoshop-medical-association-altering-contributes-unrealistic-expectations-article-1.126921.

38. Goldwert, "AMA Takes Stand on Photoshop; Medical Association: Altering Contributes to Unrealistic Expectations."

39. Goldwert, "AMA Takes Stand on Photoshop; Medical Association: Altering Contributes to Unrealistic Expectations."

40. "Ralph Lauren Apologises for Digitally Retouching Slender Model to Make Her Head Look Bigger Than Her Waist," *Daily Mail*, October 10, 2009, accessed July 27, 2017, http://www.dailymail.co.uk/news/article-1219046/Ralph-Lauren-digitally-retouches-slender-model-make-look-THINNER.html#ixzz4sbRVJU00.

41. "Ralph Lauren Apologises for Digitally Retouching Slender Model to Make Her Head Look Bigger Than Her Waist," *Daily Mail*.

42. Sheila Marikar, "Real? Or Photoshopped? 'Airbrushing' Run Amok," *ABC News*, December 19, 2008, accessed July 27, 2017, https://abcnews.go.com/Entertainment/Celebrity Cafe/story?id=6483994&page=1.

43. Rosie Baker, "Airbrushing Damages Consumer Trust in Brands," *Marketing Week*, December 6, 2011, accessed July 20, 2018, https://www.marketingweek.com/2011/12/06/airbrushing-damages-consumer-trust-in-brands/.

44. Baker, "Airbrushing Damages Consumer Trust in Brands."

45. "Kate Moss Regrets 'Nothing Tastes as Good as Skinny Feels' Comment," *BBC News*, September 14, 2018, accessed October 11, 2019, https://www.bbc.com/news/newsbeat-45522714.

46. Dan Bilefsky, "Model in Gucci Ad Is Deemed 'Unhealthily Thin' by British Regulator," *New York Times*, April 6, 2016, accessed July 1, 2017, https://www.nytimes.com/2016/04/07/business/international/gucci-ad-unhealthily-thin-model.html.

47. Bilefsky, "Model in Gucci Ad Is Deemed 'Unhealthily Thin' by British Regulator."

48. Sophia Rosenbaum, "Models Keep Getting Skinnier and Skinnier," *New York Post*, June 9, 2016, accessed July 29, 2017, https://nypost.com/2016/06/09/models-keep-getting-skinnier-and-skinnier/.

49. Audrey Gillan, "Skinny Models 'Send Unhealthy Message,'" *Guardian*, May 30, 2000, accessed July 29, 2017, https://www.theguardian.com/uk/2000/may/31/audreygillan.

50. Gillan, "Skinny Models 'Send Unhealthy Message.'"

51. "Outrage Over Magazine's Emaciated 'Corpse' Model," *New York Post*, February 26, 2015, accessed July 30, 2017, https://nypost.com/2015/02/26/fashion-magazine-faces-backlash-over-emaciated-model/.

52. "Outrage Over Magazine's Emaciated 'Corpse' Model," *New York Post*.

53. "Skinny Models Banned from Catwalk," CNN, September 13, 2006, accessed July 27, 2017, http://www.cnn.com/2006/WORLD/europe/09/13/spain.models/.

54. "Skinny Models Banned from Catwalk," CNN.

55. Amy Bonawitz, "Italy Bans 'Too-Thin' Models," *CBS News*, December 16, 2006, accessed July 27, 2017, https://www.cbsnews.com/news/italy-bans-too-thin-models/.

56. Bonawitz, "Italy Bans 'Too-Thin' Models."

57. Bonawitz, "Italy Bans 'Too-Thin' Models."

58. Mary Brophy Marcus, "Ban on Super-Thin Models Takes Effect in France," *CBS News*, May 10, 2017, accessed July 27, 2107, https://www.cbsnews.com/news/ban-on-super-thin-models-anorexia-takes-effect-in-france/.

59. Marcus, "Ban on Super-Thin Models Takes Effect in France."

60. Rosie Baker, "Advertisers Refute 'Beauty Industry Perpetuates Low Self-Esteem' Claim," *Marketing Week*, January 31, 2012, accessed July 10, 2017, https://www.marketingweek.com/2012/01/31/advertisers-refute-beauty-industry-perpetuates-low-self-esteem-claim/.

61. Baker, "Advertisers Refute 'Beauty Industry Perpetuates Low Self-Esteem' Claim."

62. Baker, "Advertisers Refute 'Beauty Industry Perpetuates Low Self-Esteem' Claim."

63. Baker, "Advertisers Refute 'Beauty Industry Perpetuates Low Self-Esteem' Claim."

64. Loulla-Mae Eleftheriou-Smith, "Dove Wins at Inaugural Body Confidence Awards," *Campaign*, April 24, 2012, accessed July 28, 2017, https://www.campaignlive.co.uk/article/dove-wins-inaugural-body-confidence-awards/1128443#1rS8gurDcKhOLZyf.99.

65. Eleftheriou-Smith, "Dove Wins at Inaugural Body Confidence Awards."

66. Amy Merrick, "Marketing 'Real' Bodies," *New Yorker*, April 1, 2014, accessed July 28, 2017, https://www.newyorker.com/business/currency/marketing-real-bodies.

67. Merrick, "Marketing 'Real' Bodies."

68. Deepa Sen, "Female-Targeted Brands Lead on Aspirational Authenticity," *Advertising Age*, November 22, 2016, accessed July 28, 2017, http://adage.com/article/agency-viewpoint/female-targeted-brands-lead-aspirational-authenticity/306815/.

69. Sen, "Female-Targeted Brands Lead on Aspirational Authenticity."

70. Jamie Feldman, "'World's First Size 22 Supermodel' Tess Holliday Lands Cover of People Magazine," *Huffington Post*, May 20, 2015, accessed March 15, 2020, https://www.huffpost.com/entry/tess-holliday-people-maga_n_7343192.

71. Emma Bazilian, "Why More Brands Are Embracing Plus-Size Models," *Adweek*, April 24, 2016, accessed July 27, 2017, www.adweek.com/brand-marketing/why-more-brands-are-embracing-plus-size-models-170984/.

72. Bazilian, "Why More Brands Are Embracing Plus-Size Models."

73. Emma Bazilian, "Teen's Petition Leads to 'Seventeen' Body Image Pledge," *Adweek*, July 3, 2012, accessed July 28, 2017, https://www.adweek.com/digital/teens-petition-leads-seventeen-body-image-pledge-141493/.

CHAPTER 9

1. Reba A. Wissner, "For Want of a Better Estimate, Let's Call It the Year 2000: The Twilight Zone and the Aural Conception of a Dystopian Future," *Music and the Moving Image* 8, no. 3 (2015): 52, doi: 10.5406/musimoviimag.8.3.0052.

2. "The Beauty Business: Pots of Promise," *Economist*, May 22, 2003, accessed July 13, 2017, https://www.economist.com/special-report/2003/05/22/pots-of-promise.

3. James Bennett, "Straps, Bandages and Tapes," Cosmetics and Skin, last modified December 6, 2017, accessed January 21, 2018, http://www.cosmeticsandskin.com/aba/straps.php.

4. Bennett, "Straps, Bandages and Tapes."

5. Natalie Kita, "The History of Plastic Surgery," Verywell Health, last modified August 5, 2019, accessed September 6, 2019, https://www.verywellhealth.com/the-history-of-plastic-surgery-2710193.

6. Martin Donohoe, "Women's Health in Context: Cosmetic Surgery Past, Present, and Future: Scope, Ethics, and Policy," *Medscape Ob/Gyn* 11, no. 2 (2006), accessed July 27, 2018, https://www.medscape.com/viewarticle/542448.

7. Donohoe, "Women's Health in Context."

8. Kita, "The History of Plastic Surgery."

9. Donohoe, "Women's Health in Context."

10. American Society of Plastic Surgeons, "2018 Plastic Surgery Statistics Report," accessed July 30, 2019, https://www.plasticsurgery.org/documents/News/Statistics/2018/plastic-surgery-statistics-full-report-2018.pdf.

11. American Society of Plastic Surgeons, "2018 Plastic Surgery Statistics Report."

12. American Society of Plastic Surgeons, "2018 Plastic Surgery Statistics Report."

13. International Society of Aesthetic Plastic Surgery, "Latest Study Shows Aesthetic Surgery Continues to Rise Worldwide," ISAPS press release, December 3, 2019, accessed March 16, 2020, https://www.prnewswire.com/in/news-releases/latest-international-study-shows-aesthetic-surgery-continues-to-rise-worldwide-853742798.html.

14. "Lunchtime Lift: Breast Enhancement Now Available in 20 Minute Procedure," *ABC News*, August 22, 2014, accessed July 28, 2017, https://abcnews.go.com/Lifestyle/lunchtime-lift-breast-enhancement-now-20-minute-procedure/story?id=25078909.

15. "Lunchtime Lift," *ABC News*.

16. "Lunchtime Lift," *ABC News*.

17. Lisa Lombardi, "Cosmetic Surgery Boom Revamps Doctors' Offices," CNN, December 2, 2009, accessed July 28, 2017, http://www.cnn.com/2009/HEALTH/12/02/plastic.surgery.cosmetic.risks/index.html.

18. Lombardi, "Cosmetic Surgery Boom Revamps Doctors' Offices."

19. "One in 5 American Women Actively Considering Plastic Surgery: Study," *New York Daily News*, February 19, 2015, accessed July 28, 2017, http://www.nydailynews.com/life-style/5-american-women-actively-plastic-surgery-article-1.2121903.

20. US Census Bureau, "Census Bureau Releases Comprehensive Analysis of Fast-Growing 90-and-Older Population," Census Bureau press release, November 17, 2011, accessed July 12, 2017, https://www.census.gov/newsroom/releases/archives/aging_population/cb11-194.html.

21. Michael Erman, Ankur Banerjee, and Julie Steenhuysen, "AbbVie Looks Beyond Humira with $63 Billion Deal for Botox-Maker Allergan," Reuters, June 25, 2019, accessed July 30, 2019, https://www.reuters.com/article/us-allergan-m-a-abbvie-idUSKCN1TQ15X.

22. "How Much Do Botox Treatments Cost?," CostHelper, accessed July 31, 2019, https://health.costhelper.com/botox.html.

23. Richard J. Crockett, Thomas Pruzinsky, and John Persing, "The Influence of Plastic Surgery 'Reality TV' on Cosmetic Surgery Patient Expectations and Decision Making," *Plastic and Reconstructive Surgery* 120, no. 1 (2007): 316–24, doi: 10.1097/01.prs.0000264339.67451.71.

24. Kathleen Doheny, "Cosmetic Surgery TV Shows Get Viewers Pondering," MedicineNet.com, August 9, 2007, accessed July 12, 2017, https://www.medicinenet.com/script/main/art.asp?articlekey=83119.

25. American Academy of Facial Plastic and Reconstructive Surgery, "Selfie Trend Increases Demand for Facial Plastic Surgery," AAFPRS press release, March 11, 2014, accessed July 28, 2017, https://www.aafprs.org/media/press_release/20140311.html.

26. American Academy of Facial Plastic and Reconstructive Surgery, "AAFPRS Annual Survey Unveils Rising Trends in Facial Plastic Surgery," January 26, 2018, accessed July 28, 2017, https://www.aafprs.org/media/press-release/20170125.html.

27. The Aesthetic Society, "Generation X May Help Fuel Anti-aging Industry," October 26, 2011, accessed July 28, 2017, https://www.surgery.org/consumers/plastic-surgery-news-briefs/generation-x-fuel-anti-aging-industry-1035740.

28. The Aesthetic Society, "Generation X May Help Fuel Anti-aging Industry."

29. Laura Donnelly, "Girls as Young as Eight Being Groomed by Cosmetic Surgery Games," *Telegraph*, June 22, 2017, accessed July 28, 2017, https://www.telegraph.co.uk/news/2017/06/22/girls-young-eight-groomed-cosmetic-surgery-games/.

30. Nuffield Council on Bioethics, "Cosmetics Procedures: Ethical Issues," accessed July 20, 2018, http://nuffieldbioethics.org/wp-content/uploads/Cosmetic-procedures-full-report.pdf.

31. Donnelly, "Girls as Young as Eight Being Groomed by Cosmetic Surgery Games."

32. Karol Markowicz, "Celebrities Are Driving the Teen Plastic-Surgery Boom," *New York Post*, August 23, 2015, accessed July 28, 2017, https://nypost.com/2015/08/23/the-modern-vanity-cult-is-prompting-a-teen-plastic-surgery-boom/.

33. American Society of Plastic Surgeons, "2018 Plastic Surgery Statistics Report."

34. American Society of Plastic Surgeons, "2018 Plastic Surgery Statistics Report."

35. American Society of Plastic Surgeons, "2018 Plastic Surgery Statistics Report."

36. American Society of Plastic Surgeons, "2018 Plastic Surgery Statistics Report."

37. American Society of Plastic Surgeons, "2018 Plastic Surgery Statistics Report."

38. Alene Dawson, "Gen X Women, Young for Their Age," *Los Angeles Times*, September 25, 2011, accessed July 11, 2017, http://articles.latimes.com/2011/sep/25/image/la-ig-beauty -genx-20110925.

39. Rachel Strugatz, "Are the Kardashians, Millennials Seeking to Look Young Causing Cosmetic Procedures Boom?," *Los Angeles Times*, March 31, 2017, accessed July 31, 2017, http://www.latimes.com/fashion/la-ig-wwd-cosmetic-procedures-kardashian-driven-millennial -led-20170331-story.html.

40. American Academy of Facial Plastic and Reconstructive Surgery, "Selfie Trend Increases Demand for Facial Plastic Surgery."

41. American Academy of Facial Plastic and Reconstructive Surgery, "Selfie Trend Increases Demand for Facial Plastic Surgery."

42. Joel Schlessinger, Daniel Schlessinger, and Bernard Schlessinger, "Prospective Demographic Study of Cosmetic Surgery Patients," *Journal of Clinical and Aesthetic Dermatology* 3, no. 11 (2010): 30–35, accessed July 28, 2017, http://jcadonline.com/prospective -demographic-study-of-cosmetic-surgery-patients/.

43. Schlessinger, Schlessinger, and Schlessinger, "Prospective Demographic Study of Cosmetic Surgery Patients."

44. Schlessinger, Schlessinger, and Schlessinger, "Prospective Demographic Study of Cosmetic Surgery Patients."

45. "One in 5 American Women Actively Considering Plastic Surgery," *New York Daily News*.

46. "One in 5 American Women Actively Considering Plastic Surgery," *New York Daily News*.

47. "One in 5 American Women Actively Considering Plastic Surgery," *New York Daily News*.

48. Nina Godlewski, "Barbie 60th Anniversary, Birthday, History and Facts about the Doll; What's Her Last Name?," *Newsweek*, March 9, 2019, accessed September 7, 2019, https://www.newsweek.com/barbie-60th-birthday-real-name-1357397.

49. Lauren Sherman, "In Depth: Barbie by the Numbers," *Forbes*, March 5, 2009, accessed September 7, 2019, https://www.forbes.com/2009/03/05/barbie-design-manufacturing -business_numbers_slide.html#2659ac9e792b.

50. Sasha Goldstein, "Barbie as a Real Woman Is Anatomically Impossible and Would Have to Walk on All Fours, Chart Shows," *New York Daily News*, April 14, 2013, accessed August 10, 2019, https://www.nydailynews.com/life-style/health/barbie-real-womaan -anatomically-impossible-article-1.1316533.

51. Katya Foreman, "The Changing Faces of Barbie," BBC, May 11, 2016, accessed July 30, 2017, http://www.bbc.com/culture/story/20160511-the-changing-faces-of-barbie.

52. Olivia Bahou, Mylan Torres, and Kerry Justich, "16 Insane Photos of Women Living as Human Dolls," *Cosmopolitan*, May 28, 2015, accessed September 7, 2019. https://www .cosmopolitan.com/lifestyle/news/g4816/photos-of-human-barbies/.

53. Alana Moorhead, "Plastic Surgeon Reveals Which Celebrity Facial Features Clients Want Most," *New York Post*, August 31, 2016, accessed July 28, 2017, https://nypost.com/ 2016/08/31/plastic-surgeon-reveals-which-celebrity-facial-features-clients-want-most/.

54. Moorhead, "Plastic Surgeon Reveals Which Celebrity Facial Features Clients Want Most."

55. Abby Ellin, "That Nose, That Chin, Those Lips," *New York Times*, January 15, 2014, accessed July 28, 2017, https://www.nytimes.com/2014/01/16/fashion/Plastic-surgery-celebrity-makeover.html.

56. "The 'Ugly Truth' about Body Dysmorphic Disorder," *BBC News*, June 21, 2015, accessed August 1, 2017, https://www.bbc.com/news/health-33190297.

57. "The 'Ugly Truth' about Body Dysmorphic Disorder," *BBC News*.

58. Andri S. Bjornsson, Elizabeth R. Didie, and Katharine A. Phillips, "Body Dysmorphic Disorder," *Dialogues in Clinical Neuroscience* 12, no. 2 (2010): 221–32, accessed July 28, 2017.

59. Kashyap K. Tadisina, Karan Chopra, and Devinder P. Singh, "Body Dysmorphic Disorder in Plastic Surgery," *Eplasty* 13 (2013): ic48, https://www.ncbi.nlm.nih.gov/pmc/articles/PMC3693597/.

60. Tadisina, Chopra, and Singh, "Body Dysmorphic Disorder in Plastic Surgery."

61. International Society of Aesthetic Plastic Surgery, "Latest Study Shows Aesthetic Surgery Continues to Rise Worldwide."

62. Juju Chang and Victoria Thompson, "South Korea's Growing Obsession with Cosmetic Surgery," *ABC News*, June 20, 2014, accessed July 29, 2017, https://abcnews.go.com/Lifestyle/south-koreas-growing-obsession-cosmetic-surgery/story?id=24123409.

63. Zara Stone, "The K-Pop Plastic Surgery Obsession," *Atlantic*, May 24, 2013, accessed July 9, 2017, https://www.theatlantic.com/health/archive/2013/05/the-k-pop-plastic-surgery-obsession/276215/.

64. Stone, "The K-Pop Plastic Surgery Obsession."

65. Steve Nolan, "Has Plastic Surgery Made These Beauty Queens All Look the Same? Koreans Complain about Pageant 'Clones,'" *Daily Mail*, April 25, 2013, accessed July 28, 2017, http://www.dailymail.co.uk/news/article-2314647/Has-plastic-surgery-20-Korean-beauty-pageant-contestants-look-Pictures-contest-hopefuls-goes-viral.html#ixzz4tPibUTuz.

66. Nolan, "Has Plastic Surgery Made These Beauty Queens All Look the Same?"

67. Deni Kirkova, "Iran Is the Nose Job Capital of the World with SEVEN Times More Procedures Than the U.S.—but Rise in Unlicensed Surgeons Poses Huge Risk," *Daily Mail*, March 5, 2013, accessed July 28, 2017, http://www.dailymail.co.uk/femail/article-2287961/Iran-named-nose-job-capital-world-SEVEN-times-rhinoplasty-operations-U-S-Iranian-women-strive-western-doll-face.html.

68. Melissa Etehad, "From L.A. to Tehran, Nose Jobs Are a Rite of Passage and a Quiet Rebellion for Many Persian Women," *Los Angeles Times*, March 31, 2017, accessed August 1, 2017, http://www.latimes.com/local/california/la-me-ln-persian-nose-job-20170130-story.html.

69. Kirkova, "Iran Is the Nose Job Capital of the World with SEVEN Times More Procedures Than the U.S."

70. Bruce Y. Lee, "In Plastic Surgery, Brazil Gets the Silver Medal," *Forbes*, August 8, 2016, accessed July 28, 2017, https://www.forbes.com/sites/brucelee/2016/08/08/in-plastic-surgery-brazil-gets-the-silver-medal-behind/#3f254ebd3642.

71. Lee, "In Plastic Surgery, Brazil Gets the Silver Medal."

72. Jonathan Watts, "Why Brazil Loves Nip and Tuck, as Told by Country's Plastic Surgery 'Maestro,'" *Guardian*, September 24, 2014, accessed July 28, 2017, https://www.theguardian.com/world/2014/sep/24/brazil-loves-nip-tuck-plastic-surgeon-ivo-pitanguy.

73. Sarah Boseley, "Cosmetic Surgery Advertising Ban Urged by Leading Surgeons," *Guardian*, January 22, 2012, accessed July 28, 2017, https://www.theguardian.com/lifeand style/2012/jan/22/ban-advertising-cosmetic-surgery.

74. Boseley, "Cosmetic Surgery Advertising Ban Urged by Leading Surgeons."

75. Edward J. Huth and T. Jock Murray, eds., *Medicine in Quotations: Views of Health and Disease Through the Ages*, 2nd ed. (Philadelphia: American College of Physicians, 2006), 341. The original quote appeared in Gaspare Tagliacozzi, *De Curtorum Chirurgia per Insitionem, Libri Duo* (Venezia: apud Gasparem Bindonum iuniorem, 1597), accessed July 28, 2017, https://archive.org/details/decurtorumchirur02tagl.

76. Heidi J. Hennink-Kaminski and Tom Reichert, "Using Sexual Appeals in Advertising to Sell Cosmetic Surgery: A Content Analysis from 1986 to 2007," *Sexuality & Culture* 15, no. 1 (2010): 41–55, accessed July 27, 2018, doi: 10.1007/s12119-010-9081-y.

77. Hennink-Kaminski and Reichert, "Using Sexual Appeals in Advertising to Sell Cosmetic Surgery," 42.

78. Hennink-Kaminski and Reichert, "Using Sexual Appeals in Advertising to Sell Cosmetic Surgery," 42.

79. Natasha Singer, "In Hard Times, a Cosmetic Hard Sell," *New York Times*, November 5, 2008, accessed July 31, 2017, https://www.nytimes.com/2008/11/06/fashion/06skin.html.

80. Singer, "In Hard Times, a Cosmetic Hard Sell."

81. Hennink-Kaminski and Reichert, "Using Sexual Appeals in Advertising to Sell Cosmetic Surgery," 42.

82. "Social Responsibility: Body Image," Advertising Standards Authority (ASA), June 14, 2019, accessed August 10, 2019, https://www.asa.org.uk/advice-online/social-responsibility -body-image.html.

83. "ASA Ruling on MYA Cosmetic Surgery Ltd.," Advertising Standards Authority (ASA), October 17, 2018, accessed September 7, 2019, https://www.asa.org.uk/rulings/mya -cosmetic-surgery-ltd-a18-459775.html.

84. Daniel J. Gould et al., "Emerging Trends in Social Media and Plastic Surgery," *Annals of Translational Medicine* 4, no. 23 (2016): 455, doi: 10.21037/atm.2016.12.17.

85. Kari Paul, "Study Reveals the Dangers of Plastic Surgery Advertisements on Instagram," *MarketWatch*, August 30, 2017, accessed November 18, 2017, https://www.market watch.com/story/a-surprising-trend-fueling-plastic-surgery-instagram-2017-02-15.

86. Paul, "Study Reveals the Dangers of Plastic Surgery Advertisements on Instagram."

87. Lisa Schencker, "Real Plastic Surgeons Not Behind Most Instagram Posts Offering Nips, Tucks and Nose Jobs: Study," *Chicago Tribune*, August 30, 2017, accessed November 18, 2017, http://www.chicagotribune.com/business/ct-instagram-plastic-surgery-study-0830-biz -20170829-story.html.

88. Schencker, "Real Plastic Surgeons Not Behind Most Instagram Posts Offering Nips, Tucks and Nose Jobs."

89. Schencker, "Real Plastic Surgeons Not Behind Most Instagram Posts Offering Nips, Tucks and Nose Jobs."

90. Joel Samaha, *Criminal Procedure*, 8th ed. (Belmont, CA: Wadsworth, 2012), 10–12; International Association for Physicians in Aesthetic Medication, "FDA Law Enforcers Crack Down on Illegal Botox Scammers," *Aesthetic Medicine News*, February 24, 2010, accessed August 27, 2018, https://aestheticmedicinenews.com/fda-law-enforcers-crack-down-on-illegal -botox-scammers.htm.

91. "Illegal Injections Killing, Maiming Women Seeking Cheap Alternative to Plastic Surgery," *Fox News*, August 5, 2013, accessed July 9, 2017, http://www.foxnews.com/health/2013/08/05/buttocks-injections-killing-maiming-some-women-who-seek-cheap-alternative-to.html.

92. "Illegal Injections Killing, Maiming Women Seeking Cheap Alternative to Plastic Surgery," *Fox News*.

93. "Illegal Injections Killing, Maiming Women Seeking Cheap Alternative to Plastic Surgery," *Fox News*.

94. "Big Butts Are Becoming a Booming Business," *New York Post*, November 11, 2014, accessed July 29, 2017, https://nypost.com/2014/11/11/bigger-butts-are-a-booming-business/.

95. Rachael Rettner, "Illegal Silicone Butt Injections Cause Host of Health Problems," *Live Science*, June 18, 2015, accessed July 29, 2017, https://www.livescience.com/51275-silicone-butt-injections-health-problems.html.

96. Joel Stein, "Nip. Tuck. Or Else," *Time*, June 17, 2015, accessed July 29, 2017, http://time.com/3926042/nip-tuck-or-else/.

97. Stein, "Nip. Tuck. Or Else."

98. Stein, "Nip. Tuck. Or Else."

99. Monica Anderson, "Americans Aren't Sold on Plastic Surgery: Few Have Had It Done, Opinions Mostly Mixed," Pew Research Center, October 18, 2016, accessed July 29, 2017, http://www.pewresearch.org/fact-tank/2016/10/18/americans-arent-sold-on-plastic-surgery-few-have-had-it-done-opinions-mostly-mixed/.

100. Anderson, "Americans Aren't Sold on Plastic Surgery."

101. Stein, "Nip. Tuck. Or Else."

102. Stein, "Nip. Tuck. Or Else."

103. Seyed Reza Mousavi, "The Ethics of Aesthetic Surgery," *Journal of Cutaneous and Aesthetic Surgery* 3, no. 1 (2010): 39, accessed July 31, 2017, doi: 10.4103/0974-2077.63396. Quote adapted from Giovanni Maio, "Is Aesthetic Surgery Still Really Medicine? An Ethical Critique [Ist die ästhetische Chirurgie überhaupt noch Medizin? Eine ethische Kritik]," *Handchirurgie Mikrochirurgie Plastische Chirurgie* 39, no. 3 (2007); 189–94, discussion 195–96, doi: 10.1055/s-2007-965328.

CONCLUSION

1. Yardley London, "Royal Warrants," accessed March 15, 2020, https://www.yardleylondon.co.uk/royal-warrant.

2. "Swinging 60s—Capital of Cool," History.com, accessed May 11, 2018, https://www.history.co.uk/history-of-london/swinging-60s-capital-of-cool.

3. Yardley London, "Yardley London Historical Timeline," accessed June 6, 2018, http://www.yardleylondon.co.uk/media/our-world/Yardley-London-Historical-Timeline.pdf.

4. "Company News; SmithKline to Sell Yardley," *New York Times*, April 13, 1990, accessed May 11, 2018, https://www.nytimes.com/1990/04/13/business/company-news-smithkline-to-sell-yardley.html.

5. Emma Hall, "News: Linda Evangelista Stars in Yardley Launch Ad," *Campaign*, September 13, 1996, accessed May 11, 2018, https://www.campaignlive.co.uk/article/news-linda-evangelista-stars-yardley-launch-ad/22987.

6. "Britain's Yardley Placed in Receivership," *Los Angeles Times*, August 27, 1998, accessed May 11, 2018, http://articles.latimes.com/1998/aug/27/business/fi-16944.

7. Yardley London, "Yardley London Historical Timeline."

8. Bhatnagar Parija, "P&G Has a Good Hair Day," CNN, March 18, 2003, accessed March 15, 2020, https://money.cnn.com/2003/03/18/news/companies/Procter/.

9. Rumman Ahmed and Dhanya Ann Thoppil, "Wipro Buys Lornamead's Yardley Assets," *Wall Street Journal*, November 5, 2009, accessed April 25, 2018, https://www.wsj.com/articles/SB10001424052748704013004574516670901869720.

10. "Yardley London Launches First Ad Campaign in 16 Years," *Drum*, April 18, 2012, accessed June 6, 2018, https://www.thedrum.com/news/2012/04/18/yardley-london-launches-first-ad-campaign-16-years.

11. Becky Bargh, "Yardley London Reinvigorates Brand with New Fragrance Launch for Millennials," Cosmetics Business, April 12, 2018, accessed June 6, 2018, https://www.cosmeticsbusiness.com/news/article_page/Yardley_London_reinvigorates_brand_with_new_fragrance_launch_for_millennials/141759.

12. Sharon Terlep, "Aging Beauty Brands Want a Facelift," *Wall Street Journal*, February 5, 2018, accessed April 24, 2018, https://www.wsj.com/articles/aging-beauty-brands-want-a-facelift-1517826601.

13. Stephanie Hoi-Nga Wong, "The Latest Acquisition Targets Are Indie Beauty Brands," *Bloomberg Businessweek*, March 23, 2017, accessed August 21, 2019, https://www.bloomberg.com/news/articles/2017-03-23/the-latest-acquisition-targets-are-indie-beauty-brands.

References

Abrahamson, David, and Marcia R. Prior-Miller. *The Routledge Handbook of Magazine Research: The Future of the Magazine Form*. New York: Routledge, 2015.

"Ad Age Advertising Century: Top 10 Slogans." *Advertising Age*, March 29, 1999. Accessed July 15, 2017. http://adage.com/article/special-report-the-advertising-century/ad-age-advertising-century-top-10-slogans/140156/.

Ad Age Datacenter. "Ad Age Leading National Advertising 2019 Fact Pack," *Ad Age*, June 23, 2019. https://adage.com/article/datacenter/ad-age-leading-national-advertisers-2019-index/2178026.

Ad Standards Canada. "The Canadian Code of Advertising Standards." Accessed July 1, 2017. https://adstandards.ca/code/the-code-online/.

———. "Gender Portrayal Guidelines." Accessed August 1, 2017. https://adstandards.ca/code/gender-portrayal-guidelines/.

Advertising Self-Regulatory Council. "ASRC Procedures." Accessed July 17, 2017. www.asrcreviews.org/asrc-procedures/.

Advertising Standards Authority. "Advertising Codes." Accessed July 1, 2017. https://www.asa.org.uk/codes-and-rulings/advertising-codes.html.

———. "Depictions, Perceptions and Harm: A Report on Gender Stereotypes in Advertising." Last modified October 9, 2017. Accessed November 1, 2017. https://www.asa.org.uk/genderresearch.html.

"Advertising Watchdog to Get Tough on Gender Stereotypes." *BBC News*, July 18, 2017. Accessed July 20, 2017. https://www.bbc.com/news/business-40638343.

"Adverts Banned for Promoting the Benefits of Botox." *BBC News*, January 15, 2014. Accessed July 28, 2017. http://www.bbc.co.uk/newsbeat/article/25744497/adverts-banned-for-promoting-the-benefits-of-botox.

The Aesthetic Society. "Generation X May Help Fuel Anti-aging Industry." October 26, 2011. Accessed July 28, 2017. https://www.surgery.org/consumers/plastic-surgery-news-briefs/generation-x-fuel-anti-aging-industry-1035740.

Agnone, Sarah. "The Zero Epidemic." *Michigan Daily*, March 22, 2017. Accessed March 30, 2018. https://www.michigandaily.com/section/arts/zero-epidemic.

Ahmed, Rumman, and Dhanya Ann Thoppil. "Wipro Buys Lornamead's Yardley Assets." *Wall Street Journal*, November 5, 2009. Accessed April 25, 2018. https://www.wsj.com/articles/SB10001424052748704013004574516670901869720.

Alexander, Brian. "Ideal to Real: What the 'Perfect' Body Really Looks Like for Men and Women." *Today*, June 23, 2016. Accessed July 4, 2017. https://www.today.com/health/ideal-real-what-perfect-body-really-looks-men-women-t83731.

Alkon, Amy. "The Truth about Beauty." *Psychology Today*, November 1, 2010. Accessed July 6, 2017. https://www.psychologytoday.com/us/articles/201011/the-truth-about-beauty.

Alter, Adam. "Does Beauty Drive Economic Success?" *New Yorker*, December 19, 2013. Accessed January 12, 2018. https://www.newyorker.com/business/currency/does-beauty-drive-economic-success.

American Academy of Facial Plastic and Reconstructive Surgery. "AAFPRS Annual Survey Unveils Rising Trends in Facial Plastic Surgery." January 26, 2017. Accessed July 28, 2017. https://www.aafprs.org/media/press-release/20170125.html.

———. "Selfie Trend Increases Demand for Facial Plastic Surgery." AAFPRS press release, March 11, 2014. Accessed July 28, 2017. https://www.aafprs.org/media/press_release/20140311.html.

American Board of Cosmetic Surgery. "Cosmetic Surgery vs. Plastic Surgery." Accessed July 28, 2017. https://www.americanboardcosmeticsurgery.org/patient-resources/cosmetic-surgery-vs-plastic-surgery/.

American Cancer Society. "Cosmetics." May 28, 2014. Accessed July 17, 2017. https://www.cancer.org/cancer/cancer-causes/cosmetics.html.

American Chemical Society. "Ancient Egyptian Cosmetics: 'Magical' Makeup May Have Been Medicine for Eye Disease." ACS press release, January 11, 2010. Accessed July 21, 2017. https://www.acs.org/content/acs/en/pressroom/newsreleases/2010/january/ancient-egyptian-cosmetics.html.

American Society of Plastic Surgeons. "Briefing Paper: Plastic Surgery for Teenagers." Accessed July 15, 2017. https://www.plasticsurgery.org/news/briefing-papers/briefing-paper-plastic-surgery-for-teenagers.

———. "New Plastic Surgery Statistics Reveal Focus on Face and Fat." ASPS press release, March 1, 2017. Accessed July 28, 2017. https://www.plasticsurgery.org/news/press-releases/new-plastic-surgery-statistics-reveal-focus-on-face-and-fat.

———. "New Statistics Reflect the Changing Face of Plastic Surgery." ASPS press release, February 25, 2016. Accessed July 20, 2018. https://www.plasticsurgery.org/news/press-releases/new-statistics-reflect-the-changing-face-of-plastic-surgery.

———. "New Statistics Reveal the Shape of Plastic Surgery." ASPS press release, March 1, 2018. Accessed July 20, 2018. https://www.plasticsurgery.org/news/press-releases/new-statistics-reveal-the-shape-of-plastic-surgery.

———. "2018 Plastic Surgery Statistics Report." Accessed July 30, 2019. https://www.plastic-surgery.org/documents/News/Statistics/2018/plastic-surgery statistics-full-report-2018.pdf.

Ancient China Facts. "Ancient Chinese Make Up." Ancient Chinese Civilization. Accessed July 17, 2018. http://www.ancientchinalife.com/ancient-chinese-make-up.html.

Andersen, Kurt. "The Best Decade Ever? The 1990s, Obviously." *New York Times*, February 6, 2015. Accessed August 30, 2019. https://www.nytimes.com/2015/02/08/opinion/sunday/the-best-decade-ever-the-1990s-obviously.html.

Anderson, Monica. "Americans Aren't Sold on Plastic Surgery: Few Have Had It Done, Opinions Mostly Mixed." Pew Research Center, October 18, 2016. Accessed July 29, 2017. http://www.pewresearch.org/fact-tank/2016/10/18/americans-arent-sold-on-plastic -surgery-few-have-had-it-done-opinions-mostly-mixed/.

Anderson, Taylor. "How the 'Ideal' Body Shape Has Changed over the Last 100 Years." *Cosmopolitan*, January 19, 2015. Accessed October 29, 2019. https://www.cosmopolitan.com/ uk/body/news/a32749/perfect-body-has-changed-over-100-years/.

Andriotis, AnnaMaria. "10 Things the Beauty Industry Won't Tell You." *MarketWatch*, April 20, 2011. Accessed July 10, 2017. https://www.marketwatch.com/story/10-things-the -beauty-industry-wont-tell-you-1303249279432.

Angell, Elizabeth. "What's Beautiful Now?" *Allure*, March 29, 2011. Accessed August 1, 2017. https://www.allure.com/story/whats-beautiful-now.

Angyal, Chloe. "The 'Thinspiration' Behind an Impossible Ideal of Beauty." *Nation*, April 23, 2013. Accessed July 4, 2017. https://www.thenation.com/article/thinspiration-behind -impossible-ideal-beauty/.

Anschutz, Doeschka J., Rutger C. M. E. Engles, Eni S. Becker, and Tatjana van Strien. "The Effects of TV Commercials Using Less Thin Models on Young Women's Mood, Body Image and Actual Food Intake." *Body Image* 6, no. 4 (2009): 270–76. Accessed July 29, 2017. doi: 10.1016/j.bodyim.2009.07.007.

"Anthony Overton." In *Wikipedia*. Last modified August 8, 2018. Accessed July 27, 2017. https://en.wikipedia.org/wiki/Anthony_Overton.

Apaolaza-Ibañez, Vanessa, Patrick Hartmann, Sandra Diehl, and Ralf Terlutter. "Women Satisfaction with Cosmetic Brands: The Role of Dissatisfaction and Hedonic Brand Benefits." *African Journal of Business Management* 5, no. 3 (2011): 792–802. Accessed July 7, 2017. doi: 10.5897/AJBM10.305.

"Archetype/Stereotype." *Advertising Age*, September 15, 2003. Accessed July 3, 2017. http://adage.com/article/adage-encyclopedia/archetype-stereotype/98323/.

Arizona State University. "Study: Ads with Plus-Size Models Unlikely to Work." *ASU Now*, March 22, 2010. Accessed July 28, 2017. https://asunow.asu.edu/content/study-ads-plus -size-models-unlikely-work.

Armstrong, Cory L., ed. *Media Disparity: A Gender Battleground*. Lanham, MD: Lexington Books, 2013.

Arnold, Andrew. "Why YouTube Stars Influence Millennials More Than Traditional Celebrities." *Forbes*, June 20, 2017. Accessed July 28, 2019. https://www.forbes.com/sites/under 30network/2017/06/20/why-youtube-stars-influence-millennials-more-than-traditional -celebrities/#795f3c2e48c6.

"Art Deco." The Art Story. Accessed September 1, 2019. https://www.theartstory.org/move ment/art-deco/.

"ASA Ruling on MYA Cosmetic Surgery Ltd." Advertising Standards Authority (ASA), October 17, 2018. Accessed September 7, 2019. https://www.asa.org.uk/rulings/mya-cosmetic -surgery-ltd-a18-459775.html.

Ashikali, Eleni-Marina, and Helga Dittmar. "The Effect of Priming Materialism on Women's Responses to Thin-Ideal Media." *British Journal of Social Psychology* 51, no. 4 (2012): 514–33. Accessed July 10, 2017. doi: 10.1111/j.2044-8309.2011.02020.x.

Atasoy, Ozgun. "You Are Less Beautiful Than You Think." *Scientific American*, May 21, 2013. Accessed July 20, 2017. https://www.scientificamerican.com/article/you-are-less-beautiful -than-you-think/.

Athavaley, Anjali. "It's Just Lip Gloss, Mom." *Wall Street Journal*, February 3, 2011. Accessed July 15, 2017. https://www.wsj.com/articles/SB10001424052748703445904576118032658742632.

"Audrey Hepburn Biography." Biography.com. Last modified April 27, 2017. Accessed July 7, 2017. https://www.biography.com/people/audrey-hepburn-9335788.

"Audrey Hepburn: Style Icon." *BBC News*, May 4, 2004. Accessed July 7, 2017. http://news.bbc.co.uk/2/hi/entertainment/3667517.stm.

"Axe Excite: Angels." *Advertising Age*, January 30, 2011. Accessed September 20, 2019. https://adage.com/creativity/work/angels/22274.

"Axe/Lynx Excite Variant—Even Angels Will Fall Making-of." Ad Forum, BBH London, United Kingdom. Accessed August 16, 2019. https://www.adforum.com/creative-work/ad/player/34462167/even-angels-will-fall-making-of/axelynx-excite-variant.

Baack, Daniel W., Eric G. Harris, and Donald Baack. *International Marketing*. Thousand Oaks, CA: Sage, 2012.

Bacchilega, Cristina. *Postmodern Fairy Tales: Gender and Narrative Strategies*. Philadelphia: University of Pennsylvania Press, 1997.

Baer, Drake. "Why South Korea Is the Plastic Surgery Capital of the World." *Business Insider*, September 22, 2015. Accessed July 28, 2017. https://www.businessinsider.com/south-korea-is-the-plastic-surgery-capital-of-the-world-2015-9.

Bahadur, Nina. "It's Amazing How Much the 'Perfect Body' Has Changed in 100 Years." *Huffington Post*, February 13, 2014. Accessed November 24, 2017. https://www.huffingtonpost.com/entry/perfect-body-change-beauty-ideals_n_4733378.html.

Bahou, Olivia, Mylan Torres, and Kerry Justich. "16 Insane Photos of Women Living as Human Dolls." *Cosmopolitan*, May 28, 2015. Accessed September 7, 2019. https://www.cosmopolitan.com/lifestyle/news/g4816/photos-of-human-barbies/.

Baker, Katie. "The Problem with *The Great Gatsby*'s Daisy Buchanan." *Daily Beast*, May 10, 2013. Accessed July 21, 2018. https://www.thedailybeast.com/the-problem-with-the-great-gatsbys-daisy-buchanan.

Baker, Rosie. "Advertisers Refute 'Beauty Industry Perpetuates Low Self-Esteem' Claim." *Marketing Week*, January 31, 2012. Accessed July 10, 2017. https://www.marketingweek.com/2012/01/31/advertisers-refute-beauty-industry-perpetuates-low-self-esteem-claim/.

———. "Airbrushing Damages Consumer Trust in Brands." *Marketing Week*, December 6, 2011. Accessed July 20, 2018. https://www.marketingweek.com/2011/12/06/airbrushing-damages-consumer-trust-in-brands/.

Barakat, Christie. "Emotional Branding and the Emotionally Intelligent Consumer." *Adweek*, January 12, 2014. Accessed July 30, 2017. https://www.adweek.com/digital/emotional-branding-emotionally-intelligent-consumer/.

Barford, Vanessa. "Royal Warrants: What They Tell Us about the Royal Family." *BBC News*, July 12, 2013. Accessed May 11, 2018. https://www.bbc.com/news/magazine-23255710.

Bargh, Becky. "Yardley London Reinvigorates Brand with New Fragrance Launch for Millennials." Cosmetics Business, April 12, 2018. Accessed June 6, 2018. https://www.cosmeticsbusiness.com/news/article_page/Yardley_London_reinvigorates_brand_with_new_fragrance_launch_for_millennials/141759.

Barker, Chris. "Reports of Counterfeit Estee Lauder Cosmetics Grow in the Bay Area." CosmeticsDesign.com-USA. Last modified December 12, 2013. Accessed July 14, 2017. https://www.cosmeticsdesign.com/Article/2013/11/27/Reports-of-counterfeit-Estee-Lauder-cosmetics-grow-in-the-Bay-area.

Barrett, Julia R. "Chemical Exposures: The Ugly Side of Beauty Products." *Environmental Health Perspectives* 113, no. 1 (2005): A24. Accessed July 15, 2017. doi: 10.1289/ehp.113-a24.

Bartky, Sandra Lee. *Femininity and Domination: Studies in the Phenomenology of Oppression.* New York: Routledge, 1990.

Baumann, Leslie. "Read the Fine Print: Watch Out for 'In-Vitro' Testing." *Miami Herald*, June 26, 2012. Accessed July 17, 2017. https://www.miamiherald.com/living/health-fitness/skin-deep/article1940828.html.

Baumeister, Roy F., and Kathleen D. Vohs, eds. "Objectification Theory." In *Encyclopedia of Social Psychology.* http://dx.doi.org/10.4135/9781412956253.n377.

Bazilian, Emma. "Ad of the Day: Liquid-Plumr Gives Housewives More Erotic Cleaning Fantasies." *Adweek*, July 25, 2013. Accessed August 17, 2019. https://www.adweek.com/brand-marketing/ad-day-liquid-plumr-gives-housewives-more-erotic-cleaning-fantasies-151441/.

———. "Teen's Petition Leads to 'Seventeen' Body Image Pledge." *Adweek*, July 3, 2012. Accessed July 28, 2017. https://www.adweek.com/digital/teens-petition-leads-seventeen-body-image-pledge-141493/.

———. "Why More Brands Are Embracing Plus-Size Models." *Adweek*, April 24, 2016. Accessed July 27, 2017. https://www.adweek.com/brand-marketing/why-more-brands-are-embracing-plus-size-models-170984/.

Beall, Abigail. "Gender Stereotypes Are Holding Strong: Beliefs about the Roles of Men and Women Are 'as Firmly Held Now as They Were in 1980.'" *Daily Mail.* Last modified March 9, 2016. Accessed August 31, 2019. https://www.dailymail.co.uk/sciencetech/article-3482589/Gender-stereotypes-holding-strong-Beliefs-roles-men-women-firmly-held-1980.html.

Beans, Laura. "22 Cosmetics Companies File for 'Trade Secret' Status to Skirt Toxins Law." EcoWatch, January 30, 2014. Accessed July 8, 2017. https://www.ecowatch.com/22-cosmetics-companies-file-for-trade-secret-status-to-skirt-toxins-la-1881858579.html.

"Beauty." In *Merriam-Webster.* Accessed June 3, 2017. https://www.merriam-webster.com/dictionary/beauty.

"Beauty." In *New World Encyclopedia.* Accessed July 6, 2017. http://www.newworldencyclopedia.org/entry/Beauty.

"Beauty & Personal Care." Statista. Accessed August 29, 2019. https://www.statista.com/outlook/70000000/109/beauty-personal-care/united-states.

"The Beauty Business: Pots of Promise." *Economist*, May 22, 2003. Accessed July 13, 2017. https://www.economist.com/special-report/2003/05/22/pots-of-promise.

"Beauty History: Cosmetics in the Edwardian Era." Beautiful with Brains. Accessed August 8, 2019. https://www.beautifulwithbrains.com/beauty-history-cosmetics-in-the-edwardian-era/.

"Beauty History: The Elizabethan Era." Beautiful with Brains. Accessed August 21, 2019. https://www.beautifulwithbrains.com/beauty-history-the-elizabethan-era/.

"The Beauty Obsession Feeding Iran's Voracious Cosmetic Surgery Industry." *Guardian*, March 1, 2013. Accessed July 28, 2017. https://www.theguardian.com/world/iran-blog/2013/mar/01/beauty-obsession-iran-cosmetic-surgery.

Beck, Ernest. "Yardley Put into Receivership Amid Mounting Debts, Losses." *Wall Street Journal*, August 27, 1998. Accessed May 11, 2018. https://www.wsj.com/articles/SB904165247115663500.

Beer, Jeff. "Ronda Rousey Updates the Classic Pantene Slogan to 'Don't Hate Me Because I'm Strong.'" *Fast Company*, December 7, 2016. Accessed July 24, 2017. https://www.fast

company.com/3066353/ronda-rousey-updates-the-classic-pantene-slogan-to-dont-hate-me-because-im-strong.

"Behind the Color, Legacy." Revlon. Accessed August 17, 2019. http://en.revlon.com.hk/behind-the-color/legacy.

Belmas, Genelle, Jason M. Shepard, and Wayne E. Overbeck. *Major Principles of Media Law, 2017 Edition.* Boston, MA: Cengage Learning, 2017.

Beltrone, Gabriel. "Pantene Reimagines 'Don't Hate Me Because I'm Beautiful' to Celebrate LGBTQ+ Pride." *Adweek*, June 18, 2019. Accessed August 17, 2019. https://www.adweek.com/creativity/pantene-reimagines-dont-hate-me-because-im-beautiful-to-celebrate-lbtq-pride/.

"Benefits and Applications." Nano.gov. Accessed July 17, 2017. https://www.nano.gov/you/nanotechnology-benefits.

Bennett, James. "Arsenic-Eaters and Cucumber Creams." Cosmetics and Skin, June 2, 2014. Accessed July 10, 2018. http://cosmeticsandskin.com/ded/arsenic.php.

———. "Cover Girl." Cosmetics and Skin. Last modified February 28, 2018. Accessed August 17, 2019. http://www.cosmeticsandskin.com/companies/cover-girl.php.

———. "Max Factor." Cosmetics and Skin. Last modified March 30, 2018. Accessed July 27, 2018. http://www.cosmeticsandskin.com/companies/max-factor.php.

———. "Maybelline." Cosmetics and Skin. Last modified March 30, 2018. Accessed July 27, 2018. http://www.cosmeticsandskin.com/companies/max-factor.php.

———. "Pond's Extract Company." Cosmetics and Skin. Last modified January 5, 2018. Accessed June 4, 2018. http://cosmeticsandskin.com/companies/ponds.php.

———. "Revlon." Cosmetics and Skin. Last modified March 2, 2018. Accessed April 4, 2018. http://www.cosmeticsandskin.com/companies/revlon.php.

———. "Rouge." Cosmetics and Skin. Last modified August 8, 2017. Accessed September 7, 2018. http://cosmeticsandskin.com/bcb/rouge.php.

———. "Straps, Bandages and Tapes." Cosmetics and Skin. Last modified December 6, 2017. Accessed January 21, 2018. http://www.cosmeticsandskin.com/aba/straps.php.

———. "Yardley (post-1945)." Cosmetics and Skin. Last modified January 22, 2018. Accessed August 17, 2019. http://cosmeticsandskin.com/companies/yardley-1945.php.

Bennett, Jessica. "Are We Turning Tweens into 'Generation Diva'?" *Newsweek*, March 29, 2009. Accessed July 15, 2017. https://www.newsweek.com/are-we-turning-tweens-generation-diva-76425.

Berl, Rachel Pomerance. "How Safe Are Your Cosmetics?" *U.S. News & World Report*, July 31, 2012. Accessed July 11, 2017. https://health.usnews.com/health-news/articles/2012/07/31/how-safe-are-your-cosmetics.

Berman, Eliza. "This Is What the Ideal Woman Looked Like in the 1930s." *Time*, July 2, 2015. Accessed July 5, 2017. http://time.com/3860561/ideal-woman-1930s/.

Bessenoff, Gayle R. "Can the Media Affect Us? Social Comparison, Self-Discrepancy, and the Thin Ideal." *Psychology of Women Quarterly* 30, no. 3 (2006): 239–51. Accessed July 29, 2017. doi:10.1111/j.1471-6402.2006.00292.x.

Beyer, Alisa Marie. "The Art of Online Beauty Advertising." *Global Cosmetic Industry*, August 27, 2012. Accessed July 12, 2017. https://www.gcimagazine.com/business/marketing/167601455.html.

BeYu. "German Cosmetics Brand BeYu Launches in the US." BeYu press release, February 11, 2016. Accessed July 18, 2017. https://www.prnewswire.com/news-releases/german-cosmetics-brand-beyu-launches-in-the-us-300218308.html.

"Big Butts Are Becoming a Booming Business." *New York Post*, November 11, 2014. Accessed July 29, 2017. https://nypost.com/2014/11/11/bigger-butts-are-a-booming-business/.

Bilefsky, Dan. "Model in Gucci Ad Is Deemed 'Unhealthily Thin' by British Regulator." *New York Times*, April 6, 2016. Accessed July 1, 2017. https://www.nytimes.com/2016/04/07/business/international/gucci-ad-unhealthily-thin-model.html.

Bingham, John. "Three-year-old Girls Worry about Their Weight, Study Finds." *Telegraph*, November 26, 2009. Accessed July 27, 2017. https://www.telegraph.co.uk/news/health/news/6655447/Three-year-old-girls-worry-about-their-weight-study-finds.html.

"The Biology of Beauty." *Newsweek*, June 2, 1996. Accessed July 23, 2017. https://www.newsweek.com/biology-beauty-178836.

Biron, Bethany. "Beauty Has Blown Up to Be a $532 Billion Industry—And Analysts Say That These 4 Trends Will Make It Even Bigger." *Business Insider*, July 9, 2019. Accessed November 1, 2019. https://www.businessinsider.com/beauty-multibillion-industry-trends-future-2019-7.

Bjornsson, Andri S., Elizabeth R. Didie, and Katharine A. Phillips. "Body Dysmorphic Disorder." *Dialogues in Clinical Neuroscience* 12, no. 2 (2010): 221–32. Accessed July 28, 2017. https://www.ncbi.nlm.nih.gov/pmc/articles/PMC3181960/.

Blumenfeld, Warren J. "Examining Media's Socialization of Gender Roles." *Huffington Post*. Last modified October 8, 2013. Accessed July 10, 2017. https://www.huffingtonpost.com/entry/examining-medias-socializ_b_3721982.html.

Boddewyn, Jean J. "Controlling Sex and Decency in Advertising around the World." *Journal of Advertising* 20, no. 4 (1991): 25–35. Accessed July 1, 2017. doi: 10.1080/00913367.1991.10673352.

The Body Shop. "Chemicals Strategy." July 2008. Accessed July 14, 2017. http://www.thebodyshop.ch/media/wysiwyg/pdf/umweltschutz/2BSI_Chemicals_Strategy.pdf.

Bolton, Amanda. "All-Natural Beauty Products Most Popular Among Millennials." *Defy Media*. January 4, 2017. Accessed July 7, 2017. http://defymedia.com/2017/01/04/natural-beauty-products-popular-among-millennials/.

Bonawitz, Amy. "Italy Bans 'Too-Thin' Models." *CBS News*, December 16, 2006. Accessed July 27, 2017. https://www.cbsnews.com/news/italy-bans-too-thin-models/.

"Booming: Industries Benefiting from the Aging Population." IBISWorld, November 17, 2014. Accessed July 31, 2017. https://www.ibisworld.com/media/2014/11/17/booming-industries-benefiting-aging-population/.

Boorstin, Julia. "The Scent of Celebrity." *Fortune*, November 14, 2005. Accessed July 27, 2017. http://archive.fortune.com/magazines/fortune/fortune_archive/2005/11/14/8360679/index.htm.

Booth, Barbara. "Real Men Don't Cry—but They Are Exfoliating. Say Hello to 'Mampering.'" CNBC, September 16, 2015. Accessed July 18, 2017. https://www.cnbc.com/2014/12/05/real-men-dont-cry-but-they-are-exfoliating.html.

Borghini, Andrea. "How Do Philosophers Think about Beauty?" ThoughtCo. Last modified April 7, 2018. Accessed July 8, 2018. https://www.thoughtco.com/how-do-philosophers-think-about-beauty-2670642.

Boseley, Sarah. "Cosmetic Surgery Advertising Ban Urged by Leading Surgeons." *Guardian*, January 22, 2012. Accessed July 28, 2017. https://www.theguardian.com/lifeandstyle/2012/jan/22/ban-advertising-cosmetic-surgery.

Bowen, Jane. "Eye Makeup Trends by Decade: The Shadow, Mascara, and More That Ruled the Last 100 Years." *Elle*, September 1, 2016. Accessed July 5, 2017. https://www.elle.com/beauty/makeup-skin-care/g28604/best-eye-makeup-trends-every-decade/.

Brand Finance. "Cosmetics 50 2019: The Annual Report on the Most Valuable and Strongest Cosmetics Brands," May 2019. Accessed October 23, 2019. https://brandfinance.com/knowledge-centre/reports/brand-finance-cosmetics-50-2019/.

———. "Johnson & Johnson Looking Pretty with Top Cosmetics Brands." Brand Finance press release. Accessed July 15, 2018. http://brandfinance.com/news/press-releases/johnson-and-johnson-looking-pretty-with-top-cosmetics-brands/.

Brauneis, Sabrina. *The Relationship of Body Weight and Skepticism Towards Advertising*. Heidelberg, DE: Springer Gabler, 2016. doi: 10.1007/978-3-658-14861-4.

"Brazilians Transfixed by Recent Anorexia Deaths." *NBC News*, December 27, 2006. Accessed July 27, 2017. http://www.nbcnews.com/id/16370676/ns/health-mental_health/t/brazilians-transfixed-recent-anorexia-deaths/#.W32MmvZFxPZ.

"A Brief History of Cosmetics 2: Dark Ages to Mid-20th Century." BareFacedTruth.com, January 25, 2012. Accessed July 21, 2017. http://barefacedtruth.com/2012/01/25/cosmetics-through-history-part-2-dark-ages-to-mid-20th-century/.

"Bristol-Myers Squibb Co." *Advertising Age*, September 15, 2003. Accessed August 21, 2018. http://adage.com/article/adage-encyclopedia/bristol-myers-squibb/98543/.

"Britain's Yardley Placed in Receivership." *Los Angeles Times*, August 27, 1998. Accessed May 11, 2018. http://articles.latimes.com/1998/aug/27/business/fi-16944.

Brown, Rachel. "Social Media in the Beauty Landscape." *Women's Wear Daily*, February 16, 2016. Accessed July 12, 2017. https://wwd.com/beauty-industry-news/beauty-features/beauty-industry-social-media-10347599/.

Brucculieri, Julia. "'Snapchat Dysmorphia' Points to a Troubling New Trend in Plastic Surgery." *Huffington Post*, February 22, 2018. Accessed November 3, 2019. https://www.huffpost.com/entry/snapchat-dysmorphia_n_5a8d8168e4b0273053a680f6?guccounter=1&guce_referrer=aHR0cHM6Ly93d3cuZ29vZ2xlLmNvbS8&guce_referrer_sig=AQAAALq6P4rtAy1J7XLj_3hZmFPPd_aVIwvNmXA1lK3vfSjRoixmwpeFCML2TfO4MS.

Bukszpan, Daniel. "'DADvertising': How Realistic Images of Dads Took Over TV Ads." *Fortune*, June 19, 2016. Accessed July 31, 2017. http://fortune.com/2016/06/19/dadvertising-commercials-fathers-day-ads/.

Burge, David A. *Patent and Trademark Tactics and Practice*, 3rd ed. Hoboken, NJ: Wiley, 1999. doi: 10.1002/9780470172285.

Burton, Thomas M. "FDA Official Rejects Cosmetics Firms' Safety Proposal." *Wall Street Journal*, March 6, 2014. Accessed July 8, 2017. https://www.wsj.com/articles/no-headline-available-1394143998.

Bushak, Lecia. "History of Body Image in America: How the 'Ideal' Female and Male Body Has Changed over Time." *Medical Daily*, November 6, 2015. Accessed July 4, 2017. https://www.medicaldaily.com/history-body-image-america-how-ideal-female-and-male-body-has-changed-over-360492.

"Business: The Company File: Yardley Faces Collapse." *BBC News*, August 26, 1998. Accessed August 21, 2019. http://news.bbc.co.uk/2/hi/business/158758.stm.

"Business: The Company File: Yardley Sold to Wella." *BBC News*, November 23, 1998. Accessed May 11, 2018. http://news.bbc.co.uk/2/hi/business/220200.stm.

Butterly, Amelia. "Plastic Surgery App Game Aimed at Children Taken Down." BBC, January 15, 2014. Accessed July 28, 2017. http://www.bbc.co.uk/newsbeat/article/25741350/plastic-surgery-app-game-aimed-at-children-taken-down.

"Buzz Words That Sell." *Global Cosmetic Industry*, August 7, 2008. Accessed July 16, 2017. https://www.gcimagazine.com/business/marketing/19293699.html.

Calaor, Jesa Marie. "Beauty by Numbers: 12 Fun Facts Shampoo and Its History." *Allure*, February 16, 2018. Accessed November 15, 2019. https://www.allure.com/story/shampoo -facts-history.

Caldbeck, Ryan. "Why You Should Think about Investing in Beauty Instead of Bitcoin." *Forbes*, February 6, 2014. Accessed July 22, 2017. https://www.forbes.com/sites/ ryancaldbeck/2014/02/06/why-you-should-think-about-investing-in-beauty-instead-of -bitcoin/#a125ea16f841.

California Department of Public Health. "California Safe Cosmetics Program." Accessed July 17, 2017. https://www.cdph.ca.gov/Programs/CCDPHP/DEODC/OHB/CSCP/Pages/ CSCP.aspx.

"Calvin Klein, Inc.—Company Profile, Information, Business Description, History, Background Information on Calvin Klein, Inc." In *Reference for Business*. Accessed August 15, 2019. https://www.referenceforbusiness.com/history2/92/Calvin-Klein-Inc.html.

"Calvin Klein, Inc." In *International Directory of Company Histories*. Encyclopedia.com. Accessed July 24, 2018. https://www.encyclopedia.com/social-sciences-and-law/economics -business-and-labor/businesses-and-occupations/calvin-klein-inc#2845900031.

Campaign for Safe Cosmetics. "Butylated Compounds." Accessed August 22, 2019. http:// www.safecosmetics.org/get-the-facts/chemicals-of-concern/butylated-compounds/#sthash .NAARvqzR.dpuf.

———. "International Laws." Accessed July 14, 2017. http://www.safecosmetics.org/get-the-facts/regulations/international-laws/.

———. "Phthalates." Accessed March 16, 2020. http://www.safecosmetics.org/get-the-facts/ chemicals-of-concern/phthalates/.

———. "State Laws." Accessed August 22, 2019. http://www.safecosmetics.org/get-the-facts/ regulations/state-laws/.

Canby, William C., Jr., and Ernest Gellhorn. "Physician Advertising: The First Amendment and the Sherman Act." *Duke Law Journal* 1978, no. 2 (1978): 543–85. Accessed July 28, 2017. doi: 10.2307/1372239.

Carmichael, Mary. "How Reality TV Influences Plastic-Surgery Patients." *Newsweek*, July 23, 2007. Accessed July 4, 2017. https://www.newsweek.com/how-reality-tv-influences-plastic-surgery-patients-104443.

"Case Study: Always #LikeAGirl." *Campaign*, October 12, 205. Accessed August 12, 2019. https://www.campaignlive.co.uk/article/case-study-always-likeagirl/1366870.

Castillo, Michelle. "L'Oréal Receives Warning Letter from FDA over Claims on Anti-aging Products." *CBS News*, September 12, 2012. Accessed July 14, 2017. https://www.cbsnews .com/news/loreal-receives-warning-letter-from-fda-over-claims-on-anti-aging-products/.

———. "Phthalate Exposure in Pregnancy May Increase Preterm Birth Risk." *CBS News*, November 19, 2013. Accessed July 14, 2017. https://www.cbsnews.com/news/phthalate -exposure-in-pregnancy-may-increase-preterm-birth-risk/.

Caulfield, Timothy. "The Pseudoscience of Beauty Products." *Atlantic*, May 5, 2015. Accessed July 11, 2017. https://www.theatlantic.com/health/archive/2015/05/the-pseudoscience-of -beauty-products/392201/.

"Celebrities' Endorsement Earnings on Social Media." *Economist*, October 17, 2016. Accessed July 24, 2017. https://www.economist.com/graphic-detail/2016/10/17/celebrities -endorsement-earnings-on-social-media.

Celkyte, Aiste. "Ancient Aesthetics." In *The Internet Encyclopedia of Philosophy*. Accessed July 4, 2017. https://www.iep.utm.edu/anc-aest/.

Centers for Disease Control and Prevention. "Phthalates Factsheet." National Biomonitoring Program. Last modified April 7, 2017. Accessed July 15, 2017. https://www.cdc.gov/biomonitoring/phthalates_factsheet.html.

Chan, Emily. "'Successful Marriages Start in the Kitchen!' Outrageous Retro Advertising Slogans Reveal the Sexist Marketing Ploys Once Used to Sell Everything from Lingerie to Washing Machines." *Daily Mail*, January 9, 2018. Accessed July 10, 2018. http://www.dailymail.co.uk/femail/article-5249797/Adverts-1940s-50s-60s-world-changed.html.

Chan, Mi-Anne. "How Social Media Has Changed the Beauty Industry." *Refinery29*. Last modified November 8, 2016. Accessed July 7, 2017. https://www.refinery29.com/2015/12/99728/beauty-industry-social-media-effect.

Chan, Wilfred. "Thai Beauty Ad: 'Just Being White, You Will Win.'" CNN. Last modified January 8, 2016. Accessed July 4, 2017. https://www.cnn.com/2016/01/08/asia/thai-racist-white-beauty-ad/index.html.

"Chanel No 5: The Story Behind the Classic Perfume." *BBC News*, May 29, 2011. Accessed November 23, 2017. https://www.bbc.com/news/world-13565155.

Chang, Juju, and Victoria Thompson. "South Korea's Growing Obsession with Cosmetic Surgery." *ABC News*, June 20, 2014. Accessed July 28, 2017. https://abcnews.go.com/Lifestyle/south-koreas-growing-obsession-cosmetic-surgery/story?id=24123409.

Chapman, Catherine. "Women with Toned and Muscular Bodies Are Now Seen as MORE Attractive Than Those with Slim Figures." *Daily Mail*, January 25, 2018. Accessed October 29, 2019. https://www.dailymail.co.uk/sciencetech/article-5312187/Thinness-no-longer-considered-ideal-body-type-women.html.

Chatterjee, Sumeet. "Wipro Buys Some Yardley Operations for $45.5 Mln." Reuters, November 4, 2009. Accessed April 25, 2018. https://www.reuters.com/article/idINIndia-43698620091105.

Chemical Inspection & Regulation Service. "EU Cosmetics Regulations and Registration." Accessed July 14, 2017. http://www.cirs-reach.com/Cosmetics_Registration/eu_cosmetics_directive_cosmetics_registration.html.

Chesters, Anna. "A Brief History of Origins." *Guardian*, October 4, 2011. Accessed December 12, 2017. https://www.theguardian.com/fashion/fashion-blog/2011/oct/04/a-brief-history-of-origins.

Chiu, Allyson. "Patients Are Desperate to Resemble Their Doctored Selfies. Plastic Surgeons Alarmed by 'Snapchat Dysmorphia.'" *Washington Post*, August 6, 2018. Accessed November 3, 2019. https://www.washingtonpost.com/news/morning-mix/wp/2018/08/06/patients-are-desperate-to-resemble-their-doctored-selfies-plastic-surgeons-alarmed-by-snapchat-dysmorphia/.

Chiu, Joanna. "The Very Real Danger of Fake Cosmetics from China." *Mashable* (blog), November 10, 2015. Accessed July 14, 2017. https://mashable.com/2015/11/10/fake-makeup-china/#UabKuFALxPqj.

Chown, Marcus. "The Golden Rule." *Guardian*, January 15, 2003. Accessed October 10, 2019. https://www.theguardian.com/science/2003/jan/16/science.research1.

"Chris Evans for Gucci Guilty Pour Homme Fragrance." Design Scene. Accessed August 31, 2019. https://www.designscene.net/2010/12/chris-evans-gucci-guilty-pour-homme-fragrance.html.

Clark, C. Robert, and Ignatius J. Horstmann. "A Model of Advertising Format Competition: On the Use of Celebrities in Ads." *Canadian Journal of Economics/Revue Cana-*

dienne D'Economique 46, no. 4 (2013): 1606–30. Accessed July 24, 2017. doi: 10.1111/caje.12056.

Clé de Peau Beauté. "Company Information." Accessed August 16, 2019. https://www.cledepeaubeaute.com/company-info.html.

———. Eye shadow ad featuring Amanda Seyfried. Code MM. Accessed August 16, 2019. http://www.code-mm.com/work/creative-direction/cle-de-peau-beaute-2012-aw-david-sims.

Clement, J. "Leading Beauty Brands with the Most Followers on Facebook as of October 2019 (in Millions)." Statista, October 16, 2019. Accessed October 23, 2019. https://www.statista.com/statistics/300050/beauty-brands-follower-facebook/.

Clericuzio, Peter, and The Art Story Contributors, eds. "The Arts & Crafts Movement Overview and Analysis." *The Art Story.* Accessed August 15, 2018. https://www.theartstory.org/movement-arts-and-crafts.htm.

Clinique. "Clinique Start Better Manifesto." YouTube, published May 20, 2014. Accessed August 27, 2019. https://www.youtube.com/watch?v=19_JUAw_Zeg.

Codinha, Alessandra. "Makeup for Men Is on the Rise—and No Longer a Taboo." *Daily Beast*, May 14, 2013. Accessed July 18, 2017. https://www.thedailybeast.com/makeup-for-men-is-on-the-riseand-no-longer-a-taboo.

Coffee, Patrick. "Clinique Drops Models for Influencers in New Campaign." *Adweek*, July 14, 2015. Accessed July 15, 2017. https://www.adweek.com/digital/clinique-drops-models-for-influencers-in-new-campaign/.

Cohen, Anya. IBISWorld Industry Report 32562: Cosmetic & Beauty Products Manufacturing in the US. Los Angeles: IBISWorld, 2016. https://www.ibisworld.com/united-states/market-research-reports/cosmetic-beauty-products-manufacturing-industry/.

Coleman, Claire. "Granny's Favourite Beauty Brands Have Had a Millennial Makeover! But Can Yardley and Co's New Products Compete with Their Classics?" *Daily Mail*, March 28, 2018. Accessed July 25, 2018. http://www.dailymail.co.uk/femail/article-5556613/Grannys-favourite-beauty-brands-millennial-makeover.html.

Collins, Allison. "Millennials Disrupt Beauty Industry's Antiwrinkle Agenda." *Women's Wear Daily*, April 27, 2016. Accessed July 7, 2017. https://wwd.com/beauty-industry-news/skin-care/millennial-beauty-antiwrinkle-baby-boomer-10419202/.

Collins, Gail. *When Everything Changed: The Amazing Journey of American Women From 1960 to the Present.* Boston: Little, Brown and Co., 2014.

"Company News; SmithKline to Sell Yardley." *New York Times*, April 13, 1990. Accessed May 11, 2018. https://www.nytimes.com/1990/04/13/business/company-news-smithkline-to-sell-yardley.html.

Connell, Claudia. "I've Spent £55,000 Keeping My Face Young . . . and I Don't Regret a Penny! The Women Who Blow Their Budgets for the Perfect Line-Free Skin." *Daily Mail*, September 11, 2016. Accessed July 17, 2017. http://www.dailymail.co.uk/femail/article-3784418/I-ve-spent-55-000-keeping-face-young-don-t-regret-penny-women-blow-budgets-perfect-line-free-skin.html.

"Consent Order." In *Justipedia.* Accessed July 17, 2018. https://www.justipedia.com/definition/1912/consent-order.

Cook, Ian A., and Clay Warren, Sarah K. Pajot, David Schairer, and Andrew F. Leuchter. "Regional Brain Activation with Advertising Images." *Journal of Neuroscience, Psychology, and Economics* 4, no. 3 (2011): 147–60. Accessed July 28, 2019. doi: 10.1037/a0024809.

"Corrective Advertising." *Advertising Age*, September 15, 2003. Accessed July 20, 2018. http://adage.com/article/adage-encyclopedia/corrective-advertising/98418/.

Cortese, Anthony J. *Provocateur: Images of Women and Minorities in Advertising*, 4th ed. Lanham, MD: Rowman & Littlefield, 2015.

Cosgrave, Bronwyn. "A Fragrance Debut? First, It's Lights, Camera, Action." *New York Times*, October 2, 2016. Accessed July 2, 2017. https://www.nytimes.com/2016/10/03/fashion/fragrance-film-kenzo-world.html.

"Cosmetic." In *Online Etymology Dictionary*. Accessed August 21, 2019. https://www.etymonline.com/word/cosmetic.

"Cosmetic Ingredient Labeling." CosmeticsInfo.org. Accessed July 16, 2017. https://www.cosmeticsinfo.org/label.

Cosmetic Ingredient Review. "How Does CIR Work?" Accessed July 17, 2017. https://www.cir-safety.org/how-does-cir-work.

"Cosmetics." *Advertising Age*, September 15, 2003. Accessed July 5, 2017. https://adage.com/article/adage-encyclopedia/cosmetics/98419.

"Cosmetics History and Facts." *History of Cosmetics*. Accessed July 21, 2017. http://www.historyofcosmetics.net/.

"Cosmetics, Western." Encyclopedia.com. Last modified February 28, 2020. Accessed March 15, 2020. https://www.encyclopedia.com/fashion/encyclopedias-almanacs-transcripts-and-maps/cosmetics-western.

Cosmopolitan. Hearst Corporation, 2019. Accessed July 6, 2017. https://www.hearst.com/magazines/cosmopolitan.

"Cosmopolitan Demographic Profile 2017." *Cosmopolitan*. Accessed July 6, 2017. http://www.cosmomediakit.com/r5/showkiosk.asp?listing_id=4785154&category_code=demo&category_id=77109.

Covert, Bryce. "Super Bowl Ads Serve Up Sexism." *Forbes*, February 4, 2013. Accessed July 20, 2017. https://www.forbes.com/sites/brycecovert/2013/02/04/super-bowl-ads-serve-up-sexism/#2b9eb9d44644.

Cox, Rebecca. "Watch: The New Marilyn Monroe Chanel N°5 Advert." *Glamour*, November 1, 2013. Accessed July 19, 2017. https://www.glamourmagazine.co.uk/article/chanel-reveals-its-new-no5-campaign-star.

Creswell, Julie. "Nothing Sells Like Celebrity." *New York Times*, June 22, 2008. Accessed July 24, 2017. https://www.nytimes.com/2008/06/22/business/media/22celeb.html.

Croatto, Pete. "History Lesson! Learn How Colette, Audrey Hepburn, Leslie Caron & Vanessa Hudgens Transformed *Gigi*." Broadway.com, April 6, 2015. Accessed July 10, 2018. https://www.broadway.com/buzz/180286/history-lesson-learn-how-colette-audrey-hepburn-leslie-caron-vanessa-hudgens-transformed-gigi/.

Crockett, Richard J., Thomas Pruzinsky, and John Persing. "The Influence of Plastic Surgery 'Reality TV' on Cosmetic Surgery Patient Expectations and Decision Making." *Plastic and Reconstructive Surgery* 120, no. 1 (2007): 316–24. doi: 10.1097/01.prs.0000264339.67451.71.

Crooks, Ross. "Splurge vs. Save: Which Beauty Products Are Worth the Extra Cost?" *Mint-Life*, April 11, 2013. Accessed July 18, 2017. https://blog.mint.com/consumer-iq/splurge-vs-save-which-beauty-products-are-worth-the-extra-cost-0413/?display=wide.

Crutchfield, Dean. "Celebrity Endorsements Still Push Product." *Advertising Age*, September 22, 2010. Accessed July 24, 2017. http://adage.com/article/cmo-strategy/marketing-celebrity-endorsements-push-product/146023/.

"Cult of Domesticity." In *Wikipedia*. Last modified August 7, 2019. Accessed August 30, 2019. https://en.wikipedia.org/wiki/Cult_of_Domesticity.

Currie, Dawn H. *Girl Talk: Adolescent Magazines and Their Readers*. Toronto: University of Toronto Press, 1999. doi: 10.3138/9781442675346.

CVS Pharmacy. "Nuance Salma Hayek Brand Shop." Accessed July 27, 2017. https://www.cvs.com/shopbrand/aboutnuance.

Daboll, Peter. "Celebrities in Advertising Are Almost Always a Big Waste of Money." *Advertising Age*, January 12, 2011. Accessed August 1, 2017. http://adage.com/article/cmo-strategy/celebrities-ads-lead-greater-sales/148174/.

Dahl, Darren W., Jaideep Sengupta, and Kathleen D. Vohs. "Sex in Advertising: Gender Differences and the Role of Relationship Commitment." *Journal of Consumer Research* 36, no. 2 (2009): 215–31. Accessed July 1, 2017. doi: 10.1086/597158.

Danziger, Pamela N. "6 Trends Shaping the Future of the $532B Beauty Business." *Forbes*, September 1, 2019. Accessed November 4, 2019. https://www.forbes.com/sites/pamdanziger/2019/09/01/6-trends-shaping-the-future-of-the-532b-beauty-business/#3748f8ee588d.

Dass, Mayukh, Chiranjeev Kohli, Piyush Kumar, and Sunil Thomas. "A Study of the Antecedents of Slogan Liking." *Journal of Business Research* 67, no. 12 (2014): 2504–11. Accessed July 30, 2017. doi: 10.1016/j.jbusres.2014.05.004.

"David Lynch: Commercials, Ads and Promos." LynchNet: The David Lynch Resource. Accessed August 5, 2018. http://www.lynchnet.com/ads/.

David Suzuki Foundation. "'The Dirty Dozen' Cosmetic Chemicals to Avoid." Accessed July 17, 2017. https://davidsuzuki.org/queen-of-green/dirty-dozen-cosmetic-chemicals-avoid/.

Dawson, Alene. "Clamping Down on Beauty Products Claims." *Los Angeles Times*, October 28, 2012. Accessed July 10, 2017. http://www.latimes.com/fashion/alltherage/la-ig-beauty-crackdown-20121028-story.html#axzz2lTrOmZ00.

———. "Gen X Women Aging Gracefully? Try Beautifully." *Los Angeles Times*, September 25, 2011. Accessed July 11, 2017. http://articles.latimes.com/2011/sep/25/image/la-ig-genx-side-20110925.

———. "Gen X Women, Young for Their Age." *Los Angeles Times*, September 25, 2011. Accessed July 11, 2017. http://articles.latimes.com/2011/sep/25/image/la-ig-beauty-genx-20110925.

———. "What Is Beauty and Who Has It?" CNN, June 29, 2011. Accessed July 4, 2017. http://www.cnn.com/2011/LIVING/06/29/global.beauty.culture/index.html.

Dayu, Zhang. "China Considers End to Mandatory Animal Testing on Cosmetics." CNN, November 15, 2013. Accessed July 8, 2017. https://www.cnn.com/2013/11/15/world/asia/china-cosmetics-testing.

DeBraganza, Ninoska, and Heather A. Hausenblas. "Media Exposure of the Ideal Physique on Women's Body Dissatisfaction and Mood: The Moderating Effects of Ethnicity." *Journal of Black Studies* 40, no. 4 (2010): 700–16. Accessed July 24, 2017. doi: 10.1177/0021934708317723.

DEFY Media. "Millennials Ages 13–24 Declare It's Not Just the Cord, TV Content Doesn't Cut It." Business Wire, March 3, 2015. Accessed July 30, 2017. http://defymedia.com/2015/03/03/millennials-ages-13-24-declare-just-cord-tv-content-doesnt-cut/.

Degler, Carl N. "Curves In, Curves Out." Review of *American Beauty*, by Lois W. Banner. *New York Times*, April 7, 1983. Accessed July 6, 2017. https://www.nytimes.com/1983/04/17/books/curves-in-curves-out.html.

Deloitte LLP. "Shades for Success: Influence in the Beauty Market," produced by Deloitte LLP, 2017. Accessed November 2, 2019. https://www2.deloitte.com/content/dam/Deloitte/cn/Documents/international-business-support/deloitte-cn-ibs-france-beauty-market-en-2017.pdf.

De Melker, Saskia. "Researchers Measure Increasing Sexualization of Images in Magazines." PBS, December 21, 2013. Accessed July 1, 2017. https://www.pbs.org/newshour/nation/social_issues-july-dec13-sexualization_12-21.

Dennis, Brady. "FDA Official Says Cosmetics Industry Is Trying to Undercut Government Regulations." *Washington Post*, March 6, 2014. Accessed July 8, 2017. https://www.washingtonpost.com/national/health-science/fda-official-says-cosmetics-industry-is-trying-to-undercut-government-regulations/2014/03/06/3961bae2-a55b-11e3-8466-d34c451760b9_story.html?noredirect=on&utm_term=.d26fdd982449.

Derrick, Julyne. "8 Beauty Industry Buzzwords and Phrases to Watch Out For." *LiveAbout*. Last modified March 6, 2018. Accessed July 9, 2018. https://www.liveabout.com/beauty-industry-buzzwords-and-phrases-to-watch-out-for-346967.

Dholakia, Utpal. "Can a Celebrity Endorsement Hurt the Brand?" *Psychology Today*, November 3, 2015. Accessed July 26, 2017. https://www.psychologytoday.com/us/blog/the-science-behind-behavior/201511/can-celebrity-endorsement-hurt-the-brand.

Diaz, Ann-Christine. "Extreme Sports Athletes Put Bobbi Brown's Makeup to the Test." *Advertising Age*, April 21, 2015. Accessed September 4, 2019. https://adage.com/article/behind-the-work/extreme-sports-athletes-put-bobbi-brown-s-makeup-test/298138.

DiDonato, Theresa E. "5 Research-Backed Reasons We Wear Makeup." *Psychology Today*, February 6, 2015. Accessed July 11, 2017. https://www.psychologytoday.com/us/blog/meet-catch-and-keep/201502/5-research-backed-reasons-we-wear-makeup.

"Dieting through the Decades: What We've Learned from Fads." *Shape*. Accessed July 5, 2017. https://www.shape.com/blogs/weight-loss-coach/dieting-through-decades-what-weve-learned-fads.

Diller, Vivian. "The Anti–Cosmetic Surgery League: Does It Have Unexpected Consequences?" *Psychology Today*, November 29, 2011. Accessed July 10, 2017. https://www.psychologytoday.com/us/blog/face-it/201111/the-anti-cosmetic-surgery-league-does-it-have-unexpected-consequences.

Dines, Gail, and Jean M. Humez, eds. *Gender, Race, and Class in Media: A Critical Reader*, 3rd ed. Thousand Oaks, CA: Sage, 2011.

Dion, Karen, Ellen Berscheid, and Elaine Walster. "What Is Beautiful Is Good." *Journal of Personality and Social Psychology* 24, no. 3 (1972): 285–90. Accessed July 6, 2017. doi: 10.1037/h0033731.

Dittmann, Melissa. "Plastic Surgery: Beauty or Beast?" *Monitor on Psychology* 36, no. 8 (2005): 30. American Psychological Association. Accessed July 10, 2017. http://www.apa.org/monitor/sep05/surgery.aspx.

Dittmar, Helga. "How Do 'Body Perfect' Ideals in the Media Have a Negative Impact on Body Image and Behaviors? Factors and Processes Related to Self and Identity." *Journal of Social and Clinical Psychology* 28, no. 1 (2009): 1–8. Accessed July 30, 2017. doi: 10.1521/jscp.2009.28.1.1.

Doheny, Kathleen. "Cosmetic Surgery TV Shows Get Viewers Pondering." MedicineNet.com, August 9, 2007. Accessed July 12, 2017. https://www.medicinenet.com/script/main/art.asp?articlekey=83119.

Domonoske, Camila. "Mirror, Mirror: Does 'Fairest' Mean Most Beautiful or Most White?" NPR, May 18, 2014. Accessed July 3, 2018. https://www.npr.org/sections/codeswitch/2014/05/16/313154674/mirror-mirror-does-fairest-mean-most-beautiful-or-most-white.

"The Donna Reed Show (1958)." The Movie Database (TMDb). Accessed August 31, 2019. https://www.themoviedb.org/tv/10649-the-donna-reed-show.

Donnelly, Laura. "Girls as Young as Eight Being Groomed by Cosmetic Surgery Games." *Telegraph*, June 22, 2017. Accessed July 28, 2017. https://www.telegraph.co.uk/news/2017/06/22/girls-young-eight-groomed-cosmetic-surgery-games/.

Donohoe, Martin. "Women's Health in Context: Cosmetic Surgery Past, Present, and Future: Scope, Ethics, and Policy." *Medscape Ob/Gyn* 11, no. 2 (2006). Accessed July 27, 2018. https://www.medscape.com/viewarticle/542448.

Douglas, Joanna. "The Evolution of the Perfect Female Body." *Yahoo News*, December 20, 1015. Accessed October 20, 2019. https://news.yahoo.com/photos/the-evolution-of-the-perfect-c1421446673662/1930-the-soft-siren-1450638708187.html.

Dove-Viebahn, Aviva. "Future of Feminism: No More Media Sexualization of Women." *Ms.* (blog), March 9, 2012. Accessed July 9, 2017. http://msmagazine.com/blog/2012/03/09/future-of-feminism-no-more-media-sexualization-of-women/.

Dow Jones. "International Business; Yardley Brands Are Sold." *New York Times*, November 26, 1998. Accessed April 25, 2018. https://www.nytimes.com/1998/11/26/business/international-business-yardley-brands-are-sold.html.

Downing, Sarah Jane. *Beauty and Cosmetics 1550 to 1950*. London: Bloomsbury, 2012.

Doyle, Lisa. "Not Just a Pretty Face: The Power of a Celebrity Endorsement." *Global Cosmetic Industry*, November 7, 2012. Accessed July 25, 2017. https://www.gcimagazine.com/business/marketing/Not-Just-a-Pretty-Face-The-Power-of-a-Celebrity-Endorsement-177704111.html.

Dreisbach, Shaun. "Shocking Body-Image News: 97% of Women Will Be Cruel to Their Bodies Today." *Glamour*, February 3, 2011. Accessed July 9, 2017. https://www.glamour.com/story/shocking-body-image-news-97-percent-of-women-will-be-cruel-to-their-bodies-today.

Dries, Kate. "*Cosmo* Is Taking Over the World, One International Website at a Time." *Jezebel*, January 12, 2015. Accessed July 6, 2017. https://jezebel.com/cosmo-is-taking-over-the-world-one-international-websi-1679015736.

Driessens, Olivier. "Celebrity Capital: Redefining Celebrity Using Field Theory." *Theory and Society* 42, no. 5 (2013): 543–60. Accessed July 24, 2017. doi: 10.1007/s11186-013-9202-3.

Duenwald, Mary. "The Consumer; New Creams Smooth Wrinkles, but They're Not Botox." *New York Times*, June 22, 2004. Accessed July 6, 2017. https://www.nytimes.com/2004/06/22/health/the-consumer-new-creams-smooth-wrinkles-but-they-re-not-botox.html.

Dukcevich, Davide. "Josiah Wedgwood." *Forbes*, March 15, 2004. Accessed July 24, 2017. https://www.forbes.com/2004/03/15/cx_dd_mibp_0315wedgwood.html#7cc1670b133c.

Duronio, Ben. "Some Psychologists Did a Thorough Study of the 'Lipstick' Economic Indicator." *Business Insider*, June 28, 2012. Accessed July 18, 2017. https://www.businessinsider.com/lipstick-effect-mating-pscyhology-2012-6#ixzz3CfEkr8HA.

Eagly, Alice H., Richard D. Ashmore, Mona G. Makhijani, and Laura C. Longo. "What Is Beautiful Is Good, But . . . : A Meta-analytic Review of Research on the Physical

Attractiveness Stereotype." *Psychological Bulletin* 110, no. 1 (1991): 109–28. Accessed July 6, 2017. doi: 10.1037//0033-2909.110.1.109.

Eating Disorder Hope. "Weight & Body Image Disorders: Causes, Symptoms & Signs." Accessed July 9, 2017. https://www.eatingdisorderhope.com/information/body-image.

"The Economics of Good Looks: The Line on Beauty." *Economist*, August 27, 2011. Accessed January 12, 2018. https://www.economist.com/books-and-arts/2011/08/27/the-line-of -beauty.

Editorial Board. "Do You Know What's in Your Cosmetics?" *New York Times*, February 9, 2019. Accessed September 26, 2019. https://www.nytimes.com/2019/02/09/opinion/ cosmetics-safety-makeup.html.

Editors of Encyclopedia Britannica. "Kate Moss." In *Encyclopedia Britannica*. Accessed September 19, 2019. https://www.britannica.com/biography/Kate-Moss.

———. "Mona Lisa." In *Encyclopedia Britannica*. Last modified July 18, 2919. Accessed August 29, 2019. https://www.britannica.com/topic/Mona-Lisa-painting.

Edmonds, Molly. "How Makeup Works: History of Makeup." HowStuffWorks. Accessed August 21, 2019. https://people.howstuffworks.com/about-makeup1.htm.Elbaum, Rachel. "Britain to Crack Down on Gender Stereotypes in Advertising." *ABC News*, July 18, 2017. Accessed July 30, 2017. https://www.nbcnews.com/news/europe/britain-crackdown -gender-stereotypes-advertising-n783971.

Elberse, Anita. "Risks and Rewards of Celebrity Endorsements." CNN, December 16, 2009. Accessed July 26, 2017. http://www.cnn.com/2009/OPINION/12/16/elberse.athlete .endorsements.tiger.woods/index.html.

Elberse, Anita, and Jeroen Verleun. "The Economic Value of Celebrity Endorsements." *Journal of Advertising Research* 52, no. 2 (2012): 149–65. Accessed July 24, 2017. doi: 10.2501/ JAR-52-2-149-165.

Eleftheriou-Smith, Loulla-Mae. "Dove Wins at Inaugural Body Confidence Awards." *Campaign*, April 24, 2012. Accessed July 28, 2017. https://www.campaignlive.co.uk/article/ dove-wins-inaugural-body-confidence-awards/1128443#1rS8gurDcKhOLZyf.99.

Ellin, Abby. "That Nose, That Chin, Those Lips." *New York Times*, January 15, 2014. Accessed July 28, 2017. https://www.nytimes.com/2014/01/16/fashion/Plastic-surgery -celebrity-makeover.html.

Elliott, Larry. "Into the Red: 'Lipstick Effect' Reveals the True Face of the Recession." *Guardian*, December 21, 2008. Accessed August 21, 2019. https://www.theguardian.com/ business/2008/dec/22/recession-cosmetics-lipstick.

eMarketer. "Brand Advocates: Scaling Social Media Word-of-Mouth." October 2012. Accessed July 17, 2017. http://www.emarketer.com/public_media/docs/brand_advocates_ scaling_social_media_word_of_mouth.pdf.

———. "Millennials Dominate US Beauty Market." December 14, 2016. Accessed July 12, 2017. https://www.emarketer.com/Article/Millennials-Dominate-US-Beauty-Market/ 1014857.

Engagement Labs. "Engagement Labs Releases TotalSocial® Ranking of Top Personal Care and Beauty Brands." Engagement Labs press release, June 14, 2018. Accessed August 25, 2019. https://www.engagementlabs.com/press/engagement-labs-releases-totalsocial-ranking-top -personal-care-beauty-brands/.

———. "Mirror, Mirror on the Wall, Who Are the Top Ranked Beauty Brands on Social Media of Them All?" Engagement Labs press release, August 12, 2015. Accessed July

12, 2017. https://www.engagementlabs.com/press/mirror-mirror-on-the-wall-who-are-the
-top-ranked-beauty-brands-on-social-media-of-them-all/.

Enoch, Nick, and Wills Robinson. "Too Grimm for Disney: Original Editions of Classic
Fairy Tales Offer Darker Side of Brothers Grimm Stories—Including Self-Mutilation in
Cinderella and Rapunzel Getting Pregnant in Her Tower." *Daily Mail*, November 14,
2014. Accessed January 12, 2018. http://www.dailymail.co.uk/news/article-2833782/Even
-Grimmer-English-translation-Brothers-Grimm-earliest-edition-fairy-tales-reveals-darker
-world-s-loved-children-s-stories-including-Cinderella-Rapunzel.html.

"Entrepreneurs: Merchant of Glamour." *Time*, September 8, 1975. Accessed July 11, 2017.
http://content.time.com/time/magazine/article/0,9171,917802,00.html.

Environmental Working Group. "Dirty Dozen Endocrine Disruptors." October 28,
2013. Accessed July 14, 2017. https://www.ewg.org/research/dirty-dozen-list-endocrine
-disruptors#.W32esPZFxPY.

———. "Personal Care Products Safety Act Letter to Senate Leadership." August 30, 2016.
Accessed July 15, 2017. https://www.ewg.org/testimony-official-correspondence/personal
-care-products-safety-act-letter-senate-leadership#.W32exPZFxPY.

———. "Teen Girls' Body Burden of Hormone-Altering Cosmetics Chemicals: Cosmetics
Chemicals of Concern." September 24, 2008. Accessed July 14, 2017. https://www.ewg
.org/research/teen-girls-body-burden-hormone-altering-cosmetics-chemicals/cosmetics
-chemicals-concern#.W32ez_ZFxPY.

Erman, Michael, Ankur Banerjee, and Julie Steenhuysen. "AbbVie Looks Beyond Humira
with $63 Billion Deal for Botox-Maker Allergan." Reuters, June 25, 2019. Accessed July
30, 2019. https://www.reuters.com/article/us-allergan-m-a-abbvie-idUSKCN1TQ15X.

Escobar, Sam. "The Number of Makeup Products the Average Woman Owns Is Just Plain
Shocking." *Good Housekeeping*, October 14, 2015. Accessed July 14, 2017. https://www
.goodhousekeeping.com/beauty/makeup/a34976/average-makeup-products-owned/.

"Estee Lauder Inc." Encyclopedia.com. Accessed August 21, 2019. https://www.encyclopedi
a.com/people/social-sciences-and-law/business-leaders/estee-lauder-inc.

"Estée Lauder: Marketing Cosmetics." *Who Made America?* PBS. Accessed August 22, 2019.
http://www.pbs.org/wgbh/theymadeamerica/whomade/lauder_hi.html.

"Estee Lauder: The Sweet Smell of Success." *Entrepreneur*, October 10, 2008. Accessed July
21, 2017. https://www.entrepreneur.com/article/197658.

"The Estée Story." The Estée Lauder Companies. Accessed August 8, 2019. https://www
.elcompanies.com/en/who-we-are/the-lauder-family/the-estee-story.

Etehad, Melissa. "From L.A. to Tehran, Nose Jobs Are a Rite of Passage and a Quiet Rebellion for Many Persian Women." *Los Angeles Times*, March 31, 2017. Accessed August 1,
2017. http://www.latimes.com/local/california/la-me-ln-persian-nose-job-20170130-story
.html.

European Advertising Standards Alliance. "Promoting Responsible Advertising." Accessed July
1, 2017. http://www.easa-alliance.org/about-easa/what-we-do.

———. "Welcome to EASA." Accessed October 12, 2019. https://www.easa-alliance.org/.

European Association of Communications Agencies. "Gender Portrayal and Stereotyping."
Accessed July 2, 2017. http://eaca.eu/wp-content/uploads/2018/03/Position-paper-gender
-2018.pdf.

———. "Statement of Gender Portrayal." Accessed July 29, 2019. https://eaca.eu/wp-content/
uploads/2018/03/EACA-position-statement-2018.pdf.

European Chemicals Agency. "Understanding REACH." Accessed December 12, 2017. https://echa.europa.eu/regulations/reach/understanding-reach.

"Eva Mendes Steamy Perfume Ads Banned." *Marie Claire*, August 4, 2008. Accessed June 6, 2018. https://www.marieclaire.co.uk/news/beauty-news/eva-mendes-steamy-perfume-ads -banned-184789.

Evans, Jonathan. "The NSFW History of Calvin Klein's Provocative Ads." *Esquire*, July 7, 2016. Accessed July 7, 2018. https://www.esquire.com/style/news/g2841/nsfw-history -calvin-klein-advertising/.

"'Even Pesticides' Are More Regulated Than Cosmetics: A New California Bill Wants to Change That." *The Fashion Law*, March 28, 2019. Accessed September 26, 2019. https:// www.thefashionlaw.com/home/even-pesticides-are-more-regulated-than-cosmetics-a-new -california-bill-wants-to-change-that.

"Facing the Facts." *Economist*, August 13, 2014. Accessed July 6, 2017. https://www .economist.com/science-and-technology/2014/08/13/facing-the-facts.

Fan, J. "Perception of Body Appearance and Its Relation to Clothing." In *Clothing Appearance and Fit* (2004), Internal Representation, *ScienceDirect*. Accessed September 4, 2019. https://www.sciencedirect.com/topics/engineering/internal-representation.

Farhi, Paul. "Obsession for 'Twin Peaks.'" *Washington Post*, August 16, 1990. Accessed July 19, 2018. https://www.washingtonpost.com/archive/lifestyle/1990/08/16/obsession-for -twin-peaks/8c83b84a-2d10-4c58-aacf-7987c1c9e28e/?noredirect=on&utm_term =.edac8231d3be.

Farkas, Brian. "Trade Secret Basics FAQ." Nolo.com. Accessed August 4, 2018. https://www .nolo.com/legal-encyclopedia/trade-secret-basics-faq.html.

Faulke, Judith E. "Cosmetic Labeling." *FindLaw*, September 24, 1996. Accessed July 16, 2017. https://corporate.findlaw.com/law-library/cosmetic-labeling.html.

"FDA/Company Cosmetic Registration Program." CosmeticsInfo.org. Accessed July 17, 2017. https://www.cosmeticsinfo.org/VCRP.

"FDA Issues Warning Letter to Lancôme USA about Génifique Line of Products." *Dermatologist*, September 19, 2012. Accessed July 17, 2017. https://www.the-dermatologist.com/ content/fda-issues-warning-letter-lancôme-usa-about-génifique-line-products.

Federal Communications Commission. "The FCC and Freedom of Speech." Accessed October 25, 2019. https://www.fcc.gov/consumers/guides/fcc-and-freedom-speech.

"Federal Food, Drug, and Cosmetic of 1938." Ballotpedia. Accessed August 22, 2019. https:// ballotpedia.org/Federal_Food,_Drug,_and_Cosmetic_Act_of_1938.

Federal Trade Commission. "Advertisement Endorsements." Accessed July 17, 2017. https:// www.ftc.gov/news-events/media-resources/truth-advertising/advertisement-endorsements.

———. "Advertising and Marketing." Accessed July 1, 2017. https://www.ftc.gov/tips-advice/ business-center/advertising-and-marketing.

———. "Advertising Substantiation Principles." Accessed July 17, 2017. https://www.ftc.gov/ sites/default/files/attachments/training-materials/substantiation.pdf.

———. "A Brief Overview of the Federal Trade Commission's Investigative, Law Enforcement, and Rulemaking Authority." Last modified July 2008. Accessed July 17, 2017. https://www .ftc.gov/about-ftc/what-we-do/enforcement-authority.

———. "Consumer Protection 2016.0: Challenges in Advertising." By Jessica Rich, Director, Bureau of Consumer Protection, April 7, 2016. Accessed July 17, 2017. https://www .ftc.gov/system/files/documents/public_statements/944423/160407digitalrevolutionadver tising.pdf.

———. "Division of Advertising Practices." Accessed July 2, 2017. https://www.ftc.gov/about-ftc/bureaus-offices/bureau-consumer-protection/our-divisions/division-advertising-practices.

———. "Four Companies Agree to Stop Falsely Promoting Their Personal-Care Products as 'All Natural' or '100% Natural'; Fifth Is Charged in Commission Complaint." FTC press release, April 12, 2016. Accessed July 15, 2017. https://www.ftc.gov/news-events/press-releases/2016/04/four-companies-agree-stop-falsely-promoting-their-personal-care.

———. "FTC Approves Final Order Settling Charges That L'Oréal USA, Inc. Made Deceptive Advertising Claims for Its Anti-aging Cosmetics." FTC press release, September 26, 2014. Accessed July 17, 2017. https://www.ftc.gov/news-events/press-releases/2014/09/ftc-approves-final-order-settling-charges-loreal-usa-inc-made.

———. "FTC Policy Statement on Deception." Letter from James C. Miller, III, Chairman, Federal Trade Commission, to Representative John D. Dingell, Chairman, House Committee on Energy and Commerce. October 14, 1983. Appended to Cliffdale Associates, Inc., 103 F.T.C. 110, 174 (1984). Accessed July 15, 2017. https://www.ftc.gov/system/files/documents/public_statements/410531/831014deceptionstmt.pdf.

———. "FTC Policy Statement Regarding Advertising Substantiation." March 11, 1983. Accessed July 16, 2017. https://www.ftc.gov/public-statements/1983/03/ftc-policy-statement-regarding-advertising-substantiation.

———. "L'Oréal Settles FTC Charges Alleging Deceptive Advertising for Anti-aging Cosmetics." FTC press release, June 30, 2014. Accessed July 17, 2017. https://www.ftc.gov/news-events/press-releases/2014/06/loreal-settles-ftc-charges-alleging-deceptive-advertising-anti.

———. "Truth in Advertising." Accessed July 17, 2017. https://www.ftc.gov/news-events/media-resources/truth-advertising.

Feldman, Jamie. "'World's First Size 22 Supermodel' Tess Holliday Lands Cover of People Magazine." *Huffington Post*, May 20, 2015. Accessed March 15, 2020. https://www.huffpost.com/entry/tess-holliday-people-maga_n_7343192.

Feldman, Sally. "The Enduring Appeal of Makeup." *New Humanist*, January 25, 2016. Accessed July 21, 2017. https://newhumanist.org.uk/articles/4990/the-enduring-appeal-of-makeup.

Felix, Samantha. "18 Ads That Changed How We Think about Women." *Business Insider*, October 28, 2012. Accessed July 10, 2017. https://www.businessinsider.com/18-ads-that-changed-the-way-we-think-about-women-2012-10?op=1#ixzz2l6anenfc.

Felton, George. *Advertising: Concept and Copy*, 3rd ed. New York: Norton, 2013.

"Feminism, Impact of." *Advertising Age*, September 15, 2003. Accessed July 2, 2017. http://adage.com/article/adage-encyclopedia/feminism-impact/98471/.

Feng, Charles. "Looking Good: The Psychology and Biology of Beauty." *Journal of Young Investigators* 6, no. 6 (2002). Accessed July 6, 2017. http://legacy.jyi.org/volumes/volume6/issue6/features/feng.html.

Ferguson, Kelly K., Thomas F. McElrath, and John D. Meeker. "Environmental Phthalate Exposure and Preterm Birth." *JAMA Pediatrics* 168, no. 1 (2014): 61–67. Accessed July 14, 2017. doi:10.1001/jamapediatrics.2013.3699.

Ferguson, Sarah. "How Much Does Your Face Cost? A New Survey Finds That the Average Woman in the U.S. Will Spend Up to $300,000 on Beauty Products in Her Lifetime." *Daily Mail*, April 6, 2017. Accessed July 31, 2017. http://www.dailymail.co.uk/femail/article-4383930/How-Women-U-S-Spend-Beauty-Products.html#ixzz4wGrd8onn.

Festinger, Leon. "A Theory of Social Comparison Processes." *Human Relations* 7, no. 2 (1954): 117–40. Accessed July 29, 2017. doi: 10.1177/001872675400700202.

Feto, John. "Where's the Lovin'?" *Advertising Age*, February 2, 2011. Accessed July 1, 2017. http://adage.com/article/american-demographics/lovin/42214.

"Few Women Over 50 Like Their Bodies, Study Shows." *Huffington Post*, October 24, 2013. Accessed July 9, 2017. https://www.huffingtonpost.com/2013/10/24/women-body -image_n_4156825.html.

"50+ Sexist Vintage Ads So Bad, You Almost Won't Believe They Were Real." Click Americana. Accessed August 16, 2019. https://clickamericana.com/topics/culture-and-lifestyle/ 50-sexist-vintage-ads-so-bad-you-almost-wont-believe-they-were-real.

Fitch, Dede. "Celebrity Power: Can Less Be More?" Millward Brown's POV, December 2006. Accessed July 25, 2017. http://www.millwardbrown.com/docs/default-source/insight -documents/points-of-view/MillwardBrown_POV_CelebrityPower.pdf.

"Flatteners." In *Encyclopedia of Fashion*. Accessed July 6, 2017. http://www.fashion encyclopedia.com/fashion_costume_culture/Modern-World-1919-1929/Flatteners.html.

Foltz, Kim. "All About/Cover Girls; The Look That Sells Is Both Girl-Next-Door and Celebrity." *New York Times*, May 24, 1992. Accessed July 19, 2018. https://www.nytimes .com/1992/05/24/business/all-about-cover-girls-the-look-that-sells-is-both-girl-next-door -and-celebrity.html.

———. "The Media Business: Advertising; A New Twist for Klein's Obsession." *New York Times*, August 15, 1990. Accessed July 19, 2018. https://www.nytimes.com/1990/08/15/ business/the-media-business-advertising-a-new-twist-for-klein-s-obsession.html.

"For Millennial Women, Beauty Is Fun." MillennialMarketing.com, August 2012. Accessed July 7, 2017. http://www.millennialmarketing.com/2012/08/for-millennial-women -beauty-is-fun/.

Foreman, Katya. "The Changing Faces of Barbie." BBC, May 11, 2016. Accessed July 30, 2017. http://www.bbc.com/culture/story/20160511-the-changing-faces-of-barbie.

Franke-Ruta, Garance. "The Natural Beauty Myth." *Wall Street Journal*, December 15, 2006. Accessed July 10, 2017. https://www.wsj.com/articles/SB116615895325651304.

Frazier, Mya. "Honor Your Mother: Don't Watch That Patronizing Viral Ad." *New Republic*, May 8, 2014. Accessed July 3, 2017. https://newrepublic.com/article/117693/mothers -advertising-regressive-stereotypes-dominate-pg-and-others.

Fredrickson, Barbara L., and Tomi-Ann Roberts. "Objectification Theory: Toward Understanding Women's Lived Experiences and Mental Health Risks." *Psychology of Women Quarterly* 21, no. 2 (1997): 173–206. Accessed July 2, 2017. doi: 10.1111/j.1471-6402.1997 .tb00108.x.

Freeman, Laurie. "John Peoples Pantene Prov-V." *Advertising Age*, July 4, 1994. Accessed August 5, 2018. http://adage.com/article/news/john-peoples-pantene-pro-v/91281.

"French and Raven's Five Forms of Power." MindTools. Accessed August 10, 2019. https:// www.mindtools.com/pages/article/newLDR_56.htm.

Friedan, Betty. *The Feminine Mystique*. New York: Norton, 1963.

Friedman, Vanessa. "Underage Models Return to the Runway and Reignite a Debate." *New York Times*, July 22, 2015. Accessed July 27, 2017. https://www.nytimes.com/2015/07/23/ fashion/underage-models-return-to-the-runway-and-reignite-a-debate.html?mcubz=0.

Frith, Katherine T., and Barbara Mueller. *Advertising and Societies: Global Issues*, 2nd ed. Bern, CH: Peter Lang, 2010.

"From Mass to Class—the Future of Masstige." Cosmetics Business, August 12, 2010. Accessed July 21, 2017. https://www.cosmeticsbusiness.com/news/article_page/From_mass_to_class_-_the_future_of_masstige/55985.

Frucht, Corey S., and Arisa E. Ortiz. "Nonsurgical Cosmetic Procedures for Men: Trends and Technique Considerations." *Journal of Clinical and Aesthetic Dermatology* 9, no. 12 (2016): 33–43. Accessed July 28, 2017. https://www.ncbi.nlm.nih.gov/pmc/articles/PMC5300725/pdf/jcad_9_12_33.pdf.

Furnham, Adrian, and James Levitas. "Factors That Motivate People to Undergo Cosmetic Surgery." *Canadian Journal of Plastic Surgery* 20, no. 4 (2012): e47–e50. *Europe PMC*. Accessed July 28, 2019. doi: 10.1177/229255031202000406.

Fury, Alexander. "Men's Grooming Is Now a Multi-Billion Pound Worldwide Industry." *Independent*, January 14, 2016. Accessed July 18, 2017. https://www.independent.co.uk/life-style/fashion/features/mens-grooming-is-now-a-multi-billion-pound-worldwide-industry-a6813196.html.

Gabler, Neal. "The Brief Half-Life of Celebrity." *New York Times*, October 16, 1994. Accessed September 27, 2019. https://www.nytimes.com/1994/10/16/arts/the-brief-half-life-of-celebrity.html.

Gage, Eleni N. "What Are Parabens—and Do I Need to Worry about Them?" *Real Simple*. Accessed July 15, 2017. https://www.realsimple.com/beauty-fashion/skincare/worry-about-parabens.

Galindo, Brian. "'Noxzema Girl' Was Rebecca Gayheart's Biggest Contribution to the '90s." *BuzzFeed*, March 25, 2013. Accessed August 17, 2019, https://www.buzzfeed.com/brian galindo/noxzema-girl-was-rebecca-gayhearts-biggest-contribution-to-t.

Garcia, Tonya. "Promoting a Positive Body Image Doesn't Mean Banishing All Thin Models." *Adweek*, July 30, 2015. Accessed July 27, 2017. https://www.adweek.com/digital/womens-running-positive-body-image/.

Gardner, Eriq. "Judge Agrees Broadcasters Have First Amendment Right to Refuse Advertisements." *Hollywood Reporter*, May 24, 2017. Accessed July 15, 2018. https://www.hollywoodreporter.com/thr-esq/judge-agrees-broadcasters-have-first-amendment-right-refuse-advertisements-1007317.

Garrison, Cassandra. "UK Watchdog to Crack Down on Gender Stereotypes in Adverts in Britain." Reuters. July 18, 2017. Accessed July 30, 2017. https://www.reuters.com/article/us-britain-adverts-idUSKBN1A31IO?il=0.

Gartner. "Gartner L2 Digital IQ Index: Beauty U.S. 2018." Gartner for Marketers Research, March 9, 2018. Accessed August 27, 2019. https://www.gartner.com/en/marketing/research/beauty-us-2018.

Gartrell, Ellen. "Emergence of Advertising in America: 1850–1920, Pond's Advertisements." John W. Hartman Center for Sales, Advertising & Marketing History. Duke University Rare Book, Manuscript, and Special Collections Library. Accessed August 9, 2019. https://library.duke.edu/rubenstein/scriptorium/eaa/ponds.html.

Gavron, Darlene. "Portrait of the Times Is Winner." *Chicago Tribune*, July 17, 1988. Accessed August 8, 2019. https://www.chicagotribune.com/news/ct-xpm-1988-07-17-8801160123-story.html.

Gee, Rachel. "Influencers Top List of the Biggest Celebrity Endorsers in 2016." *Marketing Week*, January 24, 2017. Accessed July 27, 2017. https://www.marketingweek.com/2017/01/24/top-20-endorsers-2016/.

———. "The Representation of Women in Advertising Hasn't Improved in a Decade." *Marketing Week*, June 21, 2017. Accessed July 2, 2017. https://www.marketingweek.com/ 2017/06/21/representation-women-ads/.

Geena Davis Institute on Gender in Media. "Gender Bias in Advertising: Research, Trends and New Visual Language." Accessed August 1, 2017. https://seejane.org/research-informs -empowers/gender-bias-advertising/.

Gellad, Ziad F., and Kenneth W. Lyles. "Direct-to-Consumer Advertising of Pharmaceuticals." *American Journal of Medicine* 120, no. 6 (2007): 475–80. Accessed July 28, 2017. doi: 10.1016/j.amjmed.2006.09.030.

"Gender Advertisement." In *Wikipedia*. Last modified June 3, 2019. Accessed August 31, 2019. https://en.wikipedia.org/wiki/Gender_advertisement.

Gerbner, George. "Cultivation Analysis: An Overview." *Mass Communication and Society* 1, nos. 3–4 (1998): 175–94. Accessed July 1, 2017. doi: 10.1080/15205436.1998.9677855.

Gianatasio, David. "Hunkvertising: The Objectification of Men in Advertising." *Adweek*, October 7, 2013. Accessed July 2, 2017. https://www.adweek.com/brand-marketing/ hunkvertising-objectification-men-advertising-152925/.

"The Gibson Girl's America: Drawings by Charles Dana Gibson." Library of Congress. Accessed August 30, 2019. https://www.loc.gov/exhibits/gibson-girls-america/the-gibson-girl -as-the-new-woman.html.

Gillan, Audrey. "Skinny Models 'Send Unhealthy Message.'" *Guardian*, May 30, 2000. Accessed July 29, 2017. https://www.theguardian.com/uk/2000/may/31/audreygillan.

Glamour Daze. "Max Factor, Elizabeth Arden and Helena Rubinstein." November 30, 2009. Accessed August 21, 2019. https://glamourdaze.com/2009/11/history-of-glamour -makeup-max-factor.html.

Gleason-Allured, Jeb. "Beauty Brands Winning without Traditional Advertising." *Global Cosmetic Industry*, September 20, 2015. Accessed July 12, 2017. https://www.gcimagazine .com/business/marketing/Beauty-Brands-Winning-without-Traditional-Advertising— 328426401.html.

"Global Anti-aging Market 2017 Is Growing Rapidly and Expected to Reach $331.41 Billion by 2021—Orbis Research." MarketersMedia press release, June 19, 2017. Accessed July 17, 2018. https://marketersmedia.com/global-anti-aging-market-2017-is-growing-rapidly -and-expected-to-reach-331-41-billion-by-2021-orbis-research/209086.

"Global Cosmetics Market 2018—Industry Analysis, Size, Share, Strategies and Forecast to 2025. *MarketWatch* press release, September 4, 2018. Accessed July 28, 2019, https://www .marketwatch.com/press-release/global-cosmetics-market-2018-industry-analysis-size -share-strategies-and-forecast-to-2025-2018-09-04.

Glynn, Taylore. "In Honor of the Queen's Birthday, 5 Royal Family-Approved Beauty Brands." *Marie Claire*, April 21, 2018. Accessed May 11, 2018. https://www.marieclaire .com/beauty/makeup/g4602/royal-family-beauty-favorites/.

Godlewski, Nina. "Barbie 60th Anniversary, Birthday, History and Facts about the Doll; What's Her Last Name?" *Newsweek*, March 9, 2019. Accessed September 7, 2019. https:// www.newsweek.com/barbie-60th-birthday-real-name-1357397.

Goffman, Erving. *Gender Advertisements*. New York: Harper & Row, 1979. http://public collectors.org/Goffman_Gender.pdf.

Gold, Tanya. "Body Confidence Awards: A Start in Fightback Against Image-Makers." *Guardian*, April 20, 2012. Accessed July 28, 2017. https://www.theguardian.com/fashion/2012/ apr/20/body-confidence-awards-fightback.

———. "L'Oréal's Pulled Adverts: This Ideal of Female Beauty Is an Abomination." *Guardian*, July 29, 2011. Accessed July 10, 2017. https://www.theguardian.com/commentis free/2011/jul/29/loreal-adverts-pulled-by-asa-beauty-tanya-gold.

Goldberg, Hannah. "This Ad Completely Redefines the Phrase 'Like a Girl.'" *Time*, June 26, 2014. Accessed August 12, 2019. https://time.com/2927761/likeagirl-always-female -empowerment/.

Goldberg, Lesley. "Jessica Biel Goes Glam for Revlon." *Hollywood Reporter*, November 13, 2010. Accessed September 1, 2019. https://www.hollywoodreporter.com/news/jessica-biel -glam-revlon-44803.

Goldhill, Olivia. "Are We Falling Out of Love with Barbie?" *Telegraph*, October 17, 2014. Accessed July 31, 2017. https://www.telegraph.co.uk/women/womens-life/11169524/Are -we-falling-out-of-love-with-Barbie.html.

Goldstein, Sasha. "Barbie as a Real Woman Is Anatomically Impossible and Would Have to Walk on All Fours, Chart Shows." *New York Daily News*, April 14, 2013. Accessed August 10, 2019. https://www.nydailynews.com/life-style/health/barbie-real-womaan-anatomically -impossible-article-1.1316533.

Goldwert, Lindsay. "AMA Takes Stand on Photoshop; Medical Association: Altering Contributes to Unrealistic Expectations." *New York Daily News*, June 24, 2011. Accessed July 27, 2017. http://www.nydailynews.com/life-style/fashion/ama-takes-stand-photoshop-medical -association-altering-contributes-unrealistic-expectations-article-1.126921.

———. "Axe 'Angels' Deodorant Ad Yanked for Offending Christians." *New York Daily News*, October 29, 2011. Accessed July 4, 2017. http://www.nydailynews.com/life-style/fashion/ axe-angels-deodorant-ad-yanked-offending-christians-article-1.968858.

Goode, Erica. "Study Finds TV Alters Fiji Girls' View of Body." *New York Times*, May 20, 1999. Accessed July 27, 2017. https://www.nytimes.com/1999/05/20/world/study-finds -tv-alters-fiji-girls-view-of-body.html.

GoPro. "Bobbi Brown Cosmetics Selects Female GoPro Brand Ambassadors." GoPro press release, April 2015. Accessed September 4, 2019. https://gopro.com/en/us/news/bobbi -brown-cosmetics-selects-female-gopro-brand-ambassadors.

Goudreau, Jenna. "The 10 Worst Stereotypes about Powerful Women." *Forbes*, October 24, 2011. Accessed July 4, 2017. https://www.forbes.com/sites/jennagoudreau/2011/10/24/ worst-stereotypes-powerful-women-christine-lagarde-hillary-clinton/#1a666e5761ca.

Gould, Daniel J., Hyuma A. Leland, Adelyn L. Ho., and Ketan M. Patel. "Emerging Trends in Social Media and Plastic Surgery." *Annals of Translational Medicine* 4, no. 23 (2016): 455. Accessed July 27, 2017. doi:10.21037/atm.2016.12.17.

Government of Canada. "Cosmetic Ingredient Hotlist: Prohibited and Restricted Ingredients." November 11, 2011. Accessed July 28, 2018. https://www.canada.ca/en/health -canada/services/consumer-product-safety/cosmetics/cosmetic-ingredient-hotlist-prohibited -restricted-ingredients.html.

Graff, Amy. "'Don't Let Them Call You Skinny': Vintage Ads Push Women to Gain Weight." *SFGate*, July 16, 2012. Accessed September 25, 2019. https://blog.sfgate.com/ sfmoms/2012/07/16/dont-let-them-call-you-skinny-vintage-ads-push-women-to-gain -weight/#photo-129217.

Granero, Kristin. "What Is J-Beauty? Best Japanese Beauty Skin Care Products." *Today*, May 9, 2019. Accessed August 21, 2019. https://www.today.com/style/what-j-beauty-best -japanese-beauty-skin-care-products-t150969.

Gray, Emma. "The 'Perfect Woman' in 1912, Elsie Scheel, Was 171 Pounds and Loved Beefsteaks." *Huffington Post*, December 26, 2012. Accessed July 27, 2018. https://www.huffingtonpost.com/2012/12/26/perfect-woman-1912_n_2365529.html.

Greenspan, Jesse. "The Dark Side of the Grimm Fairy Tales." History.com, September 17, 2013. Accessed January 12, 2018. https://www.history.com/news/the-dark-side-of-the-grimm-fairy-tales.

Greenwood, Elizabeth. "'Mirror Mirror' Shows That the Evil Witch Is the Real Hero of 'Snow White.'" *Atlantic*, March 30, 2012. Accessed July 3, 2018. https://www.theatlantic.com/entertainment/archive/2012/03/mirror-mirror-shows-that-the-evil-witch-is-the-real-hero-of-snow-white/255248/.

Greer, Germaine. *The Female Eunuch*. New York: Harper Perennial, 1970.

Gregoire, Carolyn. "Body Image Issues among Young Women More Influenced by Peers Than TV, Study Finds." *Huffington Post*, January 31, 2013. Accessed July 9, 2017. https://www.huffingtonpost.com/2013/01/31/body-image-issues-for-you_n_2590719.html.

Grimm, Jacob, and Wilhelm Grimm. *The Annotated Brothers Grimm*. Edited and translated by Maria Tatar. New York: Norton, 2004.

Grinberg, Emanuella. "How to Create Ads That Don't Objectify Women." CNN. Last modified February 18, 2016. Accessed July 4, 2017. http://www.cnn.com/style/article/women-not-objects-madonna-badger-feat/index.html.

Griner, David. "Powerful Ads Use Real Google Searches to Show the Scope of Sexism Worldwide." *Adweek*, October 18, 2013. Accessed July 20, 2017. https://www.adweek.com/creativity/powerful-ads-use-real-google-searches-show-scope-sexism-worldwide-153235/.

Grogan, Sarah. *Body Image: Understanding Body Dissatisfaction in Men, Women and Children*, 3rd ed. London: Routledge, 2016.

Gunter, Barrie. *Celebrity Capital: Assessing the Value of Fame*. London: Bloomsbury, 2014.

Gurari, Inbal, John J. Hetts, and Michael J. Strube. "Beauty in the 'I' of the Beholder: Effects of Idealized Media Portrayals on Implicit Self-Image." *Basic and Applied Social Psychology* 28, no. 3 (2006): 273–82. Accessed July 27, 2017. doi: 10.1207/s15324834basp2803_6.

Guttman, A. "Advertising Spending in the Perfumes, Cosmetics, and Other Toilet Preparations Industry in the United States from 2010 to 2017 (in Million U.S. Dollars)." Statista. Last modified November 29, 2018. Accessed August 29, 2019. https://www.statista.com/statistics/470467/perfumes-cosmetics-and-other-toilet-preparations-industry-ad-spend-usa/.

Haines, Elizabeth L., Kay Deaux, and Nicole Lofaro. "The Times They Are A-Changing . . . or Are They Not? A Comparison of Gender Stereotypes, 1983–2014." *Psychology of Women Quarterly* 40, no. 3 (2016): 353–63. Accessed July 2, 2017. doi: 10.1177/0361684316634081.

Hall, Emma. "News: Linda Evangelista Stars in Yardley Launch Ad." *Campaign*, September 13, 1996. Accessed May 11, 2018. https://www.campaignlive.co.uk/article/news-linda-evangelista-stars-yardley-launch-ad/22987.

———. "U.K. Bans Gender Stereotypes in Ads." *Ad Age*, July 18, 2017. Accessed July 30, 2017. http://adage.com/article/global-news/u-k-bands-gender-stereotypes-ads/309785/.

Halliwell, Emma, and Helga Dittmar. "Does Size Matter? The Impact of Model's Body Size on Women's Body-Focused Anxiety and Advertising Effectiveness." *Journal of Social and Clinical Psychology* 23, no. 1 (2004): 104–22. Accessed July 30, 2017. doi: 10.1521/jscp.23.1.104.26989.

Halzack, Sarah. "The Sephora Effect: How the Cosmetics Retailer Transformed the Beauty Industry." *Washington Post*, March 9, 2015. Accessed July 17, 2017. https://www

.washingtonpost.com/news/business/wp/2015/03/09/the-sephora-effect-how-the-cosmetics
-retailer-transformed-the-beauty-industry/?utm_term=.83713a75db3f.

———. "Women Are Scrimping on Clothes, but Splurging on This." *Washington Post*, March 30, 2016. Accessed July 11, 2017. https://www.washingtonpost.com/news/business/wp/2016/03/30/women-are-scrimping-on-clothes-but-splurging-on-this/?noredirect=on&utm_term=.f9abd9b37246.

"'Harmful' Gender Stereotypes in Adverts Banned." *BBC News*, June 14, 2019. Accessed September 1, 2019. https://www.bbc.com/news/business-48628678.

Harper, Brit, and Marika Tiggemann. "The Effect of Thin Ideal Media Images on Women's Self-Objectification, Mood, and Body Image." *Sex Roles* 58, no. 9 (2008): 649–57. Accessed July 29, 2017. doi: 10.1007/s11199-007-9379-x.

Harrington, Kevin. "Celebrity Branding Is Making a Comeback—Tips for Success." *Forbes*, August 18, 2014. Accessed July 25, 2017. https://www.forbes.com/sites/kevinharrington/2014/08/18/celebrity-branding-is-making-a-comeback-tips-for-success/#1b61236465d0.

———. "Save Your Money: Celebrity Endorsements Not Worth the Cost." *Forbes*, January 31, 2014. Accessed August 1, 2017. https://www.forbes.com/sites/kevinharrington/2014/01/31/save-your-money-celebrity-endorsements-not-worth-the-cost/#1120578c24f3.

Harrington, Rory. "Scientist Defends Study Linking Phthalates to Feminising Boys." Food-Navigator.com. Last modified November 19, 2009. Accessed July 14, 2017. https://www.foodnavigator.com/Article/2009/11/19/Scientist-defends-study-linking-phthalates-to-feminising-boys#.

Harris, Neil. *Business Economics: Theory and Application*. London: Routledge, 2007.

Hawkins, Nicole, P. Scott Richards, H. Mac Granley, and David M. Stein. "The Impact of Exposure to the Thin-Ideal Media Image on Women." *Eating Disorders: The Journal of Treatment & Prevention* 12, no. 1 (2004): 35–50. Accessed July 27, 2017. doi: 10.1080/10640260490267751.

Hawley, Julia. "Top 5 Companies Owned by Estee Lauder (EL)." In *Investopedia*, October 5, 2018. https://www.investopedia.com/articles/markets/022016/top-5-companies-owned-estee-lauder-el.asp.

Hayzlett, Jeffrey. "What Does It Mean to Be a Good Brand Ambassador?" *Entrepreneur*, June 25, 2015. Accessed July 16, 2017. https://www.entrepreneur.com/article/246773.

Heckle, Harold. "Madrid Fashion Show Bans 5 Thin Models." *Washington Post*, September 16, 2006. Accessed July 27, 2017. http://www.washingtonpost.com/wp-dyn/content/article/2006/09/16/AR2006091600431.html.

Heikkila, Caitlin. "21 Beauty Products That Every '80s Kid Remembers." *Allure*, August 18, 2015. Accessed August 9, 2019. https://www.allure.com/gallery/80s-beauty-products.

Heller, Dana, ed. *Makeover Television: Realities Remodelled*. London: I.B. Tauris, 2007.

Hemsley, Steve. "Brands Need to Ensure Their Designs Are Age-Agnostic." *Marketing Week*, March 24, 2016. Accessed July 18, 2017. https://www.marketingweek.com/2016/03/24/appeal-to-consumers-across-generations-by-adopting-an-age-agnostic-approach-to-design/.

Heussner, Ki Mae. "Science of Beauty: What Made Elizabeth Taylor So Attractive?" *ABC News*, March 23, 2011. Accessed July 6, 2017. https://abcnews.go.com/Technology/elizabeth-taylor-science-great-beauty/story?id=13203775.

Higgins, Wendy. "Wendy Higgins: Animal Testing Is the Beauty Industry's Well-Kept Ugly Secret." *Independent*, July 31, 2012. Accessed July 15, 2017. https://www.independent.co.uk/voices/wendy-higgins-animal-testing-is-the-beauty-industry-s-well-kept-ugly-secret-7987460.html.

Hill, Sarah. "Lipstick, the Recession and Evolutionary Psychology." *Scientific American* (guest blog), June 27, 2012. Accessed July 17, 2017. https://blogs.scientificamerican.com/guest -blog/lipstick-the-recession-and-evolutionary-psychology/.

Hill, Sarah E., Christopher D. Rodeheffer, Vladas Griskevicius, Kristina Durante, and Andrew Edward White. "Boosting Beauty in an Economic Decline: Mating, Spending, and the Lipstick Effect." *Journal of Personality and Social Psychology* 103, no. 2 (2012): 275–91. Accessed July 17, 2017. doi: 10.1037/a0028657.

"History 1910–1920." *Advertising Age*, September 15, 2003. Accessed July 6, 2017. http:// adage.com/article/adage-encyclopedia/history-1910-1920/99072/.

"History 1920s." *Advertising Age*, September 15, 2003. Accessed July 4, 2017. http://adage .com/article/adage-encyclopedia/history-1920s/98699/.

"A History of Cosmetics from Ancient Times." CosmeticsInfo.org. Accessed July 21, 2017. https://cosmeticsinfo.org/Ancient-history-cosmetics.

Hitti, Miranda. "Thin Ads + Low Body Image = Stress." *CBS News*, October 27, 2006. Accessed July 9, 2017. https://www.cbsnews.com/news/thin-ads-plus-low-body-image-stress/.

Hix, Lisa. "Selling Shame: 40 Outrageous Vintage Ads Any Woman Would Find Offensive." *Mental Floss*, September 6, 2010. Accessed July 17, 2017. http://mentalfloss .com/article/67885/selling-shame-40-outrageous-vintage-ads-any-woman-would-find -offensive.

Hobbs, Thomas. "Plastic Surgery Ad Banned for 'Exploiting' Young Women's Insecurities." *Marketing Week*, April 19, 2017. Accessed July 29, 2017. https://www.marketingweek .com/2017/04/19/exploitative-plastic-surgery-ad-banned/.

Hodgson, Kendra, Jeremy Earp, and Jason Young, eds. *Media Education Foundation Study Guide: Killing Us Softly 4: Advertising's Image of Women.* Media Education Foundation. Accessed August 21, 2018. https://www.mediaed.org/discussion-guides/Killing-Us-Softly -4-Discussion-Guide.pdf.

Hoff, Joan. *Law, Gender, and Injustice: A Legal History of U.S. Women*, rev. ed. New York: New York University Press, 1994.

Hofstede Insights. "Country Comparison." Accessed August 31, 2019. https://www.hofstede -insights.com/country-comparison/.

Hollis, Nigel. *The Global Brand: How to Create and Develop Lasting Brand Value in the World Market*, rev. ed. New York: St. Martin's Griffin, 2010.

Holloway, April. "Donkey Milk: Ancient Elixir of Life Experiences Modern-Day Resurgence." *Ancient Origins*, December 17, 2014. Accessed July 21, 2017. https://www .ancient-origins.net/news-general/donkey-milk-ancient-elixir-life-experiences-modern-day -resurgence-002502.

Holmes, Anna. "Plastic Surgery Doesn't Work—but Neither Does Our Standard of Beauty." *Time*, August 5, 2013. Accessed July 20, 2017. http://ideas.time.com/2013/08/05/plastic -surgery-doesnt-work-but-neither-does-our-standard-of-beauty/#ixzz2lTaPoMzP.

Holmes, Elizabeth. "Dude, Pass the Exfoliator." *Wall Street Journal*, April 26, 2012. Accessed July 18, 2017. https://www.wsj.com/articles/SB10001424052702304811304577365902173161004.

———. "In Aisle Five, $50 Skin Cream." *Wall Street Journal*, January 15, 2014. Accessed July 7, 2017. https://www.wsj.com/articles/in-aisle-five-50-skin-cream-1389831096www.wsj .com/articles/in-aisle-five-50-skin-cream-1389831096.

Holmes, Stephanie. "Scandinavian Split on Sexist Ads." *BBC News*, April 25, 2008. Accessed July 2, 2017. http://news.bbc.co.uk/2/hi/europe/7365722.stm.

Holst, Arne. "Number of Smartphone Users Worldwide from 2016 to 2021 (in Billions)." *Statista.* Last modified July 26, 2019. Accessed August 29, 2019. https://www.statista.com/ statistics/330695/number-of-smartphone-users-worldwide/.

Honigman, Roberta, and David J. Castle. "Aging and Cosmetic Enhancement." *Clinical Interventions in Aging* 1, no. 2 (2005): 115–19. Accessed July 9, 2017. doi: 10.2147/ ciia.2006.1.2.115.

Horovitz, Bruce. "Great Year for Bad Ads, Say Sponsors of 'Lemon Awards.'" *Los Angeles Times,* December 4, 1991. Accessed August 17, 2019. https://www.latimes.com/archives/ la-xpm-1991-12-04-fi-296-story.html.

Hovland, Roxanne, Joyce M. Wolburg, and Eric E. Haley. *Readings in Advertising, Society, and Consumer Culture.* New York: Routledge, 2014.

"How Important Are Celebrity Endorsements in Personal Care Purchases?" *Beauty Packaging,* August 12, 2015. Accessed July 27, 2017. http://www.beautypackaging.com/contents/ view_breaking-news/2015-08-12/how-important-are-celebrity-endorsements-in-personal -care-purchases.

"How Much Do Botox Treatments Cost?" CostHelper. Accessed July 31, 2019. https://health .costhelper.com/botox.html.

Howard, Jacqueline, and Anna Ginsburg. "The History of the 'Ideal' Woman and Where That Has Left Us." CNN, March 9, 2018. Accessed August 30, 2019. https://www.cnn .com/2018/03/07/health/body-image-history-of-beauty-explainer-intl/index.html.

Huang, Shaojie. "China Ends Animal Testing Rule for Some Cosmetics." *New York Times,* June 30, 2014. Accessed December 12, 2017. https://sinosphere.blogs.nytimes.com/ 2014/06/30/china-ends-animal-testing-rule-for-some-cosmetics/.

Huddleston, Tom, Jr. "L'Oréal USA Settles with FTC over Deceptive Skin Care Ads." *Fortune,* June 30, 2014. Accessed August 1, 2017. http://fortune.com/2014/06/30/loreal-usa-ftc/.

Humane Society International. "Be Cruelty-Free Campaign." Accessed July 15, 2017. http:// www.hsi.org/issues/becrueltyfree/facts/infographic/en/?referrer=https://www.google.com/.

———. "China Implements Rule Change in First Step Towards Ending Animal Testing of Cosmetics." HSI press release, June 30, 2014. Accessed July 15, 2017. http://www.hsi.org/ news/press_releases/2014/06/china-implements-rule-change-063014.html.

The Humane Society of the United States. "Cosmetics Testing FAQ." Accessed July 15, 2017. http://www.humanesociety.org/issues/cosmetic_testing/qa/questions_answers.html.

———. "Federal Bill to End Cosmetics Testing on Animals Introduced." HSUS press release, June 23, 2015. Accessed July 8, 2017. https://www.humanesociety.org/news/federal-bill -end-cosmetics-testing-animals-introduced.

Hunt, Kenneth A., Jennifer Fate, and Bill Dodds. "Cultural and Social Influences on the Perception of Beauty: A Case Analysis of the Cosmetics Industry." *Journal of Business Case Studies* 7, no. 1 (2011): 1–10. Accessed July 21, 2017. doi: 10.19030/jbcs.v7i1.1577.

Huth, Edward J., and T. Jock Murray, eds. *Medicine in Quotations: Views of Health and Disease Through the Ages,* 2nd ed. Philadelphia: American College of Physicians, 2006.

Hyde, Nina S. "The Beautiful Billion-Dollar Business of Black Cosmetics." *Washington Post,* July 9, 1977. Accessed July 2, 2017. https://www.washingtonpost.com/archive/ lifestyle/1977/07/09/the-beautiful-billion-dollar-business-of-black-cosmetics/5a690143 -de1a-4778-900a-ac093ebe4e34/?noredirect=on&utm_term=.075c08499d9a.

"Illegal Buttocks Injections Kill, Maim U.S. Women." *USA Today,* August 5, 2013. Accessed July 29, 2017. https://www.usatoday.com/story/news/nation/2013/08/05/illegal-buttocks -injections-kill-maim-us-women/2618887/.

"Illegal Injections Killing, Maiming Women Seeking Cheap Alternative to Plastic Surgery." *Fox News*, August 5, 2013. Accessed July 9, 2017. http://www.foxnews.com/health/2013/08/05/buttocks-injections-killing-maiming-some-women-who-seek-cheap-alternative-to.html.

"Industry Self-Regulation." In *Wikipedia*. Last modified July 21, 2019. Accessed August 24, 2019. https://wiki2.org/en/Industry_self-regulation.

Information Resources Management Association, ed. *Digital Multimedia: Concepts, Methodologies, Tools, and Applications*. Hershey, PA: IGI Global, 2018.

Ingrassia, Michele. "Calvin Klein on 'Kiddie Porn' Advertisements." *Newsweek*, September 10, 1995. Accessed July 2, 2017. https://www.newsweek.com/calvin-klein-kiddie-porn-advertisements-182964.

Insel, Paul, Don Ross, Kimberley McMahon, and Melissa Bernstein. *Discovering Nutrition*, 6th ed. Burlington, MA: Jones & Bartlett Learning, 2019.

Insights Association. "Advertising Substantiation and Standards for Conducting Research for Advertising Claims." Last modified April 15, 2015. Accessed July 16, 2017. https://www.insightsassociation.org/issues-policies/best-practice/advertising-substantiation-and-standards-conducting-research.

International Chamber of Commerce. "ICC Advertising and Marketing Communications Code." Accessed July 1, 2017. https://iccwbo.org/publication/advertising-and-marketing-communication-practice-consolidated-icc-code/.

International Society of Aesthetic Plastic Surgery. "ISAPS International Survey on Aesthetic/Cosmetic Procedures Performed in 2018." Accessed March 16, 2020, https://www.isaps.org/wp-content/uploads/2019/12/ISAPS-Global-Survey-Results-2018-new.pdf.

———. "Latest Study Shows Aesthetic Surgery Continues to Rise Worldwide." ISAPS press release, December 3, 2019. Accessed March 16, 2020. https://www.prnewswire.com/in/news-releases/latest-international-study-shows-aesthetic-surgery-continues-to-rise-worldwide-853742798.html.

Internet Movie Database. *The Devil Wears Prada* (2006). Accessed August 6, 2018. https://www.imdb.com/title/tt0458352/plotsummary.

Jackall, Robert, and Janice M. Hirota. *Image Makers: Advertising, Public Relations, and the Ethos of Advocacy*. Chicago: University of Chicago Press, 2003.

Jacobsen, Thomas. "Beauty and the Brain: Culture, History and Individual Differences in Aesthetic Appreciation." *Journal of Anatomy* 216, no. 2 (2009): 184–91. Accessed July 17, 2017. doi: 10.1111/j.1469-7580.2009.01164.x.

James, Caryn. "Audrey Hepburn, Actress, Is Dead at 63." *New York Times*, January 21, 1993. Accessed July 7, 2017. https://www.nytimes.com/1993/01/21/movies/audrey-hepburn-actress-is-dead-at-63.html.

James, Michael S. "The 2000s: A Decade of Doom or Diversions?" *ABC News*, November 25, 2009. Accessed November 25, 2017. https://abcnews.go.com/Technology/Decade/defining-2000s-decade-doom-digital-divas/story?id=9174978.

Jamieson, Patrick, and Daniel Romer. *The Changing Portrayal of Adolescents in the Media Since 1950*. New York: Oxford University Press, 2008.

"Jane Fonda's First Workout Video Released." History.com, April 24, 1982. Last modified July 27, 2019. https://www.history.com/this-day-in-history/jane-fondas-first-workout-video-released.

Jankowski, Paul. "9 Steps to Creating Successful Brand/Celebrity Partnerships." *Forbes*, March 2, 2015. Accessed July 27, 2017. https://www.forbes.com/sites/pauljankowski/2015/03/02/9-steps-to-creating-successful-brandcelebrity-partnerships/#70ad63c1ed6e.

Jeffers, Michelle. "Behind Dove's 'Real Beauty.'" *Adweek*, September 12, 2005. Accessed July 31, 2017. https://www.adweek.com/brand-marketing/behind-doves-real-beauty-81469/.

"Jennifer Lopez Launches New Fragrance." CosmeticsDesign.com-USA. Last modified July 19, 2008. Accessed October 11, 2019. https://www.cosmeticsdesign.com/Article/2005/02/17/Jennifer-Lopez-launches-new-fragrance.

Jha, Alok Kumar, Amrita Raj, and Dr. Rachana Gangwar. "A Semiotic Analysis of Portraying Gender in Magazine Advertisements." *IOSR Journal of Humanities and Social Science* 22, no. 5, ver. 11 (2017): 1–8. Accessed July 3, 2017. doi: 10.9790/0837-2205110108.

Johnson & Johnson Consumer Inc. "Our Mission." Last modified July 9, 2018. Accessed August 16, 2019. https://www.johnsonsbaby.com/our-mission.

"Johnson & Johnson to Phase Out Potentially Harmful Chemicals by 2015." *CBS News*, August 15, 2012. Accessed July 7, 2017. https://www.cbsnews.com/news/johnson-johnson-to-phase-out-potentially-harmful-chemicals-by-2015/.

Johnson, Caitlin. "Cutting through Advertising Clutter." *CBS News*, September 17, 2006. Accessed July 1, 2017. https://www.cbsnews.com/news/cutting-through-advertising-clutter/.

Johnson, Lauren. "L'Oréal Will Add Makeup to Selfies as the First Beauty Brand Snapchat Lens." *Adweek*, June 3, 2016. Accessed July 11, 2017. https://www.adweek.com/digital/loreal-will-add-makeup-selfies-first-beauty-brand-snapchat-lens-171810/.

———. "Unilever's Dove Promotes Beauty Products through Multichannel Digital Effort." *Mobile Marketer*. Accessed July 17, 2017. https://www.mobilemarketer.com/ex/mobilemarketer/cms/news/advertising/12710.html.

Johnson, Vera Stiefler. "Internalizing Beauty Ideals: The Health Risks of Adult Women's Self-Objectification." NYU-Steinhardt *Applied Psychology OPUS* (Fall 2014). Accessed July 1, 2017. https://steinhardt.nyu.edu/appsych/opus/issues/2014/fall/stieflerjohnson.

Jones, Geoffrey. *Beauty Imagined: A History of the Global Beauty Industry*. New York: Oxford University Press, 2011.

———. "Globalizing the Beauty Business before 1980." Harvard Business School, July 11, 2006. Accessed March 15, 2020. https://hbswk.hbs.edu/item/globalizing-the-beauty-business-before-1980.

Jones, Kim. "Can a Pill Really Make You Beautiful? We Put Anti-ageing Tablets to the Test." *Mirror*, June 21, 2016. Accessed July 11, 2017. https://www.mirror.co.uk/3am/style/3am-fashion-celebrity-beauty/can-pill-really-make-you-1858910.

Joosen, Vanessa. *Critical and Creative Perspectives on Fairy Tales: An Intertextual Dialogue between Fairy-Tale Scholarship and Postmodern Retellings*. Detroit: Wayne State University Press, 2011.

JWT.com, aka J. Walter Thompson Worldwide. "Unpacking Gender Bias in Advertising." June 21, 2017. Accessed July 31, 2017. https://www.jwt.com/en/news/unpacking-gender-bias-in-advertising.

Kahn, Mattie. "Always Redefines What It Means to Run 'Like a Girl.'" *ABC News*, July 1, 2014. Accessed August 12, 2019. https://abcnews.go.com/Lifestyle/redefines-means-run-girl/story?id=24377039.

Kalb, Ira. "Sexy Celebrity Ads Are the Worst Thing Companies Can Do for Their Sales." *Business Insider*, February 22, 2013. Accessed December 23, 2017. https://www.businessinsider.com.au/despite-what-you-believe-celebrities-sex-doesnt-sell-2013-2.

Kamouni, Sara. "Beauty Icons: How Audrey Hepburn Is the Ultimate Beauty Icon, According to New Survey." *Sun*, December 21, 2016. Accessed July 7, 2017. https://www.thesun.co.uk/news/2449770/how-audrey-hepburn-is-the-ultimate-beauty-icon-according-to-new-survey/.

Kantar Millward Brown. "Brands Articulate Viewpoints on Beauty and Social Mission." BrandZ. Accessed July 16, 2017. http://www.millwardbrown.com/brandz/rankings-and -reports/top-global-brands/2015/brand-categories/personal-care.

Kaplan, Sheila. "Cosmetics May Face New Safety Regulation—and, Surprisingly, the Industry Is on Board." *STAT News*, September 27, 2016. Accessed July 17, 2017. https://www .statnews.com/2016/09/27/cosmetics-fda-congress-safety/.

"Kate Moss Regrets 'Nothing Tastes as Good as Skinny Feels' Comment." *BBC News*, September 14, 2018. Accessed October 11, 2019. https://www.bbc.com/news/newsbeat -45522714.

Katz, Brigit. "New Study Shows Impact of Social Media on Beauty Standards." *Women in the World*, April 3, 2015. Accessed July 12, 2017. https://womenintheworld.com/2015/04/03/ new-study-shows-impact-of-social-media-on-beauty-standards/.

Kavoussi, Bonnie. "'The Lipstick Effect': Women Spend More on Beauty Products During Recessions, Study Says." *Huffington Post*, June 19, 2012. Accessed July 10, 2017. https://www.huffingtonpost.com/2012/06/19/the-lipstick-effect-women-beauty-recessions _n_1606298.html.

Kay, Jane. "Johnson & Johnson Removes Some Chemicals from Baby Shampoo, Other Products." *Scientific American*, May 6, 2013. Accessed July 7, 2017. https://www.scientific american.com/article/johnson-and-johnson-removes-some-chemicals-from-baby-shampoo -other-products/.

Keller, Kevin Lane. *Strategic Brand Management: Building, Measuring, and Managing Brand Equity*, 4th ed. Hoboken, NJ: Pearson, 2013.

Ketchum, Dan. "The Persuasion Techniques of Beauty Product Advertising." *Houston Chronicle*. Accessed July 10, 2017. https://smallbusiness.chron.com/persuasion-techniques -beauty-product-advertising-22993.html.

Khanom, Roshida. "The Evolution of Celebrity Endorsement in Beauty." Mintel (blog), April 12, 2017. Accessed July 27, 2017. http://www.mintel.com/blog/beauty-market-news/the -evolution-of-celebrity-endorsement-in-beauty.

Kiderra, Inga, and Joyann Callender. "The Measure of a Woman?" UC San Diego press release, December 16, 2009. Accessed August 19, 2018. https://ucsdnews.ucsd.edu/archive/ newsrel/soc/12-09Beauty.asp.

Kiefaber, David. "Axe's Fallen Angels Banned in South Africa." *Adweek*, October 31, 2011. Accessed July 4, 2017. https://www.adweek.com/creativity/axes-fallen-angels-banned -south-africa-136190/.

———. "Taylor Swift's CoverGirl Ad Is Pulled over Bogus Eyelashes." *Adweek*, December 23, 2011. Accessed July 17, 2017. https://www.adweek.com/creativity/taylor-swifts-covergirl -ad-pulled-over-bogus-eyelashes-137269/.

Kilbourne, Jean. "Beauty . . . and the Beast of Advertising." Original article in *Media & Values: Redesigning Women* 49 (Winter 1990). Center for Media Literacy. Accessed July 1, 2017. http://www.medialit.org/reading-room/beautyand-beast-advertising.

———. *Killing Us Softly 4: Advertising's Image of Women*. Media Education Foundation. Accessed August 21, 2018. https://shop.mediaed.org/killing-us-softly-4-p47.aspx.

Kinonen, Sarah. "Millennial Women Want More Green Beauty Products." *Allure*, November 24, 2016. Accessed July 28, 2019. https://www.allure.com/story/millennial-women-green -beauty.

Kirkova, Deni. "Are YOU Swayed by a Famous Face? Women Buy Twice as Many Celebrity-Endorsed Products as Men." *Daily Mail*, May 30, 2014. Accessed July 27, 2017. http://

www.dailymail.co.uk/femail/article-2641476/Susceptible-women-buy-twice-celebrity
-endorsed-products-men.html#ixzz4rjgoLh7j.

———. "Iran Is the Nose Job Capital of the World with SEVEN Times More Procedures Than the U.S.—but Rise in Unlicensed Surgeons Poses Huge Risk." *Daily Mail*, March 5, 2013. Accessed July 28, 2017. http://www.dailymail.co.uk/femail/article-2287961/Iran-named -nose-job-capital-world-SEVEN-times-rhinoplasty-operations-U-S-Iranian-women-strive -western-doll-face.html.

Kita, Natalie. "The History of Plastic Surgery." Verywell Health. Last modified August 5, 2019. Accessed September 6, 2019. https://www.verywellhealth.com/the-history-of-plastic -surgery-2710193.

Klara, Robert. "How Clairol Hair Color Went from Taboo to New You." *Adweek*, February 28, 2013. Accessed July 3, 2017. https://www.adweek.com/brand-marketing/how-clairol -hair-color-went-taboo-new-you-147480/.

———. "The Rise and Fall of the World's Most Hated Clothing Brand." *Adweek*, November 2, 2014. Accessed July 20, 2018. https://www.adweek.com/brand-marketing/rise-and-fall -worlds-most-hated-clothing-brand-161153/.

Klausner, Alexandra. "Real-Life Barbie and Ken Ditch Love for Plastic." *New York Post*, August 25, 2016. Accessed July 28, 2017. https://nypost.com/2016/08/25/real-life-barbie-and -ken-dolls-ditch-love-for-plastic/.

Klein, Karin. "Digital Anorexia." *Los Angeles Times*, October 16, 2009. Accessed July 9, 2017. http://opinion.latimes.com/opinionla/2009/10/ralph-lauren-photoshop-filippa-anorexiea -eating-disorder-bulimina.html.

Kleinman, Susan. "Challenging Body Distortions through the Eyes of the Body." Psych Central. Accessed July 9, 2017. https://psychcentral.com/lib/challenging-body-distortions -through-the-eyes-of-the-body/.

Klich, Tanya Benedicto. "How the Beauty Industry Continues to Crack the Bro Code." *Entrepreneur*, March 25, 2015. Accessed July 18, 2017. https://www.entrepreneur.com/ article/244344.

Knapton, Sarah. "Four in Five Beauty Claims Cannot Be Substantiated." *Telegraph*, July 28, 2015. Accessed July 15, 2017. https://www.telegraph.co.uk/news/science/science-news/ 11768390/Four-in-five-beauty-claims-cannot-be-substantiated.html.

Koehn, Nancy F. "Building a Powerful Prestige Brand: Estée Lauder and the Department Store Cosmetics Counter." *Harvard Business School Working Knowledge*, October 30, 2000. Accessed July 21, 2017. https://hbswk.hbs.edu/archive/building-a-powerful-prestige-brand -est-eacute-e-lauder-and-the-department-store-cosmetics-counter.

———. "How to Get a Celebrity Endorsement from the Queen of England." National Public Radio, May 21, 2012. Accessed August 5, 2018. https://www.npr.org/sections/ money/2012/05/21/153199679/how-to-get-a-celebrity-endorsement-from-the-queen-of -england.

Komar, Marlen. "Revlon's Fire & Ice Campaign in 1952 Was the First Ad to Acknowledge Women Wear Makeup for Themselves." *Bustle*, October 9, 2018. Accessed November 10, 2019. https://www.bustle.com/p/revlons-fire-ice-campaign-in-1952-was-the-first-ad-to -acknowledge-women-wear-makeup-for-themselves-12159808.

Konstan, David. *Beauty: The Fortunes of an Ancient Greek Idea*. Oxford: Oxford University Press, 2015.

Kotler, Philip T., and Gary Armstrong. *Principles of Marketing*, 15th ed. Upper Saddle River, NJ: Prentice Hall, 2013.

Kraft, Amy. "Most 'Scientific' Beauty Product Claims Are Bogus, Study Finds." *CBS News*, July 28, 2015. Accessed July 16, 2017. https://www.cbsnews.com/news/most-beauty -product-claims-are-bogus/.

Kretzer, Michelle. "Countries Around the World Work to Ban Cosmetics Testing on Animals." People for the Ethical Treatment of Animals, July 21, 2015. Accessed July 15, 2017. https://www.peta.org/blog/countries-around-the-world-work-to-ban-cosmetics-testing-on -animals/.

Kuo, Lily. "This Phone App Lets Chinese Women Try on Plastic Surgery for Size." *Quartz*, July 9, 2013. Accessed July 9, 2017. https://qz.com/101914/this-phone-app-lets-chinese -women-try-on-plastic-surgery-for-size/.

Kushner, Dale M. "How Snow White's Cruel Stepmother Helps Us Cope with Evil." *Psychology Today*, June 26, 2017. Accessed October 12, 2018. https://www.psychologytoday.com/ us/blog/transcending-the-past/201706/how-snow-whites-cruel-stepmother-helps-us-cope -evil.

Lachapelle, Tara. "Secrets of the Booming Beauty Business." *Washington Post*, December 20, 2018. Accessed November 2, 2019. https://www.washingtonpost.com/business/secrets -of-the-booming-beauty-business/2018/12/20/8d86ea52-0479-11e9-958c-0a601226ff6b_ story.html.

Lafky, Sue, Margaret Duffy, Mary Steinmaus, and Dan Berkowitz. "Looking through Gendered Lenses: Female Stereotyping in Advertisements and Gender Role Expectations." *Journalism and Mass Communication Quarterly* 73, no. 2 (1996): 379–88. Accessed July 8, 2017. doi: 10.1177/107769909607300209.

Lague, Louise. "How Thin Is Too Thin?" *People*, September 20, 1993. Accessed August 2, 2017. https://people.com/archive/cover-story-how-thin-is-too-thin-vol-40-no-12/.

Lah, Kyung. "Plastic Surgery Boom as Asians Seek 'Western' Look." CNN, May 23, 2011. Accessed July 28, 2017. http://www.cnn.com/2011/WORLD/asiapcf/05/19/korea.beauty/ index.html.

Landau, Elizabeth. "Beholding Beauty: How It's Been Studied." CNN, March 3, 2012. Accessed July 4, 2017. https://www.cnn.com/2012/03/02/health/mental-health/beauty -brain-research/index.html.

———. "'Plastic Micro Beads' to Be Removed from Soap." CNN, January 8, 2013. Accessed July 11, 2017. https://www.cnn.com/2013/01/07/health/microplastics-soap-unilever/.

Langton, Rae. *Sexual Solipsism: Philosophical Essays on Pornography and Objectification*. New York: Oxford University Press, 2009.

Lantos, Geoffrey Paul. *Consumer Behavior in Action: Real-Life Applications for Marketing Managers*. New York: Routledge, 2015.

LaPorte, Nicole. "How Ipsy Founder Michelle Phan Is Using Influencers to Reinvent the Cosmetics Industry." *Fast Company*, January 11, 2016. Accessed July 12, 2017. https:// www.fastcompany.com/3054926/how-ipsy-founder-michelle-phan-is-using-influencers-to -reinvent-the-cosmeti.

Lavine, Howard, Donna Sweeney, and Stephen H. Wagner. "Depicting Women as Sex Objects in Television Advertising: Effects on Body Dissatisfaction." *Personality and Social Psychology Bulletin* 25, no. 8 (1999): 1049–58. Accessed July 1, 2017. doi: 10.1177/01461672992511012.

Law360. "Nano-Cosmetics: Beyond Skin Deep." LexisNexis, February 15, 2011. Accessed July 14, 2017. https://www.law360.com/classaction/articles/225932/nano-cosmetics -beyond-skin-deep.

Leagle. *U.S. Nature Products Corp. v. Schaffer*, 125 F. Supp. 374 (1954). Accessed September 25, 2019. https://www.leagle.com/decision/1954499125fsupp3741418.

Lee, Bruce Y. "In Plastic Surgery, Brazil Gets the Silver Medal." *Forbes*, August 8, 2016. Accessed July 28, 2017. https://www.forbes.com/sites/brucelee/2016/08/08/in-plastic -surgery-brazil-gets-the-silver-medal-behind/#3f254ebd3642.

Lennon, Christine. "Beauty: Smiling for Dollars." *Time*, September 11, 2006. Accessed July 26, 2017. http://content.time.com/time/magazine/article/0,9171,1533550,00.html.

Levine, Bettijane. "Cosmetics Queen Put New Face on Beauty Industry." *Los Angeles Times*, April 26, 2004. Accessed July 21, 2017. http://articles.latimes.com/2004/apr/26/local/ me-lauder26.

Lewak, Doree, and Jane Ridley. "Inside the Terrifying Tactics Models Use to Stay Thin." *New York Post*, February 8, 2017. Accessed July 27, 2017. https://nypost.com/2017/02/08/ models-tell-all-before-new-york-fashion-week/.

Liang, Bryan A., and Kurt M. Hartman. "It's Only Skin Deep: FDA Regulation of Skin Care Cosmetics Claims." *Cornell Journal of Law and Public Policy* 8, no. 2, article 2 (1999): 249–80. Accessed July 17, 2017. https://scholarship.law.cornell.edu/cgi/viewcontent .cgi?article=1249&context=cjlpp.

Liberto, Daniel. "The Wealth Effect." In *Investopedia*, June 26, 2019. Accessed October 19, 2019. https://www.investopedia.com/terms/w/wealtheffect.asp.

"Lipstick Effect." In *Investopedia*. Accessed July 7, 2017. https://www.investopedia.com/ terms/l/lipstick-effect.asp.

Little, Anthony C., Benedict C. Jones, and Lisa M. DeBruine. "Facial Attractiveness: Evolutionary Based Research." *Philosophical Transactions of the Royal Society B: Biological Sciences* 366 (2011): 1638–59. doi:10.1098/rstb.2010.0404.

Littlejohn, Stephen W., and Karen A. Foss, eds. *Encyclopedia of Communication Theory*. Thousand Oaks, CA: Sage, 2009.

Loeb, Walter. "Estée Lauder—a Beauty Company to Be Reckoned With." *Forbes*, September 9, 2013. Accessed July 11, 2017. https://www.forbes.com/sites/walterloeb/2013/09/09/ estee-lauder-a-beauty-company-to-be-reckoned-with/1.

Lohani, Alka, Anurag Verma, Himanshi Joshi, Niti Yadav, and Neha Karki, "Nanotechnology-Based Cosmeceuticals," *ISRN Dermatology* 2014, no. 843687 (2014): 14 pages. https://doi .org/10.1155/2014/843687.

Lohr, Steve. "Photoshopped or Not? A Tool to Tell." *New York Times*, November 28, 2011. Accessed July 9, 2017. https://www.nytimes.com/2011/11/29/technology/software-to-rate -how-drastically-photos-are-retouched.html?_r=0%27.

Lombardi, Lisa. "Cosmetic Surgery Boom Revamps Doctors' Offices." CNN, December 2, 2009. Accessed July 28, 2017. http://www.cnn.com/2009/HEALTH/12/02/plastic.surgery .cosmetic.risks/index.html.

London, Bianca. "A Fifth of Girls as Young as 12 Won't Leave Home without Full Make-up—and over Half of Under-14s Wear Cosmetics EVERY Day." *Daily Mail*, August 13, 2014. Accessed July 15, 2017. http://www.dailymail.co.uk/femail/article-2723853/ Would-YOU-let-12-year-old-wear-make-Over-HALF-14s-wear-EVERY-day-nearly-fifth -wont-leave-home-without-cosmetics-on.html#ixzz4byMDSaLC.

———. "Plastic Surgery Addicts Who Have Spent $500,000 on 350 Cosmetic Procedures Admit Their Obsession Has RUINED Their Love Lives." *Daily Mail*, August 25, 2016. Accessed July 28, 2017. http://www.dailymail.co.uk/femail/article-3758164/Plastic

-surgery-addicts-ve-spent-380-000-350-cosmetic-procedures-vow-live-real-life-Barbie
-Ken-obsession-ruins-love-life.html#ixzz4t83GeXVQ.

"A Look Back at Portrayals of Women in Advertising." *Advertising Age*, September 2, 2014. Accessed July 3, 2017. http://adage.com/article/news/a-back-portrayals-women-advertising/294756/.

Lopaciuk, Aleksandra, and Miroslaw Loboba. "Global Beauty Industry Trends in the 21st Century." Paper presented at the Management, Knowledge and Learning International Conference, Zadar, Croatia, June 19–21, 2013. Accessed July 17, 2017. http://www.toknowpress.net/ISBN/978-961-6914-02-4/papers/ML13-365.pdf.

L'Oréal. "Because You're Worth It: The Story Behind the Legendary Phrase." Accessed July 19, 2017. https://www.lorealparisusa.com/about-loreal-paris/because-youre-worth-it.aspx.

Lorenzetti, Laura. "FTC Goes After 5 'Natural' Companies for False Claims." *Fortune*, April 13, 2016. Accessed July 17, 2017. http://fortune.com/2016/04/13/ftc-natural-personal-care-false/.

Lovett, Edward. "Most Models Meet Criteria for Anorexia, Size 6 Is Plus Size: Magazine." *ABC News*, January 13, 2012. Accessed July 9, 2017. https://abcnews.go.com/News/most-models-meet-criteria-for-anorexia-size-6-is-plus-size-magazine/blogEntry?id=15350058.

Ludacer, Randy. "Formula No. 9." *Box Vox*, July 1, 2011. Accessed July 17, 2017. https://beachpackagingdesign.com/boxvox/formula-no-9.

"Lunchtime Lift: Breast Enhancement Now Available in 20 Minute Procedure." *ABC News*, August 22, 2014. Accessed July 28, 2017. https://abcnews.go.com/Lifestyle/lunchtime-lift-breast-enhancement-now-20-minute-procedure/story?id=25078909.

Lupkin, Sydney. "Women Put an Average of 168 Chemicals on Their Bodies Each Day, Consumer Group Says." *ABC News*, April 27, 2015. Accessed July 14, 2017. https://abcnews.go.com/Health/women-put-average-168-chemicals-bodies-day-consumer/story?id=30615324.

Lutz, Ashley. "Baby Boomers Are the Sexiest Consumers in Retail." *Business Insider*, June 2, 2015. Accessed July 17, 2017. https://www.businessinsider.com/baby-boomers-spend-the-most-money-2015-6.

———. "The Fashion World Is Embracing 'Heroin Chic' Again." *Business Insider*, September 6, 2012. Accessed September 19, 2019. https://www.businessinsider.com/heroin-chic-looks-at-new-york-fashion-week-2012-9.

Maas, Lauren. "A History of Blush." *Into the Gloss*. Accessed July 9, 2018. https://intothegloss.com/2015/01/history-of-makeup-blush/.

Maio, Giovanni. "Is Aesthetic Surgery Still Really Medicine? An Ethical Critique. [Ist die ästhetische Chirurgie überhaupt noch Medizin? Eine ethische Kritik]." *Handchirurgie Mikrochirurgie Plastische Chirurgie* 39, no. 3 (2007); 189–94, discussion 195–96. doi: 10.1055/s-2007-965328.

"Majority of Beauty Ads Digitally Enhanced: Report." *Huffington Post*. Last modified May 25, 2011. Accessed November 2, 2019. https://www.huffpost.com/entry/majority-of-beauty-ads-di_n_517276.

"Make-up Tips of the Women in the Tang Dynasty." ChinaCulture.org, April 1, 2014. Accessed July 7, 2018. http://en.chinaculture.org/chineseway/2014-04/01/content_518065.htm.

"Male Vanity Spurs the Development of Skin Care." *NBC News*, July 19, 2005. Accessed July 18, 2017. http://www.nbcnews.com/id/8631299/ns/business-us_business/t/male-vanity-spurs-development-skin-care/#.V7m6u_krLIU.

Malkan, Stacy. "Johnson & Johnson Is Just the Tip of the Toxic Iceberg." *Time*, March 2, 2016. Accessed July 14, 2017. http://time.com/4239561/johnson-and-johnson-toxic-ingredients/.

Mandavilli, Apoorva. "Nanocosmetics: Buyer Beware." *MIT Technology Review*, March 1, 2007. Accessed July 18, 2017. https://www.technologyreview.com/s/407397/nanocosmetics -buyer-beware/.

Mannes, Marya. *But Will It Sell?* Philadelphia: Lippincott, 1964.

Mapes, Diane. "Dove Ad Highlights Women's Distorted Self-Image." *Today*, April 17, 2013. Accessed July 9, 2017. https://www.today.com/health/dove-ad-highlights-womens -distorted-self-image-1C9406053.

———. "Frozen in Time: Botox over the Years." *NBC News*, October 22, 2007. Accessed July 28, 2017. http://www.nbcnews.com/id/21369061/ns/health-skin_and_beauty/t/frozen -time-botox-over-years/#.W33JDuhKhPY.

———. "It's Never Too Early for Botox, Doctor Says." *Today*, September 18, 2013. Accessed July 28, 2017. https://www.today.com/health/its-never-too-early-botox-doctor-says -4B11187467.

———. "Suffering for Beauty Has Ancient Roots." *NBC News*, January 11, 2008. Accessed July 21, 2017. http://www.nbcnews.com/id/22546056/ns/health/t/suffering-beauty-has -ancient-roots/.

Marcus, Mary Brophy. "Ban on Super-Thin Models Takes Effect in France." *CBS News*, May 10, 2017. Accessed July 27, 2017. https://www.cbsnews.com/news/ban-on-super-thin -models-anorexia-takes-effect-in-france/.

Maresca, Rachel. "Paris Hilton Returns in New Carl's Jr. Ad with Sports Illustrated Model Hannah Ferguson." *New York Daily News*, July 25, 2014. Accessed August 1, 2017. http://www.nydailynews.com/entertainment/tv/paris-hilton-returns-carl-jr-commercial -article-1.1879980.

Marikar, Sheila. "Real? Or Photoshopped? 'Airbrushing' Run Amok." *ABC News*, December 19, 2008. Accessed July 27, 2017. https://abcnews.go.com/Entertainment/CelebrityCafe/ story?id=6483994&page=1.

Mark, Margaret, and Carol S. Pearson. *The Hero and the Outlaw: Building Extraordinary Brands Through the Power of Archetypes*. New York: McGraw-Hill, 2001.

Markowicz, Karol. "Celebrities Are Driving the Teen Plastic-Surgery Boom." *New York Post*, August 23, 2015. Accessed July 28, 2017. https://nypost.com/2015/08/23/the-modern -vanity-cult-is-prompting-a-teen-plastic-surgery-boom/.

Marsh, Sarah. "'Many Suffer but No One Talks about It': The Rise of Eating Disorders in Japan." *Guardian*, May 17, 2016. Accessed July 27, 2017. https://www.theguardian.com/ world/2016/may/17/many-suffer-but-no-one-talks-about-it-the-rise-of-eating-disorders -in-japan.

Marshall, P. David, and Sean Redmond, eds. *A Companion to Celebrity*. Hoboken, NJ: Wiley- Blackwell, 2015.

Marx, Patricia. "About Face." *New Yorker*, March 23, 2015. Accessed July 6, 2017. https:// www.newyorker.com/magazine/2015/03/23/about-face.

Mask, Lisa, and Céline M. Blanchard. "The Effects of 'Thin Ideal' Media on Women's Body Image Concerns and Eating-Related Intentions: The Beneficial Role of an Autonomous Regulation of Eating Behaviors." *Body Image* 8, no. 4 (2011): 357–65. Accessed July 29, 2017. doi: 10.1016/j.bodyim.2011.06.003.

"Masstige." In *Wikipedia*. Last modified June 6, 2019. Accessed August 8, 2019. https:// en.wikipedia.org/wiki/Masstige.

Matthews, Imogen. "Genderless Beauty Creates New Opportunities for Brands." Cosmetics Business, April 18, 2017. Accessed July 31, 2017. https://www.cosmeticsbusiness .com/news/article_page/Genderless_beauty_creates_new_opportunities_for_brands/ 128205.

Matusow, Jamie. "Shakeup in the Beauty World." *Beauty Packaging*, November 2, 2015. Accessed July 21, 2017. http://www.beautypackaging.com/heaps/view/2017/1/.

Matusow, Jamie, and Joanna Cosgrove. "Re-Formulating Strategies in the Beauty World." *Beauty Packaging*, November 2, 2017. Accessed July 15, 2018. http://www.beautypackaging .com/issues/2017-10-01/view_features/re-formulating-strategies-in-the-beauty-world -143009/?widget=suggestedbox.

"Mauritania Struggles with Love of Fat Women." *NBC News*, April 16, 2007. Accessed July 27, 2017. http://www.nbcnews.com/id/18141550/ns/health-health_care/t/mauritania -struggles-love-fat-women/.

Max Factor, "A Glamorous NOW . . . a lovelier TOMORROW" (1947). Duke University Libraries Digital Repository, John W. Hartman Center for Sales, Advertising & Marketing History. Accessed August 17, 2019. https://idn.duke.edu/ark:/87924/r4wd3qn8g.

Maxwell, Sophie. "What Is Premiumization?" *Brandingmag*, April 9, 2014. Accessed July 18, 2017. https://www.brandingmag.com/2014/04/09/what-is-premiumization/.

McCarthy, Kelly. "Calvin Klein's New, Racy Ad Campaign Sparks Controversy." *ABC News*, May 12, 2016. Accessed July 2, 2017. https://abcnews.go.com/Lifestyle/calvin-kleins-racy -ad-campaign-sparks-controversy/story?id=39057405.

McCracken, Grant. "Who Is the Celebrity Endorser? Cultural Foundations of the Endorsement Process." *Journal of Consumer Research* 16, no. 3 (1989): 310–21. Accessed July 24, 2017. doi: 10.1086/209217.

McDermott, Nick. "Huge Rise in Men with Eating Disorders Is 'Fueled by Social Media.'" *New York Post*, July 24, 2017. Accessed March 15, 2018. https://nypost.com/2017/07/24/ huge-rise-in-men-with-eating-disorders-is-fueled-by-social-media/.

McDonough, John, and Karen Egolf. *The Advertising Age Encyclopedia of Advertising*, 1st ed. New York: Routledge, 2002.

McDonough, Katie. "Hate Women, Make Money: 8 Ads and Products That Take Sexism to New Lows." *Salon*, September 10, 2013. Accessed July 20, 2017. https://www .salon.com/2013/09/10/hate_women_make_money_9_ads_and_products_that_take_ sexism_to_new_lows/.

McDougall, Andrew. "Beauty Marketers Falling Short When It Comes to Advertising." CosmeticsDesign.com-USA. Last modified February 16, 2015. Accessed July 18, 2017. https:// www.cosmeticsdesign.com/Article/2015/02/16/Beauty-marketers-falling-short-when-it -comes-to-advertising.

———. "Fragrance Brands Will Continue to Push the Boundaries Because Ultimately, Sex Sells." CosmeticsDesign-Asia.com. Last modified November 23, 2011. Accessed July 1, 2017. https://www.cosmeticsdesign-asia.com/Article/2011/11/23/Fragrance-brands-will -continue-to-push-the-boundaries-because-ultimately-sex-sells.

———. "Growing Natural Trend and Intense Competition in Anti-ageing Market." CosmeticsDesign-Europe.com. Last modified May 23, 2014. Accessed July 18, 2017. https://www .cosmeticsdesign-europe.com/Article/2014/05/23/Growing-natural-trend-and-intense -competition-in-anti-ageing-market.

———. "Is It Time for Cosmetics Industry to Change Ads Following Further FDA Claim Crackdowns?" CosmeticsDesign.com-USA. Last modified September 20, 2012. Ac-

cessed July 20, 2017. https://www.cosmeticsdesign.com/Article/2012/09/20/Is-it-time-for
-cosmetics-industry-to-change-ads-following-further-FDA-claim-crackdowns.

McKee, Melinda. "Beauty Brands You Thought Were Cruelty-Free but Aren't." People for the
Ethical Treatment of Animals, March 24, 2015. Accessed July 15, 2017. https://www.peta
.org/living/personal-care-fashion/companies-test-on-animals/.

McKenzie, Richard. "Decade of Greed?" *National Review*, June 10, 2004. Accessed July 5,
2017. https://www.nationalreview.com/2004/06/decade-greed-richard-mckenzie/.

McNeilly, Mark. "Is Celebrity Branding Worth the Price Tag?" *Fast Company*, January 22,
2013. Accessed July 25, 2017. https://www.fastcompany.com/3004910/celebrity-branding
-worth-price-tag.

McNew, Bradley Seth. "This Cosmetics Giant Owns Most of America's Favorite Brands."
The Motley Fool. February 10, 2017. Accessed July 13, 2017. https://www.fool.com/
investing/2017/02/10/this-cosmetics-giant-owns-most-of-americas-favorit.aspx.

"Media and Entertainment." Vault.com. Accessed December 12, 2017. http://www.vault
.com/industries-professions/industries/media-and-entertainment.aspx.

"Media Conglomerate." In *Wikipedia*. Last modified August 29, 2019. Accessed August 29,
2019. https://en.wikipedia.org/wiki/Media_conglomerate.

Melina, Remy. "How Advertisements Seduce Your Brain." *Live Science*, September 11, 2011.
Accessed September 2, 2019. https://www.livescience.com/16169-advertisements-seduce
-brain.html.

Meredith Corporation. "Women 2020: Meredith's Exclusive Research Study Reveals Weight
Acceptance and Wage Equality Top Issues Facing Millennial Women Today." Meredith
Corporation press release, August 6, 2015. Accessed July 18, 2017. http://meredith
.mediaroom.com/2015-08-06-Women-2020-Merediths-Exclusive-Research-Study-Reveals
-Weight-Acceptance-And-Wage-Equality-Top-Issues-Facing-Millennial-Women-Today.

Merrick, Amy. "Marketing 'Real' Bodies." *New Yorker*, April 1, 2014. Accessed July 28, 2017.
https://www.newyorker.com/business/currency/marketing-real-bodies.

Michael Ochs Archives. "Marilyn Monroe with Chanel No. 5." Photos.com by Getty Images.
Accessed August 16, 2019. https://photos.com/featured/marilyn-monroe-with-chanel-no
-5-michael-ochs-archives.html.

Minnick, Mimi. "Breck Girls." *Smithsonian Magazine*, January 1, 2000. Accessed July 4,
2017. https://www.smithsonianmag.com/arts-culture/breck-girls-60936753/#1Q7YVmcd
8Tk4iUbi.99.

Mintel. "Mintel Announces Four Beauty Trends Set to Impact Global Markets by 2025."
Mintel press release, December 1, 2015. Accessed July 12, 2017. http://www.mintel
.com/press-centre/beauty-and-personal-care/mintel-announces-four-beauty-trends-set-to
-impact-global-markets-by-2025.

———. "Mintel Beauty & Personal Care Announces 'Active Beauty' as a Key Trend for 2017."
Mintel press release, February 16, 2017. Accessed July 31, 2017. http://www.mintel.com/
press-centre/beauty-and-personal-care/beauty-and-personal-care-trend-2017.

Mitchell, Elizabeth S. "Liquid-Plumr Turns a Clogged Drain into an Erotic Fantasy. Again."
Adweek, July 29, 2013. Accessed July 2, 2017. https://www.adweek.com/digital/liquid
-plumr-turns-a-clogged-drain-into-an-erotic-fantasy-again/.

Monllos, Kristina. "Ad of the Day: Ronda Rousey Shows 'Strong is Beautiful' in This New
Pantene Campaign." *Adweek*, December 7, 2016. Accessed July 24, 2017. https://www
.adweek.com/brand-marketing/ad-day-ronda-rousey-shows-strong-beautiful-new-pantene
-campaign-174984/.

———. "Brands Are Throwing Out Gender Norms to Reflect a More Fluid World." *Adweek*, October 17, 2016. Accessed July 4, 2017. https://www.adweek.com/brand-marketing/brands-are-throwing-out-gender-norms-reflect-more-fluid-world-174070/.

———. "Men Appear in Ads 4 Times More Than Women, According to Research Revealed at Cannes." *Adweek*, June 21, 2017. Accessed July 31, 2017. https://www.adweek.com/brand-marketing/men-appear-in-ads-4-times-more-than-women-according-to-research-revealed-at-cannes/.

———. "These Empowering Ads Were Named the Best of #Femvertising." *Adweek*, July 17, 2015. Accessed July 3, 2017. https://www.adweek.com/brand-marketing/these-women-empowering-ad-campaigns-win-inaugural-femvertising-awards-165949/.

Monllos, Kristina, and Patrick Coffee. "Why the U.S. Ad Industry Will Never Regulate Gender Stereotypes." *Adweek*, July 20, 2017. Accessed July 28, 2017. https://www.adweek.com/brand-marketing/why-the-u-s-ad-industry-will-never-regulate-gender-stereotypes/.

Monro, Fiona B., and Gail Huon. "Media-Portrayed Idealized Images, Body Shame, and Appearance Anxiety." *International Journal of Eating Disorders* 38, no. 1 (2005): 85–90. Accessed July 19, 2017. doi: 10.1002/eat.20153.

Moodie, Alison. "Is Botox as Safe as We Think It Is?" *Guardian*, August 27, 2016. Accessed July 28, 2017. https://www.theguardian.com/lifeandstyle/2016/aug/27/botox-safe-new-research-testing-toxins-fda.

Moorhead, Alana. "Plastic Surgeon Reveals Which Celebrity Facial Features Clients Want Most." *New York Post*, August 31, 2016. Accessed July 28, 2017. https://nypost.com/2016/08/31/plastic-surgeon-reveals-which-celebrity-facial-features-clients-want-most/.

Morais, Richard C. "The Color of Beauty." *Forbes*, November 27, 2000. Accessed July 2, 2017. https://www.forbes.com/forbes/2000/1127/6614170a.html#3faa33a951ec.

Morgan, Penny. "Estée Lauder Expands Business through Brand Acquisitions." Market Realist, August 28, 2015. Accessed July 23, 2017. https://marketrealist.com/2015/08/estee-lauder-expands-business-brand-acquisitions.

Moriarty, Sandra, Nancy Mitchell, Charles Wood, and William D. Wells. *Advertising & IMC: Principles and Practice*, 11th ed. Hoboken, NJ: Pearson, 2019.

"Most Women 'Unhappy with Their Bodies.'" *Daily Mail*. Accessed July 20, 2017. http://www.dailymail.co.uk/news/article-146021/Most-women-unhappy-bodies.html.

Mousavi, Seyed Reza. "The Ethics of Aesthetic Surgery." *Journal of Cutaneous and Aesthetic Surgery* 3, no. 1 (2010): 38–40. Accessed July 31, 2017. doi: 10.4103/0974-2077.63396.

Mueller, Barbara. *Dynamics of International Advertising: Theoretical and Practical Perspectives*, 2nd ed. New York: Peter Lang, 2011.

Muller, Marissa G. "Katy Perry Wore Brand New CoverGirl Makeup to the 2017 Grammy Awards." *Self*, February 13, 2017. Accessed July 26, 2017. https://www.self.com/story/katy-perry-covergirl-makeup-2017-grammy-awards.

Mulvey, Jeanette. "Why Sex Sells . . . More Than Ever." *Business News Daily*, June 7, 2012. Accessed July 1, 2017. https://www.businessnewsdaily.com/2649-sex-sells-more.html.

Murphy, Andrea, Jonathan Ponciano, Sarah Hansen, and Halah Touryalai. "Global 2000: The World's Largest Public Companies," *Forbes*, May 15, 2019. Accessed August 19, 2019. https://www.forbes.com/global2000/#39edcff5335d.

Mustafa, Nadia. "Iman." *Time*, February 9, 2004. Accessed July 5, 2017. http://content.time.com/time/specials/packages/article/0,28804,2015519_2015510_2015477,00.html.

Muto, Jordan. "What Beauty Brands Are Big with Millennials? See the Top 25 Brands They Love." *Today*, June 14, 2015. Accessed July 7, 2017. https://www.today.com/style/new-report-looks-millennials-beauty-habits-t25956.

Myers, Philip N., Jr., and Frank A. Biocca. "The Elastic Body Image: The Effect of Television Advertising and Programming on Body Image Distortions in Young Women." *Journal of Communication* 42, no. 3 (1992): 108–33. Accessed July 29, 2017. doi: 10.1111/j.1460-2466.1992.tb00802.x.

Myint, B. "5 Facts about the Brothers Grimm." Biography.com, December 22, 2014. Accessed December 12, 2017. https://www.biography.com/news/brothers-grimm-facts.

N., Pam M.S. "Gender Role." In *PsychologyDictionary.org*, May 11, 2013. Accessed August 31, 2019. https://psychologydictionary.org/gender-role/.

"Nano, Nano on the Wall . . ." *Bloomberg Businessweek*, December 11, 2005. Accessed July 17, 2017. https://www.bloomberg.com/news/articles/2005-12-11/nano-nano-on-the-wall-dot-dot-dot.

"Nanotechnology—Keeping Cosmetics Out of the Courtroom." Cosmetics Business, April 7, 2011. Accessed July 18, 2017. https://www.cosmeticsbusiness.com/technical/article_page/Nanotechnology__keeping_cosmetics_out_of_the_courtroom/60306.

Naravan, Priyanka. "The Cosmetics Industry Has Avoided Strict Regulation for Over a Century. Now Rising Health Concerns Has FDA Inquiring." CNBC, August 2, 2018. https://www.cnbc.com/2018/08/01/fda-begins-first-inquiry-of-lightly-regulated-cosmetics-industry.html.

National Coalition Against Censorship. "Sex and Censorship: Dangers to Minors and Others?" May 1, 2013. Accessed August 20, 2018. https://ncac.org/selected-resources/sex-and-censorship-dangers-to-minors-and-others-2.

Nauert, Rick. "Acquaintances Can Influence Body Image." Psych Central. Accessed July 27, 2017. https://psychcentral.com/news/2019/01/31/acquaintances-can-influence-body-image/142516.html.

———. "Cosmetics Industry Driven by Emotions." Psych Central, July 25, 2011. Accessed July 7, 2017. https://psychcentral.com/news/2011/07/25/cosmetics-industry-driven-by-emotions.

"Neanderthal 'Make-up' Containers Discovered." *BBC News*, January 9, 2010. Accessed July 21, 2017. http://news.bbc.co.uk/2/hi/sci/tech/8448660.stm.

Neff, Jack. "Clinique Sees Hope in a Fresh Start." *Advertising Age*, July 28, 2014. Accessed July 15, 2017. http://adage.com/article/cmo-strategy/clinique-sees-hope-a-fresh-start/294329/.

———. "Coming Next: Cosmetics Ads Featuring You as the Model." *Advertising Age*, November 5, 2014. Accessed July 5, 2017. http://adage.com/article/digital/coming-cosmetics-ads-featuring-model/295715/.

———. "Estee Lauder Gets Women Ready for Their Social-Media Close-ups." *Advertising Age*, October 7, 2009. Accessed July 11, 2017. http://adage.com/article/news/marketing-estee-lauder-promotion-connects-social-media/139524/.

———. "Unilever Unleashes 'Onslaught' on Beauty Industry." *Advertising Age*, October 2, 2007. Accessed July 10, 2017. http://adage.com/article/news/unilever-unleashes-onslaught-beauty-industry/120886/.

Neimark, Jill. "The Culture of Celebrity." *Psychology Today*, May 1, 1995. Accessed July 24, 2017. https://www.psychologytoday.com/us/articles/199505/the-culture-celebrity.

Nelson, Dean. "India Bans 'Overtly Sexual' Deodorant Ads." *Telegraph*, May 27, 2011. Accessed July 2, 2017. https://www.telegraph.co.uk/news/worldnews/asia/india/8541292/India-bans-overtly-sexual-deodorant-ads.html.

"New Poll Reveals US United against Cosmetics Animal Tests." Cruelty Free International, September 12, 2019. Accessed October 19, 2019. https://www.crueltyfreeinternational.org/what-we-do/latest-news-and-updates/new-poll-reveals-us-united-against-cosmetics-animal-tests.

Newman, Andrew Adam. "Clean & Clear Videos Dare Not Speak Blemish's Name." *New York Times*, March 12, 2014. Accessed July 3, 2017. https://www.nytimes.com/2014/03/13/business/media/clean-clear-videos-dare-not-speak-blemishs-name.html.

———. "Mascara Ads: Thick Lashes, Fine Print." *New York Times*, November 12, 2013. Accessed July 16, 2017. https://www.nytimes.com/2013/11/14/fashion/Mascara-Ads-Draw-Criticisms.html.

Newman, Cathy. "The Enigma of Beauty." *National Geographic*, January 2000. Accessed July 10, 2017. https://www.nationalgeographic.com/science/health-and-human-body/human-body/enigma-beauty/.

Nichols, James Michael. "Secret Deodorant Debuts Groundbreaking Transgender Ad." *Huffington Post*, November 3, 2016. Accessed July 28, 2017. https://www.huffingtonpost.com/entry/secret-pro-transgender-commercial_us_58122d5de4b0390e69ce9a4b.

Nichols, Nancy A. "Whatever Happened to Rosie the Riveter?" *Harvard Business Review*, July–August 1993. Accessed July 31, 2017. https://hbr.org/1993/07/whatever-happened-to-rosie-the-riveter.

Nickles, Liz, and Savita Iyer. *Brandstorm: Surviving and Thriving in the New Consumer-Led Marketplace*. New York: Palgrave Macmillan, 2012.

Nielsen. "Advertising & Audiences: State of the Media," May 2014. Accessed July 16, 2017. http://www.nielsen.com/content/dam/nielsenglobal/jp/docs/report/2014/Nielsen_Advertising_and_%20Audiences%20Report-FINAL.pdf.

———. "Age Before Beauty: Treating Generations with a Personal Touch in Beauty Advertising," February 5, 2015. Accessed July 12, 2017. http://www.nielsen.com/us/en/insights/news/2015/age-before-beauty-treating-generations-with-a-personal-touch-in-beauty-advertising.html.

———. "Facts of Life: As They Move through Life Stages, Millennials' Media Habits Are Different and Distinct," March 24, 2016. Accessed July 12, 2017. http://www.nielsen.com/us/en/insights/news/2016/facts-of-life-as-they-move-through-life-stages-millennials-media-habits-are-different.html.

———. "Nielsen's N-Score Now Provides Enhanced Talent Analytics Based on Fan Affinity," June 22, 2016. Accessed July 25, 2017. http://www.nielsen.com/us/en/press-room/2016/nielsens-n-score-now-provides-enhanced-talent-analytics-based-on-fan-affinity.html.

Nigam, Pramod Kumar, and Anjana Nigam. "Botulinum Toxin." *Indian Journal of Dermatology* 55, no. 1 (2010): 8–14. Accessed July 28, 2017. doi: 10.4103/0019-5154.60343.

"1980: Brooke Shields Sparks Controversy in Calvin Klein Jeans." 4A's. Accessed September 1, 2019. https://www.aaaa.org/timeline-event/brooke-shields-sparks-controversy-calvin-klein-jeans/.

"1930s USA Camay Magazine Advert." Advertising Archives. Accessed August 16, 2019. http://www.advertisingarchives.co.uk/index.php?service=search&action=do_quick_search&language=en&q=camay.

Niven-Phillips, Lisa. "The New Face of No.5: Marilyn Monroe." *Vogue*, October 16, 2013. Accessed July 19, 2017. https://www.vogue.co.uk/article/marilyn-monroe-new-face-of -chanel-no5-perfume.

"No Brand Loyalty among Millennials, Cosmetics Consumer Study Says." *Beauty Packaging*, December 24, 2014. Accessed July 30, 2017. http://www.beautypackaging.com/contents/ view_breaking-news/2014-12-24/no-brand-loyalty-among-millennials-cosmetics-consumer -study-says.

Nolan, Steve. "Has Plastic Surgery Made These Beauty Queens All Look the Same? Koreans Complain about Pageant 'Clones.'" *Daily Mail*, April 25, 2013. Accessed July 28, 2017. http://www.dailymail.co.uk/news/article-2314647/Has-plastic-surgery-20-Korean-beauty -pageant-contestants-look-Pictures-contest-hopefuls-goes-viral.html#ixzz4tPibUTuz.

Nolo. "Seven Guidelines for Honest Advertisers." *Forbes*, August 18, 2006. Accessed July 17, 2018. https://www.forbes.com/2006/08/18/ftc-advertising-fraud-cx_nl_0818nolo .html#16fdd619256a.

"Not a Very Good Endorsement." *Independent*, March 31, 2005. Accessed August 21, 2019. https://www.independent.co.uk/news/media/not-a-very-good-endorsement-8592.html.

"Now Walmart Targets EIGHT-year-olds with a New Range of 'Anti-aging' Make-up." *Daily Mail*, January 26, 2011. Accessed July 15, 2017. http://www.dailymail.co.uk/ news/article-1350857/Walmart-Geo-Girl-anti-aging-make-targets-EIGHT-year-olds .html#ixzz4bycupMDE.

NSF Cosmetics and Personal Care Program. "Claims Substantiation and Testing Services." Accessed July 17, 2017. http://www.nsf.org/newsroom_pdf/cos_claims_testing_services.pdf.

Nudd, Tim. "Ad of the Day: Axe Gets Inclusive in a Remarkable Ad That's Really Pretty Magical." *Adweek*, January 14, 2016. Accessed November 23, 2017. https://www.adweek .com/brand-marketing/ad-day-axe-gets-inclusive-remarkable-ad-thats-really-pretty-magical -168996/.

———. "10 Sexist Ads Made by Total Pigs." *Adweek*, July 13, 2011. Accessed July 20, 2017. https://www.adweek.com/creativity/10-sexist-ads-made-total-pigs-133401/.

Nudelman, Janet. "Federal Personal Care Products Safety Act (S.1014)." Campaign for Safe Cosmetics," May 28, 2015. Accessed July 15, 2017. http://www.safecosmetics.org/wp -content/uploads/2015/06/Personal-Care-Products-Safety-Act-SB-1014-factsheet.pdf.

Nuffield Council on Bioethics. "Cosmetics Procedures: Ethical Issues." Accessed July 20, 2018. http://nuffieldbioethics.org/wp-content/uploads/Cosmetic-procedures-full-report.pdf.

"Number 12 Looks Just Like You," *The Twilight Zone* (1964). In *Wikipedia*. Last modified May 22, 2019. Accessed August 1, 2019. https://en.wikipedia.org/wiki/Number_12_ Looks_Just_Like_You.

Nussbaum, Martha C. "Objectification." *Philosophy and Public Affairs* 24, no. 4 (1995): 249–91. Accessed July 2, 2017. doi: 10.1111/j.1088-4963.1995.tb00032.x.

Nussbaum, Rachel. "CVS Will No Longer Photoshop Its Beauty Ads." *Glamour*, January 15, 2018. Accessed November 5, 2019. https://www.glamour.com/story/cvs-beauty-mark -photoshop.

O'Connor, Clare. "How Glossier's Emily Weiss Is Using the Internet to Build a Beauty Brand for Generation Instagram." *Forbes*, August 2, 2016. Accessed July 7, 2017. https:// www.forbes.com/sites/clareoconnor/2016/08/02/how-glossiers-emily-weiss-is-using-the -internet-to-build-a-beauty-brand-for-generation-instagram/#220b8bed6208.

Ogilvy, David. *Ogilvy on Advertising*. New York: Vintage Books, 1985.

O'Guinn, Thomas C., Chris Allen, and Richard J. Semenk. *Promo2*, 2nd ed. Boston: Cengage, 2012.

Olenski, Steve. "The Branding of Dead Celebrities." *Forbes*, June 12, 2017. Accessed July 24, 2017. https://www.forbes.com/sites/steveolenski/2017/06/12/the-branding-of-dead -celebrities/#4c3151da6d80.

———. "How Brands Should Use Celebrities for Endorsements." *Forbes*, July 20, 2016. Accessed July 26, 2017. https://www.forbes.com/sites/steveolenski/2016/07/20/how-brands -should-use-celebrities-for-endorsements/#3e3c4b755593.

Oliver, Amy. "Vanity Mirror Used by Tragic 18th Century Society Beauty, 27, Who Died of Make-up Poisoning Sells for £300,000." *Daily Mail*, May 29, 2012. Accessed September 21, 2019. https://www.dailymail.co.uk/news/article-2151541/Vanity-mirror-used -tragic-18th-century-society-beauty-27-died-make-poisoning-sells-300-000.html.

Oliver, Dana. "The 'Most Unforgettable Women in the World' Turn Heads in This 1989 Revlon Commercial." *Huffington Post*, April 5, 2014. Accessed July 5, 2017. https://www .huffingtonpost.com/2014/04/05/most-unforgettable-women-in-the-world-revlon _n_5092021.html.

Olya, Gabrielle. "The Rise of 'Brotox': More Men Are Getting Botox Than Ever Before." *People*, October 6, 2015. Accessed July 18, 2017. https://people.com/bodies/the-rise-of -brotox-more-men-are-getting-botox-than-ever-before/.

"One in 5 American Women Actively Considering Plastic Surgery: Study." *New York Daily News*, February 19, 2015. Accessed July 28, 2017. http://www.nydailynews.com/life -style/5-american-women-actively-plastic-surgery-article-1.2121903.

Oneill, Therese. "6 Terrifying Beauty Practices from History." *Mental Floss*, February 2, 2018. Accessed October 19, 2019. https://mentalfloss.com/article/69360/7-terrifying-beauty -practices-history.

"Oops! L'Oreal's Diane Keaton Golden Globes Ad Is Busted by Unphotoshopped Reality We Saw Just Seconds Earlier." *Daily Mail*, January 14, 2014. Accessed July 18, 2017. http://www.dailymail.co.uk/femail/article-2538813/LOreal-accused-heavily-Photo shopping-Diane-Keaton-ad-aired-IMMEDIATELY-retouched-Golden-Globes-speech .html#ixzz4IAWIaeLc.

O'Reilly, Lara. "Unilever Seeks to Premiumise Its Personal Care Portfolio." *Marketing Week*, May 9, 2014. Accessed July 22, 2017. https://www.marketingweek.com/2014/05/09/ unilever-seeks-to-premiumise-its-personal-care-portfolio/.

"Our Purpose and Strategy." Advertising Standards Authority. Accessed August 11, 2019. https://www.asa.org.uk/about-asa-and-cap/about-regulation/our-purpose-and-strategy .html.

"Outrage over Magazine's Emaciated 'Corpse' Model." *New York Post*, February 26, 2015. Accessed July 30, 2017. https://nypost.com/2015/02/26/fashion-magazine-faces-backlash -over-emaciated-model/.

Øvreberg, Elisabeth. "Why Women Want Plastic Surgery." *ScienceNorway*, October 16, 2012. Accessed July 10, 2017. http://sciencenordic.com/why-women-want-plastic-surgery.

Paglia, Camille. *Sexual Personae: Art and Decadence from Nefertiti to Emily Dickinson*. New York: Vintage Books, 1991.

Pai, Deanna. "CoverGirl's New Brand Ambassador Is Muslim Beauty Blogger Nura Afia." *Glamour*, November 2, 2016. Accessed September 2, 2019. https://www.glamour.com/ story/covergirl-nura-afia-muslim-beauty-blogger.

Pallett, Pamela M., Stephen Link, and Kang Lee. "New 'Golden' Ratios for Facial Beauty." *Vision Research* 50, no. 2 (2010): 149–54. Accessed July 4, 2017. doi: 10.1016/j.visres .2009.11.003.

Pantene. "The History of Pantene." Accessed August 5, 2018. https://www.pantene.com.ph/ en-ph/about-us/the-history-of-pantene.

Papadaki, Evangelia. "Feminist Perspectives on Objectification." In *Stanford Encyclopedia of Philosophy*, edited by Edward N. Zalta. Last modified December 1, 2015. Accessed July 18, 2018. https://plato.stanford.edu/archives/sum2018/entries/feminism-objectification/.

Pappas, Stephanie. "Our Brains See Men as Whole and Women as Parts." *Scientific American*, July 25, 2012. Accessed July 8, 2017. https://www.scientificamerican.com/article/our -brains-see-men-as-whole-women-as-parts/.

———. "Sexy Advertising on the Rise." *Live Science*, June 6, 2012. Accessed July 1, 2017. https://www.livescience.com/20773-sexy-advertising-increasing.html.

Parija, Bhatnagar. "P&G Has a Good Hair Day." CNN, March 18, 2003. Accessed March 15, 2020. https://money.cnn.com/2003/03/18/news/companies/Procter/.

Parker-Pope, Tara. "The Dark Side of the Beauty Industry, in 60 Seconds." *New York Times*, October 15, 2007. Accessed July 10, 2017. https://well.blogs.nytimes.com/2007/10/15/ the-beauty-industrys-dark-side-in-60-seconds/.

Parsons, Sarah. "Jennifer Lopez Fragrance Relaunches with Designer Parfums." Cosmetics Business, April 10, 2017. Accessed July 26, 2017. https://www.cosmeticsbusiness.com/ news/article_page/Jennifer_Lopez_fragrance_relaunches_with_Designer_Parfums/127984.

Pathak, Shareen. "Why Fashion and Beauty Brands Love Instagram." *Digiday*, August 11, 2015. Accessed July 17, 2017. https://digiday.com/marketing/fashion-beauty-brands -instagram/.

Patterson, Martha H., ed. *The American New Woman Revisited: A Reader, 1894–1930*. New Brunswick, NJ: Rutgers University Press, 2008.

Paul, Kari. "Study Reveals the Dangers of Plastic Surgery Advertisements on Instagram." *MarketWatch*, August 30, 2017. Accessed November 18, 2017. https://www.marketwatch.com/ story/a-surprising-trend-fueling-plastic-surgery-instagram-2017-02-15.

Paul, Pamela. "Flattery Will Get an Ad Nowhere." *New York Times*, December 10, 2010. Accessed July 10, 2017. https://www.nytimes.com/2010/12/12/fashion/12Studied.html ?_r=0.

Peacock, Louisa. "The Pursuit of Beauty: What Compels Women to Go Under the Knife?" *Telegraph*, May 22, 2013. Accessed July 9, 2017. https://www.telegraph.co.uk/women/ womens-life/10071794/Cosmetic-surgery-What-compels-women-to-go-under-the-knife .html.

Pearce, Olivia. "Unilever to Acquire Murad Skincare; Follows Acquisitions of Dermalogica, Kate Somerville & REN." World Branding Forum, July 6, 2015. Accessed July 13, 2017. https://brandingforum.org/news/unilever-to-acquire-murad-skincare-follows-acquisitions -of-dermalogica-kate-somerville-ren/.

Pearson, Carol S. "Branding." Archetypal Narrative Intelligence. Accessed July 3, 2017. http:// www.carolspearson.com/archetypal-branding/archetypes/organizational-branding/.

———. "Caregiver." Archetypal Narrative Intelligence. http://www.carolspearson.com/ archetypes/caregiver/.

———. "Innocent." Archetypal Narrative Intelligence. http://www.carolspearson.com/ archetypes/innocent/.

———. "Lover." Archetypal Narrative Intelligence. http://www.carolspearson.com/archetypes/lover/.

———. "Magician." Archetypal Narrative Intelligence. http://www.carolspearson.com/archetypes/magician/.

Peck, Emily. "Advertisers Are Actually Teaming Up to Fight Sexism. For Real." *Huffington Post*, June 20, 2017. Accessed July 4, 2017. https://www.huffpost.com/entry/advertising-sexism-unstereotype-alliance_n_59482fa0e4b07499199ddfeb.

Peiss, Kathy. *Hope in a Jar: The Making of America's Beauty Culture*. Philadelphia: University of Pennsylvania Press, 2011.

Perera, Kathryn. "Time to Kick Sexism Out of Advertising." *Guardian*, June 29, 2010. Accessed July 20, 2017. https://www.theguardian.com/commentisfree/2010/jun/29/kick-sexism-out-of-advertising.

"Perfect Illusions: "Eating Disorders and the Family." PBS.org. Accessed July 27, 2017. http://www.pbs.org/perfectillusions/eatingdisorders/preventing_facts.html.

"A Perfect Wife . . . until 6 p.m." Lysol Disinfectant for Feminine Hygiene. https://i.pinimg.com/736x/6f/36/43/6f3643072eeaa8e9a7dd31b9653d5bb5.jpg.

"The 'Perfect' Body: 100 Years of Our Changing Shape." *Today*. Last modified February 24, 2014. Accessed November 25, 2017. https://www.today.com/slideshow/perfect-body-100-years-our-changing-shape-54454777.

"Perfume." *Advertising Age*, September 15, 2003. Accessed July 2, 2017. http://adage.com/article/adage-encyclopedia/perfume/98816/.

"The Perfume Shop Names Chanel No.5 Most Iconic Scent." Cosmetics Business, April 14, 2016. Accessed July 19, 2017. https://www.cosmeticsbusiness.com/news/article_page/%20The_Perfume_Shop_names_Chanel_No5_most_iconic_scent/117369.

Perrigo, Billy. "The U.K. Just Banned 'Harmful Gender Stereotypes' in Advertising." *Time*, June 14, 2019. Accessed September 1, 2019. https://time.com/5607209/uk-gender-stereotypes-adverts/.

Persaud, Raj, and Peter Bruggen. "The Lipstick Effect: How Boom or Bust Effects Beauty." *Psychology Today*, October 10, 2015. Accessed August 21, 2017. https://www.psychologytoday.com/us/blog/slightly-blighty/201510/the-lipstick-effect-how-boom-or-bust-effects-beauty.

Phelps, Nicole. "Sex Sells: Calvin Klein's 1990s Ads Stirred Libidos and Controversies in Equal Measure." *Vogue*, September 1, 2015. Accessed July 2, 2017. https://www.vogue.com/article/calvin-klein-jeans-90s-ads-kate-moss-mark-wahlberg-controversy.

Phillips, Cara. "The Beauty Advantage: Six Ugly Secrets of the Cosmetics Counter." *Newsweek*, July 19, 2010. Accessed July 18, 2017. https://www.newsweek.com/beauty-advantage-six-ugly-secrets-cosmetics-counter-74319.

Phillips, Tom. "'Everyone Knew She Was Ill. The Other Girls, the Model Agencies . . . Don't Believe It When They Say They Didn't.'" *Guardian*, January 13, 2007. Accessed July 27, 2017. https://www.theguardian.com/lifeandstyle/2007/jan/14/fashion.features4.

"Physical Attractiveness." In *Wikipedia*. Last modified August 29, 2019. Accessed August 29, 2019. https://en.wikipedia.org/wiki/Physical_attractiveness.

Pilditch, David. "Perfume Ad Featuring Naked Cara Delevingne Cleared After Complaints It Objectified Women." *Daily Express*, April 29, 2015. Accessed July 1, 2017. https://www.express.co.uk/life-style/style/573549/Tom-Ford-perfume-advert-naked-Cara-Delevingne-cleared-ASA-complaints.

Pitman, Simon. "Beauty Industry Blamed for Making Women Feel Bad about Themselves." CosmeticsDesign-Europe.com. Last modified July 19, 2008. Accessed July 10, 2017. https://www.cosmeticsdesign-europe.com/Article/2006/06/26/Beauty-industry-blamed-for-making-women-feel-bad-about-themselves.

———. "German Color Cosmetics Brand BeYu Targets US Masstige Market." CosmeticsDesign.com-USA, February 16, 2016. Accessed July 18, 2017. https://www.cosmeticsdesign.com/Article/2016/02/16/German-color-cosmetics-brand-BeYu-targets-US-masstige-market.

———. "Rise of Male Star Endorsed Cosmetics." CosmeticsDesign.com-USA. Last modified July 19, 2008. Accessed July 27, 2017. https://www.cosmeticsdesign.com/Article/2007/01/11/Rise-of-male-star-endorsed-cosmetics.

"Plastic Chemicals 'Feminise Boys.'" *BBC News*, November 16, 2009. Accessed July 31, 2017. http://news.bbc.co.uk/2/hi/health/8361863.stm.

"Plato's Aesthetics." In *The Stanford Encyclopedia of Philosophy*. Last modified July 13, 2016. Accessed July 30, 2017. https://plato.stanford.edu/entries/plato-aesthetics/#ForBea.

"Plus-Size Models May Boost Body Image, Study Says." *New York Daily News*, November 9, 2012. Accessed July 28, 2017. http://www.nydailynews.com/life-style/health/plus-size-models-boost-body-image-study-article-1.1199412.

Pols, Mary. "*Snow White and the Huntsman*: The Fairest Feminist of Them All." *Time*, May 31, 2012. Accessed October 12, 2018. http://entertainment.time.com/2012/05/31/step-monster-snow-white-and-the-huntsman/.

Pool, Robert. *Fat: Fighting the Obesity Epidemic*. Oxford: Oxford University Press, 2001.

Postrel, Virginia. "The Truth about Beauty." *Atlantic*, March 1, 2007. Accessed July 2, 2017. https://www.theatlantic.com/magazine/archive/2007/03/the-truth-about-beauty/305620/.

Poulter, Sean. "Banned, Nivea Ad That Made Model of 62 Look Younger: Watchdog Bans Advert After It Misled Customers Over Effects of Using Anti-ageing Cream." *Daily Mail*, August 27, 2013. Accessed July 5, 2017. http://www.dailymail.co.uk/femail/article-2403530/Banned-Nivea-anti-ageing-cream-advert-model-look-younger-digital-airbrushing.html.

Powers, Katie. "Shattering Gendered Marketing." *Marketing Week*, September 3, 2019. Accessed September 20, 2019. https://www.ama.org/marketing-news/shattering-gendered-marketing/.

Prigg, Mark, and Katharine Barney. "Doctors Urge Fashion Bosses to Put Ban on 'Clearly Anorexic' Girls; The Size Zero Debate," excerpt from *London Evening Standard*. Questia. Accessed September 5, 2019. https://www.questia.com/newspaper/1G1-152651045/doctors-urge-fashion-bosses-to-put-ban-on-clearly.

Pringle, Hamish. *Celebrity Sells*. Hoboken, NJ: Wiley, 2004.

"Prohibitions on Cosmetics Testing in the EU and Elsewhere." Cruelty Free International. Accessed August 24, 2019. https://www.crueltyfreeinternational.org/what-we-do/corporate-partnerships/eu-ban-cosmetics-testing.

Pullano, Chelsea. "How Revlon's Charles Revson Pioneered the Cosmetics Industry." *Journal*. December 12, 2016. Accessed July 11, 2017. https://journal.media/how-revlon-s-charles-revson-pioneered-the-cosmetics-industry.

Quenqua, Douglas. "Graduating from Lip Smackers." *New York Times*, April 28, 2010. Accessed July 16, 2017. https://www.nytimes.com/2010/04/29/fashion/29tween.html.

Rainey, Sarah. "High Street Skeletons: We All Know about Painfully Thin Catwalk Stars. Here We Reveal the Deeply Worrying Vital Statistics of Models for High Street Chains."

Daily Mail, October 28, 2015. Accessed July 27, 2017. http://www.dailymail.co.uk/femail/article-3294113/High-street-skeletons-know-painfully-catwalk-stars-reveal-deeply-worrying-vital-statistics-models-high-street-chains.html#ixzz4sJ7nYQIq.

Raj, Silpa, Shoma Jose, U.S. Sumod, and Mangalathillam Sabitha. "Nanotechnology in Cosmetics: Opportunities and Challenges." *Journal of Pharmacy and Bioallied Sciences* 4, no. 3 (2012): 186–93. Accessed July 18, 2017. doi: 10.4103/0975-7406.99016.

"Ralph Lauren Apologises for Digitally Retouching Slender Model to Make Her Head Look Bigger Than Her Waist." *Daily Mail*, October 10, 2009. Accessed July 27, 2017. http://www.dailymail.co.uk/news/article-1219046/Ralph-Lauren-digitally-retouches-slender-model-make-look-THINNER.html#ixzz4sbRVJU00.

"Ralph Lauren Tender Romance." Sephora.com. Accessed September https://www.sephora.com/product/tender-romance-P405915.19, 2019.

"Ralph Lauren Tender Romance Fragrance 2016." Models.com. Accessed September 19, 2019. https://models.com/work/ralph-lauren-tender-romance-fragrance-2016/505964.

Rankin, Jennifer. "Plastic Surgery App for Nine-Year-Olds Sparks Outrage on Twitter." *Guardian*, January 14, 2014. Accessed July 28, 2017. https://www.theguardian.com/technology/2014/jan/14/plastic-surgery-app-apple-google-children-twitter.

Raphael, Rina. "What's Driving the Billion-Dollar Natural Beauty Movement?" *Fast Company*, May 26, 2017. Accessed July 31, 2017. https://www.fastcompany.com/3068710/whats-driving-the-billion-dollar-natural-beauty-movement.

Rattue, Petra. "Plastic Surgery—Enormous Increase in Uptake by Younger Women." *Medical News Today*, March 16, 2012. Accessed July 9, 2017. https://www.medicalnewstoday.com/articles/243034.php.

Redding, Marie. "3 Indie Brands That Are Driving Innovation & Leveraging Social Media." *Beauty Packaging*, August 31, 2015. Accessed July 15, 2017. http://www.beautypackaging.com/contents/view_online-exclusives/2015-08-31/3-indie-brands-that-are-driving-innovation-leveraging-social-media.

Reed, Julia. "Estée Lauder's Growing Beauty Empire." *Wall Street Journal*, February 12, 2015. Accessed July 22, 2017. https://www.wsj.com/articles/estee-lauders-growing-beauty-empire-1423753606.

Regensdorf, Laura. "Watch Kate Moss in Never-Before-Seen Footage from Calvin Klein's '90s Obsession Campaign." *Vogue*, June 20, 2017. https://www.vogue.com/article/kate-moss-original-1993-calvin-klein-obsession-perfume-campaign-images-new-obsessed-perfume.

Reichert, Tom, and Courtney Carpenter. "An Update on Sex in Magazine Advertising: 1983 to 2003." *Journalism and Mass Communication Quarterly* 81, no. 4 (2004): 823–37. Accessed July 24, 2017. doi: 10.1177/107769900408100407.

Reichert, Tom, and Jacqueline Lambiase, eds. *Sex in Advertising: Perspectives on the Erotic Appeal.* New York: Routledge, 2012.

Reid, Chip. "FDA Accuses Avon, Lancôme, Other Cosmetic Companies of Making Ad Claims That Go Too Far." *CBS News*, October 18, 2012. Accessed July 14, 2017. https://www.cbsnews.com/news/fda-accuses-avon-lancome-other-cosmetic-companies-of-making-ad-claims-that-go-too-far/.

Reily, Stephen. "What Do Boomer Women Want from Cosmetic Companies? Not What They're Selling." Mediapost.com, March 12, 2012. Accessed July 11, 2017. https://www.mediapost.com/publications/article/169776/what-do-boomer-women-want-from-cosmetic-companies.html.

Reimel, Erin. "Manny Gutierrez Is the First Man to Star in a Maybelline Campaign, and It's a Huge Deal." *Glamour*, January 4, 2017. Accessed July 31, 2017. https://www.glamour .com/story/manny-gutierrez-maybelline-campaign.

Rendle, Karla. "Millennial and Gen-Z Beauty Consumers." *Beauty Packaging*, March 6, 2016. Accessed July 7, 2017. http://www.beautypackaging.com/issues/2016-03-01/view_columns/ millennial-and-gen-z-beauty-consumers.

Reporters Committee for Freedom of the Press. "Government Censorship (Prior Restraints)." Accessed July 15, 2018. https://www.rcfp.org/digital-journalists-legal-guide/government -censorship-prior-restraints.

ReportLinker. "Global Cosmeceuticals Market Outlook 2022." RNCOS, May 2019. https:// www.reportlinker.com/p01103487/Global-Cosmeceuticals-Market-Outlook.html.

"Researchers Discover New 'Golden Ratios' for Female Facial Beauty." *(e) Science News*, December 16, 2009. Accessed July 31, 2019. http://esciencenews.com/articles/2009/12/16/ researchers.discover.new.golden.ratios.female.facial.beauty.

Rettner, Rachael. "Illegal Silicone Butt Injections Cause Host of Health Problems." *Live Science*, June 18, 2015. Accessed July 29, 2017. https://www.livescience.com/51275-silicone -butt-injections-health-problems.html.

Reuters. "Bikini Ad Prompts a Sexual Harassment Lawsuit." *New York Times*, November 9, 1991. Accessed August 17, 2019. https://www.nytimes.com/1991/11/09/us/bikini-ad -prompts-a-sexual-harassment-suit.html.

"Revlon Inc.—Company Profile, Information, Business Description, History, Background Information on Revlon Inc." In *Reference for Business*. Accessed July 11, 2017. http://www .referenceforbusiness.com/history2/10/Revlon-Inc.html.

Revlon, Inc. "Our Company—Our Founders." Accessed August 8, 2019. https://www.revlon inc.com/our-company/our-founders.

Rich, Nathaniel. "American Dreams: 'The Stepford Wives' by Ira Levin." *Daily Beast*, August 24, 2012. Accessed August 1, 2017. https://www.thedailybeast.com/american-dreams-the -stepford-wives-by-ira-levin.

Rickey, Melanie. "The Fashion Police Have Felt the Frayed Collars of Two of Britain's Best Young Actors. Melanie Rickey Senses a Miscarriage of Justice." *Independent*, March 6, 1998. Accessed August 21, 2019. https://www.independent.co.uk/life-style/when-the-cameras -stop-rolling-dress-to-please-yourselves-1148563.html.

"Rihanna Rogue Perfume Ad Restricted Due to 'Sexually Suggestive' Image." *Guardian*, June 4, 2014. Accessed July 1, 2017. https://www.theguardian.com/media/2014/jun/04/ rihanna-rogue-perfume-ad-restricted-sexually-suggestive.

Roberts, Mary Lou, and Perri B. Koggan. "How Should Women Be Portrayed in Advertisements?—A Call for Research." *NA—Advances in Consumer Research* 06 (1979): 66–72. http://acrwebsite.org/volumes/9532/volumes/v06/NA-06.

Robinson, Julian. "Yves Saint Laurent Is Accused of 'Degrading' Models and 'Inciting Rape' with French Ad Campaign Featuring Women Opening Their Legs and Bending over Furniture." *Daily Mail*, March 6, 2017. Accessed July 3, 2017. http://www.dailymail.co.uk/news/ article-4286442/Yves-Saint-Laurent-accused-degrading-models.html.

Robson, David. "The Myth of Universal Beauty." BBC, June 23, 2015. Accessed July 4, 2017. http://www.bbc.com/future/story/20150622-the-myth-of-universal-beauty.

Roderick, Leonie. "Brands Face Crackdown on Gender Stereotypes in Advertising." *Marketing Week*, July 18, 2017. Accessed July 30, 2017. https://www.marketingweek .com/2017/07/18/brands-stricter-rules-gender-stereotypes/.

————. "Tackling Gender Stereotypes: Are New Ad Rules the Answer?" *Marketing Week*, July 20, 2017. Accessed July 22, 2017. https://www.marketingweek.com/2017/07/20/gender -stereotypes-advertising/.

Rodriguez, Juan Carlos. "Estee Lauder Faces False Ad Suit Over 'Night Repair' Products." Law360, August 22, 2013. Accessed July 11, 2017. https://www.law360.com/ articles/466828/estee-lauder-faces-false-ad-suit-over-night-repair-products.

Rogers, Abby. "13 Brands That Use Sex to Sell Their Products." *Business Insider*, February 3, 2012. Accessed July 20, 2018. https://www.businessinsider.com/13-brands-that-use-sex -to-sell-their-products-2012-2#tom-fords-clothing-advertisements-are-considered-hyper sexual-9.

Romanowski, Perry. "Product Categories in the Cosmetic Industry." Chemists Corner, August 14, 2015. Accessed July 31, 2019. https://chemistscorner.com/product-categories-in-the -cosmetic-industry/.

Romeyn, Kathyrn, "Lily James, New Face of My Burberry Black, Talks Scent Memories and Power Dressing." *Hollywood Reporter*, August 22, 2016. Accessed September 2, 2019. https://www.hollywoodreporter.com/news/lily-james-my-burberry-black-921426.

Rooney, Emma. "The Effects of Sexual Objectification on Women's Mental Health." NYU-Steinhardt *Applied Psychology OPUS* (Spring 2016). Accessed July 1, 2017. https:// steinhardt.nyu.edu/appsych/opus/issues/2016/spring/rooney.

Rosen, Elisabeth. "Top 10 Beauty Brands in Digital." Gartner L2, December 17, 2015. Accessed July 17, 2017. https://www.l2inc.com/daily-insights/top-10-beauty-brands-in -digital.

Rosenbaum, Sophia. "Models Keep Getting Skinnier and Skinnier." *New York Post*, June 9, 2016. Accessed July 29, 2017. https://nypost.com/2016/06/09/models-keep-getting -skinnier-and-skinnier/.

"Rosie the Riveter." History.com. Accessed July 4, 2017. https://www.history.com/topics/ world-war-ii/rosie-the-riveter.

Ross, Carolyn Coker. "Why Do Women Hate Their Bodies?" Psych Central. Accessed July 9, 2017. https://psychcentral.com/blog/why-do-women-hate-their-bodies/.

Rossman, Sean. "Americans Are Spending More Than Ever on Plastic Surgery." *USA Today*, April 12, 2017. Accessed July 28, 2017. https://www.usatoday.com/story/news/nation -now/2017/04/12/americans-spending-more-than-ever-plastic-surgery/100365258/.

Roth, Mark. "Plastic Surgery Puts Focus on Women's Psyches." *Pittsburgh Post-Gazette*, December 6, 2010. Accessed July 10, 2017. http://www.post-gazette.com/science/2010/12/06/ Plastic-surgery-puts-focus-on-women-s-psyches/stories/201012060200.

Rubin, Courtney. "Makeup for the Selfie Generation." *New York Times*, September 22, 2015. Accessed July 18, 2017. https://www.nytimes.com/2015/09/24/fashion/selfie-new-test -makeup.html.

Rubino, Jessica. "Natural Marketplace Sees Personal Care Industry Shift to Organic." New Hope Network, May 11, 2015. Accessed July 18, 2017. https://www.newhope.com/nfm -market-overview/natural-marketplace-sees-personal-care-industry-shift-organic.

Rudd, Vivienne. "The Mature Beauty Market—Time for Brands to Grow Up?" Mintel (blog), September 24, 2013. Accessed July 7, 2017. http://www.mintel.com/blog/beauty-market -news/mature-beauty-market.

Rufus, Anneli. "The Cosmetics Racket: Why the Beauty Industry Can Get Away with Charging a Fortune for Makeup." *AlterNet*, September 11, 2010. Accessed July 10, 2017. https://www .democraticunderground.com/discuss/duboard.php?az=view_all&address=103x559653.

Runfola, Cristin D., Ann Von Holle, Christine M. Peat, Danielle A. Gagne, Kimberly A. Brownley, Sara M. Hofmeier, and Cynthia M. Bulik. "Characteristics of Women with Body Size Satisfaction at Midlife: Results of the Gender and Body Image (GABI) Study." *Journal of Women and Aging* 25, no. 4 (2013): 287–304. Accessed July 9, 2017. doi: 10.1080/08952841.2013.816215.

"Safety Fears over Nanocosmetics." *BBC News*, November 5, 2008. Accessed July 18, 2017. http://news.bbc.co.uk/2/hi/health/7706818.stm.

Samaha, Joel. *Criminal Procedure*, 8th ed. Belmont, CA: Wadsworth, 2012.

Samocha, Leeor. "'We Were Both Naked and Had Just Met!' Evan Rachel Wood Spills on Steamy Gucci Guilty Shoot with Chris Evans." *Daily Mail*, November 11, 2016. Accessed August 16, 2019. https://www.dailymail.co.uk/tvshowbiz/article-3928358/We-naked-just -met-Evan-Rachel-Wood-spills-steamy-Gucci-Guilty-shoot-Chris-Evans.html.

Sartwell, Crispin. "Beauty." In *Stanford Encyclopedia of Philosophy*, edited by Edward N. Zalta. Last modified October 5, 2016. Accessed July 6, 2017. https://plato.stanford.edu/archives/ win2017/entries/beauty/.

Sayeed, Layla. "Stand Up to Unilever's Hypocrisy over Skin-Lightening." *Guardian*, July 16, 2010. Accessed July 14, 2017. https://www.theguardian.com/commentisfree/2010/jul/16/ unilever-hypocritical-promoting-skin-lightening.

Schaefer, Katie. "PCPC Announces Support for Cosmetic Safety Amendments Act of 2012." *Cosmetics & Toiletries*, April 19, 2012. Accessed July 17, 2017. https://www.cosmeticsand toiletries.com/regulatory/region/northamerica/148134875.html.

Schaefer, Wolfgang. "3 Ways Prestige Beauty Brands Can Preserve Their Allure in the Digital Age." *Adweek*, May 3, 2015. Accessed July 7, 2017. https://www.adweek.com/brand -marketing/3-ways-prestige-beauty-brands-can-preserve-their-allure-digital-age-164458/.

Scheel, Judy. "EDs Across Cultures—Increasing in Prevalence & Awareness?" *Psychology Today*, February 5, 2013. Accessed July 27, 2017. https://www.psychologytoday .com/us/blog/when-food-is-family/201302/eds-across-cultures-increasing-in-prevalence -awareness.

Schencker, Lisa. "Real Plastic Surgeons Not Behind Most Instagram Posts Offering Nips, Tucks and Nose Jobs: Study." *Chicago Tribune*, August 30, 2017. Accessed November 18, 2017. http://www.chicagotribune.com/business/ct-instagram-plastic-surgery-study -0830-biz-20170829-story.html.

Schiro, Anne-Marie. "For Skins of All Shades, New Cosmetics." *New York Times*, May 15, 1987. Accessed July 5, 2017. https://www.nytimes.com/1987/05/15/style/for-skins-of-all -shades-new-cosmetics.html.

Schlessinger, Joel, Daniel Schlessinger, and Bernard Schlessinger. "Prospective Demographic Study of Cosmetic Surgery Patients." *Journal of Clinical and Aesthetic Dermatology* 3, no. 11 (2010): 30–35. Accessed July 28, 2017. http://jcadonline.com/prospective-demographic -study-of-cosmetic-surgery-patients/.

Schreiber, Katherine. "What Does Body Positivity Actually Mean?" *Psychology Today*, August 11, 2016. Accessed July 4, 2017. https://www.psychologytoday.com/us/blog/the-truth -about-exercise-addiction/201608/what-does-body-positivity-actually-mean.

Schulman, Bruce J. *The Seventies: The Great Shift in American Culture, Society, and Politics*. New York: Free Press, 2001.

Schultz, E. J. "Ad Age Picks the Top 10 Female Ad Icons of All Time." *Advertising Age*, September 24, 2012. Accessed July 3, 2017. http://adage.com/article/special-report-100-most -influential-women-in-advertising/ad-age-picks-top-10-female-ad-icons-time/237369/.

———. "A Century of Women in Advertising." *Advertising Age*, September 23, 2012. Accessed July 3, 2017. http://adage.com/article/special-report-100-most-influential-women-in-advertising/a-century-women-advertising/237137/.

Scott, A. O. "In 'The Devil Wears Prada,' Meryl Streep Plays the Terror of the Fashion World." Review of *The Devil Wears Prada*, directed by David Frankel. *New York Times*, June 30, 2006. Accessed July 27, 2017. https://www.nytimes.com/2006/06/30/movies/30devi.html?mcubz=1.

Seaman, Andrew M. "Chemicals in Plastics and Cosmetics Tied to Early Births." *Chicago Tribune*, November 18, 2013. Accessed July 14, 2017. http://articles.chicagotribune.com/2013-11-18/lifestyle/sns-rt-us-chemicals-cosmetics-20131118_1_phthalates-dehp-shanna-swan.

Segran, Elizabeth. "Female Shoppers No Longer Trust Ads or Celebrity Endorsements." *Fast Company*, September 28, 2015. Accessed July 28, 2019. https://www.fastcompany.com/3051491/female-shoppers-no-longer-trust-ads-or-celebrity-endorsements.

"Self-objectification." In *Wikipedia*. Last modified March 29, 2018. Accessed June 15, 2018. https://en.wikipedia.org/wiki/Self-objectification.

Sen, Deepa. "Female-Targeted Brands Lead on Aspirational Authenticity." *Advertising Age*, November 22, 2016. Accessed July 28, 2017. http://adage.com/article/agency-viewpoint/female-targeted-brands-lead-aspirational-authenticity/306815/.

Seth, Abhishek. "How Baywatch Unknowingly Changed the World: The Untapped Power of TV Shows." *Huffington Post*, November 25, 2013. Accessed July 6, 2017. https://www.huffingtonpost.com/abhishek-seth/how-baywatch-unknowingly-changed-the-world_b_3891368.html.

"Sex DOES Sell . . . and Here's Why: Attractive Men and Women in Adverts Affect Our Capacity for Rational Thought." *Daily Mail*, September 22, 2011. Accessed July 1, 2017. http://www.dailymail.co.uk/sciencetech/article-2040218/Sex-DOES-sell-Attractive-men-women-ads-affect-capacity-rational-thought.html.

"Sex in Advertising." *Advertising Age*, September 15, 2003. Accessed July 2, 2017. http://adage.com/article/adage-encyclopedia/sex-advertising/98878/adage.com/article/adage-encyclopedia/sex-advertising/98878/.

"Sexism." In *Wikipedia*. Last modified July 12, 2019. Accessed August 9, 2019. https://en.wikipedia.org/wiki/Sexism.

"The Sexist Adverts of Yesteryear That Said Women Should Lose Weight by Doing the Housework and Wives Were There to Cook (and Those Are the Less Offensive Ones!)." *Daily Mail*, March 30, 2013. Accessed July 10, 2017. http://www.dailymail.co.uk/news/article-2301242/Sexist-magazine-TV-adverts-yesterday-Kelloggs-Kenwood-Motorola-more.html#ixzz2lPrMN5RN.

Shahbandeh, M. "Cosmetics Industry in the U.S.—Statistics & Facts." Statista, August 21, 2018. Accessed August 29, 2019. https://www.statista.com/topics/1008/cosmetics-industry/.

———. "Revenue of the Leading 20 Beauty Manufacturers Worldwide in 2018 (in Billion U.S. Dollars)." Statista. Last modified March 11, 2019. Accessed August 29, 2019. https://www.statista.com/statistics/243871/revenue-of-the-leading-10-beauty-manufacturers-worldwide/.

———. "Size of the Global Men's Grooming Products Market from 2018 to 2024 (in Billion U.S. Dollars)." Statista, October 29, 2019. Accessed November 10, 2019. https://www.statista.com/statistics/287643/global-male-grooming-market-size/.

Shandrow, Kim Lachance. "10 Questions to Ask When Designing Your Company's Logo." *Entrepreneur*, February 25, 2015. Accessed August 1, 2017. https://www.entrepreneur.com/article/243181.

Shapouri, Beth. "The Way We Buy Beauty Now." *Racked*, May 26, 2016. Accessed July 17, 2017. https://www.racked.com/2016/5/26/11674106/buying-beauty-sephora-department.

Shayon, Sheila. "CoverGirl Redefines Role Models with Diversity, Inclusivity." Brandchannel, November 3, 2016. Accessed July 4, 2017. https://www.brandchannel.com/2016/11/03/covergirl-diversity-inclusivity-110316/.

Shea, Christopher. "The Lipstick Effect: In Recessions, Women Still Buy Beauty Products." *Wall Street Journal*, July 31, 2012. Accessed July 18, 2017. https://blogs.wsj.com/ideas-market/2012/07/31/the-lipstick-effect-in-recessions-women-buy-beauty-products/.

Sherman, Lauren. "In Depth: Barbie by the Numbers." *Forbes*, March 5, 2009. Accessed September 7, 2019. https://www.forbes.com/2009/03/05/barbie-design-manufacturing-business_numbers_slide.html#2659ac9e792b.

Sherrow, Victoria L. *For Appearance Sake: The Historical Encyclopedia of Good Looks, Beauty, and Grooming*. Westport, CT: Greenwood, 2001.

Shiel Jr., William C. "Medical Definition of Cosmeceutical." MedicineNet. Last modified December 21, 2018. Accessed August 25, 2019. https://www.medicinenet.com/script/main/art.asp?articlekey=25353.

Shirk, Adrian. "The Death of the Cool Feminist Smoker." *Atlantic*, January 30, 2014. Accessed September 1, 2019. https://www.theatlantic.com/health/archive/2014/01/the-death-of-the-cool-feminist-smoker/283273/.

Shorty Awards. From the 7th Annual Shorty Awards. "Clinique #StartBetter, Entered in Fashion, Beauty and Luxury." Accessed July 15, 2017. https://shortyawards.com/7th/clinique-startbetter.

Sieghart, Mary Ann. "Cosmetic Surgery Is Bad. That Women Feel the Need for It Is Worse." *Independent*, January 2, 2013. Accessed July 20, 2017. https://www.independent.co.uk/voices/comment/cosmetic-surgery-is-bad-that-women-feel-the-need-for-it-is-worse-8435780.html.

Sifferlin, Alexandra. "Botox: The Drug That's Treating Everything." *Time*, January 5, 2017. Accessed July 28, 2017. http://time.com/magazine/us/4623396/january-16th-2017-vol-189-no-3-u-s/.

———. "That Makeup Ad Is Probably Lying to You." *Time*, July 27, 2015. Accessed July 16, 2017. http://time.com/3973031/cosmetic-ads/.

———. "Women Are Still Doing Most of the Housework." *Time*, June 18, 2014. Accessed July 4, 2017. http://time.com/2895235/men-housework-women/.

Silva, Belisa. "Indie Brands Lead Beauty Industry Growth." *Beauty Packaging*, November 2, 2016. Accessed July 12, 2017. http://www.beautypackaging.com/issues/2016-10-01/view_features/indie-brands-lead-beauty-industry-growth.

Simmons, Rachel. "How Social Media Is a Toxic Mirror." *Time*, August 19, 2016. Accessed July 27, 2017. http://time.com/4459153/social-media-body-image/.

Singer, Natasha. "F.D.A. Orders Warning Label for Botox." *New York Times*, April 30, 2009. Accessed July 28, 2017. https://www.nytimes.com/2009/05/01/business/01botox.html?mcubz=0.

———. "In Hard Times, a Cosmetic Hard Sell." *New York Times*, November 5, 2008. Accessed July 31, 2017. https://www.nytimes.com/2008/11/06/fashion/06skin.html.

———. "Skin Deep; Nutri-Cosmetics: Eat, Drink and Be Skeptical." *New York Times*, December 14, 2006. Accessed July 13, 2017. https://www.nytimes.com/2006/12/14/style/health/skin-deep-nutricosmetics-eat-drink-and-be-skeptical.html.

Sivulka, Juliann. *Soap, Sex, and Cigarettes: A Cultural History of American Advertising*, 2nd ed. Boston: Wadsworth, 2012.

"Skinny Models Banned from Catwalk." CNN, September 13, 2006. Accessed July 27, 2017. http://www.cnn.com/2006/WORLD/europe/09/13/spain.models/.

Smink, Frédérique R. E., Daphne van Hoeken, and Hans W. Hoek. "Epidemiology of Eating Disorders: Incidence, Prevalence and Mortality Rates." *Current Psychiatry Reports* 14, no. 4 (2012): 406–14. Accessed July 27, 2017. doi: 10.1007/s11920-012-0282-y.

Smith, Lauren. "THIS Is the Average Age Girls Now Start Wearing Make-up." *Glamour*, March 26, 2014. Accessed July 15, 2017. https://www.glamourmagazine.co.uk/article/average-age-women-girls-start-wearing-make-up-drops.

Smith, Scott S. "Estee Lauder Built a Beauty Empire on High Quality." *Investor's Business Daily*, January 7, 2014. Accessed July 22, 2017. https://www.investors.com/news/management/leaders-and-success/estee-lauder-pioneered-cosmetics-marketing/.

Smolak, Linda, and Michael P. Levine, eds. *The Wiley Handbook of Eating Disorders: Assessment, Prevention, Treatment, Policy, and Future Directions*. Hoboken, NJ: Wiley-Blackwell, 2015.

"Social Listening." TrackMaven. Accessed August 10, 2019. https://trackmaven.com/marketing-dictionary/social-listening/.

"Social Responsibility: Body Image," Advertising Standards Authority (ASA), June 14, 2019. Accessed August 10, 2019, https://www.asa.org.uk/advice-online/social-responsibility-body-image.html.

Socolovsky, Jerome. "Spain Bans Overly Skinny Models from Fashion Shows." National Public Radio, September 19, 2006. Accessed July 27, 2017. https://www.npr.org/templates/story/story.php?storyId=6103615?storyId=6103615.

Soley, Lawrence C., and Leonard N. Reid. "Taking It Off: Are Models in Magazine Ads Wearing Less?" *Journalism and Mass Communication Quarterly* 65, no. 4 (1988): 960–66. Accessed July 11, 2017. doi: 10.1177/107769908806500419.

Solomon, Michael R. *Consumer Behavior: Buying, Having, and Being*, 8th ed. Hoboken, NJ: Pearson, 2009.

———. *Consumer Behavior: Buying, Having, and Being*, 12th ed. Hoboken, NJ: Pearson, 2016.

Somerville, Heather. "Women's Consumer Advocates Take on Cosmetics Industry." *Mercury News*, August 12, 2016. Accessed July 15, 2017. https://www.mercurynews.com/2013/10/08/womens-consumer-advocates-take-on-cosmetics-industry/.

Spade, Joan Z., and Catherine G. Valentine, eds. *The Kaleidoscope of Gender: Prisms, Patterns, and Possibilities*, 3rd ed. Thousand Oaks, CA: Sage, 2010.

Spector, Nicole. "Going 'Rouge': How Beauty Brands Are Winning at E-Commerce." *NBC News*, May 15, 2017. Accessed August 3, 2017. https://www.nbcnews.com/business/consumer/going-rouge-how-beauty-brands-are-winning-e-commerce-n759431.

"Spending on Luxury Fashion Is Down, Yet Cosmetics Sales Rise." *Fashion Law*, June 3, 2016. Accessed July 18, 2017. http://www.thefashionlaw.com/home/spending-on-luxury-fashion-is-down-yet-cosmetics-sales-rise.

Spettigue, Wendy, and Katherine A. Henderson. "Eating Disorders and the Role of the Media." *Canadian Child and Adolescent Psychiatry Review* 13, no.1 (2004): 16–19. Accessed July 27, 2017. https://psycnet.apa.org/record/2004-18850-006.

Spilson, Sandra V., Kevin C. Chung, Mary Lou V. H. Greenfield, and Madonna Walters. "Are Plastic Surgery Advertisements Conforming to the Ethical Codes of the American Society of Plastic Surgeons?" *Plastic and Reconstructive Surgery* 109, no. 3 (2002): 1181–86. Accessed July 29, 2017. doi: 10.1097/00006534-200203000-00063.

Spivack, Emily. "The History of the Flapper, Part 2: Makeup Makes a Bold Entrance." *Smithsonian Magazine*, February 7, 2013. Accessed July 6, 2017. https://www.smithsonian mag.com/arts-culture/the-history-of-the-flapper-part-2-makeup-makes-a-bold-entrance -13098323/#JjLoF46SrZdkWxD1.99.

———. "The History of the Flapper, Part 3: The Rectangular Silhouette." *Smithsonian Magazine*, February 19, 2003. Accessed July 6, 2017. https://www.smithsonianmag.com/arts -culture/the-history-of-the-flapper-part-3-the-rectangular-silhouette-20328818/.

Srinivas, Val, and Urval Goradia. "The Future of Wealth in the United States: Mapping Trends in Generational Wealth." Deloitte Insights, November 9, 2015. Accessed July 17, 2017. https://www2.deloitte.com/insights/us/en/industry/investment-management/ us-generational-wealth-trends.html.

Stampler, Laura. "How Men and Women Differ When Drawing Up the 'Perfect Body.'" *Time*, April 17, 2014. Accessed July 8, 2017. http://time.com/65901/how-men-and-women -differ-when-drawing-up-the-perfect-body/.

———. "These Modern Ads Are Even More Sexist Than Their 'Mad Men' Era Counterparts." *Business Insider*, April 10, 2012. Accessed July 20, 2017. https://www.business insider.com/these-modern-ads-are-even-more-sexist-than-their-mad-men-era-counterparts -2012-4?op=1#ixzz2lHSU5oec.

Stankiewicz, Julie M., and Francine Rosselli. "Women as Sex Objects and Victims in Print Advertisements." *Sex Roles* 58, no. 7–8 (2008): 579–89. Accessed July 2, 2017. doi: 10.1007/ s11199-007-9359-1.

State of California. Department of Justice. Office of the Attorney General. "Attorney General Kamala D. Harris Announces Settlement Requiring Honest Advertising over Brazilian Blowout Products." OAG press release, January 30, 2012. Accessed July 17, 2017. https:// oag.ca.gov/news/press-releases/attorney-general-kamala-d-harris-announces-settlement -requiring-honest.

Stein, Joel. "Nip. Tuck. Or Else." *Time*, June 17, 2015. Accessed July 29, 2017. http://time .com/3926042/nip-tuck-or-else/.

Stein, Lindsay. "Cannes Bans Gender Bias with Help from #WomenNotObjects." *Ad Age*, February 6, 2017. Accessed July 1, 2017. http://adage.com/article/agency-news/cannes -bannes-gender-bias-womennotobjects/307847/.

"The Stepford Syndrome." WebMD. Accessed July 3, 2017. https://www.webmd.com/ beauty/features/stepford-syndrome#1.

Stevens, Tiffany. "Sex in Advertising Has Increased, UGA Study Finds." *Athens Patch*, June 7, 2012. Accessed July 1, 2017. https://patch.com/georgia/athens/uga-study-finds-sex-in -advertisement-has-increased.

Stewart, Dodai. "Max Factor: The Man Behind the Makeup." *Jezebel*, August 25, 2008. Accessed August 16, 2019. https://jezebel.com/max-factor-the-man-behind-the-makeup-5041399.

———. "Photoshop of Horrors Hall of Shame, 2000–2009." *Jezebel*, December 16, 2009. Accessed July 17, 2017. https://jezebel.com/5426296/photoshop-of-horrors-hall-of -shame-2000-2009/.

———. "Why Won't Sexist Advertising Go Away?" *Jezebel*, December 9, 2008. Accessed July 10, 2017. https://jezebel.com/5105524/why-wont-sexist-advertising-go-away.

Stice, Eric, Diane L. Spangler, and W. Stewart Agras. "Exposure to Media-Portrayed Thin-Ideal Images Adversely Affects Vulnerable Girls: A Longitudinal Experiment." *Journal of Social and Clinical Psychology* 20, no. 3 (2001): 270–88. Accessed July 28, 2017. doi: 10.1521/jscp.20.3.270.22309.

Stilinovic, Milly. "Premiumization: The Most Affluent Retail Trend of 2016." *Forbes*, June 16, 2016. Accessed July 18, 2017. https://www.forbes.com/sites/millystilinovic/2016/06/16/premiumisation-the-most-affluent-retail-trend-of-2016/#b42fd9c5d07a.

Stone, Zara. "The K-Pop Plastic Surgery Obsession." *Atlantic*, May 24, 2013. Accessed July 9, 2017. https://www.theatlantic.com/health/archive/2013/05/the-k-pop-plastic-surgery-obsession/276215/.

Strauss, William, and Neil Howe. *Generations: The History of America's Future, 1584 to 2069.* New York: William Morrow, 1991.

Strugatz, Rachel. "Are the Kardashians, Millennials Seeking to Look Young Causing Cosmetic Procedures Boom?" *Los Angeles Times*, March 31, 2017. Accessed July 31, 2017. http://www.latimes.com/fashion/la-ig-wwd-cosmetic-procedures-kardashian-driven-millennial-led-20170331-story.html.

———. "Bloggers and Digital Influencers Are Reshaping the Fashion and Beauty Landscape." *Los Angeles Times*, April 10, 2016. Accessed July 16, 2017. http://www.latimes.com/fashion/la-ig-bloggers-20160809-snap-story.html.

Suess, Jeff. "Our History: Odorono Ads Made Us Realize We Needed Deodorant." *USA Today*, February 14, 2017. Accessed July 6, 2017. https://www.usatoday.com/story/news/2017/02/14/odorono-ads-made-us-realize-we-needed-deodorant/97922010/.

Sullivan, Deborah A. "Advertising Cosmetic Surgery." *Virtual Mentor* 12, no. 5 (2010): 407–11. Accessed July 28, 2017. doi: 10.1001/virtualmentor.2010.12.5.mhst1-1005.

Sun, Feifei. "Estée Lauder (1908–2004)." *Time*, November 18, 2010. Accessed July 11, 2017. http://content.time.com/time/specials/packages/article/0,28804,2029774_2029776_2031810,00.html.

Sundar, Sindhu. "L'Oréal Can't Shake False Ad Claims over Wrinkle Creams." Law360, December 12, 2013. Accessed July 14, 2017. https://www.law360.com/articles/495217/l-oreal-can-t-shake-false-ad-claims-over-wrinkle-creams.

"Supermodel." In *Wikipedia*. Last modified September 6, 2018. Accessed July 19, 2018. https://en.wikipedia.org/wiki/Supermodel.

Swan, Shanna H. "Pilot Study Relates Phthalate Exposure to Less-Masculine Play by Boys." University of Rochester Medical Center, November 16, 2009. Accessed July 14, 2017. https://www.urmc.rochester.edu/news/story/2689/pilot-study-relates-phthalate-exposure-to-less-masculine-play-by-boys.aspx.

Swan, Shanna H., Fan Liu, Melissa Hines, Robin Kruse, Christina Wang, J. Bruce Redmon, Amy Sparks, and Bernard Weiss. "Prenatal Phthalate Exposure and Reduced Masculine Play in Boys." *International Journal of Andrology* 33, no 2. (2010): 259–69. Accessed July 14, 2017. doi: 10.1111/j.1365-2605.2009.01019.x.

Sweney, Mark. "Beyoncé Knowles: L'Oreal Accused of 'Whitening' Singer in Cosmetics Ad." *Guardian*, August 8, 2008. Accessed July 18, 2017. https://www.theguardian.com/media/2008/aug/08/advertising.usa.

———. "Botox Ads Banned over 'Beauty Treatment' Claims." *Guardian*, January 15, 2014. Accessed July 28, 2017. https://www.theguardian.com/media/2014/jan/15/botox-ads-banned-asa-crackdown.

———. "Standards Body Unveils Plan to Crack Down on Sexist Advertisements." *Guardian*, July 17, 2017. Accessed July 30, 2017. https://www.theguardian.com/media/2017/jul/18/new-measures-announced-to-crack-down-on-sexist-adverts.

———. "Unilever Vows to Drop Sexist Stereotypes from Its Ads." *Guardian*, June 22, 2016. Accessed July 2, 2017. https://www.theguardian.com/media/2016/jun/22/unilever-sexist-stereotypes-ads-sunsilk-dove-lynx.

"Swinging 60s—Capital of Cool." History.com. Accessed May 11, 2018. https://www.history.co.uk/history-of-london/swinging-60s-capital-of-cool.

Swinson, Jo. "False Beauty in Advertising and the Pressure to Look 'Good.'" CNN, August 10, 2011. Accessed July 8, 2017. http://www.cnn.com/2011/OPINION/08/08/swinson.airbrushing.ads/.

Szymanski, Dawn M., Lauren B. Moffitt, and Erika R. Carr. "Sexual Objectification of Women: Advances to Theory and Research." *Counseling Psychologist* 39, no. 1 (2010): 6–38. Accessed July 1, 2017. doi: 10.1177/0011000010378402.

Taber, Kimberly Conniff. "With Model's Death, Eating Disorders Are Again in Spotlight—Americas—International Herald Tribune." *New York Times,* November 20, 2006. Accessed July 29, 2019. https://www.nytimes.com/2006/11/20/world/americas/20iht-models.3604439.html.

TABS Analytics. "Millennial Women Key to Growth in Cosmetics Industry: TABS Analytics" (blog), January 20, 2016. Assessed November 4, 2019. https://www.tabsanalytics.com/blog/millennial-women-key-to-growth-in-cosmetics-industry.

———. "2017 TABS Cosmetics Study." November 27, 2017. Accessed August 4, 2018. https://cdn2.hubspot.net/hubfs/544043/2017_Webinars/2017%20Cosmetics/White%20Paper/11-21-17%20Cosmetics%20Survey%20FINAL.pdf?t=1511794533245.

TABS Group, Inc. "TABS Group 2015 U.S. Cosmetics Study Finds Millennial Women Buyers Reign in $13 Billion Dollar Cosmetics Market." TABS Group, Inc. press release, December 9, 2015. Accessed July 12, 2017. http://www.prweb.com/releases/2015/12/prweb13121205.htm.

Tadisina, Kashyap K., Karan Chopra, and Devinder P. Singh. "Body Dysmorphic Disorder in Plastic Surgery." *Eplasty* 13 (2013): ic48. Accessed July 28, 2017. https://www.ncbi.nlm.nih.gov/pmc/articles/PMC3693597/.

Tagliacozzi, Gaspare. *De Curtorum Chirurgia per Insitionem, Libri Duo.* Venezia: apud Gasparem Bindonum iuniorem, 1597.

Talbot, Margaret. "A Stepford for Our Times." *Atlantic*, December 2003. Accessed July 4, 2017. https://www.theatlantic.com/magazine/archive/2003/12/a-stepford-for-our-times/302852/.

Tatar, Maria. "Snow White: Beauty Is Power." *New Yorker*, June 8, 2012. Accessed January 12, 2018. https://www.newyorker.com/books/page-turner/snow-white-beauty-is-power.

Taylor, Catharine P. "Botox Wants to Show Us Some Emotion." *Adweek*, February 2, 2007. Accessed July 28, 2017. https://www.adweek.com/creativity/botox-wants-show-us-some-emotion-17783/.

Taylor, Elise. "Farrah Fawcett Almost Didn't Get to Wear Her Iconic Red Swimsuit." *Vanity Fair*, August 27, 2015. Accessed August 30, 2019. https://www.vanityfair.com/style/2015/08/farrah-fawcett-red-swimsuit-bruce-mcbroom-history-of-fashion.

Taylor, Paul, and George Gao. "Generation X: America's Neglected 'Middle Child.'" Pew Research Center, June 5, 2014. Accessed July 18, 2017. http://www.pewresearch.org/fact-tank/2014/06/05/generation-x-americas-neglected-middle-child/.

Taylor, Peter Lane. "'Brotox': It's Time for Men to Come Out of the Closet." *Forbes*, May 31, 2016. Accessed July 31, 2017. https://www.forbes.com/sites/petertaylor/2016/05/31/three-reasons-why-botox-will-change-every-mans-job-and-online-dating-prospects/#f965e352eb09.

Tehseem, Tazanfal, and Arooj Hameed. "Celebrities Endorsement in Conflating Beauty Adverts: A Feministic Perspective." *European Journal of English Language, Linguistics and Literature* 2, no. 2 (2015): 18–38. Accessed July 25, 2017. https://www.idpublications.org/wp-content/uploads/2015/06/CELEBRITIES-ENDORSEMENT-IN-CONFLATING-BEAUTY-ADVERTS-A-FEMINISTIC-PERSPECTIVE.pdf.

Terlep, Sharon. "Aging Beauty Brands Want a Facelift." *Wall Street Journal*, February 5, 2018. Accessed April 24, 2018. https://www.wsj.com/articles/aging-beauty-brands-want-a-facelift-1517826601.

———. "Millennials Change the Complexion of the Beauty Business." *Wall Street Journal*, May 3, 2016. Accessed July 11, 2017. https://www.wsj.com/articles/millennials-change-the-complexion-of-the-beauty-business-1462317335.

"The Thin Ban." *USA Today*, September 14, 2006. Accessed July 26, 2017. http://usatoday30.usatoday.com/news/opinion/editorials/2006-09-14-thin_x.htm.

"The Thin Ideal." In *Wikipedia*. Last modified June 22, 2019. Accessed September 5, 2019. https://en.wikipedia.org/wiki/The_Thin_Ideal.

"Thinness in Media Feeds Body Size Obsession, Researchers Say." *BBC News*, November 8, 2012. Accessed July 27, 2017. https://www.bbc.com/news/uk-england-tyne-20251825.

Thomas, Ellen. "Pantene Signs Priyanka Chopra for 'Strong Is Beautiful' Campaign." *Los Angeles Times*, December 22, 2016. Accessed July 24, 2017. http://www.latimes.com/fashion/la-ig-wwd-pantene-priyanka-chopra-20161220-story.html.

Thomas, Katie. "Johnson & Johnson to Remove Formaldehyde from Products." *New York Times*, August 15, 2012. Accessed July 14, 2017. https://www.nytimes.com/2012/08/16/business/johnson-johnson-to-remove-formaldehyde-from-products.html.

———. "The 'No More Tears' Shampoo, Now with No Formaldehyde." *New York Times*, January 18, 2014. Accessed July 7, 2017. https://www.nytimes.com/2014/01/18/business/johnson-johnson-takes-first-step-in-removal-of-questionable-chemicals-from-products.html?_r=0.

Thompson, Derek. "Are TV Ads Getting More Sexist?" *Atlantic*, October 31, 2011. Accessed July 10, 2017. https://www.theatlantic.com/business/archive/2011/10/are-tv-ads-getting-more-sexist/247545/.

Thompson, Lana. *Plastic Surgery*. Westport, CT: Greenwood, 2011.

Thompson, William E., Joseph V. Hickey, and Mica L. Thompson. *Society in Focus: An Introduction to Sociology*, 8th ed. Lanham, MD: Rowman & Littlefield, 2016.

Thorbecke, Catherine. "UK Watchdog Cracking Down on Ads with 'Harmful' Gender Stereotypes." *ABC News*, July 19, 2017. Accessed July 26, 2017. https://abcnews.go.com/Business/uk-watchdog-cracking-ads-harmful-gender-stereotypes/story?id=48730884.

Tice, Carol. "How Social Media Is Fueling the Next $1B Beauty Brand." *Forbes*, January 22, 2014. Accessed July 8, 2017. https://www.forbes.com/sites/caroltice/2014/01/22/girlfriend-power/#5adaef673683.

"Tired Brands: Yardley Cosmetics." Brand Failures—and Lessons Learned! (blog), April 18, 2007. Accessed May 11, 2018. http://brandfailures.blogspot.com/2007/04/tired-brands-yardley-cosmetics.html.

Trager, Robert, Susan Dente Ross, and Amy Reynolds. *The Law of Journalism and Mass Communication*, 6th ed. Washington, DC: CQ Press, 2017.

Trampe, Debra, Diederik A. Stapel, and Frans W. Siero. "The Self-Activation Effect of Advertisements: Ads Can Affect Whether and How Consumers Think about the Self." *Journal of Consumer Research* 37, no. 6 (2011): 1030–45. Accessed July 10, 2017. doi: 10.1086/657430.

Tran, Khanh T.L. "Turning Nominations into Celebrity Endorsements." *Women's Wear Daily*, February 24, 2016. Accessed July 26, 2017. https://wwd.com/eye/people/oscar-nomination-celebrity-endorsement-kate-winslet-10366351/.

Trefis Team. "Reasons Behind Estee Lauder's Sudden Acquisition Spree." *Forbes*, January 5, 2015. Accessed July 23, 2017. https://www.forbes.com/sites/greatspeculations/2015/01/05/reasons-behind-estee-lauders-sudden-acquisition-spree/#3a7dea515757.

———. "The Secret Sauce for Success in the Aggressive Beauty Business." *Forbes*, April 13, 2015. Accessed July 22, 2017. https://www.forbes.com/sites/greatspeculations/2015/04/13/the-secret-sauce-for-success-in-the-aggressive-beauty-business/#5d9bab20543c.

———. "Why Is Unilever Rushing Towards Premium Personal Care Brands?" *Forbes*, August 18, 2015. Accessed July 22, 2017. https://www.forbes.com/sites/greatspeculations/2015/08/18/why-is-unilever-rushing-towards-premium-personal-care-brands/#1bf97c96688d.

Tsouderos, Trine. "Do Anti-aging Skin Creams Work?" *Chicago Tribune*, January 31, 2011. Accessed July 31, 2017. http://www.chicagotribune.com/lifestyles/health/ct-met-skin-creams-20110131-story.html.

Turner, Leigh. "Cosmetic Surgery: The New Face of Reality TV." *BMJ: British Medical Journal* 328, no. 7449 (2004): 1208. Accessed June 6, 2018. https://www.ncbi.nlm.nih.gov/pmc/articles/PMC411119/.

Tuten, Tracey L., and Michael R. Solomon. *Social Media Marketing*. Hoboken, NJ: Pearson, 2013.

Tuttle, Brad. "Consumer Phrase of the Day: 'Lipstick Effect.'" *Time*, April 19, 2011. Accessed July 10, 2017. http://business.time.com/2011/04/19/consumer-phrase-of-the-day-lipstick-effect/.

"'TV Brings Eating Disorders to Fiji.'" *BBC News*, May 20, 1999. Accessed July 26, 2017. http://news.bbc.co.uk/2/hi/health/347637.stm.

"TV Urges Fairness Doctrine Not Be Applied to Ads." *New York Times*, March 29, 1972. Accessed July 15, 2018. https://www.nytimes.com/1972/03/29/archives/tv-urges-fairness-doctrine-not-be-applied-to-ads.html.

"The 'Ugly Truth' about Body Dysmorphic Disorder." *BBC News*, June 21, 2015. Accessed August 1, 2017. https://www.bbc.com/news/health-33190297.

Um, Nam-Hyun. "The Role of Culture in Creative Execution in Celebrity Endorsement: The Cross-Cultural Study." *Journal of Global Marketing* 26, no. 3 (2013): 155–72. Accessed July 24, 2017. doi: 10.1080/08911762.2013.804613.

UN Women. "UN Women Ad Series Reveals Widespread Sexism," October 21, 2013. Accessed July 19, 2017. http://www.unwomen.org/en/news/stories/2013/10/women-should-ads.

Uniform Law Commission. "Trade Secrets Act Summary." Accessed July 16, 2017. https://www.uniformlaws.org/committees/community-home?communitykey=3a2538fb-e030-4e2d-a9e2-90373dc05792&tab=groupdetails.

Uniform Trade Secrets Act, with 1985 Amendments. Drafted by the National Conference of Commissioners on Uniform State Laws. Section 1(4)(i) and (ii). Accessed September 26, 2019. https://www.wipo.int/edocs/lexdocs/laws/en/us/us034en.pdf.

Unilever. "Launch of Unstereotype Alliance Set to Eradicate Outdated Stereotypes in Advertising." Unilever press release, June 20, 2017. Accessed September 1, 2019. https://www
.unilever.com/news/Press-releases/2017/launch-of-unstereotype-alliance-set-to-eradicate
-outdated-stereotypes-in-advertising.html.

Unilever USA. "Personal Care—Dove." Accessed August 16, 2019. https://www.unileverusa
.com/brands/personal-care/dove.html.

US Bureau of Economic Analysis. "State Personal Income Rises in 2017." BEA press release, March 22, 2018. Accessed July 10, 2018. https://www.bea.gov/news/blog/2018-03-22/
state-personal-income-rises-2017.

US Census Bureau. "Census Bureau Releases Comprehensive Analysis of Fast-Growing 90-and-Older Population." Census Bureau press release, November 17, 2011. Accessed July 18, 2017. https://www.census.gov/newsroom/releases/archives/aging_population/
cb11-194.html.

———. "Millennials Outnumber Baby Boomers and Are Far More Diverse, Census Bureau Reports." Census Bureau press release, June 25, 2015. Accessed July 18, 2017. https://www
.census.gov/newsroom/press-releases/2015/cb15-113.html.

US Congress. Senate. Personal Care Products Safety Act, S.1014, 114th Congress (2015–2016). Introduced in Senate April 20, 2015. Accessed August 17, 2018. https://www
.congress.gov/bill/114th-congress/senate-bill/1014.

US Consumer Product Safety Commission. "About CPSC." Accessed August 27, 2019. https://www.cpsc.gov/About-CPSC/.

US Food and Drug Administration. "Animal Testing & Cosmetics." Last modified November 25, 2017. Accessed December 16, 2017. https://www.fda.gov/cosmetics/scienceresearch/
producttesting/ucm072268.htm.

———. "'Cosmeceutical.'" Last modified February 22, 2018. Accessed March 17, 2018. https://www.fda.gov/Cosmetics/Labeling/Claims/ucm127064.htm.

———. "Cosmetics Guidance & Regulation." Last modified July 24, 2018. Accessed July 30, 2018. https://www.fda.gov/Cosmetics/GuidanceRegulation/.

———. "Cosmetics Labeling Guide." Last modified November 5, 2017. Accessed January 16, 2018. https://www.fda.gov/cosmetics/labeling/regulations/ucm126444.htm. Also accessed August 21, 2019. https://www.fda.gov/cosmetics/cosmetics-labeling-regulations/cosmetics
-labeling-guide.

———. "Cosmetics Nanotechnology." Last modified November 22, 2017. Accessed January 2, 2018. https://www.fda.gov/Cosmetics/ScienceResearch/Nanotech/default.htm.

———. "FDA Authority Over Cosmetics: How Cosmetics Are Not FDA-Approved, but Are FDA-Regulated." Last modified July 24, 2018. Accessed July 28, 2018. https://www.fda
.gov/Cosmetics/GuidanceRegulation/LawsRegulations/ucm074162.htm.

———. "'Hypoallergenic' Cosmetics." Last modified November 3, 2017. Accessed January 13, 2018. https://www.fda.gov/Cosmetics/Labeling/Claims/ucm2005203.htm.

———. "Is It a Cosmetic, a Drug, or Both? (Or Is It Soap?)." Last modified March 6, 2018. Accessed August 2, 2018. https://www.fda.gov/Cosmetics/GuidanceRegulation/Laws
Regulations/ucm074201.htm.

———. "'Organic' Cosmetics." Last modified November 5, 2017. Accessed January 10, 2018. https://www.fda.gov/Cosmetics/Labeling/Claims/ucm203078.htm#Does_FDA.

———. "Parabens in Cosmetics." Last modified February 22, 2018. Accessed July 28, 2018. https://www.fda.gov/Cosmetics/ProductsIngredients/Ingredients/ucm128042.htm.

———. "Product Testing of Cosmetics," October 5, 2016. Accessed July 16, 2017. https://www.fda.gov/Cosmetics/ScienceResearch/ProductTesting/default.htm.

———. "Prohibited & Restricted Ingredients in Cosmetics." Last modified November 3, 2017. Accessed August 22, 2019. https://www.fda.gov/cosmetics/cosmetics-laws-regulations/prohibited-restricted-ingredients-cosmetics.

———. "Summary of Cosmetics Labeling Requirements." Last modified November 5, 2017. Accessed December 11, 2017. https://www.fda.gov/Cosmetics/Labeling/Regulations/ucm126438.htm.

———. "'Trade Secret' Ingredients." Last modified November 4, 2017. Accessed July 16, 2018. https://www.fda.gov/cosmetics/cosmetics-labeling/trade-secret-ingredients.

———. "Voluntary Cosmetic Registration Program." Last modified December 4, 2017. Accessed February 22, 2018. https://www.fda.gov/cosmetics/registrationprogram/default.htm#register.

US Library of Congress. Congressional Research Service. "Protection of Trade Secrets: Overview of Current Law and Legislation," by Brian T. Yeh, April 22, 2016. Accessed September 26, 2019. https://fas.org/sgp/crs/secrecy/R43714.pdf.

US Senate. "Vetoes by President Dwight D. Eisenhower." Virtual Reference Desk. Accessed August 22, 2019. https://www.senate.gov/reference/Legislation/Vetoes/EisenhowerDD.htm.

US Senator for California Dianne Feinstein. "Senators Introduce Bill to Strengthen Personal Care Product Oversight." United States Senator for California Dianne Feinstein press release, April 20, 2015. Accessed July 17, 2017. https://www.feinstein.senate.gov/public/index.cfm/2015/4/feinstein-collins-introduce-bill-to-strengthen-oversight-of-personal-care-products.

Utroske, Deanna. "Millennial Buying Power Is Set to Transform the Beauty Business." CosmeticsDesign.com-USA, August 18, 2015. Accessed July 18, 2017. https://www.cosmeticsdesign.com/Article/2015/08/18/Millennial-buying-power-is-set-to-transform-the-beauty-business.

———. "Retail Trend: Digital Beauty Brands Opening Storefront Shops." CosmeticsDesign.com-USA. Last modified July 30, 2015. Accessed July 12, 2017. https://www.cosmeticsdesign.com/Article/2015/07/30/Retail-Trend-Digital-beauty-brands-opening-storefront-shops.

Valenti, Lauren. "The Supermodels of the 1980s." *Marie Claire*, April 7, 2014. Accessed March 15, 2020. https://www.marieclaire.com/fashion/g2168/supermodels-of-the-80s/.

Van Vonderen, Kristen E., and William Kinnally. "Media Effects on Body Image: Examining Media Exposure in the Broader Context of Internal and Other Social Factors." *American Communication Journal* 14, no. 2 (2012): 41–57. Accessed July 27, 2017. https://ac-journal.org/journal/pubs/2012/SPRING%202012/McKinnally3.pdf.

Vanallen, Amanda, Vanessa Weber, and Sarah Kunin. "Are Tweens Too Young for Makeup?" *ABC News*, January 27, 2011. Accessed July 18, 2017. https://abcnews.go.com/US/tweens-young-makeup/story?id=12777008.

"Variety Launches Vscore to Measure Actors' Value." *Variety*, August 6, 2014. Accessed July 25, 2017. https://variety.com/2014/biz/news/johnny-depp-value-jennifer-lawrence-variety-vscore-1201263164/.

"Venetian Ceruse." In *Wikipedia*. Last modified May 22, 2019. Accessed August 8, 2019. https://en.wikipedia.org/wiki/Venetian_ceruse.

Venison, Alexandra. "Gone Rouge: The History of Lipstick and the Color Red." *Vogue*, July 29, 2019. Accessed August 21, 2019. https://en.vogue.me/beauty/history-of-lipstick-and-the-color-red/.

Venkat, Ramesh, and Harold Ogden. "Advertising-Induced Social Comparison and Body-Image Satisfaction: The Moderating Role of Gender, Self-Esteem and Locus of Control." *Journal of Consumer Satisfaction, Dissatisfaction and Complaining Behavior* 15 (2002): 51–67. Accessed July 27, 2017.

Victor, Peter. "Yardley, No Longer Smelling of Roses, Goes into Receivership." *Independent*, August 27, 1998. Accessed April 25, 2018. https://www.independent.co.uk/news/yardley-no-longer-smelling-of-roses-goes-into-receivership-1174316.html.

Villafranco, John E., and Katherine E. Riley. "So You Want to Self-Regulate? The National Advertising Division as Standard Bearer." *Antitrust* 27, no. 2 (2013): 79–84. Accessed July 17, 2017.

Vince, Gaia. "Cosmetic Chemicals Found in Breast Tumours." *New Scientist*, January 12, 2004. Accessed July 15, 2017. https://www.newscientist.com/article/dn4555-cosmetic-chemicals-found-in-breast-tumours/.

Vizard, Sarah. "Clinique Aims to Move Beyond Beauty with First Major Global Digital Campaign." *Marketing Week*, July 14, 2015. Accessed July 15, 2017. https://www.marketingweek.com/2015/07/14/clinique-aims-to-move-beyond-beauty-with-first-major-global-digital-campaign/.

Vora, Shivani. "Not Your Grandmother's Skin Care?" *New York Times*, November 20, 2013. Accessed July 27, 2017. https://www.nytimes.com/2013/11/21/fashion/New-beauty-lines-including-family-secrets-gain-popularity.html?mcubz=0.

Walker, Joseph. "Botox Itself Aims Not to Age." *Wall Street Journal*, May 18, 2014. Accessed July 28, 2017. https://www.wsj.com/articles/botox-itself-aims-not-to-age-1400458129?tesla=y.

Walker, Peter. "Young, White and Super Skinny? We Don't Buy It, Women Tell Advertisers." *Guardian*, January 9, 2009. Accessed July 10, 2017. https://www.theguardian.com/lifeandstyle/2009/jan/10/realistic-advertising-women-judge-research.

Wallenstein, Andrew. "Q Scores Stats Reveal Who's More Popular: Digital Stars vs. Mainstream Celebs." *Variety*, June 21, 2016. Accessed July 26, 2017. https://variety.com/2016/digital/news/youtube-stars-traditional-celebrities-data-1201799487/.

Wallis, Lucy. "Five Photos That Sparked Body Image Debates." *BBC News*, November 13, 2012. Accessed July 9, 2017. https://www.bbc.co.uk/news/magazine-20252921.

Walsh, Kenneth T. "The 1960s: A Decade of Promise and Heartbreak." *US News & World Report*, March 9, 2010. Accessed November 10, 2019. https://www.usnews.com/news/articles/2010/03/09/the-1960s-a-decade-of-promise-and-heartbreak.

Warbanski, Misha. "The Ugly Side of the Beauty Industry." *Herizons* 21, no.1 (2007): 24. Accessed July 7, 2017. http://www.herizons.ca/node/227.

Wargo, Eric. "Beauty Is in the Mind of the Beholder." *Observer*, April 2011. Accessed July 4, 2017. https://www.psychologicalscience.org/observer/beauty-is-in-the-mind-of-the-beholder#.WWdhrIjytPY.

"Was Neanderthal Man the Original Metrosexual? New Study Suggests He Wore Make-up." *Daily Mail*, January 11, 2010. Accessed July 21, 2017. http://www.dailymail.co.uk/news/article-1242118/Neanderthal-make-discovered-Proof-human-subspecies-half-wits.html#ixzz4FM1WHVKf.

Washam, Cynthia. "Legislation: California Enacts Safe Cosmetics Act." *Environmental Health Perspectives* 114, no. 7 (2006): A402. Accessed March 15, 2020. https://doi.org/10.1289/ehp.114-a402.

Waterson, Brittany. "How Can Beauty Brands Adapt to the Digital World?" Interbrand. Accessed July 7, 2017. https://www.interbrand.com/views/how-can-beauty-brands-adapt-to-the-digital-world/.

Watts, Jonathan. "Why Brazil Loves Nip and Tuck, as Told by Country's Plastic Surgery 'Maestro.'" *Guardian*, September 24, 2014. Accessed July 28, 2017. https://www.theguardian.com/world/2014/sep/24/brazil-loves-nip-tuck-plastic-surgeon-ivo-pitanguy.

Weinbaum, Alys Eve, Lynn M. Thomas, Priti Ramamurthy, Uta G. Poiger, Madeleine Yue Dong, and Tani E. Barlow, eds. *The Modern Girl Around the World: Consumption, Modernity, and Globalization.* Durham, NC: Duke University Press, 2008.

Western Washington University. "Barefoot & Pregnant Award of the Week for Advertising Degrading to Women." Western Libraries Heritage Resources, circa 1970s. Accessed July 3, 2017. http://content.wwu.edu/cdm/ref/collection/whc_image/id/66.

Wharton School of the University of Pennsylvania. "Celebrity Advertising: What Is the ROI?" Knowledge@Wharton, November 4, 2009. Accessed July 24, 2017. http://knowledge.wharton.upenn.edu/article/celebrity-advertising-what-is-the-roi/.

Wheeler, Mark. "Buyer Beware: Advertising May Seduce Your Brain, Researchers Say." University of California–Los Angeles Department of Psychiatry and Biobehavioral Sciences press release, cited in Science News, *Science Daily*, September 21, 2011. Accessed July 1, 2017. https://www.sciencedaily.com/releases/2011/09/110920163318.htm.

White, Lawrence T. "Does Advertising Content Reflect or Shape Societal Values?" *Psychology Today*, December 26, 2015. Accessed July 3, 2017. https://www.psychologytoday.com/us/blog/culture-conscious/201512/does-advertising-content-reflect-or-shape-societal-values.

White, Tanika. "Redbook Doesn't Take Faith Hill as She Is." *Baltimore Sun*, August 1, 2007. Accessed August 6, 2018. http://articles.baltimoresun.com/2007-08-01/features/0708010198_1_faith-hill-redbook-magazine-cover.

Whitehouse, Lucy. "Studies Show Celebrity Endorsers Do Not Create Beauty Brand Loyalty." CosmeticsDesign-Europe.com, July 3, 2014. Accessed July 25, 2017. https://www.cosmeticsdesign-europe.com/Article/2014/07/04/Studies-show-celebrity-endorsers-do-not-create-beauty-brand-loyalty.

Whitelocks, Sadie. "Being Force Fed 16,000 Calories and Wearing a Lip Plate: The Most Bizarre Beauty Trends around the World Revealed." *Daily Mail*, September 23, 2016. Accessed July 6, 2017. http://www.dailymail.co.uk/travel/travel_news/article-3803885/Being-force-fed-16-000-calories-wearing-lip-plate-bizarre-beauty-trends-world-revealed.html.

"Why Peer-to-Peer Marketing Does More Than Celebrity Endorsements." *Adweek*, August 12, 2016. Accessed July 11, 2017. https://www.adweek.com/digital/why-peer-to-peer-marketing-does-more-than-celebrity-endorsements/.

Wielebinkski, Grace Intern. "'Skinny Girls Don't Have Oomph!': Vintage Weight Gain Ads." *Bust*. Accessed September 25, 2019. https://bust.com/style/8208-skinny-girls-dont-have-oomph-vintage-weight-gain-ads.html.

Wilkinson, Isabel. "The Story Behind Brooke Shields's Famous Calvin Klein Jeans." *New York Times*, December 2, 2015. Accessed August 9, 2019. https://www.nytimes.com/2015/12/02/t-magazine/fashion/brooke-shields-calvin-klein-jeans-ad-eighties.html.

Willens, Max. "Paris Hilton, SI Swimsuit Model Lay It on Thick for Thickburger." *Advertising Age*, July 25, 2014. Accessed August 1, 2017. http://adage.com/article/cmo-strategy/paris-hilton-s-tv-ad-carl-s-jr-hardee-s-thickburger/294347/.

Willett, Julie, ed. *The American Beauty Industry Encyclopedia*. Westport, CT: Greenwood, 2010.

Willett, Megan. "How Designers in 18 Different Countries Photoshopped This Model After Being Told to Make Her Beautiful." *Business Insider*, August 23, 2015. Accessed July 4, 2017. https://www.businessinsider.com/perceptions-of-beauty-around-the-world-2015-8/#here-was-the-original-picture-found-on-shutterstock-fractl-sent-the-image-to-freelance-graphic-designers-with-the-message-photoshop-her-form-the-idea-is-to-photoshop-and-retouch-this-woman-to-make-her-more-attractive-to-the-citizens-of-your-country-1.

Willett, Megan, and Skye Gould. "These 7 Companies Control Almost Every Single Beauty Product You Buy." *Business Insider*, May 18, 2017. Accessed July 31, 2017. https://www.businessinsider.com/companies-beauty-brands-connected-2017-5.

Williams, Rachel. "Deadly Beauty: The Fake Makeup That May Contain Cyanide or Arsenic." *Guardian*, May 18, 2015. Accessed July 14, 2017. https://www.theguardian.com/uk-news/shortcuts/2015/may/18/deadly-beauty-fake-makeup-contain-cyanide-arsenic-counterfeiters.

Wills, David. "The Importance of Being Audrey." Biography.com, January 19, 2017. Accessed July 7, 2017. https://www.biography.com/news/audrey-hepburn-style-david-wills.

Wilson, Allycia. "Skincare, Makeup, Fragrance Sales Trends, Market Data, Statistics, 2016, 2017, 2018 Forecast: What Beauty Brands & Products Are Best Selling, Growing." Beautystat.com, February 23, 2016. Accessed July 21, 2017. http://beautystat.com/site/makeup/skincare-makeup-fragrance-sales-trends-market-data-statistics-2016-2017-2018-forecast-what-beauty-brands-products-are-best-selling-growing/.

Wipro Consumer Care. "About Us—Our Growth." Accessed August 21, 2019. https://wiproconsumercare.com/about-us/wipro-consumer-care/.

Wisconsin Historical Society. "1930s Permanent Wave Machine," September 20, 2007. Accessed July 11, 2017. https://www.wisconsinhistory.org/Records/Article/CS2671.

Wissner, Reba A. "For Want of a Better Estimate, Let's Call It the Year 2000: The Twilight Zone and the Aural Conception of a Dystopian Future." *Music and the Moving Image* 8, no. 3 (2015): 52. doi: 10.5406/musimoviimag.8.3.0052.

Witcomb, Gemma L., Jon Arcelus, and Jue Chen. "Can Cognitive Dissonance Methods Developed in the West for Combatting the 'Thin Ideal' Help Slow the Rapidly Increasing Prevalence of Eating Disorders in Non-Western Cultures?" *Shanghai Archives of Psychiatry* 25, no. 6 (2013): 332–40. Accessed March 29, 2018. https://psycnet.apa.org/record/2015-36526-002.

Wojcicki, Susan. "Ads That Empower Women Don't Just Break Stereotypes—They're Also Effective." *Adweek*, April 24, 2016. Accessed July 3, 2017. https://www.adweek.com/brand-marketing/ads-empower-women-don-t-just-break-stereotypes-they-re-also-effective-170953/.

Wolchover, Natalie. "The Real Skinny: Expert Traces America's Thin Obsession." *Live Science*, January 26, 2012. Accessed July 27, 2017. https://www.livescience.com/18131-women-thin-dieting-history.html.

Wolf, Naomi. *The Beauty Myth: How Images of Beauty Are Used Against Women*. New York: Harper Perennial, 2002.

Wolfson, Alisa. "Why Companies Like Dove Are Ditching Photoshop in Their Ad Campaigns." *MarketWatch*, June 26, 2018. Accessed November 5, 2019. https://www.market

watch.com/story/why-companies-like-dove-are-ditching-photoshop-in-their-ad-campaigns -2018-06-26.

Wolfson, Paula. "The Truth about Anti-aging 'Cosmeceuticals.'" *WTOP News*, July 31, 2014. Accessed July 18, 2017. https://wtop.com/news/2014/07/the-truth-about-anti-aging -cosmeceuticals/.

"Women: Representations in Advertising." *Advertising Age*, September 15, 2003. Accessed July 3, 2017. http://adage.com/article/adage-encyclopedia/women-representations -advertising/98938/.

"Women 'Suffer Poor Self-Esteem Due to Airbrushing in Advertising.'" *Telegraph*, November 27, 2009. Accessed July 9, 2017. https://www.telegraph.co.uk/news/uknews/6662958/ Women-suffer-poor-self-esteem-due-to-airbrushing-in-advertising.html.

"#WomenNotObjects." By Badger & Winters, posted on YouTube on January 11, 2016. Accessed October 12, 2019. https://www.youtube.com/watch?v=5J31AT7viqo.

"Women's Body Image and BMI." Rehabs.com. Accessed July 5, 2017. https://www.rehabs .com/explore/womens-body-image-and-bmi/.

Women's Voices for the Earth (WVE). "Cosmetics Companies File for 'Trade Secret' Status." Women's Voices for the Earth press release, January 28, 2014. Accessed July 8, 2017. https:// www.womensvoices.org/2014/01/28/cosmetics-companies-file-for-trade-secret-status/.

Wong, Stephanie Hoi-Nga. "The Latest Acquisition Targets Are Indie Beauty Brands." *Bloomberg Businessweek*, March 23, 2017. Accessed August 21, 2019. https://www .bloomberg.com/news/articles/2017-03-23/the-latest-acquisition-targets-are-indie-beauty -brands.

Wood, Zoe. "Changing Faces: Cosmetics Firms Are Forced to Find a New Image as Beauty Goes Truly Global." *Guardian*, July 2, 2011. Accessed July 19, 2017. https://www.the guardian.com/lifeandstyle/2011/jul/03/beauty-industry-turns-east.

World Intellectual Property Organization. "What Is a Trade Secret?" Accessed June 6, 2018. http://www.wipo.int/sme/en/ip_business/trade_secrets/trade_secrets.htm.

"The World's Most Counterfeited Brands Revealed." MSN.com, May 12, 2019. Accessed August 8, 2019. https://www.msn.com/en-ph/money/personalfinance/the-worlds-most -counterfeited-brands-revealed/ss-AABhajU.

Wren, Christopher S. "Clinton Calls Fashion Ads' 'Heroin Chic' Deplorable." *New York Times*, May 22, 1997. Accessed July 5, 2017. https://www.nytimes.com/1997/05/22/us/ clinton-calls-fashion-ads-heroin-chic-deplorable.html.

Yardley London. "Royal Warrants." Accessed March 15, 2020. https://www.yardleylondon .co.uk/royal-warrant.

———. "Yardley London Historical Timeline." Accessed June 6, 2018. http://www.yardley london.co.uk/media/our-world/Yardley-London-Historical-Timeline.pdf.

"Yardley London Launches First Ad Campaign in 16 Years." *Drum*, April 18, 2012. Accessed June 6, 2018. https://www.thedrum.com/news/2012/04/18/yardley-london-launches-first -ad-campaign-16-years.

"Yardley—Quintessentially British." Cosmetics Business, January 13, 2011. Accessed April 25, 2018. https://www.cosmeticsbusiness.com/technical/article_page/Yardley__quintes- sentially_British/58536.

Yeomans, Michelle. "Estee Lauder in Courts Over Anti-aging Claims." CosmeticsDesign. com-USA, September 5, 2013. Accessed July 11, 2017. https://www.cosmeticsdesign.com/ Article/2013/09/05/Estee-Lauder-in-courts-over-anti-aging-claims.

Yotka, Steff. "Calvin Klein's New Campaign Proves There's No Age Limit to Being an Underwear Model." *Vogue*, April 18, 2017. Accessed July 2, 2017. https://www.vogue.com/article/calvin-klein-lauren-hutton-underwear-ads.

Young Entrepreneur Council. "Is Your Brand a Rebel, Lover or Hero?" *Inc.*, April 24, 2015. Accessed July 3, 2017. https://www.inc.com/young-entrepreneur-council/is-your-brand-a-rebel-lover-or-hero.html.

Young, Katy. "All Hail the Pro-ageing Revolutionaries: The Celebrities Challenging Anti-ageing." *Telegraph*, April 15, 2015. Accessed July 5, 2017. http://fashion.telegraph.co.uk/beauty/news-features/TMG11537319/All-hail-the-pro-ageing-revolutionaries-the-celebrities-challenging-anti-ageing.html.

———. "Marilyn Monroe Stars in New Chanel Ad Campaign." *Telegraph*, October 16, 2013. Accessed November 23, 2017. http://fashion.telegraph.co.uk/beauty/news-features/TMG10383749/Marilyn-Monroe-stars-in-new-Chanel-ad-campaign.html.

"Young Woman's Plastic Surgery Obsession." *ABC News*, August 22, 2002. Accessed July 9, 2017. https://abcnews.go.com/Health/Cosmetic/story?id=125835.

Yurieff, Kaya. "Who's Winning in Online Beauty Right Now." TheStreet.com, February 17, 2017. Accessed July 12, 2017. https://www.thestreet.com/story/14003281/1/who-s-winning-in-online-beauty-right-now.html.

Zaczkiewicz, Arthur. "Millennials' Top Beauty Brands." *Women's Wear Daily*, June 12, 2015. Accessed July 7, 2017. https://wwd.com/business-news/marketing-promotion/millennials-top-beauty-brands-10148834/.

Zillman, Claire. "How Some of the World's Biggest Brands Are Fighting Sexism in Advertising." *Fortune*, June 20, 2017. Accessed July 4, 2017. http://fortune.com/2017/06/20/advertising-gender-stereotypes/.

Zimmerman, Amanda, and John Dahlberg. "The Sexual Objectification of Women in Advertising: A Contemporary Cultural Perspective." *Journal of Advertising Research* 48, no. 1 (2008): 71–79. Accessed July 2, 2017. doi: 10.2501/S0021849908080094.

Zimmerman, Edith. "99 Ways to Be Naughty in Kazakhstan." *New York Times*, August 3, 2012. Accessed July 30, 2017. https://www.nytimes.com/2012/08/05/magazine/how-cosmo-conquered-the-world.html.

Zinn, Sarah. "How Western Influence Caused an Identity Crisis among Women in South Korea." *The Culture-ist*, October 10, 2013. Accessed July 20, 2017. https://www.thecultureist.com/2013/10/10/plastic-surgery-in-south-korea/.

Zipes, Jack. *The Enchanted Screen: The Unknown History of Fairy-Tale Films*. New York: Routledge, 2011.

———. "How the Grimm Brothers Saved the Fairy Tale." *Humanities* 36, no. 2 (2015). Accessed January 12, 2018. https://www.neh.gov/humanities/2015/marchapril/feature/how-the-grimm-brothers-saved-the-fairy-tale.

Zotos, Yorgos C., and Eirini Tsichla. "Female Stereotypes in Print Advertising: A Retrospective Analysis." *Procedia—Social and Behavioral Sciences* 148 (2014): 446–54. Accessed July 3, 2017. doi: 10.1016/j.sbspro.2014.07.064.

Resources

Ad Standards. Formerly Advertising Standards Canada, this national nonprofit self-regulatory body is committed to safeguarding "the integrity and viability of advertising in Canada through responsible industry self-regulation." Ad Standards administers the *Canadian Code of Advertising Standards* (*Code*). The *Code* sets forth the criteria of acceptable advertising in Canada and is used as a basis for evaluating complaints from consumer, trade, and special interest groups.

Advertising Association (AA). An umbrella organization, this UK-based trade association brings together agencies, brands, and media to combine their strengths and build consensus on issues and opportunities of mutual interest.

The Advertising Club of New York (the Ad Club). The Advertising Club is a nonprofit organization that includes members from the advertising, media, marketing, and ad tech industries. The Ad Club offers career development and networking opportunities, as well as providing a forum for exchanging ideas and recognizing creative excellence.

Advertising Research Foundation (the ARF). This nonprofit organization is devoted to creating, curating, and disseminating unbiased industry-level advertising research. The ARF brings together agencies, advertisers, research houses, media firms, and ad tech companies into one conversation about how to be better at what they do.

Advertising Self-Regulatory Council (ASRC). Founded in 1971, the ASRC (formerly known as the National Advertising Review Council, NARC) sets the policies and procedures for advertising self-regulatory programs, including the National Advertising Division (NAD), Children's Advertising Review Unit (CARU), National Advertising Review Board (NARB), Electronic Retailing Self-Regulation Program (ERSP), Direct Selling Self-Regulatory Council (DSSRC), and Digital Advertising Accountability Program ("Accountability Program"). In 2019, the

ASRC merged into BBB National Programs, Inc., the national self-regulatory unit of the former Council of Better Business Bureaus (CBBB), and assumed all ASRC responsibilities, including setting policies and procedures for these programs.

Advertising Standards Authority (ASA). The goal of the ASA, an independent advertising regulator, is "to make every UK ad a responsible ad." As the sister organization of the ASA, the Committee of Advertising Practice (CAP) is responsible for revising, updating, monitoring, and enforcing the advertising codes of practice in the United Kingdom.

Alliance for Women in Media (AWM). A nonprofit organization devoted to promoting the advancement of women in the media and entertainment industry, the AWM represents a diverse community that supports women across the media industry and brings together women from all corners of media to promote innovation, education, and collaboration.

American Advertising Federation (AAF). Headquartered in Washington, DC, the AAF seeks to protect and promote the commonwealth of advertising through a coordinated network of advertisers, agencies, media companies, local advertising clubs, and college chapters.

American Association of Advertising Agencies (AAAA or 4As). The New York–based 4As is a national trade association representing the marketing communications agency business in the United States. This management-oriented association offers leadership, advocacy, and training to encourage agencies to "innovate, evolve, and grow."

American Cancer Society (ACS). The ACS funds and conducts research, furnishes expert advice, supports patients, and disseminates information about cancer prevention.

Association for Women in Communications (AWC). As a professional organization for women in the communications industry, AWC promotes the advancement of women in all areas of the communications field by recognizing excellence, promoting leadership, and placing its members at the forefront of the communications industry.

Association of National Advertisers (ANA). A trade association serving as "the voice of the marketer," the New York–based ANA offers marketing and brand-building services, advocacy and legislative leadership, marketing information and resources, professional development, and peer networking to its members.

California Safe Cosmetics Program (CSCP). Under the California Safe Cosmetics Act of 2005, manufacturers, packers, and/or distributors are required to notify the California Department of Public Health (CDPH) of all products sold in California that contain ingredients known or suspected to cause adverse health effects. The CSCP collects this data and makes it available to consumers and cosmetics industry workers through its consumer product database so that "they can make informed choices for themselves, their clients, and their families."

Campaign for Safe Cosmetics. This San Francisco–based coalition seeks to safeguard the health of consumers, workers, and the environment through public education and engagement, corporate accountability and sustainability campaigns, and legislative advocacy designed to eliminate hazardous chemicals linked to adverse health effects from cosmetic and personal care products.

Children's Advertising Review Unit (CARU). Under the purview of BBB National Programs, Inc., CARU is "the children's arm of the advertising industry's self-regulation program." CARU assesses child-targeted advertising and promotional materials across all media to promote honesty, accuracy, and consistency with respect to CARU guidelines and applicable laws.

Consumer Reports. This independent, nonprofit organization does unbiased product testing and publishes product reviews and comparisons in its non-advertiser-sponsored magazine of the same name.

Eating Disorders Coalition (EDC). A Washington, DC–based advocacy organization, the EDC strives to raise public awareness and federal recognition of eating disorders as a public health concern. The EDC lobbies Congress and federal agencies to increase funding for eating disorders research, education, and treatment.

EcoWatch. As an online platform for environmental news, EcoWatch educates and encourages people to protect human health and the environment.

Environmental Working Group (EWG). This nonprofit, nonpartisan organization is dedicated to protecting public health and the environment through research, education, and advocacy "to drive consumer choice and civic action." EWG's Skin Deep® database provides consumers with commonsense ways to guard themselves from unnecessary exposure to toxic chemicals found in cosmetic and personal care products.

European Advertising Standards Alliance (EASA). Headquartered in Brussels, the EASA serves as "the single authoritative voice of advertising self-regulation." As the organizing body for advertising self-regulatory organizations within Europe, the EASA promotes responsible advertising by providing guidance to its members on how to adhere to advertising self-regulation to benefit consumers and businesses alike.

European Association of Communications Agencies (EACA). Serving as "the voice of Europe's communications agencies and associations," the Brussels-based EACA promotes honest, effective advertising; fosters high professional standards; raises awareness about advertising's contribution to a free-market economy; and encourages cooperation between agencies, advertisers, and European media companies.

Federal Communications Commission (FCC). An independent government agency overseen by Congress, the FCC regulates interstate and international communications by radio, television, wire, satellite, and cable in all fifty states, the District of Columbia, and US territories. The FCC implements and enforces communications law and regulations in the United States.

Federal Trade Commission (FTC). The FTC is the federal agency responsible for regulating advertising and promotion at the federal level. The FTC's Division of Advertising Practices enforces truth-in-advertising laws and protects consumers from unfair or deceptive advertising and marketing practices linked to health, safety, and economic concerns.

Geena Davis Institute on Gender in Media (GDIGM). Founded by Academy Award–winning actor and advocate Geena Davis, the institute and its programming arm, See Jane, are at the vanguard of changing female portrayals and gender stereotypes in media and entertainment content and platforms through evidence-based research, education, training, strategic guidance, and advocacy programs.

Humane Society of the United States (HSUS). This nonprofit animal advocacy organization seeks to create "a humane world for people and animals alike" and drives transformational change intended to end large-scale animal cruelty.

Interactive Advertising Bureau (IAB). Headquartered in New York, IAB aims to "empower the media and marketing industries to thrive in the digital economy." The trade group provides interactive services, establishes industry standards, conducts research, and provides legal support to the online advertising industry.

International Advertising Association (IAA). The IAA is a global strategic partnership that supports the common interests of all enterprises involved in the branding, communications, and marketing disciplines.

International Association of Better Business Bureaus (IABBB). As the umbrella organization for the local, independent BBBs throughout the United States, Canada, and Mexico, the IABBB cultivates honest and responsive relationships between businesses and consumers with an eye toward "instilling consumer confidence and advancing a trustworthy marketplace for all." It also runs national programs on advertising review, dispute resolution, and industry self-regulation.

International Chamber of Commerce (ICC). As the largest and most diverse global business organization, the Paris-based ICC promotes international trade, fosters responsible business conduct and a global approach to regulation, and provides market-leading dispute-resolution services. Its Consolidated ICC Code of Advertising and Marketing Communication Practice is considered "the gold standard for self-regulation."

International Women's Media Foundation (IWMF). A nonprofit organization based in Washington, DC, the IWMF is dedicated to elevating and strengthening the status of female journalists in the news media worldwide. The IWMF grants and programs provide the resources, training, and network to move women journalists into leadership roles in the news industry.

National Advertising Division (NAD). Administered by BBB National Programs, Inc., the NAD is an investigative arm of the advertising industry's self-regulatory system. The NAD is responsible for monitoring and evaluating the truth and accuracy of national advertising in all media.

National Advertising Review Board (NARB). As the appellate body for the advertising self-regulatory system, the NARB reviews and responds to complaints from consumers, competitors, and local branches of the Better Business Bureau concerning the truthfulness and accuracy of ads.

National Association of Anorexia Nervosa and Associated Disorders (ANAD). ANAD is a nonprofit organization committed to fighting eating disorders and helping people struggling with them to find treatment and support. ANAD works in the areas of prevention, identification, education, referral, and advocacy in addition to furnishing resources for families, schools, and the eating disorders community.

National Association of Attorneys General (NAAG). The Washington, DC–based NAAG assists the fifty-six state and territorial attorneys general in fulfilling the principal duties and responsibilities of their offices and aids in the conveyance of high-quality legal services.

National Eating Disorders Association (NEDA). This nonprofit organization is dedicated to the prevention, treatment, education, and awareness of eating disorders, as well as weight and body-image concerns. Supporting individuals and families affected by eating disorders, NEDA "serves as a catalyst for prevention, cures, and access to quality care."

National Organization for Women (NOW). Headquartered in Washington, DC, NOW is the largest organization of women's rights activists in the United States. Using intersectional grassroots activism to bring about social change, NOW advocates for reproductive and economic justice and endeavors to end violence and eliminate discrimination toward women in all spheres of social and economic life.

Public Citizen. Public Citizen is a national consumer rights advocacy group and think tank based in Washington, DC. Founded in 1971 by Ralph Nader, a prominent lawyer and consumer crusader, this nonprofit, nonpartisan organization serves as "the people's voice in the nation's capital" and champions citizen interests at the seat of government.

Truth in Advertising (TINA.org). The Madison, CT–based TINA.org is an independent, nonprofit advertising watchdog group and online resource committed to "empowering consumers to protect themselves and one another against false advertising and deceptive marketing."

US Consumer Product Safety Commission (CPSC). Headquartered in Bethesda, MD, CPSC is an independent federal agency charged with promoting product safety by protecting the public against unreasonable risks of injury or death from consumer products under the agency's jurisdiction, including products that present a fire, electrical, chemical, or mechanical hazard or that can harm children.

US Environmental Protection Agency (EPA). Based in Washington, DC, the EPA is a federal regulatory agency responsible for protecting human health and the environment from major risks. The EPA sponsors and conducts research, as well as drafts and enforces environmental regulations.

US Food and Drug Administration (FDA). Part of the US Department of Health and Human Services (HHS), the FDA is responsible for safeguarding public health by ensuring the safety, efficacy, and security of human and veterinary drugs, biological products, and medical devices, as well as guarding the safety of the nation's food supply, cosmetics, and radiation-emitting products.

Women In Media & News (WIMN). A national media analysis, education, and advocacy group, WIMN works to increase women's presence and power in the public forum and promotes equity for women as subjects, sources, and producers in news and entertainment media.

Women's Media Center (WMC). A progressive nonprofit women's media organization cofounded by Jane Fonda, Robin Morgan, and Gloria Steinem, the WMC seeks "to raise the visibility, viability, and decision-making power of women and girls in media." The organization offers media and leadership training programs, performs research, produces original content and journalism, conducts media monitoring for sexism, and runs media advocacy campaigns.

Women's Voices for the Earth (WVE). The Missoula, MT–based WVE is a grass-roots environmental justice organization committed to eliminating toxic chemicals that harm human health and communities. WVE calls for creating a less toxic, thriving world.

World Federation of Advertisers (WFA). Headquartered in Brussels, WFA is a global trade organization that "brings together the biggest markets and marketers worldwide." WFA represents the common business interests of multinational advertisers and national advertiser associations, as well as advocates for responsible and effective marketing communications.

Index

About the Author

Martha Laham is a professor at Diablo Valley College, where she has taught business, marketing, and advertising for thirty years. She has authored college textbooks in marketing and selling, developed instructional materials for educational publishers, and contributed to *HuffPost*. She is the author of *The Con Game: A Failure of Trust* (2014). Martha lives in Oakland, California.